Graffiti and Street Art

D0165561

Graffiti and street art images are ubiquitous, and they enjoy a very special place in collective imaginary due to their ambiguous nature. Sometimes enigmatic in meaning, often stylistically crude and aesthetically aggressive, yet always visually arresting, they fill our field of vision with texts and images that no one can escape. As they take place on surfaces and travel through various channels, they provide viewers an entry point to the subtext of the cities we live in, while questioning how we *read*, *write* and *represent* them. This book is structured around these three distinct, albeit by definition interwoven, key frames. The contributors of this volume critically investigate underexplored urban contexts in which graffiti and street art appear, shed light on previously unexamined aspects of these practices, and introduce innovative methodologies regarding the treatment of these images. Throughout, the focus is on the relationship of graffiti and street art with urban space, and the various manifestations of these idiosyncratic meetings. In this book, the emphasis is shifted from what the physical texts *say* to what these practices and their produced images *do* in different contexts.

All chapters are original and come from experts in various fields, such as Architecture, Urban Studies, Sociology, Criminology, Anthropology and Visual Cultures, as well as scholars that transcend traditional disciplinary frameworks. This exciting new collection is essential reading for advanced undergraduates as well as postgraduates and academics interested in the subject matter. It is also accessible to a non-academic audience, such as art practitioners and policymakers alike, or anyone keen on deepening their knowledge on how graffiti and street art affect the ways urban environments are experienced, understood and envisioned.

Konstantinos Avramidis is a PhD Candidate in Architecture by Design at the University of Edinburgh, UK.

Myrto Tsilimpounidi is a Marie Curie Researcher at the Institute of Sociology, Bratislava, Slovakia.

'This essay collection yields illuminating insights into graffiti and its close cousin street art. With a globally-diverse range of sites, and contributions from leading academics, this is essential reading for anyone wishing to better understand one of the most distinctive features of twenty-first century urbanism.'

Iain Borden, University College London, UK

'With contributions by authors from diverse geographical and disciplinary backgrounds, this book pushes for new ways to understand, study and write about graffiti and street art. In doing so, this volume constitutes an important step towards breaking down disciplinary boundaries and establishing street art studies as a multifaceted academic discipline in its own right.'

Peter Bengtsen, Lund University, Sweden

Graffiti and Street Art

Reading, Writing and Representing
the City

**Edited by
Konstantinos Avramidis and
Myrto Tsilimpounidi**

Routledge
Taylor & Francis Group

LONDON AND NEW YORK

First published 2017
by Routledge
2 Park Square, Milton Park, Abingdon, Oxon OX14 4RN

and by Routledge
711 Third Avenue, New York, NY 10017

First issued in paperback 2018

Routledge is an imprint of the Taylor & Francis Group, an informa business

British Library Cataloguing in Publication Data
A catalogue record for this book is available from the British Library

Library of Congress Cataloging in Publication Data
A catalog record for this book has been requested

ISBN 13: 978-1-138-60090-4 (pbk)
ISBN 13: 978-1-472-47333-2 (hbk)

Typeset in Times New Roman
by Florence Production Limited, Stoodleigh, Devon, UK

Contents

Figures

Contributors

Editors

Konstantinos Avramidis is a practising architect in Greece and the UK (TCG/ ARB), and PhD Candidate in Architecture by Design at the University of Edinburgh. He holds a DipArch from the AU Thessaloniki and an MSc, with Distinction, in Interdisciplinary Theories and Design of Space from the NTU Athens. Konstantinos has taught architectural design, history and theory at the NTUA and UoE, his designs have been awarded, published and exhibited internationally, while his research has been presented at conferences, and published in journals and books. He is a co-founder of the architectural design research journal *Drawing On*, and co-edited its first issue. His research interests include: text in the city; systems of archiving and taxonomy; and architectural design as mode of enquiry.

Myrto Tsilimpounidi is a social researcher and photographer. After completing a DPhil at the University of Sussex, she was a post-doctoral fellow at the University of East London. She is currently Marie Curie Fellow at the Institute for Sociology of the Slovak Academy of Sciences and the co-director of Ministry of Untold Stories. Her research focuses on the interface between urbanism, culture and innovative methodologies. Past work explores empirical investigation of cosmopolitan theory in Southern Europe. Current projects focus on street politics, landscapes of belonging, and the new aesthetics of crisis in Europe. Myrto is the author of *Sociology of Crisis: Visualising Urban Austerity* (Routledge, 2016) and the editor of *Remapping 'Crisis': A Guide to Athens* (Zero Books, 2014).

Contributors

Mona Abaza is Professor of Sociology at the Department of Sociology, the American University in Cairo. She was a Visiting Professor of Islamology in the Department of Theology at Lund University (2009–2011). Visiting scholar at the Institute for South East Asian Studies, Singapore (1990–1992), Kuala Lumpur (1995–1996), l'École des Hautes Études en Sciences Sociales, Paris (1994), the Wissenschaftskolleg, Berlin (1996–1997), the International Institute for Asian Studies, Leiden (2002–2003), the Netherlands Institute for Advanced Study in the Humanities and Social Sciences, Wassenaar (2006–2007) and the Rockefeller Foundation Bellagio Center (2005). Research Fellow at Morphomata, Cologne (2014). Her books include: *The Cotton Plantation Remembered: An Egyptian Family Story* (AUC Press, 2013); *Twentieth Century Egyptian Art: The Private Collection of Sherwet Shafei* (AUC Press, 2011); *The Changing Consumer Culture of Modern Egypt, Cairo's Urban Reshaping* (Brill/AUC Press, 2006); *Debates on Islam and Knowledge in Malaysia and Egypt, Shifting Worlds* (Routledge Curzon Press, 2002); *Islamic Education, Perceptions and Exchanges: Indonesian Students in Cairo* (Cahier d'Archipel, 1994).

Sabina Andron is a PhD candidate at the Bartlett School of Architecture, University College London, with a project on graffiti, street art, and their relation to the built environment. Her research focuses on the mutual influence of surfaces and inscriptions, which she traces through visual, material and cultural coordinates. Sabina holds a BA in comparative literature from the Babes-Bolyai University of Cluj Napoca (2005) and an MA (Distinction) in visual culture from Manchester Metropolitan University (2011). She is a lecturer in architectural history, with teaching positions at University College London, Queen Mary, University of London and University of East London. She has presented her work on graffiti and street art at conferences in the UK, US, Australia and throughout Europe, has published articles in edited volumes and shown photographic work in exhibitions in Philadelphia and London. Sabina is also an arts advisor and facilitator. She runs the London-based arts organization 'I Know What I Like', where she organizes critical gallery visits and art walks, and curates exhibitions with work by international artists. See http://sabinaandron.com

Andrea Mubi Brighenti is Aggregate Professor of 'Social Theory' and 'Space & Culture' at the Department of Sociology, University of Trento, Italy. Research topics focus on space, power and society. His most recent book is *The Ambiguous Multiplicities: Materials, Episteme and Politics of some Cluttered Social Formations* (Palgrave Macmillan, 2014). Andrea is the founder and editor in chief of the independent online web journal *lo Squaderno* as well as current co-editor of *Etnografia e Ricerca Qualitativa*.

Samantha Edwards-Vandenhoek is a design researcher, digital media artist and Senior Lecturer in Communication Design at Swinburne University of Technology, Melbourne. Samantha holds a BA (Hons) in Aboriginal Prehistory and a PhD in Media and Communication Studies. Samantha's research interests combine contemporary archaeology, documentary photography and material culture studies, place-making and Indigenous knowledge systems, as well as how design as a discipline can enrich transdisciplinary collaborations. Samantha's current research explores how public art practices informed by participatory design processes can transform the experience of place in remote Indigenous communities.

Jeff Ferrell is Professor of Sociology at Texas Christian University, USA, and Visiting Professor of Criminology at the University of Kent, UK. He is author of the books *Crimes of Style*, *Tearing Down the Streets*, *Empire of Scrounge*, and with Keith Hayward and Jock Young the first and second editions of *Cultural Criminology: An Invitation*, winner of the 2009 Distinguished Book Award from the American Society of Criminology's Division of International Criminology. He is co-editor of the books *Cultural Criminology*, *Ethnography at the Edge*, *Making Trouble*, *Cultural Criminology Unleashed*, and *Cultural Criminology: Theories of Crime*. Jeff Ferrell is founding and current editor of the New York University Press book series *Alternative Criminology*, and one of the founding editors of *Crime, Media, Culture: An International Journal*, winner of the ALPSP 2006 Charlesworth Award for Best New Journal. In 1998 Ferrell received the Critical Criminologist of the Year Award from the Critical Criminology Division of the American Society of Criminology. He is currently completing a book on drift and drifters.

Kurt Iveson is an Associate Professor of Urban Geography at the University of Sydney. His fascination with the politics of urban space was in large part inspired by his engagement with graffiti writers in Sydney back in the 1990s. He is the author of *Publics and the City* (2007), co-author of *Planning and Diversity and the City* (2008), has edited a Special Issue of the journal *City* on Graffiti, Street Art and the City (2011), and has written elsewhere on urban politics and citizenship. He also writes the blog *Cities and Citizenship*.

Alexander Lamazares is Chairperson of the Department of Modern Languages at Bronx Community College of the City University of New York. He is Associate Professor of Spanish and Portuguese. He received his MA from the University of Chicago, and his doctorate from the University at Albany, SUNY. He is a specialist in Cuban and Brazilian art and visual culture. His current research projects focus on Portuguese linguistics, and artistic representations in São Paulo and Havana.

Deborah Landry is a full time contract Replacement Professor in Criminology at the University of Ottawa, Canada. Her research focuses on how municipalities manage the aesthetics of urban spaces as a project of security (economic and environmental). Her ethnographic research focuses on the regulation of urban art communities (busking, graffiti, urban art). Her blog *KulturBurn* critiques and documents many of the tensions that have unfolded in the Ottawa graffiti scene over the past few years.

Panos Leventis is Associate Professor at the Hammons School of Architecture of Drury University in Springfield, Missouri. He holds a BArch from USC, an MArch in Urban Design from UCLA, and a PhD in the History and Theory of Architecture from McGill University. He served as Director of Drury's Study Abroad Center in Greece, taught for USC in Milan and Como, for McGill in Montréal, and for the University of Cyprus in Nicosia. His research engages the past and future of cities. He is the author of *Twelve Times in Nicosia. Nicosia,*

Cyprus, 1192–1570: Architecture, Topography and Urban Experience in a Diversified Capital City. He is a licensed and practising Architect in Cyprus and Greece. He has recently been focusing on the socio-urban upheavals that sprang forth in a post-2008 context, writing on graffiti, street art and urban resistance movements as understood via the lens of public space and participatory urban processes.

Lachlan MacDowall is an artist, researcher and Head of the Centre for Cultural Partnerships in the Faculty of VCA and MCM, University of Melbourne, Australia. His research examines the history and aesthetics of graffiti and street art, particularly in relation to cultural heritage and digital media. He has published and presented widely in this area, most recently in Lossau and Stevens (eds), *The Uses of Art in Public Space* (2015), a commissioned essay in the 'Wall to Wall: Graffiti Art' issue of *Artlink* (2014) and in Schacter (ed.), *The World Atlas of Street Art and Graffiti* (2013). See graffitistudies.info

Rafael Schacter is an anthropologist and curator from London. He is currently a British Academy Postdoctoral Fellow (2014–2017) in the Anthropology Department at University College London (UCL). Rafael has been undertaking research on graffiti and street-art for over ten years. He has curated a number of high-profile exhibitions including the iconic show *Street-Art* at the Tate Modern in 2008 (which he co-curated), as well as *Mapping the City* and *Venturing Beyond* at Somerset House in 2015 and 2016 respectively. He is the author of two books: the award winning *World Atlas of Street Art and Graffiti* (2013) published by Yale University Press, and *Ornament and Order: Graffiti, Street Art and the Parergon* (2014) published by Ashgate.

Gregory J. Snyder is an Associate Professor at Baruch College, City University of New York. His research focuses on urban subcultures such as graffiti writers, musicians and professional skateboarders, with an emphasis on subculture theory, urban space and issues of social justice. He is the author of *Graffiti Lives: Beyond the Tag in New York's Urban Underground* (NYU Press, 2009) and has just completed his second book titled, *Skatelife LA: Professional Street Skateboarding in Public Space* (NYU Press, 2017).

Stavros Stavrides is Associate Professor at the School of Architecture, National Technical University of Athens Greece, where he teaches a graduate course on social housing, as well as a postgraduate course on the meaning of metropolitan experience. He has published numerous articles as well as books on spatial theory: *The Symbolic Relation to Space* (Athens, 1990); *Advertising and the Meaning of Space* (Athens, 1996); *The Texture of Things* (Athens, 1996); *From the City-as-Screen to the City-as-Stage* (Athens, 2002 National Book Award); *Suspended Spaces of Alterity* (Athens, 2010), *Towards the City of Thresholds* (Professional Dreamers, 2011), and *Common Space: The City as Commons* (Zed Books, 2016). His research is currently focused on forms of emancipating spatial practices and urban commoning.

Stephen Luis Vilaseca is an Associate Professor of Spanish at Northern Illinois University and a co-Associate Editor of the *Journal of Urban Cultural Studies*. He is the author of *Barcelonan Okupas: Squatter Power!* (Fairleigh Dickinson University Press, 2013) as well as of articles in the *Bulletin of Hispanic Studies* (2006), *Letras Hispanas: Revista de Literatur y Cultura* (2009), the *Arizona Journal of Hispanic Cultural Studies* (2010), *Transitions: Journal of Franco-Iberian Studies* (2012), the *Journal of Urban Cultural Studies* (2014) and the *Journal of Spanish Cultural Studies* (2015).

Alison Young is the Francine V. McNiff Professor of Criminology in the School of Social and Political Sciences at the University of Melbourne, Adjunct Professor in the Griffith Law School and Honorary Professor in the Law School at City University, London. She is the author of *Street Art World* (2016), *Street Art, Public City* (2014), *The Scene of Violence* (2010), *Street/Studio* (2010) and *Judging the Image* (2005), as well as numerous articles on the intersections of law, crime and culture. She has been researching graffiti and street art in Melbourne and internationally since 1996.

Acknowledgements

We would like to extend our gratitude to many people who were instrumental in getting this volume to publication. The idea for the need of this book emerged in the conference *Disrespectful Creativity*, hosted by the Onassis Cultural Center in June 2014, where we first met some of the contributors of the collection. The conference was organized by Marilena Karra to whom we are grateful for creating such an inspiring platform for dialogue and creative meetings. We are also greatly indebted to Professor Georgios Parmenidis for his support for the realization of the conference and the accompanying exhibition.

Our immense thanks go to research partners and mentors from our institutions for their constant guidance and support in the materialization of this project: Dr Ella Chmielewska and Dr Dorian Wiszniewski from the Edinburgh School of Architecture and Landscape Architecture of the University of Edinburgh, as well as Dr Miroslav Tizik and Professor Silvia Mihalikova from the Institute for Sociology of the Slovak Academy of Sciences. Thank you also to Professor Mark Dorrian, Dr Konstantina Drakopoulou, Dr Anna Carastathis, Dr Penny Travlou and Dr Pavel Suska for their advice and stimulating conversations all these years.

We would like to thank Claire Jarvis and Lianne Sherlock for their enthusiasm and encouragement in the early stages of this endeavour and particularly Neil Jordan and Shannon Kneis who made working on this book a truly enjoyable experience. Also, we are thankful to our copy-editor Jane Fieldsend, project managers Julia Hanney and Megan Symons, and production editor Adam Guppy, who ensured the smoothness of the whole process. We are most thankful to artists Christos Tzaferos and Grigoris Paragrigoriou from the Blaqk crew who not only created the stunning artwork that adorns the cover of this book but also kindly provided the photograph.

Yeoryia Moustaka and Aylwyn Walsh have been the greatest intellectual companions from the early conceptualization of this project and we most gratefully thank them for their love and support – this project would not have been possible without you. Konstantinos would like to extend his warmest thanks to his family for the love and constant encouragement, his graffiti family for being an inexhaustible source of inspiration and excitement, and his co-students for the numerous creative exchanges. Myrto wants to wholeheartedly thank her mum Mairi and Theodora for their love, patience and for tagging her on the wall when necessary.

Last, but certainly not least, with great fanfare we want to thank all our authors for their willingness and eagerness to contribute to the volume, their inspiring chapters and their patience when working through the drafts. Thank you all for the rich material you have provided, the inspirational conversations, the critical edges and your commitment to follow the writings on the walls. As editors we could not ask for better collaborators and a more eclectic mixture of scholars. We would also like to thank those who wished to participate in this project but, for one reason or another, were not unable to do so.

This book is dedicated to the anonymous protagonists, the ones holding spray cans and paste-ups, who challenge how we read, write and represent our cities.

Graffiti and street art

Reading, writing and representing the city

Konstantinos Avramidis and
Myrto Tsilimpounidi

This is a volume dedicated to graffiti and street art. More precisely, this book is a testament to the multiple modes by which graffiti and street art have changed our ways of seeing, knowing and representing urban environments.[1] Thus, we think it is only appropriate that the structure of this introductory chapter follows the traditional stages of graffiti production. This choice reflects our deep appreciation for the art of wall writing, but most importantly seeks to highlight the similarities between scholarly and graffiti writing: the attentiveness to the words, the placement of the ideas, and the small details when drawing an outline to name a few.

As with every design endeavour or scholarly piece, *first goes the 'sketch'*, which provides the framework and the conceptual position of the volume; this section is the basis for our final product and contains the justification behind our aesthetic and political choices. *Then, comes the 'background'*, which is not just a thing on the back, but the spine that supports a graffiti piece and in our case a detailed historical, conceptual and thematic review of graffiti and street art scholarship. The background is what eventually brings all the different elements of a piece (and of a scholarly volume) together; to put it differently, the background is the conceptual glue between the different parts. Once we have the sketch and the background, we can start *filling in* our piece; this is what would make the piece stand out, giving it substance and depth. In our case, this section exposes the gap in the literature and explains why this volume fills in this gap, what future trajectories it offers and its wider contribution. Afterwards, *it's time to draw the 'outlines'*, this is what connects our piece with the background, and this is the moment when the different letters, scribbles and numbers are taking shape. The moment a graffiti artist draws the outlines is the first time an observer can read the tag/slogan. Here, we draw the outline collectively, as the 'crew' of scholars in this volume is what gives it its shape, uniqueness and value. Finally, once the piece is ready, the artist *adds the final details and signs*; this is what gives a personal touch to the piece, claims authorship and distinguishes it from all the other pieces out there. In our case this comes with a series of details regarding this project, by way of an opening gesture towards the chapters that follow.

Academic and graffiti writing have many similarities and in this era of fast production and consumption of images and texts, this volume offers a pause in order to embrace the art of writing on walls and pages, and the craft of writing about the writing on the walls.

First goes the 'sketch'

> These marks made in public places, called the defacing of monuments, actually put face on an impersonal wall or oversized statue. The human hand seems to want to touch and leave its touch, even if by only obscene smears and ugly scrawls . . . surely, a city is a masterpiece of engineering form and architectural inspiration that would not be despoiled by the presence of images that reflect the 'soul' through the hand.
>
> (Hillman 2008 [1989]: 105)

American psychologist James Hillman's opening quote eloquently outlines the main tensions, inspirations and research incentives in this volume: the multilayered interrelationship between graffiti, street art and urban space. Cities are dynamic, living organisms in which space and people mutually create one another. Graffiti and street art capture these spatio-social interactions between the placing of people and the ways humans inhabit and (in)form their spaces. Thus, seeing the writing on the wall offers valuable insights of the polyvalent character of our urban realities.

'Seeing the writing on the wall' is an expression originating from the Biblical story of Balthazar's feast, where supernatural writing on the wall works as a prophecy for the forthcoming demise of the Babylonian Empire (Tsilimpounidi 2013; cf. Mieszkowski 2010). Therefore, to attribute to someone the capacity to see the writing on the wall implies the ability to know that something is about to happen, usually an inevitable decline or an end. Is this the purpose of graffiti and street art in our postmodern urban environments? To work as prophecies inscribed on the urban surface and to project images and information from the future, or as David Ley and Roman Cybriwsky argue in a similar line of thought 'today's graffiti are tomorrow's headlines' (1974: 491). We move away from the notion of prophecy and fortune telling as we claim that graffiti and street art are valuable research lenses through which to unpack some of the tensions and contradictions of urban life. In this sense, they might work as indications of the tensions that people are facing on the ground, and thus provide insights into a variety of potential futures. After all, surrealism has taught us that the culturally marginal and/or the urban quotidian have the capacity to reveal the unexpected. Turning our focus on the walls and the marks they host is not without dangers, but definitely rewarding. French surrealist poet Léo Malet could not have put it more aptly: 'the walls of the city [is] the unlimited field of poetic realisations' (Phillips 1990: 140).

Graffiti writer Boom offers a similar definition of graffiti in his famous tag: 'graffiti is a poem the city writes to itself'.[2] What Boom implies here is that the production of graffiti comes from the city itself. Other than the personification of the city as the main protagonist and not just a background for our urban stories, what is important in Boom's tag is the poetic relationship between graffiti, social conditions and urban space. Not every city produces that same graffiti and, given its ephemeral character, there is also a deep connection with the particular era even within the same city. For example, the proliferation of graffiti and street art messages during the Arab Spring in Cairo is a testament to the particularities of that moment. To put it differently, seeing the writing on the wall offers glimpses of a particular milieu and those glimpses usually originate from the margins of social production – as what is written on the wall usually contradicts the hegemonic narratives.

A completely different take on graffiti is evident in Robert Reisner's research, where the most usual answer to the question 'what is graffiti?' is 'dirty words on clean walls' (1971: 24). This early interpretation seems to be an interesting entry point on what constitutes graffiti, a statement that sounds so familiar even today. Perhaps the dirt of graffiti is associated with the disturbance of the marginal messages, with the alternative stories that are tagged on the walls. Or perhaps, with the prevailing fixation of the regime of 'law and order' which makes the supporting surface to be understood as clean and graffiti as dirt. A subversive answer to this logic comes from graffiti writers and street artists in Athens, after every major attempt by the municipality to clean the walls the same tag appeared almost overnight stating 'clean walls, dirty consciousness'. Graffiti and street art poetically break the monopoly of messages on the urban fabric, and at the same time open up questions on the nature of public space and the right to the city, but most importantly whose right and to what city.

Graffiti and street art practices inspire media hype, are visually compelling, and have reached almost mythological status among subcultures, art historians and the public. Depending on one's point of view, these two terms are synonyms with vandalism, marginal youth and delinquency, or seen as signs of free expression. What is important in critical analysis is the sense of the constant tension in which the pieces are often seen simultaneously as either social problems, or political acts, or artistic practices. In light of the recent critical turn in graffiti and street art scholarship, we envision this interdisciplinary collection as moving beyond description in order to focus on the controversies within the scene, addressing issues of methodological innovations and the multiple ways graffiti and street art are embedded in the dynamics of urbanism.

The notions 'graffiti' and 'street art' are always mercurial due to the ambiguous and flux nature of the practices they refer to. In their constant attempt to capture the essence and define the meaning of these concepts, scholars end up either distancing themselves from them or inventing new terms to frame these practices (cf. Avramidis 2012), even though they know that a part of graffiti and street art's meaning will always escape definition.[3] Of course, during the process of attempting to understand or redefine these notions, new interpretative opportunities emerge that push the field forward. We, as editors, are not so much interested in defining what graffiti and street art *are* (what counts), but what they *do*.[4] The contributions in this volume embrace the multilayered nature of graffiti and street art, and thus deliberately avoid a single, fixed and solid definition of these practices. Yet, in terms of clarity, an open-ended definition of graffiti and street art is necessary. Echoing Rafael Schacter (2015), graffiti is a specific type of writing that has its roots in the streets of Philadelphia and the subway system of New York City dating back to the late 1960s. Graffiti is an unsolicited, frequently illegal, act of image-making, usually produced by the use of spray cans. Its focus is usually on words, tags and pseudonyms and their repetitive display on all kinds of surfaces. It is a very loose term, with multiple aesthetic outcomes and practitioners. Street art is, similarly to graffiti, a practice of image-making. Here the difference is the focus which is now on images rather than words, making the 'message' less cryptic and thus its audience more broad compared to that of graffiti. Street art can be produced by spray cans, stencils, posters, photographs or a mix of all the above. It is also an illicit practice, yet in many occasions it occurs as commissioned work, and emerged from the graffiti scene in the early 1990s. The term 'street art' is also often associated with more politically engaged forms of public interventions.

Graffiti and street art have captured a global following in recent years, and the result is a proliferation of tags, paintings, stickers and stencils in slick metropolitan cities as well as unexpected locales in impoverished areas. Part of their appeal is that the forms allow viewers an understanding of the subtext of a city without resorting to mainstream accounts or official histories. They offer an alternative history; a mapping of social trails or subcultural behaviours – a voyeuristic pleasure at entering the story of the city. To put it differently, the proliferation of pieces democratizes the relationship between art and its audiences as it generates an open gallery, allowing the free enjoyment of the skill of the practitioners.[5] As such, they provide a counter-narrative to dominant urban aesthetics. From the famous May '68 tag 'Under the cobblestones, the beach' in Paris, the proliferation of 'aerosol art' in New York's subway in the 1970s, to the messages on the Berlin wall in the 1980s, graffiti provides an elaboration of aesthetic protest and dissent.

Graffiti and street art are simultaneously physical acts and cultural practices. As such, they are spatially and socially bound; they bring together the *material* and the *immaterial*. This paradoxical and controversial nature of graffiti and street art, as well as their relationship to urban space and identities are some of the reasons behind our fascination with these practices. For us the editors, coming from different disciplines, namely architecture and sociology, graffiti and street art become the ideal vehicle in order to unpack some of our common concerns: dynamics of urban space, subversive practices of citizenship and inventive methodologies for the study of urban phenomena, to name a few.

Architecture tends to view graffiti and street art as a threat, even though they share a very special reciprocal relationship. Architecture provides not only the material background for writing – which confines and, in a sense, dictates the material and visual result of the writing – but also its historical and political context – which contributes to what the writing conveys. In turn, graffiti and street art are parts of the life of architecture and constantly change the image and meaning of particular urban places. Despite this conflictual relationship, graffiti and street art fascinate architects and have a constant presence in architectural representations as well. Yet, more often than not, they play a supplementary role; they are used as signs of a 'vibrant' city and they appear in photorealistic renders to indicate the dynamism of blossoming urban cultures. What often is ignored, however, is the material sophistication, aesthetic dynamism and contextual specificity of these writing genres (Avramidis 2015).

Sociology has its own flirtation with graffiti and street art. These frequently illegal re-appropriations of public space create a spectrum of alternative, and many times subversive, urban representation that expose the untold stories on the ground. To engage with the stories written on the walls offers a polyvalent engagement with urban space, one that does not try to define it but rather invoke it through a range of approaches. Sociology tends to focus on the soft elements of these subcultural practices, in order to unpack questions of youth expression and representations, uses of public space, disaffected communities and the limits of legality of social performances. Graffiti and street art can also affect methodological choices, as they could be viewed as an expression of counter-cultural production on the micro level, as alternative urban diaries projected on urban walls (Tsilimpounidi 2015).

We have envisioned this project for some time and materialized it in June 2014 after a conference that brought many graffiti and street art scholars together in Athens.[6] As such, the cover of the book is both a reference to our initial conceptualization of this edited volume, but also a tribute to the muse of our graffiti and street art explorations: Athens. This picture also reveals a specific attitude regarding the treatment of images that we adopt and encourage in this collection: a careful reading of the singular image; an examination of its relationship with a larger set of images; and an investigation of the ways they function together in different assemblages and specific contexts. Except for some rare occasions, graffiti and street art images that appear on book covers are reduced to generic signs, devoid of any meaning and extracted from their contexts (cf. Chmielewska 2008). The reference to the piece(s) they depict is, at best, exhausted to a single copyright line. In other words, graffiti and street art are often used to seduce and attract rather than inform. Here, the cover image is treated contextually, as a prompt that offers the image what it deserves, or rather 'what it wants' (Mitchell 1996) – i.e. attention.

The cover image is from the Athens School of Fine Arts, a hub of and for graffiti writers and street artists alike. The piece is a product of the collaboration between Athenian artists Greg Papagrigoriou and Simek (aka Blaqk crew), and is characterized by a delicate combination of abstract geometric forms, calligraphy and typography. The letters and forms twist eloquently not only to produce a unique calligraphic mosaic but also to follow the physical patina of the surface. Literally a few metres away from this piece the idea for this volume was conceived back in 2014. Also, the very first lines of this introduction were written there. Yet, this is not what makes this artwork special. Apart from its obvious visual quality and undeniable synthetic sophistication, this piece serves as this collection's entry point. This is due to its capacity to incarnate tensions, open up subjects and raise questions that are pertinent to this volume. For example, is this piece graffiti or street art? Does it matter how we name it, and why? Is this a text, an image, or both? Is it legal or not? Why this image of a graffito on an abandoned building looks so familiar and stereotypical? Do we ever wonder where this piece is, or do we take for granted that it rests on an abandoned edifice in the middle of nowhere or in a degraded neighbourhood? Would it change the way you see it if you knew that it rests on one of the busiest avenues in Athens? Also, do the artists, by intervening in this particular way in this specific site, aim to promote an aesthetic agenda or do they try to make a political statement? Can any intentional aesthetic public intervention be separated from the political? But, at the same time, how does calligraphy fit in the contemporary Athenian context and how political can it be?

Further, how important is the materiality and history of the surface that supports the writing for both artists and researchers alike? Is there any way to study this piece outside of its context? In this case, which is context: the building, the photograph, or both? And what does photographing graffiti mean after Brassaï (2002 [1964])? How do we read the image on the cover: as a graffiti piece or as a representation of a piece? And how does the photographic framing affect what we see and the ways we interpret what we see? How, in turn, is the artwork affected by both the photograph and its appearance on the cover of this collection? Can we examine this piece in isolation, or do we need to investigate it as part of a local network of physical pieces in the city and, at the same time, as a component of a global scene that shares the same aesthetic and cultural characteristics? And is this enough, or do we have to follow how this piece is represented and circulated through various online and offline media, by both the artists and others? Why did artists choose this site and what does their piece do to the place? Can we ever explore this place without referring to this piece, and can we discuss the piece without its place of reference? Is the writing surface merely the background of the piece, or an element without which it would have never have come into being?

Then, comes the 'background'

Today graffiti and street art books are shelved alongside popular fashion photography, graffiti pieces are displayed in important art fairs,[7] collectors spend millions to acquire a canvas or a piece of wall that has the signature of a celebrated graffitist,[8] while, at the same time, artists erase their works from the streets to avoid exploitation and appropriation.[9] In this context, graffiti and street art have attracted academic interest resulting in a burgeoning literature. In what follows in this section, we attempt to outline the work undertaken on the subject to date and show how the scholarship has developed throughout the years. Of course, this is not an exhaustive listing of all the works produced; we focus on the key publications of the field in order to reveal which themes and contexts have been discussed, and identify potential research gaps that this collection aims to either fill in or expand and contribute to.

Graffiti's strong visual appeal and illicit nature, and perhaps a sort of trendiness of the subject that one can witness in general and in academia in particular, have resulted in a surprising amount of books, articles and analyses, especially during the past decade (cf. Austin 2013). The vast majority of these publications are non-academic and focus on contemporary (post late 1960s) New York style graffiti. These works come primarily from journalists and photographers (Mailer *et al.* 1974; Cooper and Chalfant 1984; Chalfant and Prigoff 1987),[10] and sometimes from the practitioners themselves (Powers 1999) – their main purpose, however, is not to critically engage with the subject but to document the history and development of this writing genre. An early exception is Jean Baudrillard's (1998 [1976]) brief, albeit insightful, commentary that gives a semiotic take to the study of this writing practice. Baudrillard argues that graffiti are devoid of 'content and message', they are 'empty signifiers' due to their self-referentiality, but he considers this to be their actual strength; this 'emptiness' allows them to 'scramble the signals of urbania and dismantle the order of signs' (1998: 81). Yet, this was just a short parenthesis. The tradition of illustrative books of pieces and styles prevailed and continues until today, this time with a global rather than solely New York focus, with publications such as those by Nicholas Ganz (2004) and Rafael Schacter (2013). Of course, these two are not the only ones, but perhaps the most comprehensive and successful to date. On top of these, numerous coffee table books concerned with regional styles from around the world have been published and, of course, a myriad of books on the work of the notorious British street artist Banksy. These first publications created and gradually established a particular tradition regarding the documentation and treatment of graffiti that is primarily photographic, thus marginalizing other potential means of examination that could have opened different research opportunities.

With almost a decade of delay compared to its journalist predecessors, the first academic publication on the subject makes its appearance. Thus, inaugurating what we could call the 'first academic wave' of graffiti and street art scholarship. This belongs to communication scholar Craig Castleman (1982) who, through interviews with graffitists, investigates the early scene of subway graffiti in New York. Castleman argues for the complex relationship of practitioners, authorities and media in the creation of a unique set of communication channels that challenge spatial politics. A few years later, sociologist Richard Lachmann publishes his oft-cited article *Graffiti as Career and Ideology* (1988) which, again through interviews with practitioners, examines the 'deviant careers' of New York's writers that allow them to 'develop a total art world'. Based on one of the key elements of graffiti, i.e. fame, Lachmann paves the way for many studies that will follow. An important, albeit largely ignored, reference is Kirk Varnedoe and Adam Gopnik's *High & Low* (1990), a catalogue that accompanied the homonymous MoMA exhibition concerned with the interplay of 'high' modern art and 'low' popular culture. Varnedoe and Gopnik devote a whole chapter on graffiti that traces the aesthetic origins as well as intellectual construction of the artist as public 'scribbler' while comprehensively chronicling how graffiti is intertwined with modern art. Another key article worth mentioning here comes from geographer Tim Cresswell (1992) who shifts the focus of the – still under formation – scholarship from the 'who' and the 'what' to the 'where' of graffiti, an element that he considers to be the most crucial. Based on Mary Douglas' concept 'matter out of place', Cresswell argues that graffiti writing in New York is transgressive due to its placement 'where' it shouldn't be or doesn't belong, and believes that this practice is paradigmatic of what he terms 'heretical geographies' (1996), i.e. ways of being in space that question the taken-for-granted, everyday normative landscapes.

Despite the continuous and often aggressive 'wars on graffiti', and while the surprisingly persistent 'broken windows' theory still enjoys popularity (Wilson and Kelling 1982), this subculture survives and migrates from the streets of Philadelphia and subway cars of New York to almost every city around the world. There it is transformed and mixed with the historical, aesthetic and cultural particularities of each place. Authors from other regions start examining their local scenes in relation to the particularities of their specific cultural and urban contexts. John Bushnell's *Moscow Graffiti* (1990) concentrates on different subgenres of wall writing, ranging from slogan writing to art produced by various youth subcultural groups, in several cities of the former Soviet Union. Bushnell draws linkages between the local and the global writing scenes, and asserts that the foreign language adopted by the writers not only allows them to open channels of communication with geographically and culturally distant peers but also becomes a tool to resist and bypass their isolation. Political scientist Lyman Chaffee, in his book *Political Protest and Street Art* (1993), a work that did not get the attention it deserved most probably due to its regional focus and the wide definition of what 'street art' might mean, investigates the effectiveness of street art – or what we might call 'protest' and 'activist' art – to act as a 'tool for political democratization' in Spain, Argentina and Brazil.[11] Despite its socio-political approach, this work pays great attention to the visual treatment and placement of writings, and considers street art to be not only a means of low-tech communication in a high-tech era but also 'a record of popular history'. These early studies, which turn the focus away from North America and signature graffiti, demonstrate that the line that divides these wall writing types is thin or even non-existent. They also emphatically reveal the importance of examining these cultural and material practices in their context of production and perception, thus highlighting the need to account for their special historical, social and spatial particularities and meanings.

Authored by cultural criminologist Jeff Ferrell, *Crimes of Style* (1993) is probably the founding publication of contemporary graffiti scholarship, a work that opens the 'second wave' in graffiti literature.[12] In this study, Ferrell focuses on Denver's scene, moving the focus away from his New York-centred predecessors. He follows the discourses surrounding the local writing scene and the campaigns that attempt to criminalize it. In so doing, the author argues, writers and 'moral entrepreneurs' forge a dynamic and reciprocal relationship, and together gradually construct graffiti as a 'crime of style', by both challenging and affirming the power of the 'aesthetics of authority'. Even more geographically and stylistically distant from New York, anthropologist Susan Phillips's work entitled *Wallbangin'* (1999), analyses the cultural and territorial dimensions of gang graffiti in Los Angeles and, most importantly for our current discussion, introduces useful categories and definitions about various graffiti subgenres. Sociologist Nancy Macdonald's study *The Graffiti Subculture* (2001) is based on subcultural theories and centres the discussion on the expression and formation of the (gendered) identity of the practitioners in London and New York. Historian Joe Austin, in his seminal book *Taking the Train* (2001), traces how New York graffiti was constructed, by the media and the municipal authorities, as an urban problem; while Ivor Miller's *Aerosol Kingdom* (2002) examines, using a more ethnic approach, the development and cultural influences of specific artists as well as the history and various other aspects of the 'aerosol art' movement. Around the same time, a couple of publications initiate a discussion on the pedagogical potentials of graffiti (Rahn 2002; Christen 2003), while others begin to raise concerns about its commodification (Alvelos 2004).

In a sense, the aforementioned publications close the 'second wave' of graffiti scholarship, while paving the way for the emergence of the 'third'. This also historically coincides with the establishment of the 'street art' in the visual sphere. After that time, the number of academic publications grows geometrically. Many scholars join the debate on graffiti and street art, and start critically analysing these practices, something that results in several interesting articles and book chapters. These are mostly theoretical (sometimes over-theoretical) approaches that study graffiti in plural form rather than examining each graffito in its context. In our view, an exemplar exception of this era of scholarship is Ella Chmielewska's context-considerate take on graffiti (2007) and her proposal to carefully approach and critically examine both the temporal dimension of writing and the photographic medium of its documentation (2009), thus opening up new research potentials and methodological paths. During that period, several other aspects of these practices have been examined, such as graffiti and street art's territorial dimensions (Brighenti 2010) and their relationship with spatial control (Keith 2005) and liminality (Campos 2009), or the militarization of urban environments that they invite (Iveson 2010). Also, scholars investigate the connection of graffiti and street art with cultural heritage (MacDowall 2006) and interpret it as digitally archived and constantly flowing information (Bowen 2010; Pennycook 2010). The increasing interest in graffiti in academia is highlighted by the amplified numbers of the recent special journal issues,[13] conferences[14] and courses[15] dedicated to the subject.

One more important publication that deserves to be included in this list of key scholarly works on the subject – despite the fact that it does not focus on graffiti per se but uses it as a case study – is the *Publics and the City* (2007) by geographer Kurt Iveson. The author brings together the material and immaterial dimensions of publics and public spaces through the notion of 'public address', which he considers to be a 'form of visibility' in the city. Iveson explores the scene of Sydney and claims that there is a need to move our focus from the texts on the walls to the 'forms' through which they are circulated. Lisa Gottlieb's *Graffiti Art Styles* (2008) examines graffiti from a completely different angle. Gottlieb uses Erwin Panofsky's iconographical theories and suggests a classifications system for graffiti pieces, while introducing a model that allows us to understand which graffiti can count for (non-) representational images based on their visual characteristics. Sociologist Gregory Snyder, in his thorough ethnographic study *Graffiti Lives* (2009), investigates the graffiti subculture in New York City. He is primarily concerned with the complex interweaving of style, space and market. Snyder also attempts to counter the misconceptions about writers by putting emphasis on the creative careers that practitioners follow by utilizing the skills they have acquired or further developed through their participation in writing.

In the years that follow, while several works continue to study the history and/or the aesthetics of New York graffiti (e.g. Stewart 2009; a belated publication of his 1989 work), one can witness a new trend in the scholarship. This trend attempts to challenge, rethink and redefine the terms with which the scholars of the field became too comfortable, even though these were no longer able to capture the stylistic evolution or the cultural transformations of the practice in the streets and the galleries (Dickens 2008; Thompson 2009; Wacławek 2011; Irvine 2012). Yet, in general, the key themes examined in the field are the stylistic innovation of graffiti and street, the (sub)cultural dimensions and the identity of practitioners, and the (re)actions that these practices invite, which are often associated with the politics and governance of space (e.g. Kramer 2010; McAuliffe 2012). In others words, the main focus of the majority of studies up to this historical point is on the agents, their motivations and identities rather than on the material artefacts that they leave behind, through which one can reconstruct or invent narratives of the city (e.g. Brook and Dunn 2011). Two recent studies, however, concentrate on both the material artefacts and their representations, thus approaching graffiti as a tool to explore modes of urban critique.

Visual criminologist Alison Young, after many years of study and numerous articles on the subject, in her monograph *Street Art, Public City* (2014) looks at several urban art and mark-making practices but primarily focuses on 'street art' and its 'situational' character. The author explores the ways through which artists manage to reveal a vibrant 'public city', a 'city within a city', that, in a sense, criticizes the 'legislated city' – one that is produced by sets of regulations and is associated to the notions of property and ownership – while also highlighting the differences between graffiti and street art in terms of the criminalization of their image and treatment of the practitioners. In the study *Ornament and Order* (2014), anthropologist Rafael Schacter examines graffiti and street art – or what he calls 'Independent Public Art' – and pays attention to the materiality of these objects/images as well as to the ritualistic performances of their production. Most importantly, Schacter shifts the focus from the cultural to the material impact of this practice.

A parallel set of publications focusing on rock art and ancient graffiti – which is primarily authored by classical studies and archaeology scholars – has also a lot to offer in the study of its contemporary counterparts (e.g. Fleming 2001; David and Wilson 2002; Nash and Chippindale 2002; Oliver and Neal 2010; Baird and Taylor 2011). Even though these two interrelated fields occasionally exchange ideas and methods, up until recently they remained distant from each other.

These works' most important elements are the meticulous contextualization of the case studies and the reconstruction methods they adapt; two aspects that are often missing from contemporary graffiti studies. Another interesting dimension of these studies is the way they represent the inscriptions, i.e. together with the substrate of writing. This is in contrast to some contemporary graffiti scholarly works that represent graffiti primarily photographically and consider it to be a global phenomenon with similar material results and cultural aspects, thus often ignoring the situational, regional and cultural particularities. Further, the ancient graffiti and rock-art studies blur the differences between the textual and pictorial, the material and performative, and account for the context of production and perception of the writing. In other words, they prompt us to look more carefully at the surfaces upon which these graffiti appear. In a sense, these works remind us of what Roland Barthes considered graffiti to be: 'neither the inscription nor its message but the wall, the background, the surface' (1991 [1979]: 167). Yet, the graffiti-related edited collections that recently came out (Lovata and Olton 2015; Youkhana and Förster 2015) demonstrate that the gap between those two research strands, between ancient and contemporary graffiti, has started to be bridged and initiate a new round of productive exchanges. Finally, Jeffrey Ian Ross's *Handbook of Graffiti and Street Art* (2016), which provides an extensive summary and a reflective overview of the current approaches, works as the finishing line of the 'third wave' on the topic; by providing a comprehensive account on the theme, at the same time, marks the end of an era.

Now, let's 'fill in'

We envision that this edited volume would signal the beginning of the 'fourth wave' in graffiti and street art scholarship as all the contributors are mapping new territories by offering fresh and innovative ways of approaching the topic. As such, the volume at hand commences a new wave of literature that not only continues and reflects the invaluable tradition that it inherited and that largely shaped it, but also opens new research possibilities. The goal here is to extend the literature by introducing new scholars, exploring new methods, and investigating case studies and urban contexts from cities around the world that, even though they have blossoming scenes, have not had the chance to be critically explored or commented upon as yet. Prioritizing the visual, experiential and material along with the spatial and political, this volume aims to critically unpack the idiosyncrasies of our urban environments.

Graffiti and street art are often considered as distinct practices, and as such, many of the theoretical, methodological and empirical connections between artistic/subcultural practices are lost. Thus, by including the range of forms considered under these terms, we want to include the grit, the 'beef', the territoriality that are concomitant with writing on these art practices. We hope to explode some of the definitions that delimit which practices 'count'; and we are looking to push some of the creative form inherent to the practice into the modes of writing about graffiti and street art.

Our contributors are from urban studies, architecture, sociology, criminology, geography, anthropology, cultural and visual studies, as well as scholars that transcend traditional disciplinary frameworks. This mix is about fertile conversation across disciplines. Moreover, the constructive dialogue moves also across geographical borders as the volume includes contributions spreading from South and North America to Europe and Australia. This allows the volume to work as a map for current and future researchers and practitioners.

The edited volume aims to:

- be the first systematic collection of original, critical scholarly works that explore issues related to contemporary urban public writing;
- offer context-considerate case studies grounded in different social, cultural and urban settings in order to highlight how this global phenomenon is localized and how local practices contribute to the perpetuation of the global scene;
- bring together scholars from various disciplines to not only identify the points of convergence they share, but also examine, or rather encourage and enhance, the potentials of methodological exchanges;
- encourage new ways of thinking about the field and the possibilities of destabilizing current research methods;
- explore the position of academics with their research subjects and the implications that this might entail for a sensitive research subject such as graffiti and street art.

The contributions of the edited volume focus on specific and situated instances of graffiti and street art in their spatial, social and political contexts. In terms of scale, they range from the examination of a specific artist or an event and a web platform to a piece or a local scene in its urban context. Case studies from the UK, USA, Canada, Australia, Spain, Greece, Cyprus, Egypt and Brazil, among others, seek to reveal the plurality of the uses of graffiti and street art around the globe.

The aim of collecting context-considerate analyses that investigate how graffiti and street art are read, written and represented, is to reverse the current trend in the field, i.e. over-theorizations and generalizations, and move a step further, not by applying methods but, rather, by inventing them. The contributions intend for the physical objects, actual subjects and representational material to speak for themselves. The edited volume incorporates theories and approaches that shed new light on these phenomena and it has a balance between theoretical, methodological and empirical chapters.

Given the unique nature of graffiti and street art as both physical acts and cultural practices, as local and global at the same time, as polemic yet context-dependent, we are looking to elaborate these phenomena through a set of three distinct, yet by definition interwoven, key frames: *reading*, *writing* and *representing* graffiti, street art and the city. The concept '*reading*' moves beyond the purely linguistic understanding of the text in the city and the city as text, and is seen here as both an interpretative process and a dynamic act of creating new nexuses of meaning: a 'reading anew' that makes links between graffiti, street art and the city and identifies their relationships. The notion *'writing'* is, first and foremost, an allusion to the etymological roots of graffiti which puts emphasis on the action of the practice. The contributions addressing this concept concentrate on the actions of writing in space and writing about writing in space. *'Representing'* proved to be the most difficult to define, as its understanding varies considerably among different disciplines and individuals. The treatment of the notion here ranges from actual representations of graffiti, street art and the city (e.g. in novels or online environments) to what they represent; in other words, it is seen both as a representation of and representing something.

Individual chapters can serve as valuable stand-alone resources, yet, the volume is structured as a *narrative* that covers all the stages of graffiti and street art in relation to the city: from the production, documentation and dissemination of the pieces to the reactions, criminalization and their removal.

Time to draw the 'outlines'

The sequence of drawing the outlines of a graffito is never random; nor is the sequence of the chapters in this volume. Each part includes four papers full of rich data from a variety of urban contexts and closes with one position piece that offers a series of provocations and, in that sense, maps out territories for future investigations.

Part I of this collection, *Reading graffiti, street art and the city*, considers how graffiti and street art are perceived and treated in various domains, disciplines and fields – such as the academic world, the art establishment, campaigns, cultural and educational institutions, city authorities, activist groups, legal systems. This section considers how distinct perspectives 'read' the processes and products of artists in order to raise some key questions about public space, agency, artistic merit, criminalization and relation with property. The chapters in this section map, and critically reflect upon, the reactions that graffiti and street art invite and explore the iterative formation of the subculture of writers/artists.

The opening chapter by Jeff Ferrell, *Graffiti, street art and the dialectics of the city*, eloquently maps out the existing scholarly territories; his approach is underpinned by a recognition of the politics behind the act of wall writing. This chapter is the entry point of the volume, as it carefully unpacks issues and opens up research trajectories that many of the following contributors reflect upon or extend. Supported by specific cases, Ferrell identifies the dynamics of graffiti, street art and the contemporary city as a series of 'four unfolding dialectic tensions: crisscrossing between legality and illegality, visibility and invisibility, art and action, ephemerality and elongation'. As he claims, in the street, the dynamics of the contemporary city 'are encoded in the dialectics of its art; to read one is to read the other'.

Alison Young's chapter, *Art or crime or both at the same time? On the ambiguity of images in public space*, focuses on the ambiguous nature of images in public space and investigates the difficulties of reading illicit imagery and the consequences that this entails. More specifically, she explores the contradictions arising after the cultural legitimation of street art in combination with the harsh prosecutions for graffiti, while suggesting that the division between these two is no longer adequate to grasp the complexity of images in public spaces. Examining closely specific cases in cities such as New York, London, Berlin and Melbourne, Young touches upon the delicate theme of cultural appropriation of certain practices and the limits between legality and illegality. She unpacks the complex relationship between spectator and urban image, and at the same time poses questions of authority over urban aesthetics and public space.

In the third chapter entitled *Reading between the [plot] lines: framing graffiti as multimodal practice*, Samantha Edwards-Vandenhoek uses specific photographed examples from Melbourne and Sydney to test a multimodal and intertextual reading of graffiti. The aim here is to expose 'plot lines' otherwise inaccessible and to poeticize – without romanticizing – places through the reading of their writings. Edwards-Vandenhoek proposes an outline of an interpretative framework developed to navigate the complexity of this material. The photographic framing intermingles with a discussion of Shanks's 'archaeography' and Barthes's twin concepts of the 'studium' and 'punctum', which are the main theoretical vehicles in approaching graffiti as a multimodal practice.

Sabina Andron, in her chapter *Interviewing walls: towards a method of reading hybrid surface inscriptions*, takes us to the streets of London where she conducts 'interviews' with particular surfaces. In so doing, Andron proposes a new 'reading' method to expand our understanding of unsanctioned inscriptions as situated graphic marks, and explores their relations to sanctioned inscriptions and surface environments. In a similar fashion to Edwards-Vandenhoek's work, Andron examines signs holistically and introduces the term 'hybrid surface inscriptions' which encompasses all sorts of signs on the walls, including, but not limited to, graffiti and street art. Using the concepts of 'semiotic' and 'linguistic landscapes', Andron shows how unsanctioned inscriptions, such as street art and graffiti, make use of and interact with their sanctioned counterparts (e.g. advertising and street signage), and prompts us to examine them together.

Kurt Iveson's *Graffiti, street art and the democratic city*, offers a provocative reading of graffiti and street art practices as openings towards the creation of a more democratic city. Iveson rereads graffiti and street art not merely as 'confrontations with' authority but rather as 'assertions of' alternative forms of authority. Then, he considers both the authority of 'the authorities' and the alternative authority enacted by writers and artists in relation to a model of democratic authority and, in so doing, challenges some of the well-established stereotypes on the notions of public space and urban belonging. Finally, Iveson introduces four fresh graffiti-related approaches that he considers capable of enacting and contributing to a more democratic and equal city, namely policy advocacy, permission, participation and publicization.

Part II of the book, *Writing graffiti, street art and the city*, positions the intentions, logistics and embodied nature of making pieces as examples of art interventions that make sense of urban spaces. The contributions here relate to the particularity of the form as a process. Of great importance in these chapters is a sense of aesthetics and styles, spatial tactics, language used, urban settings, materiality and locality. Yet, there is also the need to engage with the problem of writing *about* graffiti and street art and some of the chapters here engage directly with these practices *as* methodology. The section also outlines different contexts in which graffiti and street art can be found and considers the relation between graffiti, street art and contemporary 'creative' capitalism.

Rafael Schacter opens this second part of the book. In the chapter entitled *Street art is a period, PERIOD: or, classificatory confusion and intermural art*, he addresses the problem of writing about graffiti and street art, by identifying a classificatory confusion in the way these two terms are used by practitioners and scholars alike. Schacter claims that the term 'street art' is no longer capable of grasping the works produced today in the streets or the galleries while arguing that it was a 'period'. In lack of adequate terminology, he coins the term 'intermural art' in an attempt to describe, categorize and organize graffiti and street art. Schacter engages with the difficult task of arrangement and laying out, while at the same time he recognizes and embraces the complex, dynamic and contested nature of graffiti and street art that goes against fixed categories.

In the next chapter, *Expressive measures: an ecology of the public domain*, Andrea Mubi Brighenti adapts an ecological approach to explore the manifestation and significance of urban practices in the public domain. He contests the trend of street art and, to a lesser extent, graffiti to function as conveyors of 'urban creativity', a notion that, despite its ambiguous and fuzzy nature, in recent years has not only gained momentum and legitimacy but has also been projected on and linked with these practices thus transforming them into tools of economic growth. Brighenti insists that 'creativity' has become a major asset in contemporary capitalist valorisation processes, and proposes a more critical reading of these value-creation circuits through the notions of 'expressive measure' and 'artful material'. This highlights the division between creativity and expression, and, in a sense, challenges how we write about and think of graffiti and street art in the city.

Dead ends and urban insignias: writing graffiti and street art (hi)stories along the UN buffer zone in Nicosia, 2010–2014 by Panos Leventis, offers an urban walk in the streets of the buffer zone in the walled city of Nicosia. Here, the writings on the walls become the material to write short fictional urban stories. In other words, Leventis writes about writings as he voyages through the city. In this chapter research and narrative parts, images and texts, facts and fictions, are creatively interwoven. As he travels us through the city, Leventis poetically unpacks the different layers of the urban fabric and the social conditions based on which graffiti and street art images acquire their meaning. Leventis treats graffiti and street art as agent provocateurs in his evocation of the tensions and contradictions of Nicosia.

In the next chapter we move from Cyprus to the culturally and geographically neighbouring Greece. In *The December 2008 uprising's stencil images in Athens: writing or inventing traces of the future?*, Stavros Stavrides detects the traces of the 2008 revolt in Athens through an analysis of the boosting street art scene during and after the uprising. Stavrides, whose corpus consists of protest stencils, introduces the notion of 'invented traces' in his attempt to interpret the different ways street art appropriates and transforms the official city. For Stavrides, the street art pieces from the revolt are traces meant to performatively recall a shared memory-in-the-making and a call to action. These stencils are neither writings nor representations but 'images-as-presences' that aim to contribute to a collective redefinition of urban public space; they are the ideal vehicles to unpack the changing relationship between city spaces and an urban populace in search of its identity in times of crisis.

Remaining in the Mediterranean region, Mona Abaza's *Repetitive repertoires: how writing about Cairene graffiti has turned into a serial monotony*, focuses on the scene of Cairo in the context of the post-January 2011 revolution. Here graffiti not only reflects the conflictual socio-political condition, but also responds to its exploitation, thus transforming urban surfaces into channels through which writers communicate their distrust towards those who attempt to capitalize on their work. Framed by Bourdieu's theory of the 'cultural field', this chapter critically examines the situation in which artworks are produced, circulated and consumed. Abaza investigates the active role that cultural institutions and individuals (including academics) play in the commercialization and commodification of the local graffiti scene. By engaging dialectically with this complex network of 'players', she exposes its ethical paradoxes, while questioning both the role and the position of those involved in this 'field'. Abaza raises concerns about the overconsumption of Cairene graffiti as a research subject – which tends becoming repetitive and monotonous – and invites us to consider how we, as researchers, affect the very nature of graffiti and the ways it manifests in urban settings.

The accent in the chapters of the final Part III of this volume, *Representing graffiti, street art and the city* is on the ways graffiti and street art are represented and circulated, and examine how this influences these practices. Contributors here investigate how, why, and with what impact graffiti, street art and the city are represented in media, whether popular or mass, online or offline. This section moves beyond locatedness to the diffuse dissemination of pieces, and critically unpacks the relationship between practitioners and a whole ensemble of professional figures (fans and promoters, journalists and politicians, etc.).

The opening chapter of this final part of the volume concentrates on Latin America, and more specifically the rich and stylistically unique scene of São Paulo in Brazil. Alexander Lamazares, in his contribution entitled *São Paulo's pixação and street art: representations of or responses to Brazilian modernism?*, uses as a starting point de Andrade's modernist concept 'cultural cannibalism' – a symbolic metaphor and theory of cultural hybridity that permeates Brazilian modernist thought, upon which national identity was built and aesthetics was formed – to explore São Paulo's pixação and street art as a means to critically engage with its postcolonial position. He examines local graffiti as responses to a series of urban conditions that emerged from the modernist project: segregation, anonymity, monotony and verticality, among others. Investigating the special visual treatment of Paulistanos' public interventions locally and globally, Lamazares sees these as representations of the national identity that is based on modernism. Pixação challenges modernism and is presented as a dystopian representation of its failures, while street art is welcomed as it is seen as a continuation of the modernist project, representing a local and national pride.

The next chapter transfers us to the North regions of the American continent, in particular to the Canadian capital. In *Defensible aesthetics: creative resistance to urban policies in Ottawa*, Deborah Landry offers a representation of the eradication of graffiti and street art in Ottawa, as an entrance point to the discourses surrounding the right to public space and the hypocritical municipal attempts for a 'secure' city. Her ethnographic study provides first hand insights and reports from the 'front', i.e. both from the streets and the rooms where the meetings among representatives of the city take place, whose policies will eventually affect how graffiti shapes and is represented in the city. Despite city officials' alleged support for urban art, their primary concern is the promotion of a particular aesthetic agenda that can be 'defensible' to the city council. Landry aptly argues that 'irony is a key feature of graffiti' and as such the constructive and scholarly value of ironic critique is utilized as a key element throughout her contribution.

Lachlan MacDowall's *#Instafame: aesthetics, audiences, data* takes us from the physical to the digital world in an exploration of the ways through which graffiti and street art are represented as digital objects, deeply informed by the particularities of digital platforms and the online responses of the users. MacDowall focuses, in particular, on the rise of *Instagram* as an online digital platform that transmutes graffiti and street art into data. By comparing small (local) and large (global) data, he presents the dialectical relationship between the physical and digital in this subcultural context. In so doing, he proposes a different conceptualization of what (the representations of) the 'city' might mean in an era characterized by the pervasive presence of social networking platforms: 'a scenic backdrop for the production of digital content', as he puts it. MacDowall offers glimpses into the complex ecology of formats and feeds in which graffiti and street art exist and the potential of data-driven analysis for representing the global flows and fault lines of style and taste.

We remain detached from the physical reality and this time we move to fiction, as the accent of the penultimate chapter is on a novel that refers to graffiti and street art in Madrid, Spain. Stephen Luis Vilaseca's chapter *Representations of graffiti and the city in the novel* El francotirador paciente: *readings of the emergent urban body in Madrid*, combines textual criticism with social analysis and provides a fascinating mix of real urban aesthetics and socio-political issues with fictional characters from Pérez-Reverte's novel *The Patient Sniper*. By doing this, he blurs the limits between fiction and reality in an attempt to expose the obscurifications of the battle over public space and the restrictive policies related to the neoliberal city. In the polemic representation of graffiti and the city in the novel, Vilaseca diagnoses the potentials of an 'emergent urban body' in Madrid, namely a collective – constantly in the making – body that street artists are modelling in and with the city, that seeks a new type of symbiosis with the urban environment.

The last contribution takes us back to the birthplace of contemporary graffiti, New York City. In *Long live the tag: representing the foundations of graffiti*, Gregory Snyder concentrates on the most elementary, misunderstood and hated form of graffiti writing – the tag. Snyder identifies that the 'tag' is often seen as a representation of illegality and focuses on an emblematic legal piece executed with 'illegal aesthetics', i.e. with tags. In so doing, he exposes the contradictions associated with the production and perception of graffiti, and questions the simplistic polarities through which graffiti is frequently thought of (e.g. legal vs illegal, art vs vandalism, etc.). Snyder's chapter is structured in a similar way to the volume that hosts it, thus underlining once again how inextricably linked the key concepts of this collection are. For Snyder, the tag represents the foundations of this writing genre: everything begins and finishes with a tag.

Adding the final 'details' and 'sign'

When we started this collection, we had to make some choices on what to include. As with graffiti and street art production, it is impossible to capture, document and present all the themes, voices and academic production on the topic out there. After all, this is a collection and as Jean Baudrillard said, the 'miracle of collecting' is that 'what you really collect is always yourself' (1996 [1968]: 91). Thus, we are aware of the subjectivity behind our choices and, at the same time, we feel that it would be hubris to even imagine claiming that we hold any blueprint of objective inclusion and representation of the field.

As we put the final details on these pages back to the place where all this began, in the Athens School of Fine Arts, we struggle with our positions as scholars, writers, and (street) activists, but somehow feel connected to all these spectrums of our identities. Yet, in this space right now the academic self has to write the grand finale as the sound of the spray cans is approaching.

So, dear reader, here's our last provocation: someone at the edge of your city is writing on the wall. These visual markers of the shifting discourses of power struggle, authority over public space, and counter-cultures established a new paradigm of urban aesthetics. This transformation of walls into urban diaries offers glimpses of the 'soul through the hand' as the opening quote by Hillman suggests. It is in this light that graffiti and street art are remapping the city, and teach us that urban realities are never single but multiple, and if you follow the tags you might end up in a space where playfulness, desire and hope are not only permitted but necessary.

The emergent feelings aroused by the proliferation of marks, scratches and statements provide a sensation of the kind of affective landscape that is mapped across by the political and social conditions. This volume is an interdisciplinary journey into this affective landscape created by graffiti and street art in different social, cultural and urban settings. It is a journey without a final destination, no fin-de-siècle for us, urban dwellers in search of the writing on the wall. Enjoy the ride.

Signed. The editors.

Notes

1 Graffiti and street art, of course, are not merely urban phenomena as writers and artists intervene in various other locations, such as highways, trains, etc. In this edited collection, however, we limit the discussion to the urban manifestation of these practices but keep it open to include the products stemming from the city.
2 An image from Boom's famous tag is available at: http://graffquotes.com/search/the+city+is+a+poem. Accessed: 20 December 2015.
3 For a detailed genealogy of the definitional attempts on graffiti and street art see Ross 2016.
4 The need for this shift of focus has recently been raised, most notably by Jennifer Edbauer (2005) and Sonja Neef (2011) in the context of graffiti and street art as eventful, situated and performative mark-making practices (cf. Avramidis 2014).
5 In this case, skill does not only refer to the artistic capacities of the practitioners. Sometimes it is exactly the absence of artistic skill as defined in fine arts schools, that makes the work interesting and multilayered.
6 This edited volume consists of three interconnected parts that have arisen from the last global summit of graffiti and street art hosted by the Onassis Cultural Center in Athens (6 June 2014), which was facilitated by Konstantinos Avramidis.
7 The collaborative showcase 'Bridges of Graffiti', held in the Venice Biennale (9 May–22 November 2015), is emblematic of this trend. The exhibition was accompanied by a book show that attempted to reconstruct the history of publishing in graffiti. Over 140 titles were on display, the majority of which were non-academic. Available at: www.thebridgesofgraffiti.com/bookshow-info/. Accessed: 20 December 2015.
8 Famous Hollywood couple 'Brangelina' spent £1 million to acquire a Banksy in an auction (Brennan 2007). For more on wall removals and trade of street art see Bengtsen (2014) and Young (2016).
9 Famous Italian street artist Blu erased all the murals he painted in his hometown Bologna in the past 20 years to resist to the promoted commodification of his work. For a detailed report see Caprioli 2016.
10 Mutatis mutandis, the equivalent of Mailer *et al.*'s work (1974) in the context of London is Perry's book (1976) which was, however, less influential.
11 For another study that researches the political dimension of street art in Latin America, see Ryan 2017.
12 The 'first wave' focuses primarily on what graffiti *is* and how it is the expression of dissatisfied youths, while the 'second wave' concentrates on what graffiti *does* especially in relation to urban space and began in the early 1990s.
13 See for example the following special journal issues: Iveson 2010; Lennon and Burns 2013; Samutina and Zaporozhets 2015; Neves and de Freitas Simões 2015.
14 Examples of recent conferences on graffiti and street art include, but are not limited to, the following:

GraffiCity: Materialized Visual Practices in the Public Urban Space. Cologne: University of Cologne. 17–19 April 2013.
Street Art in the Changing City: Theoretical Perspectives. Moscow: National Research University, Higher School of Economics. 7–8 June 2013.
(Dis)respectful Creativity: The Impact of Graffiti & Street Art on Contemporary Society & Urban Spaces. Athens: Onassis Cultural Centre. 6 June 2014.
Street Art and Urban Creativity Conference. Lisbon: University of Lisbon. 3–5 July 2014.
Graffiti Sessions. London: University College of London. 3–5 December 2014.
Philosophy of Street Art. New York: Pratt Institute. 5–7 March 2015.

15 Examples of academic courses on graffiti and street art include, but are not limited to, the following:

Word Collector at the McGill University, organized by Angeliki Sioli. Available at: www.mcgill.ca/architecture-theory/curriculum/masters/preparation.

Text and the City at the University of Edinburgh, organized by Ella Chmielewska. Available at:www.interkultur.eca.ed.ac.uk/courses_new.html.

Street Art at the University of Melbourne, organized by Lachlan MacDowall. Available at: https://handbook.unimelb.edu.au/view/2015/CCDP20001.

Graffiti and Legislating Aesthetics and *Graffiti & Governance* at the University of Ottawa, organized by Deborah Landry. Available at: www.pedagogmob.com/laws-3903.html; www.pedagogmob.com/crm-4310.html.

Graffiti as a Medium of Communication at the John Paul II Catholic University of Lublin, organized by Małgorzata Sławek-Czochra. Available at: https://e.kul.pl/qlsale. html?op=10&zid=409747&oz_lng=2.

Special Topics in Art & Society: Graffiti and Street Art at the University of Concordia, organized by Anna Wacławek. Available at: www.concordia.ca/finearts/art-history/programs/undergraduate/courses/archives/2011–2012/summer-july/graffiti-street-art.html. Accessed: 20 December 2015.

References

Alvelos, Heitor. 2004. 'The Desert of Imagination in the City of Signs: Cultural Implications of Sponsored Transgression and Branded Graffiti'. In Ferrell, Jeff, Hayward, Keith, Morrison, Wayne and Presdee, Mike (eds), *Cultural Criminology Unleashed*. London: Glass House Press, pp. 181–191.

Austin, Joe. 2001. *Taking the Train: How Graffiti Art became an Urban Crisis in New York City*. New York, NY: Columbia University Press.

Austin, Joe. 2013. 'Academics Don't Write: A Few Brief Scribblings and Some Questions'. *Rhizomes*. 25. Available at: www.rhizomes.net/issue25/austin.html. Accessed: 20 December 2015.

Avramidis, Konstantinos. 2012. ' "Live your Greece in Myths": Reading the Crisis on Athens' Walls'. *Professional Dreamers, working paper no.8*. Available at: www. professionaldreamers.net/_prowp/wp-content/uploads/Avramides-Reading-the-Crisis-on-Athens-walls-fld.pdf. Accessed: 20 December 2015.

Avramidis, Konstantinos. 2014. 'Public [Ypo]graphy: Notes on Materiality and Placement'. In Karra, Marilena (ed.), *No Respect*. Athens: Onassis Cultural Center, pp. 21–34, 85–96.

Avramidis, Konstantinos. 2015. 'Reading an Instance of Contemporary Urban Iconoclash: A Design Report from Athens'. *The Design Journal*. 18(4): 513–534.

Baird, Jennifer and Taylor, Claire. (eds). 2011. *Ancient Graffiti in Context*. London: Routledge.

Barthes, Roland. 1991 [1979]. 'Cy Twombly: Works on Paper'. In *The Responsibility of Forms: Critical Essays on Music, Art, and Representation*. Richard Howard (trans.). Berkeley, CA: University of California Press, pp. 157–176.

Baudrillard, Jean. 1996 [1968]. *The System of Objects*. Benedict, James (trans.). London: Verso.

Baudrillard, Jean. 1998 [1976]. 'Kool Killer, or the Insurrection of Signs'. In *Symbolic Exchange and Death*. Iain Hamilton Grant (trans.). London: Sage, pp. 76–83.

Bengtsen, Peter. 2014. *The Street Art World*. Lund: Almendros de Granada Press.

Bowen, Tracey. 2010. 'Reading Gestures and Reading Codes: The Visual Literacy of Graffiti as both Physical/Performative Act and Digital Information Text'. In Raesch, Monika (ed.), *Mapping Minds*. Oxford: Inter-Disciplinary Press, pp. 85–93.

Brassaï. 2002 [1964]. *Graffiti*. Radzinowicz, David (trans.). Paris: Flammarion.

Brennan, Greg. 2007. ' "Brangelina" Spend £1 Million on Banksy Work at Contemporary Art Auction in London'. *Daily Mail*, 12 October. Available at: www.dailymail.co.uk/ tvshowbiz/article-487230/Brangelina-spend-1-million-Banksy-work-contemporary-art-auction-London.html. Accessed: 20 December 2015.

Brighenti, Andrea Mubi. 2010. 'At the Wall: Graffiti Writers, Urban Territoriality, and the Public Domain'. *Space and Culture*. 13(3): 315–332.

Brook, Richard and Dunn, Nick. 2011. *Urban Maps: Instruments of Narrative and Interpretation in the City*. Burlington, VT: Ashgate.

Bushnell, John. 1990. *Moscow Graffiti: Language and Subculture*. Winchester, MA: Unwin Hyman.

Campos, Ricardo. 2009. 'On Urban Graffiti: Bairro Alto as a Liminal Space'. In Brighenti, Andrea Mubi (ed.), *The Wall and the City*. Trento: Professional Dreamers, pp. 135–151.

Caprioli, Caria. 2016. 'Blu in Bologna: Collateral Damages. Interview with Peter Bengtsen'. *Inchiesta*, 1 April. Available at: www.inchiestaonline.it/arte-poesia/peter-bengtsen-blu-a-bologna-danni-collaterali/. Accessed: 2 April 2016.

Castleman, Craig. 1982. *Getting Up: Subway Graffiti in New York*. Cambridge, MA: MIT Press.

Chaffee, Lyman. 1993. *Political Protest and Street Art: Popular Tools for Democratization in Hispanic Countries*. Westport, CT: Greenwood Press.

Chalfant, Henry and Prigoff, James. 1987. *Spraycan Art*. New York: Thames & Hudson.

Chmielewska, Ella. 2007. 'Framing [Con]text: Graffiti and Place'. *Space and Culture*. 10(2): 145–169.

Chmielewska, Ella. 2008. 'Writing on the Ruins or Graffiti as a Design Gesture: On the Paradoxes of Lettering Place and History'. *Edinburgh Architecture Research Journal*. 31: 7–15.

Chmielewska, Ella. 2009. 'Framing Temporality: Montréal Graffiti in Photography'. In Gérin, Annie and McLean, James (eds), *Public Art in Canada: Critical Perspectives*. Toronto: University of Toronto Press, pp. 271–292.

Cooper, Martha and Chalfant, Henry. 1984. *Subway Art*. New York, NY: Holt, Rinehart & Winston.

Cresswell, Tim. 1992. 'The Crucial "Where" of Graffiti: A Geographical Analysis of Reactions to Graffiti in New York'. *Environment and Planning D: Society and Space*. 10(3): 329–344.

Cresswell, Tim. 1996. *In Place/Out of Place: Geography, Ideology, and Transgression*. Minneapolis, MN: University of Minnesota Press.

Christen, Richard. 2003. 'Hip Hop Learning: Graffiti as an Educator of Urban Teenagers'. *Educational Foundations*. 17(4): 57–82.

David, Bruno and Wilson, Meredith. (eds). 2002. *Inscribed Landscapes: Marking and Making Place*. Honolulu, HI: University of Hawaii Press.

Dickens, Luke. 2008. 'Placing Post-Graffiti: The Journey of the Peckham Rock'. *Cultural Geographies*. 15(4): 471–496.

Edbauer, Jennifer. 2005. '(Meta)Physical Graffiti: "Getting Up" as Affective Writing Model'. *JAC*. 25(1): 131–159.

Ferrell, Jeff. 1993. *Crimes of Style: Urban Graffiti and the Politics of Criminality*. New York, NY: Garland.

Fleming, Juliet. 2001. *Graffiti and the Writing Arts of Early Modern England*. London: Reaktion.

Ganz, Nicholas. 2004. *Graffiti World: Street Art from Five Continents*. Tristan Manco (ed.). New York, NY: Abrams.

Gottlieb, Lisa. 2008. *Graffiti Art Styles: A Classification System and Theoretical Analysis*. Jefferson, NC: McFarland.

Hillman, James. 2008 [1989]. 'City and Soul'. In Moore, Thomas (ed.), *The Essential James Hillman: A Blue Fire*. London: Routledge, pp. 104–111.

Irvine, Martin. 2012. 'The Work on the Street: Street Art and Visual Culture'. In Sandywell, Barry and Heywood, Ian (eds), *The Handbook of Visual Culture*. London: Berg, pp. 235–278.

Iveson, Kurt. 2007. *Publics and the City*. Oxford: Blackwell.

Iveson, Kurt. 2010. 'The Wars on Graffiti and the New Military Urbanism'. *City*. 14(1–2): 115–134.

Iveson, Kurt. (ed.). 2010. *City [Special Issue on Graffiti, Street Art and the City]*. 14(1–2): 25–134.

Keith, Michael. 2005. *After the Cosmopolitan? Multicultural Cities and the Future of Racism*. London: Routledge.

Kramer, Ronald. 2010. 'Moral Panics and Urban Growth Machines: Official Reactions to Graffiti in New York City, 1990–2005'. *Qualitative Sociology*. 33(3): 297–311.

Lachmann, Richard. 1988. 'Graffiti as Career and Ideology'. *The American Journal of Sociology*. 94(2): 229–250.

Lennon, John and Burns, Matthew. (eds). 2013. *Rhizomes [Special Issue on Graffiti]*. 25. Available at: www.rhizomes.net/issue25/index.html. Accessed: 20 December 2015.

Ley, David and Cybriwsky, Roman. 1974. 'Urban Graffiti as Territorial Markers'. *Annals of the Association of American Geographers*. 64(4): 491–505.

Lovata, Troy and Olton, Elizabeth. (eds). 2015. *Understanding Graffiti: Multidisciplinary Studies from Prehistory to the Present*. Walnut Creek, CA: Left Coast Press.

Macdonald, Nancy. 2001. *The Graffiti Subculture: Youth, Masculinity and Identity in London and New York*. London: Palgrave Macmillan.

MacDowall, Lachlan. 2006. 'In Praise of 70K: Cultural Heritage and Graffiti Style'. *Continuum: Journal of Media & Cultural Studies*. 20(4): 471–484.

McAuliffe, Cameron. 2012. 'Graffiti or Street Art? Negotiating the Moral Geographies of the Creative City'. *Journal of Urban Affairs*. 34(2): 189–206.

Mailer, Norman, Naar, Jon and Kurlansky, Mervyn. 2009 [1974]. *The Faith of Graffiti*. New York, NY: Polaris Communications.

Mieszkowski, Jan. 2010. 'The Writing is on the Wall'. *Postmodern Culture*. 21(1): Available at: www.pomoculture.org/2013/09/03/the-writing-is-on-the-wall/. Accessed: 20 February 2016.

Miller, Ivor. 2002. *Aerosol Kingdom: Subway Painters of New York City*. Jackson, MS: University Press of Mississippi.

Mitchell, W. J. T. 1996. 'What Do Pictures "Really" Want?'. *October*. 77: 71–82.

Nash, George and Chippindale, Christopher. (eds). 2002. *European Landscapes of Rock-Art*. London: Routledge.

Neef, Sonja. 2011. *Imprint and Trace: Handwriting in the Age of Technology*. Mathews, Anthony (trans.). London: Reaktion Books.

Neves, Pedro Soares and de Freitas Simões, Daniela. (eds). 2015. *Street & Urban Creativity Scientific Journal*. 1(1&2).

Oliver, Jeff and Neal, Tim. (eds). 2010. *Wild Signs: Graffiti in Archaeology and History*. Oxford: British Archaeological Reports.

Pennycook, Alastair. 2010. 'Spatial Narrations: Graffscapes and City Souls'. In Jaworski, Adam and Thurlow, Crispin (eds), *Semiotic Landscapes: Language, Image, Space.* London: Continuum, pp. 137–150.

Perry, Roger. 1976. *The Writing on the Wall: The Graffiti of London.* London: Elm Tree Books.

Phillips, Christopher. 1990. 'When Poetry Devours the Walls'. *Art in America.* 78(2): 139–145.

Phillips, Susan. 1999. *Wallbangin': Graffiti and Gangs in L.A.* Chicago, IL: University of Chicago Press.

Powers, Stephen. 1999. *The Art of Getting Over: Graffiti at the Millennium.* New York, NY: St Martin's Press.

Rahn, Janice. 2002. *Painting without Permission: Hip-Hop Graffiti Subculture.* Westport, CT: Bergin & Garvey.

Reisner, Robert. 1971. *Graffiti: Two Thousand Years of Wall Writing.* Spokane, WA: 1Cowles.

Ross, Jeffrey Ian. (ed.). 2016. *Routledge Handbook of Graffiti and Street Art.* London: Routledge.

Ryan, Holly Eva. 2017. *Political Street Art: Communication, Culture and Resistance in Latin America.* London: Routledge.

Samutina, Natalia and Zaporozhets, Oksana. (eds). 2015. *Laboratorium [Special Issue on Street Art and the City].* 7(2): 5–133.

Schacter, Rafael. 2013. *The World Atlas of Street Art and Graffiti.* New Haven, CT: Yale University Press.

Schacter, Rafael. 2014. *Ornament and Order: Graffiti, Street Art and the Parergon.* Burlington, VT: Ashgate.

Schacter, Rafael. 2015. 'The Invisible Performance/the Invisible Masterpiece: Visibility, Concealment, and Commitment in Graffiti and Street Art'. In Flynn, Alex and Tinius, Jonas (eds), *Anthropology, Theatre, and Development.* London: Palgrave Macmillan, pp. 203–223.

Snyder, Gregory. 2009. *Graffiti Lives: Beyond the Tag in New York's Urban Underground.* New York, NY: New York University Press.

Stewart, Jack. 2009. *Graffiti Kings: New York Transit Art of the 1970s.* New York, NY: Abrams.

Thompson, Margo. 2009. *American Graffiti.* New York, NY: Parkstone Press.

Tsilimpounidi, Myrto. 2013. ' "See the Writing on the Wall": Street Art and Urban Poetics'. In Borriello, Luca and Ruggiero, Christian (eds), *Inopinatum: The Unexpected Impertinence of Urban Creativity.* Rome: Arti Grafiche Boccia, pp. 215–229.

Tsilimpounidi, Myrto. 2015. ' "If these Walls could Talk": Street Art and Urban Belonging in the Athens of Crisis'. *Laboratorium.* 7(2): 71–91.

Varnedoe, Kirk and Gopnik, Adam. 1990. *High & Low: Modern Art and Popular Culture.* New York, NY: Museum of Modern Art.

Wacławek, Anna. 2011. *Graffiti and Street Art.* London: Thames & Hudson.

Wilson, James and Kelling, George. 1982. 'Broken Windows'. *The Atlantic Monthly.* (March): 29–38.

Youkhana, Eva and Förster, Larissa. (eds). 2015. *Grafficity: Visual Practices and Contestations in Urban Space.* Paderborn: Wilhelm Fink Verlag.

Young, Alison. 2014. *Street Art, Public City: Law, Crime and the Urban Imagination.* London: Routledge.

Young, Alison. 2016. *Street Art World.* London: Reaktion.

Part I

Reading graffiti, street art and the city

1 Graffiti, street art and the dialectics of the city

Jeff Ferrell

Introduction

As graffiti and street art have proliferated globally over the past half century they have become all the more complex and contradictory. This is in part a matter of scale; with the expanding cultural and geographic range of contemporary street art and graffiti has come an expanding variety of meanings and interpretations. It is also a matter of global politics. Often emerging in situations of economic inequality and social upheaval, graffiti and street art regularly come to embody the contested cultural dynamics of these situations (see for example Bushnell 1990; Lennon 2014). But above all it is a matter of the city; it is the urban character of street art and graffiti that guarantees their continued complexity and contradiction. Graffiti and street art are deeply urban phenomena, certainly the most visible forms of global urban culture and urban cultural transgression (Bofkin 2014). More than this, they are urban folk art – the distinctive folk art of the contemporary global city. To read street art and graffiti, to understand their nuances and their negations, then, we must read the contemporary global city as well. When we do, we find that the city is itself a tangle of emerging contradictions, and a place of mutating political economy. In fact, it is the changing economic and political dynamics of the global city – and the messy conflation of street art and graffiti with these new forms of urban economy and control – that shape graffiti and street art today. Caught up in the dynamics of the contemporary city, graffiti and street art unfold as a series of dialectical tensions, crisscrossing between legality and illegality, visibility and invisibility, art and action, ephemerality and elongation. In the street, the dynamics of the contemporary city are encoded in the dialectics of its art; to read one is to read the other.

Law, crime and economy in the contemporary city

During roughly the same period that street art and graffiti have emerged as global cultural phenomena, urban life has been redefined by two powerful trends. First has been the evolution of a new regime of urban social control that includes the exponential growth of urban surveillance and street policing strategies, expanding micro-governance based on risk management ideologies, and the spread of restrictive environmental designs. The global city is now permeated by motion sensors, CCTV/security cameras, sonic tracking devices, and other technologies of surveillance. Urban authorities contend that the surveillance-saturated urban environments that they engineer promote safety and reduce risk, all while enacting a form of preventative policing that obviates the need for 'reactive' policing. Beyond the pervasive surveillance cameras and sensors, this orientation is further encoded in the materiality of the city, designed into new or newly reconstructed urban environments by way of barrier planting, building sight lines, restricted walkways, closed public facilities, and other forms of what advocates call CPTED – 'crime prevention through environmental design'. Complementing these many forms of spatial and technological control is the widely used 'broken windows' approach to street policing, with its focus on physical deterioration ('broken windows'), panhandlers, loiterers, and other alleged signs of urban decay. According to the broken windows approach, and to the plethora of politicians and police chiefs who advocate and utilize it, instances of seemingly harmless, low-level urban disorder in fact dispirit everyday urban citizens, embolden more hardened criminals, and inaugurate a downward spiral of incivility, urban violence and neighbourhood destruction. By this logic, then, low-level, non-violent 'quality of life' street crimes must in fact be the focus of law enforcement, to be monitored and policed aggressively if every day urban civility is to be maintained and urban life is to prosper.

A second development in contemporary urban life might seem wholly independent from the first, occurring as it does not in the harsh realm of street policing and surveillance, but in the more indulgent worlds of shopping, dining, entertainment and fine living. This is the trend towards what its advocates call 'consumption-driven urban development' (Markusen and Schrock 2009). Under this new political economy of the city, the traditional forces of urban economy and growth – the solid sectors of urban manufacturing and production, now largely relocated elsewhere in a global race to the bottom of wages and production standards – are replaced by new forms of urban economic development founded in cultural creativity, privatized city spaces, and exclusionary zones of consumerism and residence. Here 'quality of life' emerges as a symbolic commodity to be sold to prosperous urban residents, and in turn as a signifier of urban vitality and success. Because of this the city becomes its own simulacrum, a Disneyland redesign of its former self, its image of urban hipness and metropolitan style now meticulously manufactured and marketed to those young professionals whom city leaders hope to attract. Anyone who has toured Berlin or Boston or Birmingham has seen it: in one area the old factories, warehouses and workers' quarters now repurposed as specialty shops, locavore restaurants and trendy lofts; in another the shuttered factories and working class neighbourhoods now razed and replaced with gated communities and stylish guard houses.

The first of these urban trends centres on social control, and the second on social class – but in the contemporary practice of urban life, as in the contemporary practice of street art and graffiti, the two are thoroughly entangled. Regimes of risk management, surveillance and environmental design are used to manipulate those who participate in the privatized and highly profitable night time economy of dining, dancing and music; these regimes are also deployed against those marginalized populations who would, by intention or desperation, intrude on such privatized consumption spaces. At the level of the urban simulacrum, these approaches serve more broadly to police the city's image – that is, to make invisible those who might, by their poverty or illicit mobility, sully the city's manufactured image of itself. Likewise, the aggressive 'broken windows' policing of low-level 'quality of life' crimes works to criminalize and erase unregulated urban inter-action, and to criminalize and exclude outsider populations, in this way promoting an image of urban safety while protecting the privileged urban lifestyles of young professionals and other consumers of the contemporary city (Ferrell 2001; Mitchell 2003; Beckett and Herbert 2009).

For urban graffiti and street art generally, and for those urban citizens who work as graffiti writers and street artists, the growing confluence of these two urban trends produces something else: a series of powerful contradictions that animate the contemporary practice of street art and graffiti. In an urban environment permeated by fine-grained social control and by image-conscious consumerist arrangements, street art and graffiti come to be defined as criminal threat, as creative and com-mercial endeavour, and more often as some odd combination of the two. In this environment street art and graffiti emerge as all-too-visible markers of urban decay, and at the same time as hip signifiers of youthful urban culture and urban revitalization. They lead some of their practitioners to jail or prison, some to the gallery or the design firm, and many into some odd interstitial life that hangs between the two. In the contemporary global city the pervasive visibility of street art and graffiti all but guarantees that they will be attacked, eradicated and erased on the grounds that they undermine urban safety and urban quality of life – and that they will be celebrated, made all the more visible and culturally inescapable, as signifiers of stylish quality of life in a consumerist urban environment.

It's a bit too cynical and simplistic, but in this urban context one even begins to wonder whether graffiti and street art are today distinguishable mostly by where they fall along this confluence – that is, if 'graffiti' or 'graffiti vandalism' is that which gets caught up in the panoptic gaze of urban surveillance and street polic-ing, and 'street art' that which is appropriated into new economies of urban consumerism. Certainly it is the case that aggressive anti-graffiti campaigns have carefully and intentionally constructed graffiti and unsanctioned street art both as crimes and as broken windows-style harbingers of further criminality. Nor have these campaigns been simply about street policing and arrest rates; as researchers have shown, they have employed sophisticated forms of media manipulation to portray graffiti writers as violent vandals, gang members and community threats (Ferrell 1996; Austin 2001; Young 2012). Yet it is also the case that many business owners, gallery patrons, advertisers and city developers have increasingly come to see – and more importantly, to promote and commodify – street art and even certain forms of graffiti as essential components of commercial appeal and urban creativity (Snyder 2009). Consequently, the ongoing contradictions: around the world today, in the same city at the same time, graffiti and street art are legal and illegal, celebrated and condemned, objects of both fear and infatuation. And notably, these are not contradictions amenable to being sorted out and resolved; they are contradictions that define the very nature of contemporary street art and graffiti.

An existentialist might even call these contradictions absurd. Banksy (2005), for example, is both stubbornly invisible and pervasively visible, legal and illegal, his illicit work of such commercial value that the walls on which it is painted are stolen away to be sold at art auctions, or otherwise protected by Plexiglass lest some graffiti writer ruin them with an illegal tag. Shepard Fairey is arrested in Boston for tagging – around the time of his show at Boston's Institute of Contemporary Art – then arrested a few years later for illegally putting up posters in Detroit while in town to complete an enormous mural commissioned by a real estate company and a gallery. The Los Angeles Museum of Contemporary Art's highly publicized 'Art in the Streets' exhibition is followed by loud criticism of the ancillary street graffiti that the show generates – and also followed by liberalization of Los Angeles' public mural laws. Promoting high-end tourism as part of 'The Europe Issue' of its travel section, *The New York Times* highlights '12 Treasures' that the European traveller must experience. Alongside Copenhagen design and Brussels chocolate is the street art of Berlin, where 'elaborate murals still decorate firewalls' and 'images by sprayers and stencilers pop up everywhere else' (Bradley 2014). And when the co-creator of the broken windows model, James Q. Wilson, passes away, his front-page *New York Times* obituary highlights his model and its unquestioned categorization of graffiti as crime, crime progenitor, and symbol of disorder (Weber 2012; see Wilson and Kelling 1982). Also in that edition of the *Times*: an article about Kingston, New York, where illegally stencilled graffiti images have become so popular that the local newspaper endorses them as 'a great symbol' and the mayor argues that they are 'good for Kingston's image' (Applebome 2012).

In the absurdity of these accounts we begin to see something else as well: that the contradictions are also dialectical. It is not only that graffiti and street art are both legal and illegal, condemned and encouraged; it's that these contradictory processes entangle and intertwine, with each remaking the other as part of the ongoing cultural dynamic by which graffiti and street art are produced and perceived. To begin with, graffiti writers and street artists don't simply accept the dilemma of legality and illegality in which they are caught; they regularly negotiate it, contest it, and prank it, in the process reshaping the very nature of what they do. This is the dynamic that underlies much of the work of Banksy, Shepard Fairey, and other well-known graffiti writers/artists, and it is a dynamic that has been in play for decades now, with graffiti writers and street artists painting public commentaries on anti-graffiti campaigns, tagging city halls and police cars, and otherwise converting their own criminalization into forms of accelerated artistic adventure (Ferrell 1995, 1996, 2001). Negotiating the contradiction on a more practical level, some graffiti writers and street artists carry letters of permission from property owners, knowing that they still may be arrested even while painting a legal mural if they can't prove it to be so; others carry fake letters of permission, a subterfuge and safeguard if confronted while painting an illegal piece.

On a grander scale, street artists Workhorse and PAC recently organized a secret, illegal two-year Underbelly Project in which they snuck some 100 street artists, gallery artists and graffiti writers from around the world into a disused subterranean New York City subway station, where those involved over time created a wonderland of graffiti, murals, stencils, installations and artistic manifestos. When they eventually revealed the secret project, *The New York Times'* very public front page coverage noted that the project 'defies every norm of the gallery scene' and 'goes to extremes to avoid being part of the art world, and even the world in general' (Rees 2010) – though at this very moment, of course, the project had now become very much part of the world in general. Later on, the Underbelly Project became part of the gallery scene as well, with an Underbelly gallery show staged at Art Basel in Miami and a glossy photo book brought out with art publisher Rizzoli (Workhorse and PAC 2012). Workhorse and PAC are well aware of this unresolved dialectic of legality and illegality, and Workhorse suggests that it will only continue. 'I think it's our goal for the future that each year we do two different Underbellies', he says. 'One of them is legal, one of them is illegal. The sole point of the legal one is to finance the illegal one. So with Miami, that's essentially why we did that' (in Ferrell 2013).

The work of ESPO has likewise dealt directly with this dialectic of legality and illegality. Originally a Philadelphia graffiti writer and street artist, ESPO also founded *On the Go* magazine as a media counterpoint to the local anti-graffiti campaign's demonization of graffiti writers, later morphing *On the Go* into a commercial magazine focusing on graffiti and hip hop culture. Moving to New York City, ESPO hatched a scheme in which he rebranded ESPO to denote 'Exterior Surface Painting Outreach' and went about painting over the graffiti-tagged rolldown grates of local businesses – but then, with a few quick lines, surreptitiously turned each grate he had cleaned into a giant ESPO throw up. On his way to becoming a successful gallery artist and muralist, he also quite legally published a book under his given name, Stephen Powers (Powers 1999) – but the book's ridicule of police officers and anti-graffiti campaigns spurred ESPO's/Powers' arrest and trial on serious legal charges. For all this, ESPO's ongoing engagement with the dialectics of legality and illegality was perhaps best captured in a single illegal street mural he painted while still a New York City graffiti writer and street artist. 'Greetings from Espoland, where the quality of life is offensive!' the piece said – but in a style that so perfectly mimicked vintage tourist iconography that the mural could be mistaken for a legal billboard. Using the mural to ridicule the low-order 'quality of life' crimes that so concern advocates of broken windows policing, ESPO even depicted these crimes in the mural itself (see Snyder 2009: 73–74). Here, then, was the dialectic, doubling back on itself again: an illegal graffiti mural masquerading as a legal advertisement while questioning the logic by which street graffiti is illegal and commercial advertising is not.

The tangled trajectories of Banksy, Shepard Fairey, PAC, Workhorse, and ESPO/Steve Powers – as well as those of countless lesser-known graffiti writers and street artists – suggest that the dialectics of graffiti and street art play out in yet another realm: that of one's career. Borrowing the notion of career from the world of work and occupations, scholars have argued that there can exist deviant or criminal careers as well. In the same way that occupational achievements and connections can accumulate over time into a long-term professional career, they suggest, legal entanglements, social stigma and incarceration can spawn long-term involvement in criminal worlds and enforce ongoing exclusion from mainstream society (Becker 1963). This notion appears in early academic work on graffiti and street art (Lachmann 1988), and it is certainly the case that now decades-long anti-graffiti campaigns have pushed many graffiti writers and street artists into downward-spiralling criminal or deviant careers (Macdonald 2001). Yet as this early work began to suggest, and as Gregory Snyder (2009) has more recently documented, initial involvement in illegal graffiti or illicit street art also increasingly leads to careers in gallery art, advertising, and graphic design – careers that fit nicely with consumer-driven urban development and creative quality of life. Illegal and legal careers can also unfold simultaneously, with artists oscillating between street art and gallery art worlds while attempting to maintain identities in each; pushing this dialectic further still, skills and credibility gained in illegal street practices can often underwrite artistic reputations, and in so doing prolong legal artistic careers. For Keith Haring and Jean-Michel Basquiat back in the day, for ESPO and Banksy now – and for the many graffiti writers and street artists who today move back and forth between street, court and gallery – the dialectic is the real deal.

Visibility, invisibility, and the urban ghost

In the contemporary urban context street art and graffiti likewise engage a nuanced dialectics of visibility and invisibility. To begin with, both street artist and graffiti writers paint in 'spots' that embody widely varying degrees of public visibility (Ferrell and Weide 2010). Sometimes they choose secluded spots so as to hide their work from legal authorities or to ensure a selective and appreciative audience; other times they choose highly visible spots for the sake of subcultural status, public recognition, or commercial appeal; and sometimes they choose still other spots for their cultural significance or for the distinctive cultural audiences they draw. Beyond this, while graffiti and street art may often remain highly visible, their meanings remain invisible to many. Graffiti writers and street artists regularly encrypt aesthetic allusions, subcultural histories, street beefs and urban in-jokes in their public work; operating within collective, street-level art worlds, they traffic in subtle aesthetic conventions and dense interpersonal dynamics just as do those who inhabit more established art worlds (Becker 2008 [1982]). Consequently, the subtle meanings and subcultural valences of graffiti and street art often remain hidden from everyday viewers even as the art is displayed for all to see. In the swarm of the city and the give and take of its daily life, street art and graffiti are pervasively visible and often invisible – and this dialectics of urban visibility is produced in another way as well.

For graffiti writers especially, subcultural status is often negotiated and enforced by painting over or crossing out the work of other writers judged to be rivals or inferior artists. Likewise, even in the largest of cities, only certain spots satisfy criteria of audience or status, with this paucity of subculturally useful spots forcing writers to paint over and replace existing work as these spots evolve. Aggressive urban surveillance, environmental design and broken windows policing also limit available locations for painting street art and graffiti, and promote the legal destruction of existing work. All of this is of course backed up by the daily endeavours of countless anti-graffiti contractors and graffiti clean-up crews, who busily go about buffing murals and painting over graffiti tags and throw-ups. The result is counter-intuitive but, it would seem, indisputable: as pervasively visible as we take contemporary street art and graffiti to be, the vast majority executed over the past half century is now distinctly and decidedly invisible. The street art and graffiti that we see so widely today is but a small portion of that which has been lost or is currently hidden away, and in any case only the latest layer in an urban palimpsest of spray paint and whitewash. Graffiti and street art hide their own history; their very visibility enacts their ongoing invisibility.

Graffiti and street art are in this sense ghosts in the machinery of the contemporary city. Spectral presences, they are there and not there, made to appear and disappear 'while you were sleeping', as an early graffiti zine would have it. Coming and going as a series of urban apparitions, they create a vast dialectic of hide-and-seek that is played out across the city's cultural geography, and between street artists and their various urban audiences. Though they sometimes hide in the light (Hebdige 1988; Ferrell 2009), street art and graffiti also enliven the city's lost spaces, decorating its shadows and corners, occupying urban interstices and creating new ones by their presence; after all, as Andrea Mubi Brighenti (2013: xviii) reminds us, the urban interstice 'is not simply a physical space, but very much a phenomenon "on the ground," a "happening," a "combination" or an "encounter." ' In this way street art and graffiti constitute also the ephemeral promise of an open, democratic city. A series of glancing blows against the rationalized surveillance and control of contemporary urban life, an assemblage of spectral encounters amidst the city's shadows, they write both a secret history and an alternative future for the city.

Then again, as already seen, street art and graffiti in the contemporary city can just as well bend the other way, becoming harbingers of the gentrification and consumerism to come. Yet even in their incorporation into an emerging consumerist urban culture their ghostly mysteries remain. The rebuilding of the city around exclusivity, consumerism and private space hides away whole swaths of existing street art and graffiti, while also creating new surfaces and new opportunities for painting. On these new surfaces, and on the old ones that remain, illegal graffiti is now likely to be interwoven with and largely indistinguishable from corporate-sponsored pseudo-graffiti and street art (Alvelos 2004); legal murals are likely to sit side by side with illegal ones, each a funhouse mirror of the other (Snyder 2009); and as was the case with the Los Angeles Museum of Contemporary Art show, street-style art neatly confined within a gallery's walls is in fact likely to spill out into the streets. Here the emerging political economy of the city, and its dialectics of legality and illegality, become another ghost of visibility and invisibility. Over there – is that a billboard or a piece of street art? Didn't there used to be a mural on this block? What sort of neighbourhood is this, anyway?

Art and action, now and later

If part of the dialectical complexity of street art and graffiti comes from the changing conditions under which they are painted on urban surfaces, another part results from the fact that they also constitute a fluid set of practices, performances and experiences. Put another way, if graffiti and street painting are art, they are also action. Graffiti writers and street artists produce distinctive works of art that are shaped by shared conventions of aesthetics and style; equally, they create distinctive experiences and shared artistic communities in the moments that they produce such art. And the art and the action exist not as a dualism, but as a dialectic. 'I never really worry about the final image, I paint graffiti for the process, it is only important while I am actually making it,' says SheOne (n.d.; see 2012). 'I always improvise; I like to let the paint and the situation dictate the density of the works. Once you empty the first can you get a sense of the scale of the work, then you kind of forget where you are and just get on with it.' Other street artists back him up on this. Sound-One talks about 'the act of doing graffiti' as 'performance art' (Walsh 1996: 28), and Lister characterizes his work as 'an action painter's reflection painting, a combination of instinctual balance and mindful precision' in the moment of execution (Workhorse and PAC 2012: 118). The art on the wall incorporates the action of the moment.

The immediacy of this performative action in turn incorporates larger dynamics of the art worlds and the urban worlds that graffiti and street art occupy. Collectively acquired practical and aesthetic skills are necessary for negotiating the often dangerous uncertainty of street circumstances; to create art in such circumstances requires not only artistic training, but some degree of project planning and physical prowess. With these skills in hand, graffiti writers and street artists can embrace the street's risky dynamics, and from this situated interplay of skill and risk push the boundaries of their own artistic practice. Just as highly developed skills make possible success in situations of great peril, such situations in turn polish and promote such skills; in this way both the art and the action emerge as distinctive products of the settings in which they are produced.

This spiral of art and action loops back once again as graffiti and street painting play out within the contours of the contemporary city. The precarious, uncertain dynamics that often define street art and graffiti are precisely those that regimes of urban risk management mean to eradicate; because of this, legal and political authorities find both the art and the action threatening, and so double down on their campaigns to erase graffiti and unsanctioned street art. Yet these aggressive anti-graffiti campaigns often and ironically fail; intending to stop both action and art, they instead amplify the risk associated with them, and so push practitioners to develop greater skills – thereby intensifying the experience and fulfilment of the artistic action (Ferrell 1996). The alternative increasingly offered by consumerist urban economies – legal walls and sanctioned street art events – is no less contradictory. When graffiti writers and street artists pursue this option, they forfeit the risky street situations, urban street skills and free-form experiences that define the action and the art for many of its practitioners. Haze for one argues that, 'there is no substitute for the adrenaline and heightening of the senses that kicks in once you enter an illegal zone where you constantly have to watch your back'. In this light he also echoes an earlier distinction. 'As the debate over what is graffiti or not heats up, I prefer to consider it more along these lines: it's not illegal – it's not graffiti' (in Workhorse and PAC 2012: 20–21).

Amidst all of this there is one final set of forces in urban life that increasingly confounds the already intertwined categories of art and action, legality and illegality, visibility and invisibility. These forces elongate the experience of creating graffiti and street art, and provide new sorts of aesthetic durability; they likewise liquefy the specific urban spatiality of graffiti and street art. These forces are the digital camera and the cell phone. Early on, a camera was a scarce and expensive tool to come by for graffiti writers and street artists; today it is as common as a spray can, and infinitely more powerful in its ability to disseminate an artist's work. Not unlike others in the contemporary city, graffiti writers and street artists now regularly record their lives – which in their case means photographing or filming their own art and that of those around them, posting their images to photo and video sharing sites, and broadcasting them by way of blogs, online graffiti forums, magazines and other digital and print media (Snyder 2006; MacDowall 2008; Avramidis and Drakopoulou 2015). As pervasive as it has now become, this process of digital reproduction serves to preserve now for later, to elongate the ephemerality of the action surrounding street art and graffiti, and to grant instances of street art and graffiti a kind of eternal digital life. Collectively, the ubiquitous digital recording and dissemination of graffiti and street art creates what anti-graffiti campaigns, urban redevelopment, and the scouring vulnerabilities of the street conspire to preclude: a vast, expanding and enduring visual archive of street art, graffiti and their recent history.

The widespread digital reproduction of graffiti and street art confounds now and later in the opposite way as well: it sets up a dialectical process by which the reality of digital recording and its eventual uses loops back into the art and action itself, altering the very processes through which street art and graffiti are created, perceived and controlled. Young artists now learn aesthetic conventions not only from peers on the street, but from computer screens – and once they have mastered these conventions, they can now achieve global visibility by way of those same screens. More experienced artists may now pick an illegal 'spot' not for its immediate audience, but for its desirability in producing a digitizable image amenable to a virtual audience; alternatively, they may decide on a legally sanctioned wall because such a wall offers the hours of certainty and predictability needed to produce a photo-worthy mural. For some writers, spots are no longer situated in urban space at all. As Snyder (2009: 148) says of the magazines or 'mags' devoted to graffiti, 'For some writers, the mags are not simply documents of achievement but have become the new fame spots. Writers don't have to consider the potential audience

of the actual spot; they paint, take a flick, and send it off . . . to be seen by thousands.'
Of course, among those thousands are legal authorities and anti-graffiti campaigners
as well, who can now monitor the action and track the artists from their own office
computers – and who must increasingly consider whether images of illegal art
themselves carry the pathogen of illegality. Digitized and disseminated in this way,
graffiti and street art increasingly become disassociated images available for easy
inclusion in databases, legal proceedings, public service announcements, advertising campaigns, television shows and films. Along with the art and the action, by
turns overriding them and insinuating itself into them, is the image.

Perhaps this then is the next turn in the dialectics linking street art and graffiti
to the city. The contemporary city is itself becoming a place of profligate recording
and reproduction, its public and private spaces watched over by panoptic surveillance technologies, its police armed with body cameras and digital databases,
its moments of joy and tragedy backlit by the flashes of a thousand cell phone
cameras, its economy now mostly a matter of urban images and their consumption.
Into this city graffiti writers and street artists bring their murals, tags and stencils,
flooding it with a swarm of painted walls that soon enough transform into their
own photographs, films and visual archives. All of this flowers from the physicality,
the lived cultural geography, of the city, and from its existing contradiction of
legality, illegality, visibility and invisibility – but in doing so all of this also relocates
the city to the contested realm of the reproducible image. Here the dialectics of
art and action, law and crime, the visual and the hidden are reinvented; here the
city and its artists reengage and begin to reshape each other. The ghost that is street
art and graffiti reappears, transubstantiated into new forms such as the 'projection
bombing' of city buildings – ephemeral, illicit street art written in light – and the
PublicAdCampaign's NO AD mobile app, designed to digitally transform urban
advertising into street art (publicadcampaign.com).

The dialectic continues, and the city and its art remain to be read once again.

References

Alvelos, Heitor. 2004. 'The Desert of Imagination in the City of Signs'. In Ferrell, Jeff,
    Hayward, Keith, Morrison, Wayne and Presdee, Mike (eds), *Cultural Criminology
    Unleashed*. London: Glass House Press, pp. 181–191.
Applebome, Peter. 2012. 'How Graffiti Goats became a Symbol of . . . Something'. *The
    New York Times*, 2 March. Available at: www.nytimes.com/2012/03/03/nyregion/graffiti-
    goats-in-kingston-ny-find-a-following.html?_r=0. Accessed: November 10, 2015.
Austin, Joe. 2001. *Taking the Train: How Graffiti Art Became an Urban Crisis in New
    York City*. New York, NY: Columbia University Press.
Avramidis, Konstantinos and Drakopoulou, Konstantina. 2015. 'Moving From Urban to
    Virtual Spaces and Back: Learning In/From Signature Graffiti Subculture'. In Jandrić,
    Petar and Boras, Damir (eds), *Critical Learning in Digital Networks*. New York, NY:
    Springer, pp. 133–160.
Banksy. 2005. *Wall and Piece*. London: Random House.
Becker, Howard Saul. 1963. *Outsiders: Studies in the Sociology of Deviance*. New York,
    NY: Free Press.

Becker, Howard Saul. 2008 [1982]. *Art Worlds* (25th Anniversary edn). Berkeley, CA: University of California Press.

Beckett, Katherina and Herbert, Steve. 2009. *Banished: The New Social Control in Urban America*. Oxford: Oxford University Press.

Bofkin, Lee. 2014. *Concrete Canvas: How Street Art Is Changing the Way Our Cities Look*. London: Cassell.

Bradley, Kimberly. 2014. 'Berlin: Street Art'. *The New York Times*, 17 October. Available at: www.nytimes.com/2014/10/19/travel/12-treasures-of-europe.html. Accessed: 10 November 2015.

Brighenti, Andrea Mubi. 2013. 'Introduction'. In Brighenti, Andrea Mubi (ed.), *Urban Interstices: The Aesthetics and the Politics of the In-between*. Burlington, VT: Ashgate, pp. xv–xxiii.

Bushnell, John. 1990. *Moscow Graffiti: Language and Subculture*. Winchester, MA: Unwin Hyman.

Ferrell, Jeff. 1995. 'Urban Graffiti: Crime, Control, and Resistance'. *Youth and Society*. 27(1): 73–92.

Ferrell, Jeff. 1996. *Crimes of Style: Urban Graffiti and the Politics of Criminality*. Boston, MA: Northeastern University Press.

Ferrell, Jeff. 2001. *Tearing Down the Streets: Adventures in Urban Anarchy*. New York, NY: Palgrave Macmillan.

Ferrell, Jeff. 2009. 'Hiding in the Light: Graffiti and the Visual'. *Criminal Justice Matters*. 78(1): 23–25.

Ferrell, Jeff. 2013. 'The Underbelly Project: Hiding in the Light, Painting in the Dark'. *Rhizomes*. 25. Available at: www.rhizomes.net/issue25/ferrell/. Accessed: 10 November 2015.

Ferrell, Jeff and Weide, Robert. 2010. 'Spot Theory'. *City*. 14(1–2): 48–62.

Ferrell, Jeff, Hayward, Keith and Young, Jock. 2015. *Cultural Criminology: An Invitation* (2nd edn). London: Sage.

Hebdige, Dick. 1988. *Hiding in the Light: On Images and Things*. London: Routledge.

Lachmann, Richard. 1988. 'Graffiti as Career and Ideology'. *American Journal of Sociology*. 94(2): 229–250.

Lennon, John. 2014. 'Assembling a Revolution: Graffiti, Cairo and the Arab Spring'. *Cultural Studies Review*. 20(1): 237–275.

Macdonald, Nancy. 2001. *The Graffiti Subculture: Youth, Masculinity and Identity in London and New York*. London: Palgrave Macmillan.

MacDowall, Lachlan. 2008. 'The Graffiti Archive and the Digital City'. In Butt, Danny, Bywater, Jon and Paul, Nova (eds), *Place: Local Knowledge and New Media*. Newcastle Upon Tyne: Cambridge Scholars Press, pp. 134–147.

Markusen, Ann and Schrock, Greg. 2009. 'Consumption-Driven Urban Development'. *Urban Geography*. 30(4): 344–367.

Mitchell, Don. 2003. *The Right to the City: Social Justice and the Fight for Public Space*. New York, NY: Guilford.

Powers, Stephen. 1999. *The Art of Getting Over: Graffiti at the Millennium*. New York, NY: St Martins.

Rees, Jasper. 2010. 'Street Art Way Below the Street'. *The New York Times*, 31 October. Available at: www.nytimes.com/2010/11/01/arts/design/01underbelly.html. Accessed: 10 November 2015.

SheOne. n.d. ' "SheOne on Underbelly–Paris." Interview with Helen Soteriou'. *No New Enemies*. Available at: http://nonewenemies.net/2011/12/26/sheone-on-underbelly-paris/. Accessed: 10 November 2015.

SheOne. 2012. Interview with author. 8 April.

Snyder, Gregory. 2006. 'Graffiti Media and the Perpetuation of an Illegal Subculture'. *Crime, Media, Culture*. 2(1): 93–101.

Snyder, Gregory. 2009. *Graffiti Lives: Beyond the Tag in New York's Urban Underground*. New York, NY: New York University Press.

Walsh, Michael. 1996. *Graffito*. Berkeley, CA: North Atlantic Books.

Weber, Bruce. 2012. 'James Q. Wilson Dies at 80; Originated "Broken Windows" Policing Strategy'. *The New York Times*, 2 March. Available at: www.nytimes.com/2012/03/03/nyregion/james-q-wilson-dies-at-80-originated-broken-windows-policing-strategy.html. Accessed: 10 November 2015.

Wilson, James and Kelling, George. 1982. 'Broken Windows'. *The Atlantic Monthly*. (March): 29–38.

Workhorse and PAC. 2012. *We Own the Night: The Art of the Underbelly Project*. New York, NY: Rizzoli.

Young, Alison. 2012. 'Criminal Images: The Affective Judgment of Graffiti and Street Art'. *Crime, Media, Culture*. 8(3): 297–313.

2 Art or crime or both at the same time?

On the ambiguity of images in public space

Alison Young

Introduction

When you walk along a city street, what do you see? Are you in the city centre? If so, you might be surrounded by skyscrapers, office buildings, department stores, restaurants, cinemas, and what you will see is their signage, their concrete and glass construction, entrance doors, cars, pavements and municipal street furniture such as bins, post-boxes and lampposts. Are you in the suburbs, or some outlying residential area? Skyscrapers are uncommon there, and instead you will be able to see lower-level buildings, sometimes apartments, sometimes single homes; there might be local shops or transport stops, and there will still be some kinds of municipal street furniture. What about industrial and semi-industrial zones? It's unlikely you would have arrived there on foot, so one thing you won't be likely to see is pedestrian traffic; such areas are rarely the chosen neighbourhoods for strolling (walking is such a minority activity in these areas that you might find roads without pavements). Around you, you can see warehouses, storage depots, factories; there will be street signs but few other forms of municipal amenities.

Whichever type of area you are in, all their surfaces will have been marked in some way – by the owner, the tenant, or by the local authority. Commercial enterprises put up signs; houses and apartments make decorative choices for their outer façades; roads are painted with yellow and white lines to separate traffic to left and right. Sometimes surfaces are marked by a graffiti writer or street artist.

Is it easy to discern who made the marks that colour and inscribe urban surfaces? Well-grounded assumptions tell us that a house whose outer wall is painted blue and white was given those colours by the owner or tenant. A telephone box painted grey was probably given that hue by the manufacturer or the directions of a local council. Determining the authority behind the appearance of an urban surface is fundamental to the categorization of an urban marking as lawful or not. Alterations to a surface that are deemed to lack authorization or legitimacy can prompt a series of social, legal and cultural responses ranging from the imprisonment of the individual who made the markings to sections of a wall being removed with power tools and sold at auction.

That responses to illicit markings in the streetscape can occupy a spectrum from commercial exploitation through to punishment and prosecution means that the ways in which we determine whether urban markings are lawful or illicit are deeply significant. Markings deemed to be illicit do not constitute a homogeneous group of criminal images, for example. Some might be called 'vandalism'; others get classified as murals done by a subcultural group; still others get called 'street art'. In law, these marks can variously be called 'damage to property', or 'marking graffiti'; sometimes the specificity of the activity is lost by being designated as a symptom of 'anti-social behaviour'.

In this chapter, I will examine the ways in which paint on a wall may be categorized as a valuable cultural asset, vandalism, damage to property, a recognized art practice, or an aspect of neighbourhood character. The essay draws upon research conducted in cities such as Berlin, London, Melbourne, New York, Rome, Paris and Amsterdam, examining the range of social, legal and cultural responses to illicit markings in urban spaces.[1] It builds on the arguments of Jeff Ferrell's chapter (in this volume) in respect of the tensions around the illegal or legal status of illicit markings in public space and shares with others in this section a perspective on the streetscape as open to interpretation and construction, whether by lawyers, municipal works or by the illicit writer or artist. The intention is to raise questions about the ways in which illicit markings in the streetscape are defined and categorized, as 'damage', as 'street culture', or as 'graffiti' and 'street art', and to create some volatility and contingency around the fixity of such work of categorization. Graffiti writers and street artists, when prosecuted, can face substantial fines or imprisonment, and illicit artworks in urban spaces get removed by local councils or property owners. As such, attending to processes of categorization, definition and response is crucial to an understanding of the interconnections of law, culture and urban space.

The legal ecology of the streetscape

But how do we know when words or images have been lawfully added to an urban surface? If you walk through the streets of Fitzroy, the neighbourhood in Melbourne where I live, on one street, you can of course find paint on the walls of the houses, added to the brick surfaces by the various owners of each property.[2] But there is also chalk added to one wall; a few words in copperplate lettering inscribe the name of a street artist and her upcoming gallery show. Other walls are marked by aerosol paint, indicating the tag names of a number of graffiti writers. Some tags, such as autographs, belong to the writer; others are 'shout-outs', including a series that reads 'DN, DN, DN, DN . . .', marked on several houses in a row: these are memorial tags written to acknowledge the death of a well-known local tagger. These were done without permission, to be sure, but there has been a substantial lapse of time since they were added and it could be argued that the property owners who have not cleaned 'DN' from their walls might even be consenting to its presence, providing a retrospective permission for it to mark the wall.

Walking on further, the images get even more complicated. On one wall, the outer wall of a hairdressers' premises is covered by a mural by a well-known graffiti crew, AWOL. Most of the mural was painted by an artist called Adnate, with other members of AWOL contributing sections to the piece. It is done with permission; and has been there since 2011. On the same wall, next to the AWOL mural, is a large graffiti piece, which has been there, illegally, since the early 2000s (Figure 2.1). Both are heavily photographed by pedestrians; neither has been tagged or painted over. Next to the illegal graffiti piece is an apartment complex known as the Abito building. Its design brief aimed to respond to the character of the local area by being responsive to its streetscape; to that end the architects incorporated swirling graffiti onto the outer façade, which features walls painted with graffiti and washed with pink and green. Any tags or paste-ups get removed (a recent addition states 'Keep Fitzroy Gangster', presumably indicating that *ersatz* graffiti murals washed in pastel shades lack neighbourhood authenticity).

Opposite this building is a wall that forms the side wall to a fruit and vegetable warehouse. It features a large drip tag done with a fire extinguisher, a doorway filled with paste-ups and tags. Pieces of street art were once frequently added to its main wall, but recently bill posters have commandeered it for postering, and

Figure 2.1 Mural by Adnate and AWOL, and various graffiti pieces, Fitzroy Street, Fitzroy, Melbourne.

Photograph: Alison Young.

the walls now feature thick layers of ads for bands, CD releases and sneakers. The ground alongside this wall is thickly sticky with dripped glue. Opposite the Abito apartments, we find a private house, whose creamy white side wall is frequently tagged or written on. A CCTV camera has also been added to the wall, and when it is tagged, as happens regularly, the owners call the council which send cleaning crews with paint and power hoses to wash the white surface. The cleaners ignore tags and paste-ups applied to the neighbouring walls of other houses whose owners seem to be indifferent to the presence or absence of any markings, and additions to these surfaces are left to fade or decompose in the rain and sun.

Along a short stretch of one street can be found markings done illegally and removed, done illegally but left in place, done as a result of commissioning, long-lasting or short-lived, made with paper or paint. Some tell a story of prosecution: one tag, 'Renks', is written by an individual who was arrested for train graffiti and served time in prison (on Renks's case see further Young 2013). Others, such as the AWOL mural, function as stopping points on walking tours that showcase 'street art' in Fitzroy. Some pieces of paper pasted onto walls are advertisements for CDs or clothing; others have been hand-drawn and composed specifically for this doorway or that section of wall.

For a pedestrian, the legal status of these alterations to urban surfaces may be difficult to determine with any certainty: the legality or illegality of a word or image is not necessarily apparent or obvious. But what happens when a mark is interpreted as criminal? When do we see words and images as lawful?

Finding crime in the city

Some assume that 'street art' is legal, done with the permission of the property owner, while 'graffiti' is not. Interviews with street artists and graffiti writers revealed that inquiries from the police could be fended off by categorizing an uncommissioned image or text as 'street art' rather than 'graffiti'; conversely, artists who were adding an uncommissioned image that fitted into a street art aesthetic rather than a graffiti one reported that police officers and passers-by tended to assume that permission had been granted for the work.[3] Such a position depends upon a firm distinction between graffiti and street art as aesthetic forms. It is correct to note that they are different, and among their practitioners, there has long been a separation between them. 'Graffiti' denotes writing (even if it is a writing that foregrounds the imagistic qualities of the written form). It centres on the tag, which can be written by means of a variety of media such as marker pen or paint, or etched onto surfaces. The tag can be elaborated through a 'bubble'-style writing into what is known as a 'throw-up', or into the complex and highly stylized larger works known as 'pieces'. Graffiti can be found on almost any urban surface, but writers are traditionally attracted to trains, train tunnels and the walls adjoining train lines. Linked to hip hop, breakdancing and DJ'ing, graffiti began in the late 1960s in a number of cities in the United States, and has since been exported all over the world.

Street art is more diverse, and could almost be said to include all public mark-making that is *not* graffiti. Considered by many to be more 'user-friendly' or accessible, it is often claimed by graffiti writers to be little more than an off-shoot of graffiti writing. For its practitioners, street art is more complex than this account would imply, with the diversity of its methods, styles and media creating an art form that is much harder to define than the rather more singular styles of graffiti. Street art can include pasted-up posters, paint directly applied to walls, stickers, sculpture, stencilling, crochet and knitting. While graffiti writers tend to write for an audience composed of other graffiti writers, street art is often created for a wider population and street artworks tend to be much more easily appreciated than the hard-to-decipher calligraphy of tags and graffiti pieces.

Such aesthetic differences do not, however, indicate any distinction in the legal status of marks made by graffiti writers as opposed to street artists. Street artists who do not have the property owner's permission are all committing crimes, whether they are pasting work onto walls, attaching street sculptures to surfaces or painting lyrically expressive figures within doorways. Graffiti writers who paint an elaborate piece on a wall commit a crime if the owner does not consent to its presence, but when they obtain agreement or paint onto a 'legal wall' created by a local council, no crime is committed. Aesthetic form, then, does not determine the lawfulness of mark-making, which, rather, flows from the attitudes of the individual who owns an urban surface.

Writing or painting on property belonging to another without the owner's consent can constitute any one of a number of criminal offences. Under Article 145 of the New York Penal Law, for example, one aspect of 'criminal mischief' is 'making graffiti', defined as 'etching, painting, covering, drawing upon or otherwise placing of a mark upon public or private property with intent to damage such property'. Express permission of the property owner or operator is required to avoid prosecution with this Class A misdemeanour offence. A separate offence criminalizes 'possession of graffiti instruments', meaning 'any tool, instrument, article, substance, solution or other compound designed or commonly used to etch, paint, cover, draw upon or otherwise place a mark upon a piece of property which that person has no permission or authority to etch, paint, cover, draw upon or otherwise mark, under circumstances evincing an intent to use same in order to damage such property'. Once again, the permission of the property owner features as a key element.

In some jurisdictions generic prohibitions on damaging the property of others ensure that mark-making can be categorized as illicit; sometimes these came to be regarded as an inadequate response to the activity. In England and Wales, an individual might be prosecuted for the offence of criminal damage under the Criminal Damage Act 1971, but the Clean Neighbourhoods and Environment Act 2005 also created a specific power for police officers to issue a £75 penalty notice for those caught writing on walls, and graffiti was an oft-cited justification for the social utility of Anti-Social Behaviour Orders in Britain throughout the 2000s (Brown 2004; Millie 2008).

A similar situation evolved in Australia, where many Australian states enacted specific legislation criminalizing graffiti, although it was already an offence under existing legislation. In Victoria, the Graffiti Prevention Act was enacted in 2007 although graffiti had been prosecuted for years under the Crimes Act 1958 and the Summary Offences Act 1966. Debates in the Victorian Parliament show that a specific piece of legislation was seen as necessary to provide police officers with additional powers of arrest so that prosecution of graffiti-related offences could be facilitated to create new offences for police to prosecute, and to express disapproval of graffiti in and of itself.[4] In both Victoria and in England and Wales, the existing practice of prosecuting graffiti as criminal damage is regarded as having failed to communicate the fact of social disapproval of graffiti. The activity of illicit mark-making is thus *recriminalized* through the new statutory prohibition.

Whichever offence is used for the prosecution of the activity of placing words or images without permission in spaces that may be privately owned but that adjoin or are used by members of the public, its nature as 'damage' is unquestioned.[5] In the legislation, 'damage' tends to be a noun; meaning that it names an effect of the activity of graffiti; however, 'damage' is also a verb that requires an agent, one who damages property, and the criminal law is thus positing the existence of *an individual who damages*. For illicit mark-makers, however, damage is not necessarily the aim of their actions.

For many graffiti writers in South Australia, doing graffiti is the requisite activity for belonging to graffiti culture and for engaging in social interactions with other admirers of graffiti or hip hop in the same way that those with a talent for football might seek to join a soccer team, and talented chess players join a chess club (Halsey and Young 2006). Mark Halsey and Ben Pederick (2010) found antipathy to advertising and mainstream media motivated many writers to become involved in graffiti culture, a finding that confirmed the ethnographic research done in London by Rafael Schacter (2008). In Denver, Colorado, Jeff Ferrell found that most writers valued a particular aesthetic along with a sense of subcultural belonging (1993). In research conducted in New Zealand by Michael Rowe and Fiona Hutton, creativity and aesthetics emerged as the most significant of many motivations for engaging in graffiti, with damage the least significant (2012: 78). In my own interviews with graffiti writers and street artists in cities such as London, New York, Melbourne, Paris, Rome and Berlin, their motivations ranged from the aesthetic, by using the urban environment as a backdrop for or integral aspect of a particular kind of image, to the political, by means of expressing particular views to a broad audience and encouraging citizens to see the city as a mutable entity able to be transformed by individuals. Some were attracted by the idea of belonging to a local or global culture organized around graffiti or street art practices; others aimed to make their art accessible to the broadest possible audience (see further Young 2014). Despite the diversity of writers' and artists' intentions, mark-making without permission is always damage according to the law, irrespective of aesthetics, medium of expression or style.

Finding art in the street

The lack of the property owner's permission provides the foundation for the law's construction of most mark-making as unlawful. But unlawful mark-making can sometimes be transformed into art – both in the eyes of a spectator and the law. First of all, the criminal law enfolds exceptions within its prohibitions. The various statutory provisions to do with mark-making derive their force from the absence of an owner's permission for an individual to mark their property. When permission does exist, as when a resident commissions an artist to paint a mural or a wall or when permission *is* given by the property owner, the crime does not take place, since the owner's consent means that one of the circumstances required for the prohibited conduct cannot be met. Property owners provide consent to graffiti writers and street artists in various ways: they might commission a mural for a particular wall, or provide a space in which a range of artists can paint, refreshing the surface with regularly re-painted work. Some artists door-knock, asking owners for permission to paint on a back wall; others identify heavily tagged surfaces and offer owners the opportunity to see whether a mural will deter subsequent tagging.[6] In each of these situations, the property owner provides consent; a crime is not being committed. This has not stopped some legal work resulting in arrest of an artist or the removal of the work. Spectators sometimes assume that an artist is working illegally (perhaps associating a certain aesthetic with illicit mark-making) and have called the police to have the artist arrested. Others report the completed work to council or police, asking for it to be removed. In the Australian city of Brisbane, one artist's commissioned work was twice painted over ('buffed') by the city council. On the first occasion, in September 2010, the owners of a vacant block commissioned Anthony Lister, an internationally known street and fine artist, to paint a large piece on the rear of a wall overlooking the lot. Within forty-eight hours of its completion, the council sent a cleaning crew to paint over the piece. Councillor Geraldine Knapp stated that the owners of the derelict land did not own the wall, and 'had no power to authorize the vandalism of the building' (quoted in Dickinson 2010). Three years later, another commissioned mural by Lister was partially buffed when Brisbane City Council decided that Lister had departed from an approved design by adding a small figure of a council cleaning crew employee who appears to be starting to buff the larger mural (the buffer was then buffed by the council) (Macdonald 2013).[7]

Although it is clear that spectators may have trouble imagining that a proprietor has agreed to someone marking their property, the giving of consent alters both the status and nature of the image, converting it from 'graffiti' or 'damage' into a 'mural' or 'public art'. Artists and writers on occasion encourage spectators to interpret what they are seeing as legitimate municipal activity: many of the artists interviewed in the course of my research had adopted this practice, painting during the daytime, wearing a high-visibility vest or carrying a clipboard. Such acts clearly show awareness of the ways in which the framework of the law therefore incorporates within itself ways in which an image or word can be shifted out of the category 'crime', and the terrain of criminal law, into categories such as 'legal mural' or 'public art', and the terrain of property law.

The shift can also be effected through a second factor, which relates to the existence of something rather less understood than consent or a commission. In the opening section of this chapter, I described the varying types of legal status of a range of marks on walls in Fitzroy, in Melbourne. This neighbourhood is an area in which graffiti and street art are commonplace (hence the assumption on the part of the designers of the Abito apartment building that covering the façade with pastel-washed graffiti would make it blend into the streetscape). Some residents and traders do not like graffiti or street art: they regularly call the police or the council to have surfaces cleaned. But graffiti and street art are more commonly objects of positive responses, ranging from indifference through to approbation. Many do not clean tags or throw-ups from their property, allowing them to fade and weather instead. Tourists go on walking tours to see street art in the area; people pose for photographs next to the heavily tagged walls. Fashion shoots utilize the walls as a backdrop. Artists have been commissioned to paint walls inside Fitzroy's many bars and restaurants, as proprietors seek to bring the aesthetic of the local streets into the interior of their venue.

This spectrum from indifference to enthusiasm can be found when graffiti and street art have become part of an area's character, as shown by Kim Dovey, Simon Wollan and Ian Woodcock (2012) in their study of the Melbourne neighbourhoods of Fitzroy and Brunswick. Stokes Croft in Bristol provides another instance; as do Williamsburg and Bushwick in Brooklyn. In these areas, when street art has become part of neighbourhood character, it is as if the spectator or property owner offers a kind of consent to the presence of illicit marks through a lack of their condemnation. It is not the active consent that arises when a proprietor commissions a mural, but it is also not the censorious disapproval that can lead to an arrest and prosecution. Such an interim zone of reaction to the marks made by graffiti writers and street artists is not acknowledged in law to exist.

The third factor contributing to the ability of an illicit mark to be transformed from 'crime' into 'art' arises out of the sedimenting of an informal hierarchization between 'street art' and 'graffiti'. Thus far I have tended to use the terms as it they were interchangeable, since both are illegal when they take place without the property owner's permission. Although the statutory prohibitions might not name a difference between the two cultural forms, there are significant variations in how they are treated and regarded.

The 'art/crime' distinction is one that has been around for a long time (see for example Gomez 1993), but it has tended to be used in relation to the question of whether graffiti could be art. In contrast, what we are now seeing, both in the responses of the criminal justice system and in media and public perception, is a separation of illicit mark-making activities into a binary that elevates mark-making that can be called *street art* over that which is then categorized as *graffiti crime*. As will be elaborated in what follows, no formal decriminalization has taken place; rather, the images and activities associated with street art are undergoing a process of *cultural legitimation*.

As Shyon Baumann elaborates in his 2007 analysis of how art products become, first of all, recognized as valid products, and then, second, categorized as either 'high' or 'low' art, there are identifiable processes that must be operationalized for legitimation of art worlds to occur, and once underway, in order to explain how an artwork or artistic practice may be viewed as 'serious', 'fad', or 'popular culture', and so on. According to Baumann, legitimation of an art practice depends upon the operation of three factors: 'opportunity', the 'mobilization of resources', and 'framing'. *Opportunity* designates the extent to which legitimation is amplified when the wider social context has shifted or altered in such a way that new audiences, receptive to the idea of cultural value in a particular practice, are able to emerge (2007: 52).

In the context of street art, a number of new audiences have emerged, with connections to different markets. First, specialized galleries were set up in cities such as New York, London, Berlin and Melbourne, exhibiting the work of street artists while striving to avoid the perceived elitism of the conventional gallery scene. The owner of one gallery, located in a former shop on London's Brick Lane, stated in interview with me: 'As soon as people have seen artwork on the street they're going to come into a gallery that's showing street art, because they are relating to it – this is their street, this is their artwork.'

Dedicated galleries saw the emergence of new groups of art collectors, many of whom began collecting for the first time in order to buy Banksy prints or works by other street artists. Another audience evolved through the proliferation of street art websites. *Wooster Collective, Vandalog, Hooked, Brooklyn Street Art* and *Stencil Revolution*, which appeared from 2003 onwards, have featured images of street artworks in cities all over the world, such that individuals can view street art without having to be in the street in front of it. Unlike websites providing photo-posting platforms and discussion forums about graffiti (such as *Streetpins* and *Art Crimes*), these street art websites, in particular *Brooklyn Street Art* and *Wooster Collective*, adopted an open and inclusive 'tone', such that visitors who are not themselves practising street artists nonetheless felt included within the street art 'community' to which the sites referred. Such inclusiveness of tone led to their extensive popularity, which marked the generation of a global audience of fans and consumers. Furthermore, street art spectatorship has become intimately linked to active online participation: people send their own photos to *Wooster Collective* and other sites, set up photo streams on *Flickr* and *Instagram*, and create their own blogs enumerating the various street artworks they have encountered.

Audiences are also created when street art is used as a backdrop to other cultural forms and as the pretext for cultural narratives. While the prevalence of illicit art in music videos is entirely predictable, less so is its frequent appearance in reality television shows such as *Street Art Throwdown* in the United States, crime dramas such as the British show *New Tricks* and the Australian drama *Jack Irish*, documentaries, and advertisements for banks, car insurance and cars (HSBC, Youi Insurance, Hummer, Ford, Mazda and Mitsubishi have all used street art in their campaigns).The appearance of street art in and through so many cultural forms both creates a backdrop of familiarity and neutralizes its illicit qualities.

The second of the factors identified by Baumann for the legitimation of an art practice is the *mobilization of resources* (2007: 54). In the art world, these resources can be cultural, knowledge-based or financial. Certain institutions play a signifi-cant role here: as Howard Becker makes clear (1974, 1982), museums, auction houses and art critics are of central importance as thresholds of legitimation.

Similarly, Pierre Bourdieu (1993) confirms the legitimating importance of such institutions as museums, in that they bear responsibility for conserving works of national cultural significance, and confer the imprimatur of the art establishment on their holdings. From 2007 onwards, street art began to have a presence in national museums and major art galleries. In 2008, Tate Modern gave over its façade to six international street artists; in 2010 the National Gallery of Australia exhibited some of its holdings of 400-plus works on paper by street artists; and in 2011, the Museum of Contemporary Art in Los Angeles showed 'Art in the Streets', a survey of work in public space from the 1970s to the present.

The art market is also able to influence perceptions of legitimacy. In 2007, Bonhams was the first auction house to hold dedicated sales for street artworks (creating a new name for them, 'urban art'). That the first street art auction was held at Bonhams is worthy of comment: Bonhams, founded in 1793, is one of the oldest and most prestigious auction houses in London, associated with luxury goods, fine art and the exchange of art objects at high prices. The decision by Bonhams to commence auctioning works by street artists and graffiti writers both functioned as a stamp of legitimacy in itself at the same time that it indicated the market for street art was thought to be significant.

Since then, others in London and elsewhere have followed suit (including Dreweatts in London, Doyle in New York City and Joel Leonard in Melbourne). Early urban art auctions achieved astonishing prices, part of the 'art bubble' that preceded the credit crisis of 2008 onwards (see Horowitz 2014). More recently, most auction houses have abandoned the practice of having separate 'urban art' listings, instead focusing on a smaller number of street artists whose works could fit into 'contemporary art' sales (such as the Phillips contemporary art auction in February 2014, when works by Banksy were listed alongside those by Damien Hirst and Chris Ofili). This should not be seen as an indication that the legitimation effect of the auction market is waning; on the contrary, it attests to the increasingly comfortable position of the street artwork within genres of fine art.[8]

The final component of legitimation is the *framing* of a cultural practice as legitimate (Baumann 2007: 57). While street art has not yet been awarded the unqualified status of a new art movement in art-historical terms, in the way that Pop Art or Land Art have, its move in this direction can be marked through an increase in writings about it within art journals. Recent years have seen, for example, publication of a special issue of the art journal, *Artlink* (2014) and numerous articles advising on how to collect street art.

To that extent, and in a manner related to the operation of the preceding two elements of legitimation, certain individuals or institutions function as discursive and institutional gatekeepers. In Melbourne, the National Gallery of Victoria (NGV) staged a large exhibition in 2013–2014 entitled 'Melbourne Now', showcasing the work of artists across a wide range of fields such as sculpture, painting, print-making and fashion. Two well-known street artists were included in the show: Ash Keating, who uses fire extinguishers to spray paint onto walls, and Lush, who is known for prolific tagging as well as a meta-commentary upon the street art scene in his drawings and writings. Keating was given the outer wall of one of the NGV buildings to spray with paint from a fire extinguisher (the wall was covered by vinyl sheeting so that its brickwork would not be permanently altered by the artwork) (Figure 2.2), and Lush was given an entire room in the gallery, which he rendered as a graffiti-covered streetscape complete with dumpster and rubbish (the work was entitled 'Who says graffiti doesn't belong in a gallery?') (Figure 2.3). In order to make it clear that the gallery was endorsing street art in the street as well as in the gallery, the NGV also sponsored the curation of street art in an alleyway opposite the gallery. In this dual move of financial sponsorship and curatorial inclusion, street art was being named as an art form like all the others exhibited in the museum.

Against this extensive and ongoing backdrop of normalization, street art becomes familiar and unthreatening. Banksy is in the news, photographs of images on walls are in people's smartphones. It is the object of affection, rather than fear or dislike. Distaste is reserved for graffiti, which has not been subject to any such process of cultural legitimation. In fact, the progressive familiarization

Figure 2.2 Mural by Ash Keating for the 'Melbourne Now' exhibition at the National Gallery of Victoria, Melbourne.

Photograph: Alison Young.

Figure 2.3 Installation view of 'Who says graffiti doesn't belong in a gallery?'
by Lush, for the 'Melbourne Now' exhibition, National Gallery of
Victoria, Melbourne.

Photograph: Alison Young.

of street art depends partly upon its being distinguished from graffiti. Bourdieu
(1984) writes of how distinction marks out class strata, educational attainment,
and confirms cultural capital as a desirable resource; for culture, distinction works
in a similarly hierarchical manner: the dichotomy between street art and graffiti
crime has been essential to the legitimation of street art.

Finding art and crime at the same time

In the opening section of this chapter, I described a range of streetscapes and the
various marks that can be found on their surfaces. My aim was to situate the marks
classified as street art and graffiti within a broad context of urban marks and signs,
some created at the behest of a proprietor, some done in order to encourage purchase
of goods, others considered to be present as a means of providing information to
members of the public. Sometimes it is easy to distinguish one from another; at
other times, the boundaries between these categories are more blurred. One task
that arises from these blurred categories is, as set out earlier, how we determine
the legal status of marks made in public space. The difficulty is that often there
is little to distinguish one set of marks on a wall from another in themselves – all

may be versions of paint applied to a surface, or paper stuck to a wall. One of the ways that this task can be addressed is through the issue of whether there exists consent or permission for the mark. This may be done through the presence of an explicit authorization but also arises through a series of judgements made by the spectator, by those who interact with the wall or other property, and by city authorities. Distinction – the sorting of words and images into categories of licit and illicit marks – is an effect of assessments made by reference to questions of property and propriety: such as ownership of a wall or building, aesthetic authority over public space, and the extent to which an image conforms to genres of appropriate imagery for the location, setting or surface.

In thinking about the status of graffiti and street art, both in law and in contemporary culture, it is important to hold onto an awareness that categorization of marks on urban surfaces, as 'advertisements', 'art', 'tags', 'signage', 'vandalism' and 'murals' among other possibilities, is contingent upon a series of assumptions and associations about authority and aesthetics in urban spaces. Finding 'art' and 'crime' in the street is not always straightforward. Murals done with permission have been buffed because their aesthetic was associated with illicit graffiti; spectators have called police because they assume that someone painting a graffiti mural on a house must be a criminal. Conversely, advertising agencies frequently use illicit stencils to associate particular products with urban 'coolness', while some street artists now only put work illegally in the streets when they have an upcoming gallery show to promote. Categories as rigid as 'art' and 'crime' are thus insufficiently flexible or commodious.

Instead of trying to determine a fixed allocation for urban marks such that they can be called legal or illegal, it is my proposal that their inherent ambiguity be acknowledged, as an indicator of the complexities of the relationship between spectator and urban images. In addition, instead of seeking to resolve contradictions in the status of an image, its multivalency should be embraced. The complexity of an illicit urban mark derives from the fact that it is the product of an aesthetic practice, a criminal act and a communicative act. Such an image may be meaningful, damaging, illegal, political or beautiful; and it may be *all those things at once*. Finally, an urban image is always in flux – we may find a piece of illegal mark-making one day, but if we return two weeks later, the building owners may have placed perspex over it in order to preserve it. Placed in public space, subject to the effects of the weather and the whims of passers-by and councils, the illicit word or image may last for five years or may be painted over in two days. Categories such as 'legal' or 'illegal' images, and distinctions between 'art' and 'crime', can no longer do justice to what we find in the streets of the contemporary city.

Notes

1   This research was funded by the Australian Research Council, in a project entitled 'Urban Images and the Appearance of City Spaces', examining the emergence of street art as a distinctive cultural practice, and subsequently in a project entitled 'Transforming City Spaces: Street Art, Urban Cultures and Transnational Networks', investigating

the reception and legitimation of aspects of street art culture. I'm grateful to the ARC for their support of my research.

2   Fitzroy is Melbourne's 'first suburb'; that is, the first area to be developed outside the city's central business district. It is one of the oldest areas of Melbourne, and is known today for its gentrifying street culture, entertainment precincts, and a population of residents varying from the wealthy to those living in extreme poverty or without homes. It has significance in Aboriginal culture and history, with a number of important historical meeting places for Indigenous people within its streets.

3   For example, Berlin-based artist Jaybo described an interaction with police officers in Shoreditch, London: 'I was painting something illegal, and the cops just appeared straight away, saying "I suppose this is legal?" . . . And I say "yeah" and smile. . . . They said, "are you sure?" and I kept smiling and they went away'.

4   Typical of the mood of the debates are the comments by Dr Denis Napthine, who would later become Victorian Premier: 'Anybody who tries to describe graffiti as something that is acceptable art or witty is just encouraging this form of irresponsible vandalism. Graffiti is not art; it is vandalism. It is irresponsible and illegal damage to public and private property, and it is offensive to the community. . . . [T]he bill proposes increased penalties. That is all very well and good, and we support that, but those increased penalties must be backed up by the courts . . . We have to have tougher sentences, and we have to have courts that actually administer those tougher sentences.' Second Reading of the Graffiti Prevention Bill, Assembly, 10 October 2007, 3437–3438.

5   'Damage' is a flexible concept, able to connote the way that aerosol paint might have corrosive effects on the material surface it is sprayed on, as well as an aesthetic that can harm the appearance of a neighbourhood.

6   There is evidence that rates of tagging can be reduced by the introduction of a legal mural: Craw *et al.* conducted a small-scale study investigating whether the creation of a legal mural reduced tagging in one location (Craw *et al.* 2006). The study found that the mural was tagged less often than had occurred prior to the appearance of the mural; tagging also appeared at higher rates on surfaces without murals nearby.

7   Some artists have incorporated the buff into their art practices. In London, Mobstr's work has been buffed, then repainted by him in a way that creates a dialogue with the cleaning crews, sometimes painting an instruction to the crew to 'paint here' or 'buff this'. Mobstr then photographs and compiles the resulting images over time and posts them for viewing on his website. Examples can be seen here: www.mobstr.org/red/ and www.mobstr.org/the-question-mark/. Accessed: 17 December 2015.

8   The auction of works by Banksy held at Sotheby's in June 2014 is a further example, with pieces priced from £4,000 to £500,000.

References

Baumann, Shion. 2007. 'A General Theory of Artistic Legitimation: How Art Worlds are Like Social Movements'. *Poetics*. 35: 47–65.

Becker, Howard. 1974. 'Art as Collective Action'. *American Sociological Review*. 39: 767–776.

Becker, Howard. 1982. *Art Worlds*. Berkeley, CA: University of California Press.

Bourdieu, Pierre. 1984. *Distinction: A Social Critique of the Judgment of Taste*. Cambridge, MA: Harvard University Press.

Bourdieu, Pierre. 1993. *The Field of Cultural Production*. New York, NY: Columbia University Press.

Brown, Alison P. 2004. 'Anti-social Behaviour, Crime Control and Social Control'. *Howard Journal of Criminal Justice*. 43(2): 203–11.

Craw, Penelope J., Leland, Louis S., Bussell, Michelle G., Munday, Simon J. and Walsh, Karen. 2006. 'The Mural as Graffiti Deterrence'. *Environment and Behavior*. 38(3): 422–434.

Dickinson, Alex. 2010. 'Graffiti Artwork by Anthony Lister Commissioned by Property Owner rubbed out by Brisbane City Council'. *Courier Mail*, 14 September. Available at: www.couriermail.com.au/news/queensland/graffiti-artwork-by-anthony-lister-rubbed-out-by-brisbane-city-council/story-e6freoof-1225921335596. Accessed: 17 December 2015.

Dovey, Kim, Wollan, Simon and Woodcock, Ian. 2012. 'Placing Graffiti: Creating and Contesting Character in Inner-city Melbourne'. *Journal of Urban Design*. 17(1): 21–41.

Ferrell, Jeff. 1993. *Crimes of Style: Urban Graffiti and the Politics of Criminality*. New York, NY: Garland.

Gomez, Marisa. 1993. 'The Writing on Our Walls: Finding Solutions through Distinguishing Graffiti Art from Graffiti Vandalism'. *University of Michigan Journal of Law Reform*. 26: 633–708.

Halsey, Mark and Pederick, Ben. 2010. 'The Game of Fame: Mural, Graffiti, Erasure'. *City*. 14(1–2): 82–98.

Halsey, Mark and Young, Alison. 2006. ' "Our Desires are Ungovernable": Writing Graffiti in Urban Space'. *Theoretical Criminology*. 10(3): 275–306.

Horowitz, Noah. 2014. *The Art of the Deal: Contemporary Art in a Global Financial Market*. Princeton, NJ: Princeton University Press.

Macdonald, Andrew. 2013. 'Graffiti Artist Anthony Lister Objects to City Council 'Buffing' Milton Road Mural'. *Courier Mail*, 25 September. Available at: www.couriermail.com.au/news/queensland/graffiti-artist-anthony-lister-objects-to-brisbane-city-council-8216buffing8217-milton-rd-mural/story-fnihsrf2–1226726481283. Accessed: 17 December 2015.

Millie, Andrew. 2008. 'Antisocial Behaviour, Behaviour Expectations, and an Urban Aesthetic'. *British Journal of Criminology*. 48(3): 379–94.

Rowe, Michael and Hutton, Fiona. 2012. ' "Is your City Pretty Anyway?" Perspectives on Graffiti and the Urban Landscape'. *Australian & New Zealand Journal of Criminology*. 45(1): 66–86.

Schacter, Rafael. 2008. 'An Ethnography of Iconoclash: An Investigation into the Production, Consumption and Destruction of Street-Art in London'. *Journal of Material Culture*. 13(1): 35–61.

Young, Alison. 2013. 'Criminal Images: The Affective Judgment of Graffiti and Street Art'. *Crime, Media, Culture*. 8(3): 297–314.

Young, Alison. 2014. *Street Art, Public City: Law, Crime and the Urban Imagination*. London: Routledge Glass House.

3 Reading between the [plot] lines

Framing graffiti as multimodal practice

Samantha Edwards-Vandenhoek

Introduction

This chapter outlines a reflexive and interpretative framework developed to navigate the complexity of material and temporal disclosure associated with the photographic re-framing of graffiti's traces. It is embedded in broader research that seeks to interrogate how illicit graffiti shapes and transforms place in varied spatio-temporal contexts in Sydney and Melbourne. Graffiti's transgressions are understood as a poetic process of revealing and concealing marks over time and space that leave indelible traces in the here and now, and can be read as texts, whether it be image, word, impression and/or gesture to form new or hidden narratives and places. The conceptual aim sets out to unravel the tensions and conversations embedded in graffiti's discursive relations to expose plot lines inaccessible in approaches that emphasize the disparate classification of decontextualized modes of practice. The challenge here is to ascertain how such a diverse and divergent practice with its range of modes, relations and situations that have a varied capacity for meaning making can be negotiated. The notion of meaning making being relational is twofold. It refers to the relations between or within graffiti texts, as well as the relation between the viewer and the photographic frame. This approach asserts the place and value of the materiality of graffiti as discursive sites of knowledge about the process, formation and transference of social meanings. The multimodal and intertextual handling of graffiti advanced here affords a hybrid, flexible and less discriminatory place to negotiate the discursive, expressive and socio-semiotic dimensions of graffiti practice framed *in situ*, coupled with its performative and material aspects, and spatio-temporal compression. Readings from the researcher's own empirical encounters in the landscape of graffiti production contextualize this discussion. These photographic framings embed a fertile mix of interactions, engagements and place-making that pries open graffiti's parallel discursive arena, which counters normative modes of public expression to construct a relational socio-politics of place.

The world turned upside down

Graffiti pops up everywhere. It's pervasive, ephemeral and transformative. Graffiti embeds and re-presents traces of social behaviour that exposes tensions and ontological ambiguities in the urban sphere. It destabilizes and infiltrates the formalized codification of space, with an alternative world view, turned upside down and inside out, even if only for a short period of time. As in this stencilled impression of one graffitist's point of view, it's better to be a 'spanner in the works, [rather than] a cog in the machine' (Figure 3.1). In this respect, graffiti challenges and transgresses normative conceptions of place by diverting space to serve communicative, performative or expressive endeavours counter to its intended use. As Tim Cresswell (1996) deftly argues in his critique of the recodification of space and destabilization of normative conventions of place afforded by graffiti in New York, by altering or diverting the built environment, graffiti materializes the meanings that the built environment carries about place. In this way graffiti forms a place where geography and ideology converge. It affords a shared geography, where streets are transformed into places for conversation and exchange. However, in a tightly controlled and monitored built environment, the spatial tactics of the

Figure 3.1 Paste up with tags that reads 'The World turned Upside Down' framed with stencilled iconography that reads 'don't be a cog in the machine, be a spanner in the works'. Wilson St, Enmore, October 2007.

Photograph: Samantha Edwards-Vandenhoek.

graffitist serve to detour rather than redirect space. As such, the value and legacy of graffiti's multimodality lies in its poetization rather than the domination of the urban experience.

I ventured into the encoded territories of illicit graffiti writing and urban art production armed with ontological concerns and a camera for a trowel. Bridging the fields of documentary photography and contemporary archaeology, what Michael Shanks (2004) coined 'archaeography' affords a reflexive and interpretative place in which the multimodal and intertextual traits of graffiti production can be meaningfully interpreted. Archaeography is a term that Shanks (2004) has given to formalize the working relationship between photography and archaeology, as processes of cultural production, as well as data collection modalities. It rests on the premise that photography and archaeology are reflexive mediations that breathe new life into the re-articulation of socially constructed artefacts and poetization of the urban experience. It is further embedded in Shanks's (2007) theorizing on media archaeology, a working framework for archaeologists, archivists and photographers, such as myself, who work with contemporaneous forms of archaeological intervention with material culture, and where photography functions as the principal mode and media of engagement (Shanks 2001: 284).

The points of interest in the archaeographs storied here have been conceived with Roland Barthes's (1984) twin concepts of the *studium* and *punctum* in mind. The *studium* is the essence or cultural interest of the photo as a whole and speaks to the intention of the photographer. The *punctum* is more powerful, compelling and subjective. The *punctum* is an addition, and 'what I add [as an interpreter] to the photograph and what is nonetheless already there' (Barthes 1984: 55). As an archaeographer, an understanding of *punctum* allows me to produce stronger images, as the photographs have been conceived with a clear focus – to draw out the tensions, dialogues, modal relations and poetics of place. However, as this research deals with hybridity and transience, the point or value in an archaeograph may be multifarious and shift over time. It could reference the entire frame, in terms of how things work as a whole in an evocation of the place I framed and saw. Moreover, neither photography nor archaeology creates transparent windows on the past (Shanks 2009). Images are artefacts in that they sample and shape the past in the same way that an archaeologist's trowel and photographer's lens sculpts it (2009). As a photographer and an archaeologist I strongly identify with these propositions, and how to negotiate this ambiguity has been central to the analytical framework put forward here.

The framework developed to negotiate these complexities, relations and omissions, draws on the socio-semiotic multimodality of Gunter Kress and Theo van Leeuwen (2001, 2006) and Carey Jewitt's (2009) continuing work developing tools for reading images and enhancing multimodal literacy. It rests on Barthes's notion of text as 'a tissue, a woven fabric' (1977: 159), and extends on Julia Kristeva's notion of intertextuality, which implies that 'text is constructed as a mosaic of quotations; any text is the absorption and transformation of another' (1980: 66).

As Jay Lemke (2009) furthers, meanings and identities can also then be constructed and negotiated across various discourses, media, spaces and temporalities simultaneously. It is an approach that is responsive to variation in communication, representation and practice and aims to contribute to a multimodal way of analysing everyday cultural practices.

A multimodal handling of the archaeographs also provides a discursive space where the reader replaces the graffiti writer or artist as interpreter. Signalling what Barthes (1977) famously referred to as the 'Death of the Author', rather than emitting a fixed meaning from a singular voice, image or trace, is but a tissue of quotations that are themselves references to other texts and so on. As such, there is an endless proliferation of potentially conflicting meanings, which means that the origin of a text cannot be fixed (or focused on its author). However, in this Barthesian framework decentring the graffiti practitioners concerned does not remove them from the analysis or interpretation. In this model, the graffiti practitioner returns to the status of producer, and the focus of interpretation shifts to graffiti's multi-vocal traces. Moreover, it is a place where subject–object relations can be dissolved, Kristeva (1980) attests, meaning is not transferred directly from writer to reader but instead is mediated through, or filtered by, codes imparted to the writer and reader by other texts, such as archaeographs, as is the case here.

This reorientation is further substantiated by the fact that the graffiti medium presents a visual dialogue that does not rely on face-to-face interaction or knowledge of the artist's identities, and where the interpretation of the work is often left up to the observer and the relationship the researcher (as both observer and participant) has to this cultural practice. Graffiti is very much an anonymous endeavour. There are a number of significant personalities and recognized names. Yet for the most part these practitioners remain faceless to an outside audience, though not necessarily nameless. As a citational system of illicit behaviour there is clearly a pseudonym of protection and self-preservation. Recognition and infamy are important motivators for graffiti crews and urban artists. However, the relationship between placement and cultural message does not necessarily hinge on knowledge of the artist or writer's identities.

A multimodal and intertextual approach

> The landscape is a multi-temporal and complicated, folded cultural typology, where any practice of 'deep mapping', which might aim to capture this complexity, must itself be hybrid, syncretic, diverse.
>
> (Shanks 2001: 293)

Visual culture studies offer clues and a range of singular approaches (form, content, iconology, semiotics) in which discrete aspects of the visual culture of graffiti can be examined (see Walker and Chaplin 1997; Rose 2001; Howells 2003). However, it is the concepts of multimodality and intertextuality that provide a more inclusive environment to interrogate the socio-semiotic, discursive, performative and material dimensions of graffiti's trace and its intertextual relations, framed *in situ*.

Multimodality provides tools for analysing and describing the varied semiotic resources that graffiti writers and urban artists use to communicate, represent and comment on their environment and other graffiti works (Jewitt 2009). Multimodality also concerns the role of the image, use of space, gestures, gestural marks (such as tagging, freestyle spraying and strike thru), as well as the visual and linguistic devices and codes used in these place-making activities (Jewitt 2009). Moreover, multimodality specifically concerns the analysis of fields of practice (such as graffiti) where meanings are consistently made through the use of stylistic conventions (e.g. symbols and codes) (Kress and van Leeuwen 2001). Significantly, multimodality challenges conventional notions of representation, communication and interaction as something more than language (Jewitt 2009: 1). Multimodality is a rejection of traditional linguistics where communication is rooted in language and text and the spoken word dominates (Kress and van Leeuwen 2001). Traditional linguistics works with the idea of double articulation, whereas multimodality allows for a broader model of communication, or what Kress and van Leeuwen refer to as 'multiple articulations' (2001: 4). In multimodality, modes (other than verbal language) are not simply forms of verbal communication phrased differently. Here, language is seen as 'nested among a multimodal ensemble of modes' (Jewitt 2009: 15). As such, a multimodal framework can respond to the communication of varied iconographic, readable, symbolic and figurative graffiti modes, and their material manifestations. This is because, as Kress and van Leeuwen maintain (2001), modes are not fixed, but articulated and situated. As with graffiti modes, they are shaped by their cultural, historical and social uses to realize a social purpose (Figure 3.2).

Based on local Council photos from the area, the property boundaries of 39 Phillip St Newtown framed in Figure 3.2 became an active graffiti site circa 2004. Figure 3.2a represents where I came in, mid conversation, March 2007. The archaeograph frames a hand painted statement that reads 'tags suck' tucked into Kid Kepeh's black and white pictorial and iconic stencil rendering of Frank Sinatra positioned on ground level at the intersection of two brick walls of varied heights. The iconicity of this nostalgic representation of the man known as 'old blue eyes' is signposted in Kid Kepeh's use of Sinatra's signature black tuxedo and fedora hat, taken from film posters of the time. It also signifies an attempt by the stencil artist to identify with Sinatra, as a gangster, old school crooner and ladies man, traits tied to both Sinatra's real life persona and film characters. In addition, the phrasing captures the early counter rhetoric embedded in this locale and the ensuing battle in paint and wheat paste that was to divide interests in its conquest and diversion of this particular material interface over the course of this documentation.

Tags suck and stencils are toy

Multimodality can also be harnessed to construct inventories of the semiotic resources (i.e. actions, materials and artefacts) associated with graffiti production and how they are employed.[1] Crucially, multimodality can attend to the interplay between modes at the specific site of each graffiti work and how 'each mode of

Figure 3.2 (a) 39 Phillip St, Newtown, Gladstone St face, March 2007; (b) Later evidence of strike thru. Note the spray painted tag which partially conceals Sinatra's face. Gladstone St face, July 2007.

Photographs: Samantha Edwards-Vandenhoek.

practice interacts with and contributes to the others' (e.g. strike thru, the use of imagery in pieces or re-articulation of stencils as tags) in the construction of identity, territory, power relations and knowledge (Jewitt 2009: 25) (Figure 3.2). The partially torn down paste ups and stencils struck thru by tags and performative marks in Figure 3.2b provides sustained evidence of this convoluted and persistent visual tension and modal interplay between graffiti and urban art markings at this site. The disposable nature of the paste ups ensure they are prime targets for defacement even for partial removal that leaves a more a volatile trace (as opposed to complete erasure). It is worth noting that the counter attack and addition of the stencilled boy (top right) pissing on a tag, through the use of a yellow painted line to represent the urine, connotes how urban artists can détourn modes of graffiti writing on itself. The wavy lines that cut through the faces of the stencils are reminiscent of the strike thru key on a computer used to demarcate unwanted parts of speech or text in a very direct manner. In this instance it succeeds in spoiling the aesthetic qualities of the work. It is as though this writer has decided that the green tagging did not sufficiently express his/her own position on Sinatra's presence, which now through additional strike thru reinforces the earlier sentiments. What remains is a complex and chaotic mess of scrawls and marks that carry a somewhat aggressive and negative tone. In this light, a multimodal handling furnishes a place to tackle the inter-semiotic relations between modes and to explore the interplay between graffiti and its material context, such as a wall or building interior (Jewitt 2009: 16), as is the case in Figure 3.2, and then reframed at a later date in Figure 3.3, discussed below.

The interplay between typographic and pictorial/iconic modes, as is the case of pieces and stencils, can also be considered reflexive in that their relationship affords a commentary on itself and one another, both in terms of image negation, resilience and resolution. However, as the commentary (between stencils and graffiti) that continues on at this location in Figure 3.3a suggests, do not mistake a 'piece' for 'peace'. As far as the erasure of the stencilling is concerned, out of sight is not necessarily out of mind. In this everyday contestation of space that makes rules and decides access to and visibility of certain styles, materials and traditions of works, the graffers may have won a battle, but not necessarily the war. Stencil artists are highly adaptable and opportunistic, as this next addition to Phillip St testifies (Figure 3.3b).

Parisian can-can dancers add a surprising layer of surreal beauty and intertextual communication to this already highly abstract and surreal piece. The can-can dancers' presence further distorts and destabilizes time, place and belonging in terms of what it represents, covers and counters. While the colour palette deployed in the stencils is sympathetic to those used in the mural underneath, the pictorial modality of the can-can dancers (reduced and traced), is stylistically incongruent with the mural's non pictorial abstraction. It serves to fuel the confused, musical and uncomfortable evocation of place this colliding of graffiti works generates. The movement represented in the dancers, conveys a musical quality offset by the mechanical cogs in the background scene. A highly stylized and repetitive dance in itself, the can-can lends itself to the repetition as stencils. However, it was a

Figure 3.3 (a) 'Piece'. Close up of the intersection of Gladstone St and Phillip St, Newtown, February 2009; (b) Can-can dancers, Gladstone St face, January 2010.

Photographs: Samantha Edwards-Vandenhoek.

short lived performance. These stencils were painted over when this portion of the wall was buffed and blackened out with anti graffiti paint.

Kress and van Leeuwen's emphasis on how the context of communication and the sign maker shape signs and meaning is important to my research because it puts the emphasis back on the embeddedness of socio-cultural phenomena in the spatio-temporal contexts and modes of graffiti production. To Kress and van Leeuwen, images constitute multimodal forms of communication and representation that constitute the coming together of various elements into 'meaningful wholes' such as graffiti photographs or wall surfaces (2006: 1). Kress and van Leeuwen focus on the process of sign making in which 'the signifier (form) and the signified (meaning) are relatively independent of each other until they are brought together by the sign maker in a newly made sign' (ibid.: 7). It is an open and flexible approach that focuses on situated choices of resources and where there is no fixed or pre-existing relation of sign, signifier and signified. Rather, 'signs are a product of a social process of sign making' and where relation is arbitrary (ibid.: 23).

Kress and van Leeuwen's work largely deals with formal discourses and intact communications, such as those found in newspapers, layouts, art objects, designs, conversations and technologies that rely on known principles, entities and en-gagements (2001, 2006). They provide a range of tools, resources and awareness (such as gaze, social distance, framing, composition, perspective, narrative and materiality), all of which play an important role in how meanings can be made in broader multimodal systems (see Kress and van Leeuwen 2006; Kress 2009). However, graffiti, as a product of a visual dialogue, does not constitute a formal kind of discourse. It may follow formal visual or stylistic codes or design conventions, spatial structures, rules, framing codes and so on, as in the case of pieces and tags. As previously noted, graffiti transgresses the authorized conception of public space. To reiterate, it is the inherent illicitness, as well as the hybridized nature of graffiti's visual and material signs that are crucial to signifying their lack of fit within formal spatial systems and their potency for meaning production.

This issue is further compounded by the fact that this research deals with the traces of signs mediated through images. Moreover, some graffiti expressions may resemble signs and carry an iconic dimension but their meaning may not be a direct replica of the sign, as in the case of Frank Sinatra (Figure 3.2). Rudolf Arheim (1969) and van Leeuwen (2005) have shown that much of the meaning potential in visual communication and in music comes from metaphorical association. Kress and van Leeuwen (2002) in their analysis of colour show how there are many features of colours that can create meaning on the basis of association. As every image or image of a trace has the potential to sign differently, it is important to unpack the variables that impact on the processes of semiosis and resignification and enrich the reflexive, phenomenological and expressive orientation of this research (Figure 3.4).

Sign[s] of the times

The graffiti paste up of two appropriated commercial advertisements captured in Figure 3.4a highlights the complexities associated with framing and interpretation.

It also demonstrates how the *punctum* can fluctuate in response to the affective and symbolic dimensions of the composition and timings of its intervention. My initial appraisal and point of interest was focused in on the more obvious appropriation and recontextualization of an advertisement and its embedded myth of the feminine ideal as a sign of the times in which I live. Upon further evaluation, I became drawn to a new *punctum*; the scratched out eyes and the tag SMC etched (like a swastika) into the model's forehead. It is possible that this writer was making a comment on the stereotypical representation of women in the mass media. However, strike thru is also indicative of a graffiti writer's distaste for what he or she sees as lesser or illegitimate forms of graffiti practice, such as paste ups. On a third appraisal (and in this narrative), the intertextual relations embedded in this image composition took on a new significance, and another *punctum*, as the poetry took centre stage. The content of the poem suggests that the Dior ad was chosen by the artist/poet for its visual connotations and pictorial qualities, as it mirrors the action denoted in the poem (the whisper). As such, this détournement provides a fitting emotive backdrop for the poem, as opposed to a statement about the commodification of women, which nonetheless in this storyline is drawn out.

According to Kress (1993), the meaning of a sign is shaped by how a mode has been used, what it has been repeatedly used to mean and the social conventions that it rests upon. In this particular instance, Kress is referring to more formal and observable systems. For Kress and van Leeuwen, in situations where there is an implied author or 'disembodied voice' the interpretation rests on the 'competencies shared by producer and viewer' (2006: 115–116). This distinction becomes very important for the abandoned marks of graffiti and reflexive nature of the approach taken here. Moreover, what happens if there is a rupture in the logic of time and space, such as graffiti practice? When dealing with disrupted temporality, fragmentation, erasure, omission, addition and transience – characteristic of dispersive systems such as graffiti – a purely semiotic model of multimodality is not adequately equipped to manage forms of communication, representation and interaction that are situation dependant and where the author is largely unknown or anonymous (Figure 3.4). In the case of this research, the graffer has not only fled or left the scene, his/her works remain largely unsigned and anonymous.

As a spatio-temporal rupture, the multimodal framing in Figure 3.4b evidences the removal of the second part of the paste up and poem captured in Figure 3.4a, as well as the addition of a stencil produced by an unknown practitioner. The paste up in the top left corner and first captured in Figure 3.4a, which drew attention to issues of framing and phrasing and time–space compression associated with the addition of the typed poem and placement of the work in graffiti's counter public (rather than in a magazine), as a détournement of its placing and purpose, speaks largely to the semiotic. In this later framing, the meaning potential of the paste up representation of a commodified kiss appears revitalized by the placement of the red stencilled image below it that depicts two businessmen running towards each other. This phrasing heightens the considered yet spontaneous placement of each work – depicted 'coming together' in an embrace (the kiss) or a collision (the businessmen). In this respect, it also encourages a phenomenological rendering

Figure 3.4 (a) The circled areas in these archaeographs point to the poem in full in its dual parts. It reads 'In the morning, people may whisper a word into the artist's ear. The artist then writes this word on the wall in pencil. In the afternoon, people may select a word written on the word and whisper it into the artists [sic] ear. This word is then rubbed off. The artist hides in the gallery, leaving a trail of crumbs so that people may find them.' 39 Phillip St, South Newtown, June 2007; (b) A later framing that evidences the removal of one of the pasted up advertisements that contains the second half of the poem, as well as the addition of stencilled works below, 39 Phillip St, South Newtown, July 2007.

Photographs: Samantha Edwards-Vandenhoek.

of the multimodal narratives and the whimsy and playfulness embedded in this scene first read in Figure 3.4a, enriched now by the additional *punctum(s)* I have identified here. This stencil is inspired by *Blek the Rat's* naked running men which appeared on the streets of Paris in the 1980s. It signifies how the global urban art movement continues to influence local expressions and further compound the disrupted narrative embedded in this scene, which now references different spaces (Paris) and times (1980s).

As an example of multimodal and multi-coded communication, the iconic stencil work of *Ha Ha* further evidences the layers of symbolism, iconicity and expression that dwell with a single graffiti (image). *Ha Ha* has consistently and repetitively appropriated the iconic Ned Kelly[2] figure as the basis for his early stencil work in the early 2000s (Figure 3.5). The soft, dreamy and nostalgic representation of Ned Kelly not only alludes to a more romanticized vision of our early bushrangers (as national heroes), but the illicit and edgy nature of graffiti practice and how *Ha Ha* may see himself, as a champion for the graffiti subculture; a creative outlaw and liberator of space. The illicitness of his mark is manifest not only in its illicit execution, repetition but also in its subject matter. As a symbol, the stencil functions very much like a tag. Ned Kelly has become synonymous with *Ha Ha*'s

Figure 3.5 Ha Ha's stencil of Ned Kelly. Hosier Lane, Melbourne, April 2010.
Photograph: Samantha Edwards-Vandenhoek.

identity and alter ego. They are interchangeable. The repetition is a constant reinforcement of *Ha Ha* being there, but again this interpretation would differ between readers. So, in effect the social construct of an image cannot be fixed or focused on its maker. Looking at *Ha Ha*'s Ned Kelly once more, I am drawn to its astute premonition of the hipster beard trend and resurgence of barber shops, and its signalling of the ongoing appropriation of revolutionary figures and ideologies into consumer culture; and moreover, the significance of the Hosier Lane context, which has become a major site for mainstream cultural tourism in Melbourne. This kind of cultural appropriation is indicative of how the edgy, illicit and low key semiotic resources associated with graffiti have been sold back to its members by commercial entities as illusory symbols of resistance, what Thomas Frank aptly refers to as 'hip[ster] consumerism' (1997: 26) in his ground-breaking evaluation of youth counter culture, as well as in the gentrification of the built environment, such as Hosier Lane.

Graffiti and time travel

In an examination of how media produces different meanings across divergent temporalities of games and films in 'multimedia and transmedia franchises', Lemke (2009: 140) presents a strong case for an experiential, phenomenological and affective approach to multimodality to complement its socio-semiotic work. It is also an important added dimension to my own framework. Graffiti not only carries meaning, it affords meaning (in its affective, expressive and performative attributes), and so it requires a more experiential handling. In support of this, Lemke adds that 'a phenomenological perspective . . . reminds us of the importance of time, pacing, feeling, affect and embodiment, all of which are matters that can be construed semiotically but which seem to elude being completely accounted for in formal terms', which ties the multimodal framing of the analyses back into the archaeographic imagination of this research, and its resonance with Barthes's *punctum* (Lemke 2009: 141).

As discussed, Lemke's interests are grounded in Kristeva's (1980) concept of intertextuality; the shaping of meaning over time, by what he refers to as 'co-determinants of meaning' (2009: 140). Furthered by Anna Solin (2004) in her examination of the textual relations embedded in public discourse strategies surrounding environmental debates, intertextuality offers a perspective on trace that emphasizes the relational nature of meaning; where meaning is seen as emerging from the relation texts have with other texts, over time and space (Solin 2004: 267). This kind of intertextual logic can be applied to small scale dialogues (shared between two or more graffiti texts), as in the case of image negation (Figures 3.2, 3.3 and 3.4), to large scale discourses that traverse a range of texts, temporalities, social and historical frames of reference (Figure 3.6).

The considered use of ancient motifs, Egyptian fresco imagery, typography, symbols and nostalgia in Konsumterra's[3] stencil wall mural serves to regenerate social discourses, idealisms and narratives that connect the urban present and the lives of the people in this neighbourhood with the past (Figure 3.6). At face value,

Figure 3.6 Stencil wall, Weekes Lane, Newtown, March 2010.
Photograph: Samantha Edwards-Vandenhoek.

it combines an energetic yet ad hoc layout and psychedelic colour palette with a stencilled menagerie of goats, flamingos, ibis, human faces, movie and pop culture icons, symbols, painterly constructions and text. As a discursive formation, this graffiti also serves as a trigger for further sub-texts. As the time machine stencil in the bottom right corner connotes, this wall provides a portal to earlier times by visually referencing and paying homage to its cultural, material and political traditions. Rather than moving in for the kiss (as in Figure 3.4), the positioning of the stencilled image of a suited man here, denotes mankind moving forward, as the practice of graffiti (represented by the Egyptian God) depicted with a spray can in hand, looking back and walking in the opposite direction. This playful juxtaposition destabilizes a more normative and temporally linear conception of place, and what progress and moving forward without looking back actually means. Digging deeper, the graffiti's détournement of iconic imagery has the ability to create even more powerful, stronger icons and socio-cultural messages, which demonstrates the impact of graffiti on experiences of public space and place, as a parallel discursive arena to debate cultural politics. As a quirky aside, in my search for clues from the trail of crumbs left by Konsumterra, I googled the stencilled numbers '97 AUS OC 500761' to find that it is a direct reference to a Flickr site of Flamingo photographs, perhaps employed as visual guide here. Moreover the stencilled acronym 'ST5K' references the Adelaide street art festival, a fitting context for its promotion.

Intertextuality is clearly a complex negotiation. Moreover, like photography and archaeology it is a mediated action that involves choices; about what to observe, frame, sample or ignore, or what may be lost to the passage of time. Moreover, while intertextual studies often point to compatible views on contemporary social discourses, it largely remains inharmonious (Solin 2004). Moreover, it is furthered here that although a text (or trace) may appear in isolation, there is really no such thing as a 'monologic text' (Solin 2004: 268). However, it is important to iterate that it is not always feasible to explain what I observe. However, as Kristeva (1986) points out, intertextuality provides an interpretative space where the issue of intersubjectivity can be effectively resolved. By dissolving the distinction between (often multiple and anonymous) authors and readers, intertextuality removes restrictions and opens up the possibilities of what can be observed and disseminated. To reiterate, in support of Barthes, the reader becomes 'the space on which all the quotations that make up [graffiti] writing are inscribed without any of them being lost' (1977: 148).

Reading between the [closing] lines

What I have found in a multimodal and intertextual handling of graffiti's fragmented and differentiated traces is a hybrid reflexive analytical framework that can accommodate relations between graffiti's discursive, expressive and semiotic modes, as well as attend to the performative, affective, material and spatio-temporal aspects of the graffiti captured *in situ*. Crucially, this discursive based approach to reading archaeographs has the capacity to draw out plot lines embedded in the graffiti that would be delimited by a more separatist treatment. The temporality of the image and its shifting *punctum* has enabled me to realize new connections and construct narratives of the poetics of graffiti's engagements that may have otherwise remained unscrutinized. The archaeographs themselves embed visual dialogues and material tensions that reveal small-scale conversations, contestations and debates about permissible practices, aesthetics, style, competitions for space between practitioners, with external bodies and the general public. These debates reflect broader patterns and micro-climates of contestation, trends in practice, political issues and collaborations that characterize the public face of illicit graffiti in Sydney and Melbourne at the time of this documentation.

The multimodal approach also provides a way of writing, seeing and a mode of thinking about graffiti writing and urban art practices. In this respect, the readings presented here challenge and intervene in the everyday rhetoric that surrounds graffiti – written off as a criminal act or privileged as an aesthetic object. A situated and relational framing also succeeds in restoring the graffiti to its status as physical and conceptual sites of knowledge. This is significant because there has been some resistance in the literature to critically engage with graffiti's visual codes and discursive presentations *in situ*. Attention to pace, affect, and mimesis has enabled me to narrate the ineffable and expressive nature of place constructed through the graffiti that cannot be understood in semiotic or material terms alone. In their generous incompleteness, these readings endorse an interpretative and temporally disruptive lens through which the poetization of place embedded in the graffiti can be enacted.

Notes

1 This kind of work constitutes a major component of the archivization process in the *Sydney Graffiti Archive*. The readings presented in this chapter are part of PhD research that interrogates how graffiti shapes place in a wider accumulation of interior, exterior and subterranean sites, over a five year period. The *Sydney Graffiti Archive* was built to house the archaeographs, but also to ensure the images can be searched in different categories (i.e. by mode, setting, dates, technical specification, material resources and so on). For more information, visit www.sydneygraffitiarchive.com.au. Accessed: 13 December 2015.

2 Edward (Ned) Kelly (1855–1880) was an Australian outlaw and bushranger. Over time, he reached almost mythical and legendary status in Australian folklore, despite the fact Ned Kelly and his gang were murderers and robbers, and should have excited public detestation. Despite strong calls for a reprieve, Kelly was hanged at the Melbourne gaol for his crimes. His last words were 'Ah well, I suppose it has come to this', and by another version, Barry, J. V. n.d., 'Kelly, Edward (Ned) (1855–1880)', *Australian Dictionary of Biography*, *Australian National University*. Available at: http://adb.anu.edu.au/biography/kelly-edward-ned-3933/text6187. Accessed: 29 October 2011.

3 Konsumterra is an active voice in Sydney's urban art community. Often under the pseudonym of the Crash Corporation Beast, his stencils and fly posters are anti-establishment works, inspired by 1950s cult iconography, socialist figures and films such as *Clockwork Orange*. On the whole, his works and walls provide a personal and social commentary on consumerism and the commodification of place.

References

Arheim, Rudolf. 1969. *Visual Thinking*. Berkeley, CA: University of California Press.

Barthes, Roland. 1977. *Image, Music, Text*. Stephen Heath (trans.). New York, NY: Hill & Wang.

Barthes, Roland. 1984. *Camera Lucida: Reflections on Photography*. London: Fontana.

Cresswell, Tim. 1996. *In Place/Out of Place: Geography, Ideology, and Transgression*. Minneapolis, MN: University of Minnesota Press.

Frank, Thomas. 1997. *The Conquest of Cool: Business Culture, Counterculture and the Rise of Hip Consumerism*. Chicago, IL: University of Chicago Press.

Howells, Richard. 2003. *Visual Culture*. Cambridge: Polity Press.

Jewitt, Carey. 2009. 'An Introduction to Multimodality'. In Jewitt, Carey (ed.), *The Routledge Handbook of Multimodal Analysis*. London: Routledge, pp. 14–27.

Kress, Gunther. 1993. 'Against Arbitrariness: The Social Production of the Sign as a Foundational Issue in Critical Discourse Analysis'. *Discourse & Society*. 4(2): 169–191.

Kress, Gunther. 2009. 'What is a Mode?'. In Jewitt, Carey (ed.), *The Routledge Handbook of Multimodal Analysis*. London: Routledge, pp. 54–67.

Kress, Gunther and van Leeuwen, Theo. 2001. *Multimodal Discourse: The Modes and Media of Contemporary Communication*. London: Arnold.

Kress, Gunther and van Leeuwen, Theo. 2002. 'Colour as a Semiotic Mode: Notes for a Grammar of Colour'. *Visual Communication*. 1(3): 343–368.

Kress, Gunther and van Leeuwen, Theo. 2006. *Reading Images: The Grammar of Visual Design* (2nd edn). London: Routledge.

Kristeva, Julia. 1980. *Desire in Language: A Semiotic Approach to Literature and Art.* Oxford: Blackwell.

Kristeva, Julia. 1986. 'Word, Dialogue and Novel'. In Moi, Toril (ed.), *The Kristeva Reader.* New York, NY: Columbia University Press, pp. 34–61.

Lemke, Jay. 2009. 'Multimodality, Identity and Time'. In Jewitt, Carey (ed.), *The Routledge Handbook of Multimodal Analysis.* London: Routledge, pp. 140–150.

Rose, Gillian. 2001. *Visual Methodologies: An Introduction to Researching with Visual Materials.* London: Sage.

Shanks, Michael. 2001. 'Culture/Archaeology: The Dispersion of a Discipline and its Objects'. In Hodder, Ian (ed.), *Archaeological Theory Today: Breaking the Boundaries.* Cambridge: Polity Press, pp. 284–306.

Shanks, Michael. 2004. 'About Archaeography'. *Archaeography.* Available at: http://archaeography. com/photoblog/about.shtml. Accessed: 1 March 2008.

Shanks, Michael. 2007. 'Digital Media, Agile Design, and the Politics of Archaeological Authorship'. In Clack, Timothy and Brittain, Marcus (eds), *Archaeology and the Media.* Walnut Creek, CA: Left Coast Press, pp. 273–89.

Shanks, Michael. 2009. 'The Archaeological Imagination'. Available at: http://documents. stanford.edu/michaelshanks/57. Accessed: 1 December 2009.

Solin, Anna. 2004. 'Intertextuality as Mediation: On the Analysis of Intertextual Relations in Public Discourse'. *Interdisciplinary Journal for the Study of Discourse.* 24(2): 267–96.

van Leeuwen, Theo. 2005. *Introducing Social Semiotics.* London: Routledge.

Walker, John and Chaplin, Sarah. 1997. *Visual Culture: An Introduction.* Manchester: Manchester University Press.

4 Interviewing walls

Towards a method of reading hybrid surface inscriptions

Sabina Andron

Introduction

Most of us encounter graffiti and street art as part of our everyday experiences of the city, as they occupy spots on urban surfaces and coexist alongside a wide array of urban signage. Graffiti and street art have been researched as aesthetic categories, urban cultures, legal contentions, cultural commodities and place-making tactics – but they are also, perhaps fundamentally, localized inscriptions. They take place in precise locations within the built environment, adapting to existing visual and material contexts and contributing to their appearance and development.

This chapter attempts to theorize a unifying visual-material approach to urban inscriptions, using frameworks such as multimodality (Kress and van Leeuwen 2001), geosemiotics (Scollon and Wong Scollon 2003) and semiotic landscapes (Kress and van Leeuwen 2006; Jaworski and Thurlow 2010). Starting from site-specific visual data of annotated photographs I took in London between 2012 and 2015, the chapter aims to generate a responsive, integrative discourse of sanctioned and unsanctioned surface inscriptions. These often form qualitatively different parts of the semiotic landscape but their boundaries seem to be increasingly permeable, as graffiti, street art, advertising and street signage recurrently make less distinct categories. Different types of signs form clusters of hybrid communication, using a variety of media and placement strategies within the same territories. I propose the concept of 'hybrid surface inscriptions' to bring all these signs together and accommodate the extraordinarily diverse and elusive nature of the markings it refers to.

A fundamental question I explore in this chapter is what happens when one looks at graffiti and street art as localized inscriptive artefacts, rather than focusing on their production, reception or regulation. Methodologically, this means shifting away from sociological or ethnographic studies of graffiti and street art, and into the realm of visual, textual and semiotic approaches. I propose to bracket the distinct cultures of 'graffiti' and 'street art' with their own codes and histories, and tackle them through the lens of semiotic theories instead, as part of a wider material and communicative context.

This chapter puts forward 'wall interviews' as a methodological exercise and illustrates the process through a selection of annotated visual material. These images can be studied alongside or separately from the main body of the text, as they unpack surface semiosis by referencing a diverse range of material and graphic elements. The wall interviews are supported by input from visual, linguistic and semiotic landscape theories and explore the results of reading graffiti and street art less as separate categories, and more as localized components of the urban semiotic landscape.

Urban inscriptions as textual and visual signs

The first section of this chapter deals with the textual and visual dimensions of city surface signage, and seeks to integrate both components into a discussion of signs by using linguistic and visual methodologies. The general rhetoric that accompanies urban signs is often a linguistic one, in which cities are legible, public signs are meant to be read, people who practise graffiti are writers and the city primarily creates a textual landscape around us. This is known as a 'linguistic landscape', a subfield of sociolinguistics that was first introduced by linguist Rodrigue Landry and social psychologist Richard Bourhis in 1997. Landry and Bourhis define linguistic landscapes as the sum of textual inscriptions present in an urban area that spans a variety of media and languages and offers an insight into the geographic territories occupied by minority language communities. Linguistic landscape studies are usually limited to verbal signs, often in multilingual areas, and focus mostly on quantitative research (such as counting minority language signs), analysing inscriptions according to language used, multilingualism and language policies. As Landry and Bourhis suggest:

> The language of public road signs, advertising billboards, street names, place names, commercial shop signs, and public signs on government buildings combines to form the linguistic landscape of a given territory, region or urban agglomeration.
>
> (1997: 25)

This is not meant to be an exhaustive list, and it calls for the inclusion of un-sanctioned practices that contribute to the linguistic landscape just as prominently, such as tags, stickers, graffiti throw-ups and pieces, slogans or any kind of random textual scribbling. These have been considered by a number of scholars working in the field of linguistic landscapes who have looked at graffiti in their studies: graffiti is discussed as indicative of a community's vernacular literary practices (Jaworski and Thurlow 2010); mentioned as part of the bottom-up configured linguistic landscape (Waksman and Shohamy 2010) and as part of the language of minority or excluded social groups (Marten 2010); is recognized as a literary genre (Blume 1985), and is considered as a linguistic genre that has contributed significantly to the localized study of language, through its connections to the built environment, transgression and the right to urban semiosis (Pennycook 2009; 2010; Scollon and Wong Scollon 2010; Ben-Rafael *et al.* 2010). However, as the focus of linguistic landscape studies is on language rather than image, they are limited to offering a partial insight into graffiti and other urban inscriptive practices.

Writing seems to be the concept of choice for studying many inscriptive practices, turning reading into the required action for engagement and for making sense of our urban environments. In his study of public writing and literacy in nineteenth century New York, historian David Henkin observes that 'we have come to expect cityscapes to be legible, much as we expect consumer goods to come with labels' (1998: 3). This is a telling comparison because product labels, as much as urban signs, are rarely made from bare lines of text. Text on labels is often accompanied by images and is always placed and designed in a certain way, and so are the messages on our city surfaces.

Figure 4.1 shows different types of public writing as they sit in relation to each other and display contrasting visual forms. Written text is always styled, as is apparent through the more prominent and legible messages in this frame (like the old shop sign), or the faded and unintelligible ones (like most of the text on the layered posters). Placement and design offer clues about the propriety of language on city surfaces. Here, the street number and shop sign are written in a legible typeface and therefore project a legitimate presence, while the throw-ups and posters appear to be unsanctioned, opportunistic presences.

Figure 4.1 Written texts are image signs, not just language signs. London, Spitalfields, November 2012.

Photograph: Sabina Andron.

As this first example makes apparent, a semiotic model that privileges language signs and assigns a subservient role to the image limits the potential scope of these analyses. What is needed is an approach that accounts for visual signs as much as verbal ones, as proposed by semioticians Gunther Kress and Theo van Leeuwen (2006). They stress the importance of visual literacy in today's urban environments, complementing Henkin's emphasis on reading and textual apprehension. With surface communication becoming denser and more competitive, and the battle for visibility being fought on an increasing number of fronts, images are becoming increasingly prominent components of urban environments. City surfaces are used as platforms for the gain of visibility, where images selectively attract public attention from privileged or outsider positions, some with authorization and others in spite of the lack thereof.

Cultural and visual theorist Ella Chmielewska (2005) talks about the immersive visual environment of urban inscriptions, stressing the image qualities of surface signage in addition to their textual ones. The importance of urban images gets reflected in practices such as design and advertising, with branding industries creating logos that are recognizable beyond language or culture. Even when they are words, logos function as images, communicating in a visually, rather than textually, mediated manner. The proliferation of images also gets reflected in their use by disciplines such as communication, media studies or discourse analysis, and is perhaps primarily analysed by the discipline of visual culture.

Visual culture can bring a few relevant contributions to the study of city surface inscriptions, their actual and perceived legitimacy, and their placement. Graffiti and street art have often been discussed as art-historical phenomena, but their inclusion within the remit of visual culture seems much more accurate, as it accounts not only for their aesthetic and stylistic components, but also for their cultural, affective and relational dimensions. What types of popular culture are being appropriated and produced by city surface inscriptions, how do these inscriptions alter their environments through their presence, and how do they engage with their material and communicational contexts? These are all questions that visual culture is equipped to address by exploring the powerful attributes of contextualized images.

Urban surfaces are home to a constant battle for visibility taking place between the most unequal of forces: authorities intervene with regulatory discourses such as traffic signs and public notices; public labels guide our movement and orientation through street signs; property developers promise luxurious lifestyles from the hoardings of construction sites; and commercial discourses flash posters, billboards and shop signs through our spectra of visibility. At the same time, a number of transgressive voices make their presence felt through independent inscriptive practices, strategically occupying urban surfaces in their own right. This battle is fought by prominently placing one's own inscription, but also by rendering other inscriptions visible or invisible (e.g. parasitic placement, removal of unauthorized markings or building on existing ones). Shaping and managing visibility is a practical and political issue with social and spatial implications that can be observed not only on the respective surfaces, but also way beyond them.

For example, vehicular and pedestrian flows in the city depend on the correct placement of traffic signs, sentences for graffiti writers depend on how many of their tags the police identified and recorded, and the commercial viability of a brand depends on the number of people who see and identify its logo or product (Brighenti 2007a, 2009).

The scale of visibility battles is not always prominent, and it is often on less conspicuous surfaces that they can be best observed. The wall in Figure 4.2 displays a number of interactions between sanctioned and unsanctioned texts and images, as well as between different media (from the metallic sheet of the council sign to the small paper stickers and the texts written in marker pen and aerosol, and those scratched into the supporting concrete wall). The council's directive ('No ball games') has been transformed through a series of interventions into the more relatable notice 'Ball games are great!', while some stickers have occupied the smooth surface of the plaque. From entitled prescriptive messages such as the council sign, to opportunistically placed stickers or strategic textual subversions – they are manifestations of multimodal discourse that can be encountered on many urban surfaces.

It already becomes apparent from the number of different examples of linguistic and visual landscapes that these two cannot be fully separated, and the opposition

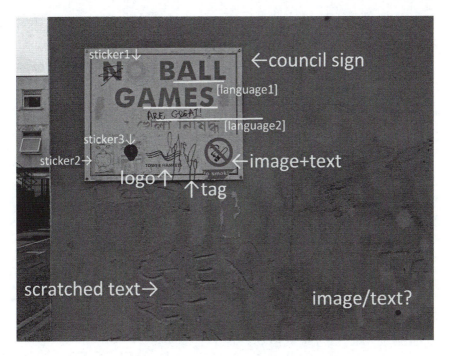

Figure 4.2 Individual signs signify through individual modes, which makes collective surface discourse multi-modal. London, Spitalfields, December 2012.

Photograph: Sabina Andron.

between text and image collapses and asks for a new reading of the complex semiological urban landscapes. This has been acknowledged from within the visual culture discipline by W.J.T. Mitchell through his argument that all media are mixed media (Mitchell, 2002), while Kress and van Leeuwen have called for a multi-modal reading of semiotic discourse that must be interdisciplinary and take into account different modes of communication at the same time, 'a theory of semiotics appropriate to contemporary semiotic practice' (2001: 2).

Similarly, James Elkins proposes that we snap out of our 'word–image trance' by using the Greek concepts *gramma* (picture, written letter and piece of writing) and *graphein* (to write, draw or scratch) instead:

> Together, gramma and graphein preserve a memory of a time when the divisions we are so used to did not exist, and they help us remember, when we need to, that picturing and writing are both kinds of 'scratching' – that is, marking on and in surfaces.
>
> (1999: 83)

Drawing, scratching and surface marking are all common attributes of graffiti definitions, and in fact graffiti shares a common etymological background with the Greek *graphein* and the Indo-European **gerebh-*, which is a general term for writing, drawing and scratching.[1] Elkins includes graffiti in the category of allographs, which he defines as forms of typography and calligraphy, namely the visual changes made to letters without affecting their alphabetic identities, or their textual communicative potential (1999: 95). Graffiti is therefore text and image at the same time, and so are many of the signs encountered on the surfaces of our cities.

City surfaces as material and territorial landmarks

The second section of this chapter looks at another essential component of surface signage semiosis, namely placement and location. The places of inscriptions are just as important as their visual and textual components, and can produce powerful contentions over permission and entitlement. Surface sites generate availability and meaning, while providing a highly influential context of reception. Signs are part of material and communicative surface networks, and undergo a process of material charting and adaptation as they occupy their spots on city surfaces. These spots are the primary connection that signs establish with the urban environment and they require as much analytical attention as the statements signs make or the messages they represent. In fact, it is often the case that physical presence itself is the message, and simply being visible on a certain surface is the most powerful content one can send across. As Chmielewska argues:

> Every urban sign, each billboard or display screen is a semiotic object whose material presence indexes and informs both the visual context and the specific

physical location. Whether the content of its message is generic or place-specific, its location creates a discrete condition of semiosis.

(2010: 277)

Physical proximity leads to friction and intermingling of cultures through their signage, so signs can offer reliable understandings of social geographies. They can reveal the language minorities in a particular area, they speak of the daily habits and customs of city dwellers, point to the degree of privatization of urban environments, offer insights into cultural trends and show which displays are allowed or not under particular circumstances, often through the traces of their removal. You can learn about a city's real estate market by looking at its signage, as you can learn about its artistic inclinations and political grievances, its social policies and cost of life, and its inhabitants' problems, passions and preoccupations. This complex semiotic system includes 'private interests, mutually indifferent pursuits, antagonistic ideologies and discrete messages' (Henkin 1998: 3), all drawing and redrawing on fluid and interactive surface territories.

The semiotic category of graffiti has received more scholarly attention than other forms of public visual discourse because it is perceived as being 'out of place', as argued by geographer Tim Cresswell (1996). Place and territory studies are important to the study of graffiti, as graffiti is very rarely perceived as pertaining to an environment, and has not undergone a process of backgrounding like other urban semiotic marks (Jaworski and Thurlow 2010: 21). Graffiti has been recognized as being a highly spatially sensitive practice, more so than its sanctioned counterparts. Ethnographic studies have pointed to the careful selection of writing spots by graffiti writers, showing how graffiti is highly controlled by its supportive environment (Ferrell and Weide 2010), and street artists have been declared adept masters of spatial semiotics on account of their engagement with the city (Irvine 2012). Cresswell (1996) talked about a hierarchy of visual rights to places and characterized graffiti as out-of-place, as it often defies expectations of legality and propriety, while geographer Luke Dickens proposed including graffiti into the 'wealth of other cultures of inscription' (2008: 472), as a means of researching the city. Chmielewska has also repeatedly emphasized the importance of researching graffiti as a localized practice (2007: 163): 'A graffito is a topo-sensitive language sign that points to itself while designating the local surface and referencing the discourse that surrounds it.'

Looking at sites in relation to graffiti has mostly been interesting because of underlying territorial contentions that rarely appear in the case of sanctioned signage. Studies of graffiti locations are more prominent than ones that look at the location of traffic signs, as the latter rarely generate territorial controversy. However, I would like to argue that sites are as important for understanding sanctioned surface marks as they are for understanding tagging or fly-posting, as they all form part of the same semiotic aggregates and signify through juxtaposition and accumulation.

Not only is any surface more than a blank canvas, but it bears upon it layers and layers of material and visual codes and it stands as part of a larger physical and inscriptive system. Surfaces are shifting, exposed territories that are constantly subject to dispute, claiming and reclaiming. Sociologist Andrea Mubi Brighenti (2010a, b) studied territories as semiotically expressed social relations that can have different degrees of material presence. Territories can exist without physical markers (publicly accessible private property is not always marked as such, but we are still aware it belongs to someone) and they are never fixed in space and time. Vulnerable, contested, and always open to dispute and change, surface territories are shifting, superimposed functions that express the dynamics of urban life in their acceptance or rejection of signage, and offer a variety of information through their shifting configuration.

Territories never exist in a fixed state, and the example in Figure 4.3 illustrates how territorial challenges can occur. These two photographs (Figure 4.3) were taken one month apart in a prime painting spot off London's Brick Lane and show how the initial sign 'Private Property, No Visitors, No Parking, No Artist [sic]' got reconfigured by the addition of 'Public Right of Way' and of successive tags and stickers. The territorial challenge goes beyond the sign itself and into the parking lot behind it, based on the public accessibility of the privately owned lot. In this particular case of territorial contestation, ownership is but one of the aspects that drives appearance, as a number of visual claims openly contest the territory of ownership.

The nature of supportive surfaces will make some signs more vulnerable than others. Ownership, materials, accessibility and exposure all get to decide the duration of signs' public lives. It is usually a regulatory or territorial claim that can make the difference between ephemeral, transient signage and sturdy, durable ones, but the physicality of both the sign and its supportive surface are also decisive factors.[2] For example, paper-based inscriptions are likely to weather away more easily than metallic plaques, irrespective of their (un)authorized nature; while anything painted on a smooth surface such as glass or metal is easier to remove and prone to a shorter life span. However, all public signs are vulnerable and are subject to responses, appropriation, collaboration, defacement, interpretation, weathering, attack and obliteration. Henkin explains this vulnerability:

> Once words have been physically and dramatically exposed to public view, they are no longer under the control of their originators. Writing assumes a life of its own in public space and becomes subject to close, literal and socially unstable reading.

(1998: 60)

When thought of as territories, urban surfaces become deeply imbued with meaning. Linguist Roy Harris uses integrational semiology to account for the importance of locational content (1995: 113): 'From an integrational point of view, the surface is not semiologically inert or valueless. It makes its contribution to the significance of what is written, and it may do so in various ways.' Harris speaks of a semiological relationship of surface to text, which is determined by

Figure 4.3 Privately owned, but publicly accessible and visible: the aspect of city surfaces should remain disputed. London, Brick Lane, December 2014 and January 2015.

Photograph: Sabina Andron.

the affinities or tensions that exist between the two. In the urban environment, inscriptions and surfaces relate through at least three different types of territories: ownership, materiality and communication.

Territorial ownership generates the most contentions in relation to uninvited inscriptions, as each publicly visible surface has a property status and belongs to someone, whether it is marked as such or not. According to Western social models, the availability of certain surfaces is strictly connected to their ownership, as they are carriers of implicit and explicit rules and codes of conduct, permission systems and legal frameworks. The first claim at territories is always associated with ownership and is often exclusionary, as the rights to public visibility and display come second to the right to property. 'Territory is a framework that pre-assigns to an official owner control or precedence over any possible object that will happen to lie within it', but this claim can always be contested, as new territories are asserted through visible graphic interventions that then become part of the territorial cycle (Brighenti 2010b: 67). City surfaces offer some of the best examples to illustrate the links between property and exclusion, but they are also the best places to look for the numerous contestations of this social postulate.

A second territorial degree is defined by the materiality of surfaces, their appearance and accessibility, or their designated purpose. The physical accessibility of a surface can be a constraint and an opportunity (e.g. placing an inscription within reach is easier as it doesn't require special equipment, but it also makes the inscription more vulnerable to future interventions), while its material features can have a major impact on the media used for its inscription (e.g. surface elevations, materials, textures, dimensions, framings and graphic saturation levels all play a role in placement).

Any added inscription will then form third and subsequent mini-territories that are generated in accordance with or in spite of initial territorial layers, staking their own claims and becoming potential backdrops for even more additions. This is a fundamental mobility for hybrid surface inscriptions, which shift their message, placement and readings according to their communicative context. They take advantage of the latency of some territories (e.g. walls where owners don't clean tags, spots where councils don't respond to fly posting, or billboard displays that aren't checked for legality), or engage in dialogue and direct reference to existing spatial and inscriptive elements (e.g. placing a sticker directly onto a traffic sign, or the practice of subvertising).

As can be seen in Figure 4.4, the simple presence of a new inscription on a surface is enough to reconfigure the whole territorial dynamics of that surface, as each sign generates a new territory in its moment of emplacement. In this particular instance, ownership territories that are often abstract become actualized through the persistent repainting (buffing) of this wall. Visibility gets policed through direct obstruction, with ownership as the underlying justification. This creates new surface geometries in the process, which then form fresh visual and material territories.

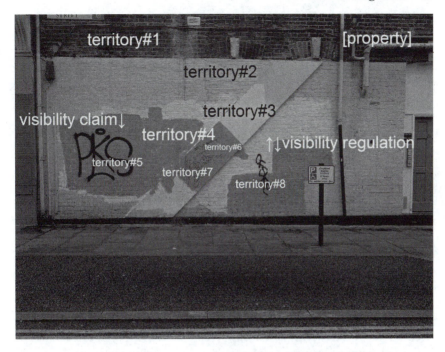

Figure 4.4 The buff appears more authoritative when it purposefully stands out and demarcates a territory. London, Bethnal Green, July 2015.

Photograph: Sabina Andron.

Multiple localized inscriptions or, the semiotic landscape

The third section of this chapter brings together previously discussed dimensions into a single inclusive method that is equipped to deal with textual, visual and territorial aspects across a wide range of city surface inscriptions, be they sanctioned or unsanctioned. Hybrid inscriptions are a sum of their media, message, linguistic and visual codes, as well as of the territories they belong to and the visual context that surrounds them. There are connections to be deciphered and layers to be read on any such type of marked urban surface, and its immediate legibility or visual appeal should not be part of our decision to do so. It is often the big, crisp and sharp signs that create a more powerful impact, as opposed to the smaller, undecipherable, and less striking ones, but they both form meaningful parts of urban cultures. In fact, the number of unsanctioned signs on city surfaces very likely exceeds their sanctioned counterparts, illustrating an urban culture that rarely behaves in a permissioned and orderly fashion. Each sign proves that a particular place is alive and inhabited, transforming surfaces into vigorous social spaces in contemporary cities.

The methodological apparatus that is needed to deal with this system must therefore be capable of handling its complexity from an interdisciplinary, inclusive perspective. Linguistic landscapes and integrational linguistics accounted for the places of language; and visual culture argued for the necessary blurring of text and image. What brings these all together in accounting for the communicational and locational diversity of urban signage is a semiotic discourse that has been proposed alternatively as 'geosemiotics' (Scollon and Wong Scollon 2003) and 'semiotic landscapes'(Kress and van Leeuwen 2006; Jaworski and Thurlow 2010). Both these theories are anchored in the multifaceted, localized nature of the semiotic sign and have the capacity to address it in all its complexity.

Geosemiotics, as introduced by Scollon and Wong Scollon (2003), foregrounds the places of discourse and is a method with a specifically urban scope. It reflects on the placement of semiotic markings within the material world, and is built on the principle that every sign is actively and intrinsically connected to its location, generating discourse and information through its simple presence. Geosemiotics can therefore be read as a theory of indexicality or localization, its purpose being to interpret the meaning systems by which textual and visual discourses are located in the material world. Lying at the intersection of visual and place semiotics, it uses tools from linguistics, cultural geography, communication, discourse analysis and sociology to generate a multimodal discourse about urban signs and their locations.

Similarly, the concept of semiotic landscape proposed by Kress and van Leeuven (2006) and further developed by Jaworski and Thurlow (2010) aims to incorporate not just textual utterances in the urban environment, but also visual and non-verbal discourses, cultural values, as well as architecture and the built environment. As Kress and van Leeuwen argue:

> The place of visual communication in a given society can only be understood in the context of, on the one hand, the range of forms or modes of public communication available in that society, and, on the other hand, their uses and valuations. We refer to this as the 'semiotic landscape'. . . . so particular modes of communication should be seen in *their* environment, in the environment of all the other modes of communication that surround them, and of their functions.

> (2006: 33)

There is a strong sense of emplacement here as well, which is not limited to looking at the places of discourse, but also includes the inherent semiotic function of those places (e.g. their assigned and disputed territorial functions). Jaworski and Thurlow go on to define semiotic landscapes as 'any (public) space with visible inscription made through deliberate human intervention and meaning making' (Jaworski and Thurlow 2010: 2) – a definition that prioritizes places over inscriptions and suggests that inscriptions can generate as much knowledge about their supportive places, as places can about their supported inscriptions.

Both these systems of categorization function less based on the messages they carry, and more based on how these messages are carried (as does indeed any semiotic theory). In the case of hybrid surface inscriptions, the main material signifiers are placement and authorization, i.e. where these messages appear and whether they are allowed to be there or not. State signage, commercial billboards, tags, notice boards, CGIs of real estate developments, discarded leaflets and artistic murals share territories all the time, and coexistence is intrinsic to their urban occupations. They each bring with them specific types of production and notions of entitlement, forming 'very complex systems of interaction of multiple semiotic systems' or, 'semiotic aggregates', as Scollon and Wong Scollon term them (2003: xii). The annotated photographs that accompany this chapter are instances of such semiotic aggregates, each with specific properties: direct linguistic reference and appropriation, visual translations of territorial claims, or material affinities between official and uninvited signage. Whatever the case, it is the complexity of these aggregates that makes them interesting for this type of reading, rather than the isolated examination of their individual elements.

For example, Figure 4.5 shows an array of inscriptions whose semiotic analysis, as an aggregate, points to a number of things. We are looking at a number of graffiti tags (or signatures), a poster, a few commercial stickers, a text-based shop sign and a painted shutter with the image of a muscular weightlifting man. Here are some observations that can be made based on this configuration of surface signage:

Figure 4.5 All graphic elements in a semiotic aggregate are significant, not just prominent ones. London, Bethnal Green, July 2015.

Photograph: Sabina Andron.

- Aerosol paintings are sought-after options for on-site commercial signage. This is a response to the wider visual context of the Brick Lane–Bethnal Green–Cambridge Heath area in London, which is very dense in aerosol inscriptions.
- Visual forms are rarely celebrated or frowned upon in themselves: it is their placement that turns the compass when it comes to acceptability. Here, tags appear both on the side wall and on the shutter, and the latter enjoys a higher degree of tolerance because it is part of an invited painting project.
- Commercial inscriptions are not to be presumed legal. Advertising is often installed without authorization, and the small commercial stickers in this image are just one instance of how this happens. In the UK, flyposting and graffiti fall under the incidence of the same legislation.[3]
- Graffiti need not have prominence in a geosemiotic study of urban surfaces. The wider the lens applied to surface inscriptions, the more diverse the information that can be obtained from their semiotic reading.

Closing the interview: graffiti and beyond, or beyond graffiti?

Human interaction in public space reveals itself through the semiosis of hybrid surface inscriptions. Each sign bears within it not just its physical presence, but has the capacity of invoking the presence of its producer and projecting intentionality in their action. For example, we know advertising is there to sell us something even when we do not actually read what it says. Moreover, we know advertising is exactly that because of the way it is placed and the visual codes it employs, this being a skill we constantly perfect as city dwellers, whether we want to or not.

Sign producers have learned to play with our sign reading proficiency and are using visual or spatial codes specific to certain signs to transmit unexpected messages. This is the case when authorities produce messages that have an independent, grassroots aesthetic; or street artists employ advertising resources to put up their art; and corporations use street art murals to promote their products. In fact, the lines between these have become so blurred, that our sign reading proficiency is often yet to keep up with the incredibly complex range of hybrid urban signage. With an increasing number of street art or graffiti works being created with permission, it often gets tricky to distinguish between sanctioned and unsanctioned signs, or legal and illegal productions.

Figures 4.6a–c show examples of how spaces, styles and visual codes get appropriated for purposes outside their conventional remit, eroding those conventions in the process. Graffiti visuals are employed to change the territorial and aesthetic praxis of commercial messages, as is the case with the spray-painted hoarding announcing the launch of a range of luxury apartments in Figure 6a. This looks like graffiti, but it is advertising, and might be illegal nonetheless. Notice how 'Eagle Black 15.05.14' was sprayed over another promotional message on the same hoarding, indicating a change of marketing strategy from the more

Figure 4.6 Graffiti and street art still seem to have a worthwhile marketing capital.
(a) London Old Street, May 2014; (b) London Brick Lane, May 2014;
(c) London Clerkenwell, July 2015.

Photographs: Sabina Andron.

conventional to what was likely perceived as an edgier approach. Similarly, the 'Original Banksy' stencil in Figure 6b was placed in one of London's most prolific street art areas by the Truman Brewery, capitalising on the presence of street work to raise interest. Follow the arrow, one might assume, and it will lead you to one of Banksy's street works. Instead, this was an advertisement for a local gallery that was selling artworks by the share (hence the £120 price per share of an artwork by Banksy).[4] One last example in Figure 6c is of the sponsored mural by prolific artist Dan Kitchener, painted with permission using fluorescent paint under the administration of Global Street Art.[5] This was paid for by corporate money and displays a logo and hashtag to mark that, but the scale of the painting makes it easy to overlook its *raison d'être*. The brand proposes itself as a supporter of creative outdoor expression, while pushing a commercial message from behind a street art aesthetic.

With these and previous examples, my proposal for a place-based semiotic reading shifted away from graffiti, in order to accommodate a wider range of city surface signs and utterances. Based on theories of geosemiotics and semiotic landscapes, this chapter introduced some samples of what a 'wall interview' might look like as a reading method, and the type of visual evidence it can produce. I like to think of the images in this chapter as snippets of 'interviewing walls', or performing a geosemiotic surface reading to reveal placements, territories and visibility battles.

What I would suggest by way of a conclusion is that a better semiotic understanding of graffiti and street art can only take place by incorporating other urban semiotic aggregates into the interpretative process, and generating a localized interpretation of their relations and territories. This can be achieved by taking up hybrid surface inscriptions and further exploring them as localized utterances of visual, textual and material composition that make up the 'surfacescapes' of our cities. Geosemiotic readings of these surface landscapes are able to reveal a great deal of information about claims, entitlements and the daily battles for visibility, which can be used to inform graffiti scholarship.

Surface signs reflect on urban cultures and rhythms and produce new cultures of their own, impacting profoundly on how cities are perceived, regulated and navigated. Hybrid surface inscriptions are not only a lens through which graffiti and street art can be read, but they are means through which urban social life constructs itself spatially and visually. I attempted to capture some of these complex urban palimpsests through the use of images as analytical tools, while providing some theoretical underpinnings for this form of city reading. Urban cultures research has a lot to gain from performing a more comprehensive reading of signs in public spaces, and graffiti can provide a generous starting point for such an endeavour.

Notes

1   The etymological root of *graffiti* can be traced through the singular *graffito*, 'a scribbling', which is the diminutive form of *graffio*, 'a scratch or scribble'. It was first used in this form in the mid-nineteenth century to refer to wall inscriptions found in

the ruins of Pompeii, and can be traced back to the Greek *gramma* and *graphein* and the Indo-European **gerebh-*, 'drawing, writing, scratching' (Elkins 1999), or 'to carve, to scratch, to write' (University of Texas Linguistic Research Centre). What is interesting about the origins of the term is that it contains both drawing and scratching within the same concept, designating an action done *on* a surface and one done *to* a surface at the same time. Both these meanings have been kept until today, as scratching and etching into surfaces and drawing on them with aerosol paint are all referred to as graffiti. More on this in Avramidis 2014.

2   See also my photographic project '100 Days of Leake Street', which follows the daily changes on walls in an uncurated legal painting spot in London. Available at: http://sabinaandron.com/leake-street/. Accessed: 29 August 2015.

3   Specifically, Part 6 of the 2003 Anti-Social Behaviour Act and Part 4 of the 2005 Clean Neighbourhoods and Environment Act.

4   The gallery is called MyArtInvest and is no longer at the aforementioned location at the time of writing (December 2015).

5   Global Street Art is one of the most prominent street art and advertising agencies in London. They organize commercial and non-commercial outdoor painting projects and manage a large number of outdoor sites across the city.

References

Avramidis, Konstantinos. 2014. 'Public [Ypo]graphy: Notes on Materiality and Placement'. In Karra, Marilena (ed.), *No Respect*. Athens: Onassis Cultural Center, pp. 21–34, 85–96.

Ben-Rafael, Eliezer, Shohamy, Elana and Barni, Monica. 2010. 'Introduction'. In Shohamy, Elana, Ben-Rafael, Eliezer and Barni, Monica (eds), *Linguistic Landscape in the City*. Bristol: Multilingual Matters, pp. xi–xxviii.

Blume, Regina. 1985. 'Graffiti'. In van Dijk, Teun Adrianus (ed.), *Discourse and Literature*. Amsterdam: Benjamins, pp. 137–148.

Brighenti, Andrea Mubi. 2007a. 'Visibility: A Category for the Social Sciences'. *Current Sociology*. 55(3): 323–342.

Brighenti, Andrea Mubi. 2007b. 'On Territory as Relationship and Law as Territory'. *Canadian Journal of Law and Society*. 21(2): 65–86.

Brighenti, Andrea Mubi. 2009. 'Walled Urbs to Urban Walls – and Return? On the Social Life of Walls'. In Brighenti, Andrea Mubi (ed.), *The Wall and the City*. Trento: Professional Dreamers, pp. 63–71.

Brighenti, Andrea Mubi. 2010a. 'At the Wall: Graffiti Writers, Urban Territoriality, and the Public Domain'. *Space and Culture*. 13(3): 315–332.

Brighenti, Andrea Mubi. 2010b. 'On Territorology: Towards a General Science of Territory'. *Theory, Culture & Society*. 27(1): 52–72.

Chmielewska, Ella. 2005. 'Logos or the Resonance of Branding: A Close Reading of the Iconosphere of Warsaw'. *Space and Culture*. 8(4): 349–380.

Chmielewska, Ella. 2007. 'Framing [Con]text: Graffiti and Place'. *Space and Culture*. 10(2): 145–69.

Chmielewska, Ella. 2010. 'Semiosis Takes Place or the Radical Uses of Quaint Theories'. In Jaworski, Adam and Thurlow, Crispin (eds), *Semiotic Landscapes: Language, Image, Space*. London: Continuum, pp. 274–291.

Cresswell, Tim. 1996. *In Place/Out of Place: Geography, Ideology, and Transgression*. Minneapolis, MN: University of Minnesota Press.

Dickens, Luke. 2008. 'Placing Post-Graffiti: The Journey of the Peckham Rock'. *Cultural Geographies*. 15(4): 471–96.

Elkins, James. 1999. *The Domain of Images*. Ithaca, NY: Cornell University Press.

Ferrell, Jeff and Weide, Robert. 2010. 'Spot Theory'. *City*. 14(1–2): 48–62.

Harris, Roy. 1995. *Signs of Writing*. London: Routledge.

Henkin, David. 1998. *City Reading: Written Words and Public Spaces in Antebellum New York*. New York, NY: Columbia University Press.

Irvine, Martin. 2012. 'The Work on the Street. Street Art and Visual Culture'. In Heywood, Ian and Sandywell, Barry (eds), *The Handbook of Visual Culture*. London: Berg, pp. 235–278.

Jaworski, Adam and Thurlow, Crispin. 2010. 'Introducing Semiotic Landscapes'. In Jaworski, Adam and Thurlow, Crispin (eds), *Semiotic Landscapes: Language, Image, Space*. London: Continuum, pp. 1–32.

Kress, Gunther and van Leeuwen, Theo. 2001. *Multimodal Discourse: The Modes and Media of Contemporary Communication*. London: Arnold.

Kress, Gunther and van Leeuwen, Theo. 2006. *Reading Images: The Grammar of Visual Design*. 2nd edn. London: Routledge.

Landry, Rodrigue and Bourhis, Richard. 1997. 'Linguistic Landscape and Ethnolinguistic Vitality: An Empirical Study'. *Journal of Language and Social Psychology*. 16(1): 23–49.

Marten, Heiko F. (2010) 'Linguistic Landscape under Strict State Language Policy: Reversing the Soviet Legacy in a Regional Centre in Latvia'. In Shohamy, Elana, Eliezer, Ben-Rafael and Barni, Monica (eds), *Linguistic Landscape in the City*. Bristol: Multilingual Matters.

Mitchell, W. J. T. 2002. 'Showing Seeing: A Critique of Visual Culture'. *Journal of Visual Culture*. 1(2): 165–181.

Pennycook, Alastair. 2009. 'Linguistic Landscapes and the Transgressive Semiotics of Graffiti'. In Shohamy, Elana and Gorter, Durk (eds), *Linguistic Landscape: Expanding the Scenery*. London: Routledge, pp. 302–312.

Pennycook, Alastair. 2010. 'Spatial Narrations: Graffscapes and City Souls'. In Jaworski, Adam and Thurlow, Crispin (eds), *Semiotic Landscapes: Language, Image, Space*. London: Continuum, pp. 137–150.

Scollon, Ron and Wong Scollon, Suzie. 2003. *Discourses in Place: Language in the Material World*. London: Routledge.

United Kingdom, Ministry of Justice. 2003. *Anti-social Behaviour Act*. Available at: www.legislation.gov.uk/ukpga/2003/38. Accessed: 29 December 2015.

United Kingdom, Ministry of Justice. 2005. *Clean Neighbourhoods and Environment Act*. Available at: www.legislation.gov.uk/ukpga/2005/16/contents. Accessed: 29 December 2015.

University of Texas Linguistic Research Centre. 'Indo-European Lexicon'. Available at: www.utexas.edu/cola/centers/lrc/ielex/X/P0579.html. Accessed: 29 December 2015.

Waksman, Shoshi and Shohamy, Elana Goldberg. 2010. 'Decorating the City of Tel Aviv-Jaffa for its Centennial: Complementary Narratives via Linguistic Landscape'. In Shohamy, Elana Goldberg, Ben-Rafael, Eliezer and Barni, Monica (eds), *Linguistic Landscape in the City*. Bristol: Multilingual Matters, pp. 57–73.

5 Graffiti, street art and the democratic city

Kurt Iveson

The right to write

So, there are writers and artists, and there are cops. And the good guys and the bad guys are locked in a battle over who has the 'right to write' on urban surfaces. Right?

Well, not quite. If your city is anything like mine (Sydney), the battle over graffiti on your streets now involves an ever-widening range of actors – the planners who (try to) regulate the uses of urban space, the politicians who make the criminal laws, the mainstream media who support the crime-fighting efforts, the government-funded youth centres who run the graffiti workshops, the galleries who put on 'urban art' shows, the companies who manufacture the paint and sponsor the shows, the publishers who make the glossy books and magazines, the shops that sell the books and the prints and the paints and the markers, the writers and artists who get the sponsorship and do the commissions and the shows, the writers who bomb the hell out of their neighbourhoods and think art is for 'fags', the anti-graffiti enterprises selling technological 'solutions' to the graffiti problem, the property owners who hate graffiti and those who want (some form of) it, and so on and so forth.

As this situation gets more and more complicated, it's increasingly difficult to think through the politics of graffiti and street art. For those of us whose passion for graffiti and street art is accompanied by commitments to urban spatial justice and democracy, the days when we could celebrate graffiti and/or street art as a kind of resistance against the evil authorities are way behind us (if they ever even existed . . .).

So, what are the politics of graffiti and street art? Can the practices of graffiti and street art contribute to the democratization of our cities? Of course, these are tricky questions to answer, not least because the meaning of each of the key terms – graffiti, street art, democracy and the city – is contested. But the stakes are high enough for us to try to work our way through these complexities. My short contribution to this volume offers a few brief thoughts in response to these questions, as part of the wider effort to help us read the complex entanglements of different forms of graffiti, street art and the city.

I approach the politics of graffiti and street art by situating these practices within a broader politics of authority in our cities. In particular, I want to make a case for thinking about the diverse practices of graffiti and street art not so much as *confrontations with* authority, but as *assertions of* authority. That is, the contest over graffiti and street art in cities is usefully conceived as a struggle over who gets to be the 'authors' of writing and work on their walls. This struggle over authorship is at the same time a struggle over authority. Indeed, the English word 'author' (defined in the Oxford English Dictionary as 'a writer' and/or 'a creator') shares an etymology with the word 'authority' (meaning 'power to enforce obedience or compliance, or a party possessing it') in the classical Latin 'auctor'.

So, the rest of this piece proceeds by considering both 'the authority of "the authorities"' – to use Alison Young's lovely phrase (2010: 113) – and the alternative or 'local' authority enacted by graffiti writers and street artists. It compares and contrasts these competing authorities with a simple, and probably unattainable, model of *democratic* authority that can guide our analysis and our practice. And it offers some thoughts about the lessons some graffiti writers and street artists are teaching us about the enactment of equality in our cities through their work.

The order of the city and the politics of urban authority

> In the end, everything in politics turns on the distribution of spaces. What are these places? How do they function? Why are they there? Who can occupy them? For me, political action always acts upon the social as the litigious distribution of places and roles. It is always a matter of knowing who is qualified to say what a particular place is and what is done in it.
>
> (Rancière 2003: 201)

The 'being together of strangers' that defines urban life is generative of a particular political dynamic (Young 1990). To put it starkly, this dynamic involves attempts to govern our 'being together' through a 'distribution of spaces' that allocates different activities, people and things to a 'proper time and place', and attempts to disrupt and transform this distribution. Jacques Rancière (1999) talks about this dynamic as a relationship between 'policing' and 'politics'. The difference between 'policing' and 'politics' for Rancière largely hinges on the forms of authority that are enacted in efforts to shape our 'being together'.

To explain: Rancière (1999) argues that democratic politics is founded on a very particular kind of authority – one that is based on the *absence* of what he calls a 'title to govern'. It's the authority of anyone at all, based on nothing more than our *equality* with one another as 'the people'. Democracy, then, is distinct from plutocracy (the rule of the wealthy), meritocracy (the rule of the cleverest), technocracy (the rule of the expert), aristocracy (the rule of the chosen), and so on. 'Democracy is equality', says Rancière (2001). That is, democracy is a practice of enacting rights that are based on the equality of each with all, thereby inscribing 'politics' in a 'police' order that seeks to dictate what is possible.

The order of the city is at least in part an *aesthetic regime* that takes the form of a 'partition of the perceptible', in which people are allocated roles to perform and then identified by the particular parts they play in society (Dikeç 2002; Davidson and Iveson 2015). 'A place for everything, and everything in its place', as the saying goes. Rancière uses the term 'police' to refer to this process of allocating and enforcing parts within the existing social order – a process that is not restricted to the operations of 'the police' in uniform (see also Iveson 2014).

Graffiti and street art certainly draw attention to the existence of competing authorities in our cities. The authority of 'the authorities' is far from democratic. The private property system is overwhelmingly (although not entirely) plutocratic and technocratic – such that the authority to determine how spaces are produced and used is enacted by those with money to purchase it, and regulated by planners using technical criteria meant to embody some minimal 'public interest'. To note that this 'public interest' is set by officials chosen at elections held once every few years is not to say that this regime is democratic! Rather, too often capitalist planning regimes tend to work by 'putting things in their place', producing a kind of 'post-political' or 'one-dimensional' city in which different practices and people are allocated a proper place and told to conform to it, and in which those places are not meant to sustain alternative uses (Swyngeodouw 2009; Tonkiss 2012).

Of course, the persistence of graffiti also illustrates the limits of these attempts to police the city through the imposition of an undemocratic urban order. As Michel de Certeau famously put it, the constructed order of the city 'is everywhere punched and torn open by elipses, drifts, and leaks of meaning: it is a sieve-order' (de Certeau 1984: 107). This is a point echoed by contemporary urban theorists such as Ash Amin and Nigel Thrift, who argue that efforts to order the city in particular ways are never complete:

> forms of governmentality may be totalizing projects, but they are not totalizations. Thus city populations can escape some of their inclinations and find new angles of declination.
>
> (2002: 108)

I am drawn back to de Certeau's classic account of everyday life because he offers us a useful term for our discussion of urban authority and its contestation. He suggests that the leakiness of the 'imposed order' of the city is the product of spatial practices that effectively enact '*local authorities*'. A local authority is defined as 'a crack in the system that saturates places with signification and indeed so reduces them to this signification that it is "impossible to breathe in them" ' (1984: 106). He goes on to note:

> It is a symptomatic tendency of functionalist totalitarianism (including its programming of games and celebrations) that it seeks precisely to eliminate these local authorities, because they compromise the univocity of the system.

Of course, de Certeau considered graffiti writing as one example of kinds of spatial practices that 'punch open' the imposed order of everyday urban life (de Certeau 1984: 102).

From the perspective I am developing here, it's important not to view struggles over the possibilities of place as a battle between 'the authorities' and 'the graffiti writers' (or 'the skateboarders' or 'the foragers' or whoever we happen to be interested in). Actually, the writers and others are asserting their own forms of authority when they do what they do. In fact, then, graffiti and street art draw our attention to the existence of *competing authorities* in our cities. Seeing things this way has important consequences. Crucially, those of us who care about urban social justice and democratization have to ask critical questions about *all* assertions of authority. On what basis do different actors claim authority to act and produce our urban spaces? As well as asking critical questions about the 'authority of the authorities', we should also ask questions about the kinds of 'local authority' asserted by writers, artists, skaters and the like. Transgression of, or resistance against, the 'dominant' urban authorities is not necessarily democratic or just. It all depends on whether the alternative or 'local' authorities are founded on the equality of each with all. So, what can we say about the kinds of authority enacted by graffiti writers and street artists in our cities?

Graffiti for a democratic city

Undoubtedly, when street artists and graffiti writers confiscate the surfaces of their city for their work, and when they do so without regard for the laws of private property and criminal damage, they are enacting a different city and asserting a different kind of authority over space. As noted above, the police order of the city is in part an aesthetic regime. The efforts of many graffiti writers and street artists show that despite the best efforts of authorities, efforts to enforce the one-dimensional city have failed, and are open to challenge.

So, street art and graffiti make a potentially important contribution to democratic urban politics through this inscription of visible *dissensus* into the policed order of the city. But having said this, countless individual acts of street art and graffiti don't necessarily add up to a democratic urban politics that produces a city in which we are 'authorized' to address each other through inscriptions on the surfaces of our urban environment as equals, regardless of wealth or age or gender. For 'local authorities' such as those asserted by graffiti writers and street artists, it is one thing to transgress the order of the city – it is another thing again to *transform* that order. A graffiti and street art practice that contributes to democratization of urban life would also involve a parallel articulation of street art and graffiti with the enactment of a democratic authority premised on our equality. This is a point Henri Lefebvre (another white Frenchman . . . sorry!) made in his musings on the 'right to the city'. Certainly, he argued, the order of the city is characterized by 'holes and chasms' that are 'the places of the possible'. However, while these actions may illustrate 'the floating and dispersed elements of the possible', do they have 'the power which could assemble them'? (Lefebvre 1996: 156).

Of course, this kind of transformation is not easy; quite the contrary. So, what kinds of approaches are emerging in contemporary graffiti and street art practice that might contribute to the projects of democracy and equality in cities? In this section, I offer four different approaches that seem to me to hold some promise in their different ways. This is far from a full catalogue, and is intended as a provocation to others to populate the list with other approaches that writers and artists are taking to enact a more democratic city in different places.

Policy

One way to try to challenge the one-dimensional city is to engage in policy advocacy and reform – effectively, supplanting one form of 'police' with another that is hopefully more democratic and equitable. As the financial and social costs of 'zero tolerance' approaches become more and more apparent (Iveson 2009), and as the commercial appeal of graffiti and street art grows (McAuliffe 2012), opportunities for this kind of policy work are likely to become increasingly common.

In the past two years, I've spent some time involved in this kind of policy work as part of a team of consultant researchers working for a progressive urban local council (our team was two academics and two artists – see Iveson *et al.* 2015). It has been a sobering experience. Even if some of the policy reforms we have suggested are implemented (and at the time of writing, this remains to be seen), I'm not sure they would do much to advance the cause of a more democratic city.

Our research certainly makes the point that for many graffiti writers and street artists, walls in public space are always going to be appropriated as spaces for public address, regardless of who owns them and the laws governing their use. And we've made the point that the obsession with rapid removal of tags will never 'work' on its own terms to stop that practice. In place of zero tolerance, we've made not-so-radical suggestions such as allowing property owners and artists to come to their own permission arrangements without needing formal planning approval from the local government (a practice that is of course already common, but not technically legal, resulting in the regular buffing of commissioned but unapproved pieces).

But ultimately, our recommendations are fairly contained with existing dominant discourses about the city – we don't really challenge the untouchable authority of private property ownership (in fact, we've tried to tactically exploit that authority to our advantage!). Nor do our recommendations challenge the authority of a rather narrow and economically driven kind of 'creativity' that has come to dominate so much discussion about the future of cities such as Sydney, influenced by the likes of Richard Florida and Charles Landry (Peck 2005). Indeed, with the official embrace of 'legal' avenues associated with creative city and place-branding strategies, we've seen the escalation of an unhelpful consolidation of the 'street art versus graffiti' discourse, as some self-declared 'street artists' offer themselves up as the best way to beat graffiti (Schacter 2014)![1] But again, we do believe that creative city discourses open up tactical opportunities for less authoritarian and punitive forms of policing.

The limits of this kind of advocacy are not surprising – it's hard to imagine the city being democratized through the implementation of an 'expert' consultant report!

This work is more about changing the way in which authority is *exercised* rather than challenging the way that authority is *constituted*. Don't get me wrong, there are better and worse forms of policing. But as Rancière (1999: 31) points out, while the differences between different forms of policing matter a great deal, in the end, '[whether] the police is sweet and kind does not make it any less the opposite of politics'. So what are some other options that exist alongside such policy advocacy? I've picked the following three emergent approaches because they seem to me to go slightly 'against the grain' of common graffiti and street art practice up to now, thereby challenging some things that we might take for granted about their politics.

Permission

Securing permission to get up on a wall might seem like the last thing we would associate with a democratic graffiti and street art practice. After all, doesn't 'permission' cede the right to write and paint to the usual 'authorities' – property owners and/or the state?

Well, not necessarily. While I'm conscious of the risks involved in making this suggestion, I think that there may indeed be a place for permission-seeking in a democratic graffiti and street art practice, if we can think through forms of permission-seeking that challenge rather than reinforce undemocratic forms of urban authority.

In some of his recent work, Stephen 'Espo' Powers might offer us a model for a democratization of permission. In his book *A Love Letter to the City* (2014), Powers documents a series of projects he has undertaken in cities across the US and beyond. These projects are of a different nature than his previous work as a more 'traditional' graffiti writer (Powers 1999). In several of those projects, he sought a kind of permission before painting, and even a kind of direction/approval for the work he did. But this permission and direction was not (only) sought from the usual 'authorities' – the property owners, or the urban planning authorities. Rather, it was sought from residents and passers-by in the localities in which he painted – that is, from the 'local authorities' whose authority was not founded in property ownership or law but on *inhabitance* (Purcell 2002). Here's how Powers sums up the outcome of working with communities in identifying both the space and the content to paint, and the inspiration he took from Brazilian twins Os Gemeos:

> This is graffiti! And it could be beating a community over the head. But it's doing the opposite: it's empowering a community, using names, color, design, and spray paint. Graffiti is putting a name on something that doesn't belong to you. But when you put up the names of the community on something, then it belongs to everybody. Os Gemeos do it every time they paint a figure on a wall; it stands for all and it claims the wall for all.
>
> (2014: 98)

This is a brilliant articulation of one way to use graffiti in pursuit of equality via a kind of 'permission' that actually extends ownership beyond the private property model to the inhabitants of a neighbourhood and a city, rather than reinforcing that private property model.

In some ways, we could say that Power's approach echoes that taken by muralist Judith Baca in her work in Los Angeles in the 1970s. As detailed by Stefano Bloch, in undertaking a large mural in the Silverlake neighbourhood in 1975, Baca took the idea of permission beyond permission of the state and property owners, and sought the permission of other 'local authorities'. As she put it:

> I wanted to make sure the actual people in these neighbourhoods accepted what I was trying to do. I needed the residents' respect, including the gang members', and I got it by showing them that they had mine. I wasn't trying to control this space or be elitist, I was trying to express a collective feeling about prevailing social issues facing the community.
>
> (quoted in Bloch 2012: 112–113)

So, while I would never advocate that graffiti writers and street artists only work with permission, I do think Powers' and Baca's approaches to permission provide us with another way to challenge undemocratic forms of urban authority founded in private property ownership and criminal law. Their approach might also be food for thought for other high-profile street artists and graffiti writers who are increasingly invited to do 'fly in, fly out' jobs in decayed urban neighbourhoods. While abandoned buildings and infrastructure can indeed make great canvases for their work, such work might be experienced by inhabitants as an external imposition that undermines their sense of belonging. Worse, such work may even contribute to the displacement of poor residents through hipsterfication and gentrification, as discussed by Lutz Henke (2015) in his piece about the artist-led buffing of iconic work by himself, Blu and JR in Berlin's Kreuzberg neighbourhood.

Participation

If we take the idea of equality seriously, does this mean that everyone's equally capable of doing good graffiti, and that we should thereby find ways to make it possible for everyone to do it? Here's Banksy (2000) on the nature of the 'graffiti problem':

> People say there is a graffiti problem. The only problem is that there isn't enough of it. Imagine a city where graffiti wasn't illegal, a city where everybody could draw wherever they liked. Where every street was awash with a million colors and little phrases. Where standing at a bus stop was never boring. A city that felt like a living breathing thing which belonged to everybody, not just the estate agents and barons of big business. Imagine a city like this and stop leaning against that wall—it's wet.

There's lots to like about this. Of course, the idea that 'everyone' can and should write graffiti or engage in street art might also seem like a recipe for the proliferation of lots of crappy work. After all, these are practices that require some skills . . . and not everyone has them! (Indeed, one of the things that annoys me most when I get into arguments about graffiti is the detractor's view that there's no skill involved!) But Banksy's formulation here evokes a city where enough space is unlocked to let countless flowers bloom.

At the very least, to take equality seriously is to embrace the notion that *anyone* could write on walls, and that the criteria for what counts as good work are never fully settled but open for debate. Such ideas would certainly be a stretch for some participants in graffiti and street art scenes – such as those who think graffiti's not for girls/women, or that stencils and characters and messages are not 'proper' graffiti, or that there's no such thing as a good tag, etc.

But we could go further, by finding ways to expand participation in the use of urban surfaces for public address (on the broader importance of the city as a site of public address, see Iveson 2007, 2012). Countless writers and artists all over the world participate in workshops with kids and adults alike with exactly this intention; indeed, one of my first jobs was working on such a project at Marrickville Youth Centre in inner-urban Sydney. And there are other ways to encourage participation. Consider the work of the Institute of Applied Autonomy and their *Graffiti Writer*.[2] The Writer was a remote-controlled car rigged with spray paint cans configured to operate like a dot-matrix printer. The IAA took their Writer to various public places, and gave people the chance to use it to write messages on the street. Here's what happened:

> We'd pull up to a park or other public space, and drive the robot around until it gathered a small crowd of interested bystanders. We'd explain exactly what the robot does, and ask for volunteers to use our machine to write a tag.
>
> Now, imagine trying the same thing with just a case of spray paint – no one would do it! With the robot, though, we always got a bunch of people really eager to participate. The volunteer would decide what the robot should write, and then operate the robot by pressing a large red button. We took photos of people using the controls, which then became our 'rogues gallery' – a collection of images of people in the act of breaking the law. We got all sorts of people to use the robot, including businessmen, homeless people, municipal workers, and once, a whole troop of girl scouts. We even got a police officer to deface public property with our machine. For the most part, people either wrote their names, or simple inspirational messages like 'The World is Yours!' All told, we did this 30 or 40 times in 5 different countries, without anyone ever getting arrested.
>
> (quoted in Iveson 2003: 77)

Through these sorts of initiatives, the authority of anyone and everyone to use the city as a space of public address is advanced well beyond the 'usual suspects' we associate with uncommissioned writing and art on the street.

Publicity

Maintaining a form of 'anonymous fame' is central to graffiti and street art practice for many, given the risks of being identified where the practice has been criminalized and is liable to violent policing and significant punishments if convicted (Iveson 2007). While anonymity has its advantages as an enabler for public participation (Warner 1990), it can also make it hard to engage the wider urban public sphere in the politics of surfaces and address.

Some artists are embracing a more aggressively 'public' approach to their graffiti and street art – by doing their work during the day, and publicly defending their illegal work in the wider public sphere. Rather than 'hiding in the light' (Hebdige 1988), they refuse to hide, performatively insisting that there's nothing wrong with what they are doing, and they have every right to do it. Espo has now resolved to write graffiti in broad daylight – while he still often conducts his work without permission, his refusal to hide is his way of declaring that he is doing nothing wrong (Powers and Vanetti 2010). I've written elsewhere (Iveson 2013) about Jordan Seiler, a New York artist who replaces outdoor advertising with his own artworks – Seiler takes a similar approach, installing his works during the day and blogging about them in his own name, as well as instigating a number of wider campaigns to reclaim outdoor media for public communication.[3]

However, I should note that this strategy is certainly not equally available to all. Consider the harsh treatment meted out to Kyle Magee in Melbourne (discussed in Young 2014). Pushing a critique of corporate advertising in outdoor spaces to its limit, he engaged in a campaign of covering up advertisements – not replacing them with art, just covering them. He has received jail time for his trouble – as have many others around the world who have been prosecuted for graffiti offences. Again, then, my point here is not to uncritically advocate that everyone 'goes public' in the ways that Powers and Seiler have. Rather, I am suggesting that their approach gestures towards another avenue for experimentation with new forms of urban authority via different kinds of publicity.

Conclusion

In this short piece, I've asked: what kind of graffiti and street art practice and advocacy might challenge the undemocratic forms of authority that dominate our cities? It's an easy question for an academic to pose, a much more difficult question for us all to answer, especially if we intend to act upon those answers. My hope is that the thoughts above are received in the spirit in which they're offered – not as a critique of people engaged in graffiti writing and street art practice, but in a spirit of excitement about some of the directions in which some people seem to be taking this work.

If we think about graffiti writers and street artists as people who are enacting their own forms of authority, rather than simply 'contesting' authority, this opens up interesting horizons for reading the politics of graffiti and street art in the city. It forces us to confront not only the problems with the authority of 'the authorities', but the limits and emancipatory potentials of the alternative or 'local' authorities that are enacted through work on the streets. Rather than arguing against 'the authorities' per se, we are invited both to critique the *naturalization* of existing forms of undemocratic authority, *and* to think through the kinds of authority we might want to enact in their place. At a time when more and more graffiti writers and street artists (and academics!) are being invited 'into the circle' by urban authorities keen to capitalize on the benefits of their work for 'place-making', it seems more important than ever that we have a framework for thinking about the kinds of places we want to make. If we want to make more democratic cities, we have to subject all urban authorities – including our own – to the test of equality.

Notes

1   This situation is parodied by LUSH in these two fantastic pieces: http://lushsux.tumblr.com/post/112119632201/get-outta-jail-free-card; http://lushsux.tumblr.com/post/111130182756/carry-on. Accessed: 20 February 2016.
2   See www.appliedautonomy.com/gw.html. Accessed: 20 February 2016.
3   See www.publicadcampaign.com. Accessed: 20 February 2016.

References

Amin, Ash and Thrift, Nigel. 2002. *Cities: Reimagining the Urban*. Oxford: Polity Press.

Banksy. 2000. *Existencilism*. London: Weapons of Mass Destruction.

Bloch, Stefano. 2012. 'The Illegal Face of Wall Space: Graffiti-Murals on the Sunset Boulevard Retaining Walls'. *Radical History Review*. (113): 111–126.

Davidson, Mark, and Iveson, Kurt. 2015. 'Recovering the Politics of the City: From the "Post-political City" to a "Method of Equality" for Critical Urban Geography'. *Progress in Human Geography*. 39(5): 543–559.

de Certeau, Michel. 1984. *The Practice of Everyday Life*. Berkeley, CA: University of California Press.

Dikeç, Mustafa. 2002. 'Police, Politics, and the Right to the City'. *GeoJournal*. 58 (2–3): 91–98.

Hebdige, Dick. 1988. *Hiding in the Light: On Images and Things*. London: Routledge.

Henke, Lutz. 2015. 'Kill your Darlings: The Auto-iconoclasm of Blu's Iconic Murals in Berlin'. *Ephemera: Theory & Politics in Organization*. 15(1): 291–295.

Iveson, Kurt. 2003. 'Automatic for the People: The Institute of Applied Autonomy'. *Graphotism*. (31): 74–77.

Iveson, Kurt. 2007. *Publics and the City*. Oxford: Blackwell.

Iveson, Kurt. 2009. 'War if Over (If you Want it): A New Approach to the Graffiti Problem'. *Australian Planner*. 46(4): 22–31.

Iveson, Kurt. 2012. 'Branded Cities: Outdoor Advertising, Urban Governance, and the Outdoor Media Landscape'. *Antipode: A Radical Journal of Geography*. 44(1): 151–174.

Iveson, Kurt. 2013. 'Cities within the City: Do-It-Yourself Urbanism and the Right to the City'. *International Journal of Urban and Regional Research*. 37(3): 941–956.

Iveson, Kurt. 2014. 'Policing the City'. In Davidson, Mark and Martin, Deborah (eds), *Urban Politics: Critical Approaches*. London: Sage, pp. 85–99.

Iveson, Kurt, McAuliffe, Cameron, Murray, Wendy and Peet, Matthew. 2015. *Reframing Graffiti and Street Art in the City of Sydney, Report of the Mural, Street Art and Graffiti Review Project*. Sydney: University of Sydney.

Lefebvre, Henri. 1996. 'The Right to the City'. In *Writings on Cities*. Kofman, Eleonore and Lebas, Elizabeth (eds; trans.). Oxford: Blackwell, pp. 61–183.

McAuliffe, Cameron. 2012. 'Graffiti or Street Art? Negotiating the Moral Geographies of the Creative City'. *Journal of Urban Affairs*. 34(2): 189–206.

Peck, Jamie. 2005. 'Struggling with the Creative Class'. *International Journal of Urban and Regional Research*. 29(4): 740–770.

Powers, Stephen. 1999. *The Art of Getting Over: Graffiti at the Millennium*. New York, NY: St Martin's Press.

Powers, Stephen. 2014. *A Love Letter to the City*. New York, NY: Princeton Architectural Press.

Powers, Stephen and Vanetti, Serena. 2010. 'Steve ESPO Powers: Writers Writing about Writing'. *Very Nearly Almost*. (13): 20–27.

Purcell, Mark. 2002. 'Excavating Lefebvre: The Right to the City and its Urban Politics of the Inhabitant'. *GeoJournal*. 58(2): 99–108.

Rancière, Jacques. 1999. *Disagreement: Politics and Philosophy*. Rose, Julie (trans.). Minneapolis, MA: University of Minnesota Press.

Rancière, Jacques. 2001. 'Ten Theses on Politics'. *Theory and Event*. 5(3).

Rancière, Jacques. 2003. 'Politics and Aesthetics: An Interview'. *Angelaki: Journal of the Theoretical Humanities*. 8(2): 191–211.

Schacter, Rafael. 2014. 'The Ugly Truth: Street Art, Graffiti and the Creative City'. *Art and the Public Sphere*. 3(2): 161–176.

Swyngeodouw, Eric. 2009. 'The Antimonies of the Postpolitical City: In Search of a Democratic Politics of Environmental Production'. *International Journal of Urban and Regional Research*. 33(3): 601–620.

Tonkiss, Fran. 2012. 'The One-dimensional City'. *City*. 16(1–2): 216–219.

Warner, Michael. 1990. *The Letters of the Republic: Publication and the Public Sphere in Eighteenth-century America*. Cambridge, MA: Harvard University Press.

Young, Alison. 2010. 'Negotiated Consent or Zero Tolerance? Responding to Graffiti and Street Art in Melbourne'. *City*. 14(1–2): 99–114.

Young, Alison. 2014. 'From Object to Encounter: Aesthetic Politics and Visual Criminology'. *Theoretical Criminology*. 18(2): 159–175.

Young, Iris Marion. 1990. *Justice and the Politics of Difference*. Princeton, NJ: Princeton University Press.

Part II
Writing graffiti, street art and the city

6 Street art is a period, PERIOD[1]

Or, classificatory confusion and intermural art

Rafael Schacter

The taxonomical imperative

Categorizing and classifying, organizing and ordering are some of the most classic of human traits. As most famously shown by the anthropologist Claude Lévi-Strauss (1962), our minds are constantly bent on cleaving the wood from the trees, finding ostensible order from within chaos, 'classify[ing] out the universe' (ibid.: 63) so as to create social and conceptual coherence in our lives.

Within the mass of material culture we today define as Art (something that is itself classified in distinction from 'mere' craft), it is through the concept of the 'period' that this taxonomical imperative can be seen to emerge. Commonly described as the 'isms' – your mannerisms, minimalisms, modernisms, maximalisms and the like – these terms codify the various movements and styles housed within the larger structure of Art itself, the distinct forms, distinct techniques, distinct visual qualities that mark out this particular type from that, that temporally and theoretically bind them as distinct, ordered practices.

Yet much like the concept of genre in literature or film, the period, like all culturally formed categories, defines more than just material characteristics. As Andrew Tudor explores specifically in relation to cinema (1974), these sub-categories come to define the wider 'moral and social world' in which these classes of objects are set (ibid.: 180), the wider values and principles that the units located within this label manifest. Moreover, these sub-structures provide the overarching frame from within which a work, a text, a film (or a species) can itself then be understood, a 'frame of reference', as Daniel Chandler explains in his wider study of Genre Theory (1997), 'which helps readers [or viewers or participants] to identify, select and interpret' them (ibid.: 7). Periodism thus plays a pivotal role in determining a work's communicable ability, defining its moral substance, providing its frame of reference, enabling its material cognizance: it impacts *how* the work is received, where it is understood to be situated in ethical and relational terms, as well as our very ability to receive it in itself, helping us to read its content rather than just its form. It not only defines from where and when the work emerges, but controls where it can then go, enabling and constraining its interpretation within the same moment.

When ambiguity or ambivalence enters the system however, when new objects or ideas defy demarcation (when one cannot, for example, distinguish between fish or fowl), our ability to not only materially but also *morally* comprehend the forms at hand becomes entirely disabled. As such, these equivocal objects present a profound danger for the broader category as a whole. They are thus classically, and as famously shown by Mary Douglas (2013 [1966]), designated as pollution, as dirt, banished in order to keep the wider social and conceptual structure intact, acting as the disarray that makes clear the array. Categories can thus be seen to be always active, always in motion, constantly subject to stresses and strains from the outside. Yet when the category *itself* starts to become contradictory, when outside pressures have modified it to the extent that it has become something entirely other itself, pollution can escape from the exterior and come to burrow itself within. Here exclusion can then be a sign of virtue, *in*clusion of inequity. Here ambiguity or ambivalence become not the exception but the rule. When Douglas's famous 'matter out of place' (ibid.: 36) thus comes paradoxically to be regarded as *in* place, only one option remains: a taxonomical restructuring, a conceptual and linguistic schism must, and almost always does, occur.

The inevitable rupture

Set within the 'Writing Graffiti, Street Art and the City' section of this volume (a subcategory that we could likewise say creates a framework for our understanding as *readers*), the task I have been set is to contextualize Graffiti and Street Art,[2] to reveal where it resides today. My task is to engage with the problems of writing about these forms, to explore the language used regarding it, to unpack the intentions of interventions that attempt to make sense of urban spaces. Yet as an aesthetic practice that I see, quite crucially, as a cohesive artistic *period* – one with distinct members, a distinct time frame, distinct styles, locations, techniques and ideologies – Street Art can today, in my belief, be seen to be positioned quite exactly within the classificatory disorder that I have outlined above. It is in a categorically ambiguous position. A state in which what is now incorporated within this designation is radically other to that was originally understood; a state in which what is incorporated either fails to fulfil the formal and moral values that the category initially implied, or has now in fact come to exceed the structural boundaries that the term itself sets up.

As such, what I will be contextualizing here is a term, the artistic period Street Art, that has today come to have been almost totally recast by the media and the market, hegemonic demarcations overpowering meanings forged from below.[3] What I will be exploring is a term not only now commonly used to denote work produced and exhibited *inside* – something that is, as what I define as a classical ornament, a basic category error and entirely (oxy)moronic[4] – but as used to describe work *outside* now denotes what is, in my belief, a superficial simulation of a previously political, conscientiously site-specific practice, an aesthetic that has today become one of pure façade. What is crucial to say, however, is that the perceived 'quality' of the works is thus not under discussion here: I am not attempting to progress a 'good art vs. bad art' form of argumentation here, nor trying to promote a hackneyed 'things used to be so much better' shtick. It is simply a terminological malfunction that I am investigating. 'Street Art', as it is now commonly understood paralyses a perspicacious reading of the contemporary artefacts set within its margins. It defines a now inapposite ethic; it provides a misleading frame of reference. It disables rather than enables a proper identification. It pollutes. And what I will hence be recounting in this essay is a scopic regime that has today been entirely turned on its head, that has become other to its nomenclature. What I will be unpacking are the new tactics of Street Art that come to make *non*-sense of space. What I will be engaging with is the impossibility of writing (or curating) Street Art with the terminological armature that we currently have.

This now inevitable rupture has been a long time coming. Since the earliest days of the term Street Art both artists and critics have been claiming its demise. Yet today the issue feels insurmountable, overwhelmingly oppressive, over. And the need,[5] not merely the desire, but the *need* for a terminological transformation, has now become, in my mind, imperative.[6]

The when, the who, the what

Perhaps we should first work backwards in order to then move forwards. If I am to claim that a new category must be coined, we must first explore what the artistic period in question really was. So what *was* Street Art? Or to start from another angle, *when* was it? My first contention is that as a defined artistic period, Street Art was operative and, crucially, innovational, between the years of 1998 and 2008. This date of inception has here been determined not through it being the year in which Street Art practices as such were first seen,[7] but, rather, due to the critical mass of practices occurring at this time. 1998 was thus the year in which I would argue that a core group of artists – approximately 100–200 artists worldwide – began to explore new ways of working both site-specifically and independently in public space. It was the year in which this group – the majority of which had come from a background in Graffiti[8] – began to explore more outwardly communicative strategies of production then antithetical to the insulated desires of this aesthetic precursor.[9] The year in which this mass – many of whom had received an art school, if not graphic design education[10] – began to merge the new visual and applied techniques learned within these sites (such as stencilling, stickering, postering, and a whole host of other techniques notable for their general movement away from the ubiquity of the spray-can) with the DIY spirit, the tools and the trades, the core ethics of Graffiti culture.

The latter date of 2008, however, is what I argue to be the year of Street Art's creative culmination. This is the point both at which all that *could* be produced within Street Art has been produced, the point at which artists began to move away from its confines and into other artistic arenas. After 2008 things may have got bigger but they did not necessarily get better. The practice may have become more renowned but it was not necessarily more innovational or pioneering.

Tate Modern's *Street Art* exhibition[11] of 2008 stands as a key boundary marker here. The massive global prominence of this event, both in terms of media attention and institutional validation, began to steer the perception of Street Art in a particular and quite singular direction. 'Street Art' became known as big, colourful, exterior paintings, as an 'edgy' muralism. Moreover, it became something that most commonly (or most visibly) occurred via the framework of *Street Art Festivals* rather than through independent action, something placing it directly on the road toward recuperation: co-opted by the Creative City discourse (as I discuss in Schacter 2014b), by the 'regenerative' urban development methodologies of Richard Florida *et al.* (a discourse harshly critiqued by scholars such as O'Connor (2010), Peck (2005) and Pratt (2011), yet one that despite this grows ever more powerful) Street Art soon came not simply to sell itself, but, more perniciously, to sell a false notion of place. It came to act as branding tool for the Creative City, parasitically utilized to amplify and magnify the process of profit, parasitically utilized to control and contain.

So that was the *when* and the *who*, now what about the *what*? What was Street Art? What defined it? What were the elements that made it a coherent artistic category? I would point to five key formal elements, five key techniques and approaches that define Street Art as a period: Spatial Assimilation, Figuration/ Iconicity, Non-Instrumentality, Institutional Autonomy and Communicative Consensuality.

The first element, *Spatial Assimilation*, marked a clear breach with Graffiti. While a deep entanglement and interaction with urban space was (and is) of course pivotal within this progenitorial practice, Graffiti artists can be understood to act antagonistically toward the surrounding architecture, to resist it, to confront it, to work at cross purpose to its normative use. Seeking to go against the flow of their prevailing medium, going over borders, across surfaces, refusing to work within its set markings, these artists thus inscribe their dissension to their physical surroundings through a refusal to conform to its architectural frame. Within Street Art however, it was the ability to play *with* rather than compete *against* the surrounding environment that was desired. It was about dialogue rather than disruption, negotiation not opposition. In this way, Street Art can be understood to have followed an idea of site specificity that was 'integrationist' and 'assimilative' rather than 'interruptive' and 'interventionist' – as Miwon Kwon (2004: 72–73) explores in terms of the history of Public Art in the 1970s and 1980s – a paradigm of site specificity believed by the artists themselves to have been 'more accessible and socially responsible' than their predecessor (ibid.: 66). Whether utilizing already existent architectural elements to complete one's work or détourning, playing with their spaces in a way to enhance rather than *oppose* them, Street Artists could be seen to have followed a more contextually 'considerate' approach in their work. They craved a clear relation with their spaces, a self-consciously produced dialogue with their environs. They yearned to create utility: to enhance, ameliorate, reform the public realm.

The second element, *Figuration/Iconicity*, likewise moved away from one of Graffiti's central tenants, typography, heading instead toward a visuality based on iconography.[12] As the 1990s progressed then, many Graffiti artists began to feel increasingly restricted by the letter form, as well as by the more dogmatic style of Graffiti that was at that time dominant. The move toward the non-textual, toward the logos, characters, ideograms and other markings that came to be produced, was thus believed to have been a pathway to more creative freedom, as well, crucially, toward a wider potential audience. While acting in a very similar way to the tags of Graffiti artists – like all logotypes being repetitive yet always singular, gaining quality through quantity, quantity in fact in some way *being* quality – the iconic turn moved past the constraints that Graffiti typography was then understood to have bestowed both in terms of innovation and reception (rather than virtuosity per se). The non-textual images produced thus not only opened up new avenues of production for the artists but were also (and perhaps more importantly) stripped of the menace that Graffiti typography has been imbued with by the media and anti-Graffiti authorities since the early 1980s. These newer works were more 'legible'. Less loaded. And they thus radically transformed the viewership of Street Art from that of an exclusive to a more inclusive public.

At the same time, however, these newly designed images were still conscientiously *Non-Instrumental*, our third element. Like Graffiti, what was key was their works' ability to sell nothing but themselves. Yet the newly formed figuration of Street Art meant they were able to do this while simultaneously hijacking the intoxicating power of corporate trademarks. Transforming the uncompromising, domineering visuality of both the State and the Market ('do this'/'buy that') into something that was literally unprofitable, Street Artists were able to take the Graffiti conception of inalienability, of production for productions sake, and yet transform it to the viewership of a wider public. The illustrative turn thus radically transformed the reach of Street Art but kept hold of the implicitly aneconomic position of Graffiti. It remained beholden to Graffiti's intrinsic purity, its total refusal to be subject to the market, yet now contained a bifold power: The power (yet not the perceived danger or dishonour) of both a Corporate and Graffiti aesthetic.

The fourth element, *Institutional Autonomy*, again surfaces through Street Art's familial relationship to Graffiti, through the always already *independent* inclinations of that practice. For Street Art then, perceived need came before authorization, perceived necessity before permission. To truly commit to the city, to commit and to place one's commitment beyond doubt, Institutional Autonomy was a basic procedural necessity. This position, one could argue however, had more to do with fidelity than legality per se: Street Art did not *need* to be illegal (unlike Graffiti one could argue). It was not about breaking laws, more about enacting them. Thou shall not stand by and watch. Thou shall communicate with the city as a whole. Thou shall engage with one's environment. What was essential was this sovereign spirit in which action was a moral obligation not a strategic act. What was crucial was this methodology in which the city was not a means to an end but an end in itself. In which the city was not a mere route to a gallery career but rather a space for communication, experience, experimentation. Institutional Autonomy was a refusal to follow the rule of the judging committee, a refusal to abide by Health and Safety. It was about spontaneity not uniformity. It was about a commitment to the city that surpassed prevailing laws, a non-instrumental conviction that Institutional Autonomy alone could permit.

The final of the five prerequisites, *Communicative Consensuality*, is, once again, set in relation to Graffiti, and is at its very basis about communication outside of one's fraternity of co-participants. Unlike the inward looking nature of Graffiti, Communicative Consensuality in Street Art was about a desire for an intersubjective relation with the wider public sphere as a whole. Consensual here thus meant appropriate, acceptable, agreeable. It meant outward facing, rational and open. It meant the simple offer of a proposition rather than the mendacious persuasion so prevalent within the commercial advertisements that dominate the public realm. Street Artists would thus produce work that was meant to be seen, to be understood, to be read, to be shared. They believed their work was more appropriate, more social, more salient than the vast majority of visual culture that lay within the street. They believed they had something important to say for everyone in the public realm. And Communicative Consensuality ensured that works could be transmitted to the public at large rather than a predefined subdivision (to those who had received an education in the arts, whether the high of the contemporary arts or the low of the low-brow). It provoked a relationship between viewer and image, a communion, a consensus, a commonality, that could not be denied. It provoked a conversation, they believed, with the public sphere as a whole.[13]

Alongside the *who*, *what* and *when* previously demarcated above then, these five distinguishing elements thus came together to create a clear periodicity for Street Art, a classificatory clarity in terms of its members, its time span, its styles, its locations, its methodologies, its beliefs. They came together not only to determine Street Art's material qualities but so too its moral ones: they created a framework in which Street Art could be understood to contain an assimilative, open, inclusive, non-instrumental, independent, consensual ethic. In which it could be read as a practice attempting to confront the dominant, corporate visuality of the public sphere. A practice that was seeking a new communicative platform, a new stage from which to create a balanced, affirmative relationship in the public sphere.

The utmost parody

So that was the *then* (an emblematic, best model of practice at the least). Now what about the *now*? In my belief, much of what is commonly termed Street Art today (by art critics, journalists, gallerists, artists, etc.) fails to uphold to the material, spatial, technical, ethical and conceptual elements of the form as related above. Much of it fails to assimilate within its site (rather coming to dominate it); much of it fails to follow its non-instrumental urge (rather acting strategically); much of it fails to contain its independent values (yet problematically acting as if autonomous); much of it fails to act consensually (and rather embraces the kitsch, seeking sentimentality or 'cool' rather than rationality or communion). And, yet at the same time, some of it, that at the very avant-garde of the practice, has equally today come to burst out of its borders, to have taken the conceptual and ethical values that it first contained and transform these into a practice that can no longer reside within the original term. So if no longer Street Art, what is it? What could we call the practices now working under its banner?

Much of what is today called Street Art should, I believe, be termed neo-Muralism (or Street Muralism perhaps – vaguely tautological but nonetheless providing an idiomatic link to Street Art). Emergent from Street Art, and utilizing many of its visual codes, neo-Muralism is Street Art turned professional, Street Art on steroids. Entranced by the belief that bigger is always better – works increasing so much in size that they have now eclipsed the capabilities of the human eye alone – what is internally called 'going big' has today come to act as such a dominant framing within Street Art that works done without this Maximalist, 'more is more' attitude have begun to almost disappear from the concept of the term itself. The point, as mentioned above, however, is not whether this monumentality produces works of good or of bad quality: what is key, rather, is that it has meant that this form of 'Street Art' is no longer (or very rarely) truly Spatially Assimilative. Acting like the purely ornamental plop art of the 1970s and 1980s explored by Kwon (2004), the 'autonomous signature-style art works sited in public places', the plop art that not only ignores the specificity of its space but that so too makes no 'genuine gestures toward public engagement' (ibid.: 65), these large-scale works more often erase rather than accentuate the particularities of place. They dominate their sites. They bypass the need to integrate. They use the wall as a blank canvas rather than as an already existent space. And they thus become the very essence of the spectacular (in both a traditional and Debordian sense).[14]

What's more, the monumentality, the visual *excess* of neo-Muralism has so too meant that this form of Street Art is no longer (or very rarely) Institutionally Autonomous. Street Art of this size and scope can very rarely *be* independent (once a cherry-picker or scaffold is involved it normally isn't).[15] And once institutions are involved, autonomy is often (not always, but often) sacrificed. As I discuss elsewhere (Schacter 2014b), it is through the technological apparatus (and institutional framework) of the *Street Art Festival* that this style of neo-Muralism most commonly emerges.[16] And the *Street Art Festival* as it now exists relies, first and foremost, on size. Size is not only 'impressive' but sellable. Size is instrumentally (rather than necessarily aesthetically) efficacious. And, in the vast majority of cases, this is what the *Street Art Festival* is for (and thus the reason for the large murals that are attached to it). It is not about engagement, let alone art. It is about two fundamental requirements; to market place and to accrue profit. As such, the art that emerges from many of these festivals can be seen to directly align with the policies of the Creative City, a practice in which the movements and developments of art are subordinated to the desires and objectives of urban planning policy – in which private sector development rather than *aesthetic* development is at the forefront. Street Art's reliance on the Festival framework has thus radically transformed its basic makeup, transformed the disruptive platform from which it used to speak into an entirely deferential one. It now feigns autonomy while being entirely recuperated, while being liable to all the bureaucratic delimitations and curatorial constraints of traditional Public Art. And once artworks are chosen by committee, sketches subject to approval, what has been termed Independent Public Art becomes nothing of the sort. It becomes Institutional Public Art. Not necessarily a good or bad thing. But, for sure, no longer Street Art.

Aside from this neo-Muralist pursuit, this Creative City Art, Street Art has also taken another clear turn, a turn toward the Kitsch (what I term, to be very harsh, a poor-man's Pop Art). Mickey Mouse snorting cocaine or seductive, half-naked women. Colourful caricatures and saccharine sentiments. It is as if the utmost parody of what Street Art once was has mistakenly become the norm, a lampoon-ery in the manner of the now absurdly successful Mr Brainwash (such a perverse, yet perfectly horrific caricature that I am still convinced his whole being is a hoax, that a guiding hand must be involved). It is the basest combination of 'edgy', 'cool' imagery. An aesthetic of transgression that is in fact utterly conformist, perfectly numb to the social realities it occludes. Appearing political while being perfectly non-partisan. An aesthetic of sentimentality, banality, one attacking our weakest emotions rather than initiating a rational discourse. Simulating the new, the visionary and unconventional, while aligning perfectly with the norms, the visions and conventions of the neoliberal city. A style that disables thought and critique, that disables either aesthetic or conceptual progression. A style that enables the existent, that enables the profusion of the 'cool' creative hubs, the 'modernistic' property development, the 'trailblazing' tourist economy that the Creative City desires.

Intermural Art

While the above section may all seem pretty harsh (and it is the extreme that I am here discussing – a hugely present extreme nonetheless), the situation for those working in Street Art today is a confusing, dispiriting, frustrating one. When much of what is termed Street Art fails to comply to the primary premises of the form, to its autonomy, its non-instrumentality, let alone its *morality*, those who are caught within its terminology can quickly become enemies to themselves. From the earliest days of Street Art, many artists drawn within the genre foresaw this impending problematic and thus tried to disassociate themselves from the form, either retreating back into the term Graffiti (even if their work was no longer typographical, no longer illegal), or withdrawing into the field of a more classical Public Art (while being indelibly influenced by their previous practices). Others simply kept on producing work in the street while attempting to ignore the terminological dispute. Kept on working and waiting, even if cognizant of the difficulties the period within which they were set came to present.

Today, however, this classificatory crisis has simply become too much to bear. I have spoken with too many artists, too many adherents and critics within the realm of Street Art who feel trapped, entirely ensnared within this period. I have spoken with too many people who realize the way it confuses and confounds, the way the works that come under its banner both exceed and disappoint its initial ideals. And this, for me, is the key point. It is not merely that what exists fails to live up to the original principles of Street Art (I am not here merely to bash what is 'bad'). It is that the artists at the avant-garde of the field are pushing at the very limits of the category as it previously existed, engaging and inhabiting the outside limits of the Street Art terrain. They are continuing to develop a practice that may have transformed itself visually, yet that retains core conceptual, methodological and ethical links to both Street Art and Graffiti. They are continuing to develop a practice that now moves between the outside and the in, yet does so in highly conscious, highly circumspect ways. A practice occupying the vital space between the street and the studio, between the independent and the intuitional; a practice occupying the spaces *in between* in disruptive, innovative, boundary shifting ways.

The term that I am thus proposing for this practice – proposing, as described above, out of need more than desire – is Intermural Art. In literal terms, Intermural Art means 'art in between the walls'. Not art inside the walls (*intra*mural), nor outside them (*extra*mural), but art *between* these same walls. As such, what is key to Intermural Art is the relationship *between* inside and outside. The way in which the inside can effect the out and the outside the in. The way the inside can critique the out and, in the same manner, the out the in.

As a practice, Intermural Art has emerged directly from both Graffiti and Street Art. Yet it is an art form that – due in main to its time frame (emerging as a wider discourse post-2008), its location (it takes as a medium both the street and the white cube) as well as its material qualities (its diverse *style*) – can no longer productively reside within these previous terminologies. Likewise it is a practice often labelled 'Contemporary Art', and while of course influenced by the myriad of practices that come under that term, is similarly obscured by its breadth (it meaning so much that it denotes almost naught). While now commonly an institutional art practice then – in that it often (but not always) occurs within galleries, within museums, and *with* authorization – Intermural Art is not merely a movement transplanting Graffiti or Street Art into this permissible realm. Rather, it is a practice utilizing these previous visual styles in three key ways:

1   as a *conceptual palette* – using Graffiti and Street Art as an aesthetic and a culture that can in itself be artistically investigated, dissected and explored;
2   as a *methodological tool* – using the procedural techniques and methods of Graffiti and Street Art yet subverting their traditional regulations and codes;
3   and as an *ethical imperative* – using the independent ethic (rather than aesthetic) of Graffiti and Street Art, using it as a way of *being* rather than a visual regime.

Of course, Graffiti and Street Art have both appeared in galleries and museums before, since their very genesis in fact. But artists are now taking the Graffiti and Street Art model – as a *concept*, as a *method*, as an *ethic* – and translating it into a new style of art. They have merged it with other movements (from Arte Povera to Pop Art, from Social Practice to New Media Art) and created something unique.

A style radically divergent from Street Art and Graffiti (yet always and already emergent from them), a style shrouded by the term Contemporary Art (yet equivalently influenced by its workings). Intermural Art is thus an art venturing beyond these previous designations, venturing beyond and between the gaps in these practices. It is an art exploring the space between the street and the studio, between Graffiti and the gallery. It is an art exploring the vibrancy of the threshold, the space in between the walls.

Inside out, upside down

While there are numerous artists[17] who could be used to exemplify this artistic period (as I would likewise claim it to be), the Berlin based, American born artist Brad Downey stands for me as one of the central figures emerging from this Intermural Art milieu. His recent work *Inside Out, Upside Down* (2014) acts as an exceptionally apposite exemplar, an archetype for Intermural Art that I shall thus briefly explore here.[18] Installing the work within the entirety of the gallery space *nun* in Berlin's Neukölln, *Inside Out, Upside Down* was produced using a singular artistic material: everyday, commonplace wall plugs (of a variety of colours and sizes). With these most mundane of objects, Downey created a series of unique, site-specific patterns and designs over the entirety of the gallery space; a triangular configuration at the intersection of walls and ceiling in the very corner of the room; a singular strip bisecting the right hand wall and half the ceiling space; a crawling line above the heating pipes navigating across three walls; an abstract accumulation migrating over four edges into the window (Figure 6.1a). Added to this, and courtesy of a close collaborator of Downey's (the French born, but also Berlin based artist Pierre-Etienne Morelle), the entrance to *Inside Out, Upside Down* was available through one means, through a handmade ladder/staircase fitted to the window of the gallery and directly down to the exterior pavement (Figure 6.1b). Viewers thus had to traverse inside from out in a manner contrary to the normative ways of entering a gallery (or a building for that matter). They had to venture beyond solely in order to witness the work itself.

While we may now have an idea of what *Inside Out, Upside Down* looked like, what is it exactly that makes it such an apposite example of Intermural Art? Well, the first clue is the location of the work itself, its positioning in a literally intermural space. Existing within the walls of the gallery, between the inside of the exhibition space and the outside of the street, *Inside Out, Upside Down* moves beyond Intermural Art as metaphor and rather realizes the term quite literally: it is art. It is intermural. It is literally intermural art. Yet if we move towards the broader understanding of Intermural Art as outlined above, we can equally see how Downey's work does not simply replicate his exterior practice within the interior realm but rather relocates the conceptual, methodological and ethical frameworks he institutes on the street (the frameworks emergent from and indelibly influenced by Graffiti and Street Art) within the site of the gallery itself. Just as his public practice of interventionism, his practice of re-appropriation and reuse, of critique and questioning, comes to explore (and upturn) the customs and

Figure 6.1 Brad Downey. *Inside Out, Upside Down*. NUN Gallery, Berlin. August 2014.
Photographs: Brad Downey. Reproduced with permission of the artist.

conventions of the street, here Downey institutes the same process in the gallery. He comes to reveal what is other to the gallery space, to reveal the space that we never encounter but which is always there, to reveal the rules (both social and spatial) that have become embedded so deeply that they are perceived as the norm. He moves beyond the restrictions of his given medium, violating and trespassing the set restrictions of the gallery's physical architecture. He moves beyond the instrumentality of his given material, transfiguring a nondescript, utilitarian object into a sublime, aesthetic one (Figure 6.2). This is an Intermural way of working, an Intermural practice. It is a mentality and methodology emergent from the street that has transformed into the gallery. Yet one that is reacting and responding to the specificities of both the *intra* and *extra*mural realms.

Just as he does in the public realm then, Downey's work acts to 'question [our] surroundings and reality', to take existing objects and spaces and 'change their composition or orientation to give them a different function and purpose' (Downey 2013). It acts in a way that may not look like Graffiti or Street Art but that smells like it. That both emerges out of and is hugely influenced by his independent public practice. That both emerges out of and is hugely influenced by a Contemporary Art practice. And that intertwines the two to create a new aesthetic terrain. Downey's work, like that of all the other artists working within Intermural Art, is thus no longer Street Art. It is no longer Street Art when in the street (it is polluted when named as such today). It is certainly not Street Art when in the gallery (in what way could it ever be)? And it so too fails to be profitably illuminated by the term Contemporary Art (actually being obscured by it). As Intermural Art it can be materially and morally comprehended. As Intermural Art it can be identified and interpreted. As Intermural Art its frame of references can be read, its desires and concepts rather than just its location or its medium deciphered. And, perhaps more importantly, as Intermural Art it can then start to encourage a new descriptive and conceptual language for other practices working within the same milieu. It can start to bind, and thus develop, the practices working both inside and outside the institution yet that emerge from the same mud-level[19] mentality. The practices that those at the very edge of what was termed Street Art are now exploring.

Street art is a period. Period.

People often criticize the pigeonholing of (art) practices. They say 'it's just a name', 'it's just a category'. They say we should spend less time thinking and more time acting. Yet these terms, these words, are hugely powerful. And this is thus far from being a simple case of pedantic semantics. These categories matter because they define *how* what is housed within them is understood. They enable not simply our ability to read these objects but effect how they are then read, dictating how they are morally comprehended and our very ability *to* morally comprehend them in themselves. And, quite crucially, when the orientation of a category has come to have been shifted from above – shifted by the market and the media rather than artists or adherents – its status becomes perilous, pollutive. Names, genres, periods matter.[20] And Street Art, as a period, is something that we must now move past.

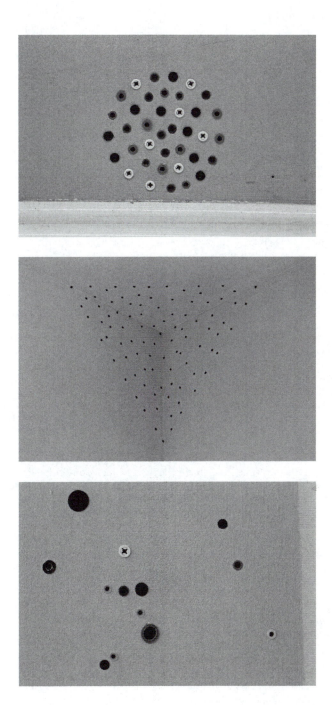

Figure 6.2 Brad Downey. *Inside Out, Upside Down* (details). NUN Gallery, Berlin. August 2014.

Photographs: Brad Downey. Reproduced with permission of the artist.

Street Art is a period. Period. A period that has now been supplanted due to its transition into something truly contaminated, corrupt. A period whose radical mantle can be seen continued today within the milieu of the intermural, within the category of Intermural Art.

Notes

1   Thanks in particular must go to Mathieu Tremblin and Jeroen Jongeleen for this title. This essay itself, however, is borne of countless conversations with artists and theorists from within this field. My thanks to all of them. Special thanks also to the editors of this volume for their perspicuous and valuable comments.

2   Both Street Art and Graffiti will be capitalized within this essay so as to identify them as specific, organized art practices rather than simply art on the street or illegal street writing.

3   Something that is also argued to have occurred with the term Graffiti: while writer or bomber were the original autochthonous terms, Lisa Gottlieb (2008: 40), quoting Jack Stewart, contends that Graffiti *Artist* was a term created by the establishment and only latterly utilized by the practitioners themselves.

4   As explained in my monograph (2014), as artefacts that are both adjunctive (a thing added) and decorative (a thing embellished), Graffiti and Street Art must be understood as ornaments in a quite classical, literal, rather than metaphorical manner. Once separated from their surface, Graffiti and Street Art hence become something entirely other, and that which is sold as 'Street Art' in galleries and auction houses is simply not thus.

5   As a curator of what is often called 'Street Art', the most common question I am asked (by both members of the public and established art critics) is 'how can you show Street Art within a gallery setting'? My answer is simple. You can't. Rather, what is being shown is art produced by artists who have produced, or still do produce, Street Art and Graffiti. This terminological need thus emerges due to the simple lack of any expression that can lucidly describe the work now being produced.

6   A number of theorists have attempted to work through this issue, utilizing helpful neologisms such as 'situational art' (Young 2014), 'Independent Public Art' (Abarca 2011), or 'politicized urban writing' (Avramidis 2012). I myself utilized the terms Consensual and Agonistic Ornamentation in my monograph (2014). However one of the issues I want to progress here is not only the fact that we are *After the End of [Street] Art* – to (mis)appropriate a famous title of Arthur Danto's – but, as we will see, that it is the relationship *between* the inside and outside realms that is becoming the key site of production today.

7   Anticipatory, proto-*Street Art* works can be seen in examples such as John Fekner's urban messages in the 1970s, Futura 2000's Graffiti abstractions in the 1980s, and REVS and COSTS stickers and sculptures in the 1990s.

8   Very few artists started directly from Street Art. While there are some notable exceptions (such as the Parisian *Invader*), the majority were primarily schooled in illegal production within the Graffiti culture.

9   As explained in Schacter 2014a, Graffiti and Street Artists can be seen, on the whole, to have quite clearly differentiated endogamous to exogamous communicative desires.

10   Undoubtedly, Street Art demonstrated the increasing influence of graphic design on graffiti artists, and an increasing usage of specialized computer software (such as Photoshop) to aid in the production of works.

11   I co-curated the Tate exhibition, curating the *Street Art Walking Tour* element of the show in which around ten site-specific works and actions were produced in the surrounding Southwark area. While not strictly a Street Art Festival (although becoming

implicitly linked to a festival-like context through acting as the opening for Tate's *Long Weekend* a 'four day festival of art and performance'), the Tate show not only served to push this concept into the stratosphere but cemented the link between Street Art and large scale muralism (as depicted on the front of the Tate) rather than with more autonomous, smaller scale practices. This is something that I have critiqued (Schacter 2014b) for its co-dependence with the Creative City discourse, and something that I believe has radically transformed the very nature of Street Art practice. What's more, while the Tate artists may have seemed to have been insulated from any commercial aspect through working with such a grand and respected institution, looking back, the warning signs were very much in place. Not only was the event sponsored by Nissan QASHQAI – a fact that the artists were not made aware of previous to their arrival in London – but their work ended up functioning as a backdrop for a photographic shoot *for* this sponsor (something very nearly leading to a revolt by the artists, and visibly recorded in the artist Blu's mural with his message 'please don't feed the sponsors'). While there were other large scale Street Art events preceding the Tate exhibition of course, such as Melbourne's Stencil Festival (active since 2004), and NuArt in Norway (active since 2005), the worldwide press attention the *Street Art* exhibition received, as well as institutional validation it gave to the genre, did I believe act as the point where Street Art began moving into new potentially awkward territory. It began to change the very nature of what Street Art was.

12 As explored by Konstantinos Avramidis (2014), through a reading of W.J.T. Mitchell and Ella Chmielewska, Graffiti, while textual, is consistently read *as* image and can thus be understood as a hybrid form.

13 One critique of Street Art is the uneasy notion of a quite *singular* public that at times emerges, occluding the true nature of our plural public*s*. In a similar way, the belief in the intrinsic ethical rightness of Street Art (by the artists themselves) can, as often seen in Social Practice Art, be problematic at points: even if one means well, a lack of criticality and a belief in a uniform 'good' means things don't necessarily always end well.

14 Of course not all large scale works do this. Many artists, such as the American neo-muralist Gaia, quite self consciously explore site specificity within their murals, and have a strong awareness of the dichotomy between placelessness and fixity that they straddle.

15 A singular exception here would be the Italian artist Blu, who has learned to paint huge walls using climbing equipment so as to resist the need for institutional support.

16 The Street Art Festival could in fact be argued to bear much of the responsibility for the reframing of Street Art itself, it being the dominant framework in which what is called 'Street Art' today appears. See http://thewynwoodwalls.com/ for a very paradigmatic example. Accessed: 1 October 2015.

17 Here, I hesitate to name any artists at the risk of producing a *Top Ten Intermural Artists List* (which I really do not want to do). However, if I had to produce some names more or less off the top of my head I would include artists such as Adams, Akay, Barry McGee, Boris Tellegen, E.B. Itso, Eltono, Filippo Minelli, Horfee, Ken Sortais, Les Frères Ripoulain, Revok and Swoon. These are all artists who have transitioned into the gallery realm while still maintaining the key conceptual, ethical and/or methodological pursuits of their independent public works. They are also all artists whose work in the public sphere continues parallel to their interior practice.

18 While Downey's work is a prime example of an Intermural practice, it is just one of a huge variety of styles that come under its auspices.

19 A term coined by the artist Akay for that which exists below the grassroots.

20 As the name of this edited volume itself does in its allusion to specific terminologies. And as the titles of my two books (2013, 2014a) do too – both containing the terms *Graffiti* and *Street Art* to my discomfort yet obvious acceptance.

References

Abarca, Javier. 2011. 'Teaching Urban Intervention, Learning to See the City Anew'. Available at: www.eksperimenta.net/ohjur/wp-content/uploads/2011/05/1101-Teaching-urban-intervention-IDEAlab-Javier-Abarca.pdf. Accessed: 1 October 2015.

Avramidis, Konstantinos. 2012. '"Live your Greece in Myths": Reading the Crisis on Athens' Walls'. Professional Dreamers, *working paper no.8*. Available at: www.profes sionaldreamers.net/_prowp/wp-content/uploads/Avramides-Reading-the-Crisis-on-Athens-walls-fld.pdf. Accessed: 1June 2015.

Avramidis, Konstantinos. 2014. 'Public [Ypo]graphy: Notes on Materiality and Placement'. In Karra, Marilena (ed.), *No Respect*. Athens: Onassis Cultural Centre, pp. 21–34, 85–96.

Chandler, Daniel. 1997. 'An Introduction to Genre Theory'. Available at: www.aber.ac.uk/media/Documents/intgenre/chandler_genre_theory.pdf. Accessed: 1 June 2015.

Douglas, Mary. 2013 [1966]. *Purity and Danger: An Analysis of Concepts of Pollution and Taboo*. New York, NY: Praeger.

Downey, Brad. 2013. Interview with author. 5 May.

Gottlieb, Lisa. 2008. *Graffiti Art Styles: A Classification System and Theoretical Analysis*. Jefferson, NC: McFarland.

Kwon, Miwon. 2004. *One Place after Another: Site-Specific Art and Locational Identity*. Cambridge, MA: MIT Press.

Lévi-Strauss, Claude. 1962. *Totemism*. Boston, MA: Beacon Press.

O'Connor, James. 2010. *The Cultural and Creative Industries: A Literature Review*. 2nd edn. Newcastle: Creativity, Culture and Education.

Peck, Jamie. 2005. 'Struggling with the Creative Class'. *International Journal of Urban and Regional Research*. 29(4): 740–70.

Pratt, Andy C. 2011. 'The Cultural Contradictions of the Creative City'. *City, Culture and Society*. 2(3): 123–130.

Schacter, Rafael. 2013. *The World Atlas of Street Art and Graffiti*. New Haven, CT: Yale University Press.

Schacter, Rafael. 2014a. *Ornament and Order: Graffiti, Street Art and the Parergon*. Burlington, VT: Ashgate.

Schacter, Rafael. 2014b. 'The Ugly Truth: Street Art, Graffiti and the Creative City'. *Art & the Public Sphere*. 3(2): 161–176.

Tudor, Andrew. 1974. *Image and Influence: Studies in the Sociology of Film*. London: George Allen & Unwin.

7 Expressive measures

An ecology of the public domain

Andrea Mubi Brighenti[1]

A time of swiftly shifting appreciations . . .

In the context of the focus in this section of the book on the writing (but also representations and reading) of graffiti and street art, it may be interesting to notice how, in the mid 2010s, a slight yet perceptible tendency to disaffiliate from the label of 'street art' has appeared. This positioning manoeuvre has been made more or less subtly and more or less contingently by some artists, and especially by various curators and gallerists. Certainly, several artists belonging to the big wave of street art of the early 2000s have sound idealistic, if not ideological reasons to be disappointed today. To them, as well as to several cultural critics, street art has, in the meantime, turned into the veritable mark of urban gentrification, the proof that capitalist dynamics have entirely recuperated the spontaneous creativity from below that characterized the early 2000s explosion of global street art.[2] Curators and gallerists might have their reasons to flee street art, too. From a commercial point of view, this genre might not be going to sell as well as it has done in the last decade. Its cutting-edge status is increasingly challenged, and cultural producers and promoters around the world feel that the label 'street art' is growing old, turning into a straightjacket that misrepresents their current research and productive efforts (see also Schacter in this volume).

So, has the whole phenomenon of street art been, economically-wise, a speculative bubble? Shall we expect that street art, also known as post-graffiti, will eventually be superseded and supplanted by *post-street art*? If street art is 'graffiti with a college degree',[3] is post-street art going to be street art with a PhD degree?

Obviously, artists do not need PhD degrees to do their work – for that matter, they don't even need art school degrees. What this metaphorical escalation of academic titles alludes to is not so much the status of producers themselves, as much as the nature of the larger social and urban sphere graffiti and street art have intercepted. Over the last decade, street art events have been caught up in official territorial marketing and tourist destination branding strategies. Major street art exhibitions, such as the one organized by Tate Modern in London in 2008, are just landmarks of a much larger trend that includes a proliferation of urban art events, galleries and organized tours. This way, graffiti art and street art have been ingrained in the official scripts of urban revitalization and urban promotion. Increasingly, contemporary art centres all over the world have opened their doors to this type of art, and the cultural policy of a number of key cities has been sensibly receptive to them. In some cases, having a local street art scene has turned into an un-disputable tourist asset – if not, in some cases, a goldmine. While in 2006 the then British Prime Minister Tony Blair was still posing before reporters with a graffiti removal hose during his visits to disadvantaged neighbourhoods (Getty Images 2006), in 2014 a senior cultural policy officer at the Greater London Authority, Adam Cooper, warmly welcomes graffiti for its 'social communal value' depicting graffiti artists as 'pioneers of a new kind of visual arts', in connection with the fact that 'culture and creativity are the essential ingredients to any successful city' (Cooper 2014).

During the last decade or so, street art has functioned as an unmistakable conveyor of 'urban creativity', a fuzzy if not hopelessly blurred notion that can be traced back to the 1990s and the rise of an array of cultural strategies and policies aimed at promoting the arts as an economic growth tool at the city as well as the national level.[4] The street art market has determined the success of galleries such as Urban Nation in Berlin and Stolen Space in London (a branch of The Whitechapel Gallery devoted to urban art), while major urban festivals such as Urban Affairs in Berlin, Upfest in Bristol, Cityleaks in Cologne, or NuArt in Stavanger, Norway, have flourished. The number of venues where street artists have been showcased has increased exponentially. Concurrently, one cannot fail to notice a trend toward gigantic operations, such as 'La Tour Paris 13' (Itinerrance 2014), defined by its organizers as 'the largest street art exhibition ever'. If La Tour Paris 13 undoubtedly shares resemblances with a kind of 'street art Disneyland', at about the same time the global street artist *par excellence* Banksy launched his Dismaland project, a post-street art operation contradistinguished by his sarcastic approach to contemporary Europe, its politics and lifestyle. Already in his first movie released in 2010, *Exit Through the Gift Shop*, Banksy ironized on how easy it can be to create a street artist *ex nihilo*. Indeed, *Exit* can be read as not only a docu-fiction, but also as a larger performance art project consisting in creating one such street artist.

Infamy and celebrity of graffiti in the public domain

This chapter is not an ethnography of producers. Rather, the theoretical proposal here is for a shift towards an 'ecological' perspective. Rather than merely confined to the impact of human industrial activities on the biosphere, an enlarged conception of the ecology also includes a human ecology, an urban ecology and a cultural ecology, or ecology of the mind. In short, an ecological approach is a theoretical approach that focuses on the relationships that are established within a heterogeneous social sphere. In other words, an ecological perspective is not meant to capture the point of view of individual actors, rather, the global pattern that derives from their intended as well as unintended moves. What is the relationship between publicness and value? How is value practically produced and measured? How can a cultural production, such as graffiti and street art, be embedded within a circuit of valorization? What are the variations and trans-formations that may occur in this circuit? These are the kind of questions that can be tackled ecologically.

Since the 1960s, in urban studies the ecological perspective has been criticized for depriving actors of their agency. Human ecology has been attacked for its weakness in taking political economy into account (York and Mancus 2009). However, that is not necessarily the case. The point with an ecological perspective is not so much erasing agency, as much as *bracketing* it. This is especially useful for investigating emotionally and morally charged phenomena; in that ecological analysis is intrinsically a-moral. The subsequent questions for social researchers, concerning how to un-bracket or unpack subjectivity and morality, and how to reconnect it to the analysis of social relations in their fullness, cannot be tackled ecologically. At some point, phenomenology is called forth to complement ecology and, an albeit apparently paradoxical synthesis – an 'ecological phenomenology' – must be envisaged.

While the farthest eco-phenomenological horizon is not part of the present inquiry, the important caveat is that the ecological perspective is far from being the ultimate perspective on social life. Nonetheless, it may turn out to be a pro-visionally helpful tool for inquiry – a Wittgenstein's ladder, so to speak. Thinking ecologically makes it possible to envisage overall patterns, or complexes of actions and reactions that allow us to gain a global insight into certain regions of social life. Such patterns can also be analysed as, diachronically, trends in transformation and, genetically, newly emerging formations. Narrowing down to a discussion of graffiti, the theoretical move proposed here enables researchers to observe what happened in the larger social and urban sphere surrounding these types of urban interventions. Elsewhere (Brighenti 2016a), I have argued that the Deleuzian notion of *divergent synthesis* might be helpful to explain the curious paths of valorization that have appeared in the field of graffiti and street art. To summarize a rather complex theoretical endeavour, Gilles Deleuze (1969) crafted the notion of divergent synthesis to overcome the traditional logical binary of conjunction and disjunction. For Deleuze, classic logic suppresses the positive presence of *difference* as a third entity that is irreducible to either affirmation or negation. In my understanding, the notion of divergent synthesis enables us to see how apparently contradictory phenomena – for instance, a tendency towards assimilation and a tendency towards expulsion of graffiti from the circuit of urban valorization – may happen. While it is impossible, and fruitless, to draw a sharp line between graffiti and street art, we observe that, on the one hand, traditional graffiti – quintessentially, tags – continues to be rejected outside the boundaries of civility, while, on the other, at least certain street art items have been accepted into mainstream art. This is a complex tendency, a divergent synthesis – simul-taneously towards expulsion and re-inscription or recapture – that needs to be untangled.

Here follows a cursory glance at the first pattern. Despite all the celebrations of street art as one of the pivotal embodiments of urban creativity, the widespread attitude against graffiti has not at all waned. Just as at the time of the broken windows theory (Wilson and Kelling 1982), graffiti remains an easily identifiable scapegoat for a vast array of urban ills. Just to mention a few cases, in 2014 the New York Police Department reported a 24 per cent increase in complaints about graffiti (Holpuch 2014). In 2015, the city of San Francisco sued graffiti artist Cozy Terry, asking for a $54,000 damage to public property, requiring to prohibit the artist from possessing spray cans and to ban him from public transport (SocketSite 2015). Graffiti writers all over the world still die in train accidents in the attempt to escape from guards and the police, not to mention accidents where the police have shot graffiti writers, frequently misjudging them for thieves. Even from an aesthetic point of view, graffiti remains defamed – not far away from the 'bastard art' Brassaï was inquiring into in the 1930s. Just to mention an example, a first-class aesthete such as the director David Lynch recently declared: 'Graffiti to me has pretty much ruined the world. It's ruined it for film. When you go to a place to film, everything is graffitied so if you don't want it, you have to paint it out' (Robertson 2015). To take another case, recently, the London-based all-city tagger Tox – technically speaking, a bomber (Van Loon 2014) – was found guilty of a string of graffiti attacks across England. Most interestingly, the public prosecutor, as well as some expert witnesses, deliberately sought to humiliate him, declaring: 'He is no Banksy. He doesn't have the artistic skills' (Davies 2011). This way, not only did an aesthetic judgement enter the legal field as a ground for incrimination, but it has crucially been employed in a shame game aimed at distinguishing *good* (artistic) and *bad* (untalented) graffiti. From an ecological perspective, Tox's point of view remains out of the picture – e.g. one cannot rule out that, after all, he might have enjoyed the 'lack-of-artistic-skill' charge on the part of a lawyer as a compliment. In this sense, in his analysis of the Sydney street art scene, Cameron McAuliffe (2012) has spoken of a 'moral geography' of the city and the citizens that is conjured up through the machinery of creativity.

The case of Tox also gives us, by contrast, an entry point into the second pattern included in the divergent synthesis. As mentioned above, this second pattern has been shaped by the eulogies to street art that have flourished since the early 2000s and that have marked the last decade especially. The examples in this vein are numerous. Let's just mention one discourse that resonates with the genre of aestheticizing gaze on street art seemingly shared by Tox's prosecutor, too. StreetARToronto is a programme run by the municipality of Toronto. Its public presentation reads as follows:

> StreetARToronto or StART is a pro-active program that aims to develop, support, promote and increase awareness of street art and its indispensable role in adding beauty and character to neighborhoods across Toronto, while counteracting graffiti vandalism and its harmful effect on communities.
>
> (City of Toronto 2013)

Here, street art is described as an urban asset for both its beautification potential as well as its community-building capacity. While the former attribute is related to the idea of art as public decoration, the latter is clearly tied to the presence of artist communities and creative milieus present in the territory. Thanks to such a rhetoric, the municipalities of large cities with active local art scenes have tried to appropriate, or at least employ, street art as an item in a Charles-Landry-Richard-Florida-type-of recipe for building their own respectable 'creative city'. The creative city literature – a large and, arguably, repetitive body of work – is sufficiently known not to be discussed in depth here. Suffice to recall how, in its unclearness, the jargon of creativity has resonated with a can-do attitude towards urban regeneration placing increasing emphasis on a kind of snapshot-language that has always been quintessential in the graffiti culture. Under the hegemony of the creative-city narrative, street art has been wielded into an urban development tool, targeting specific areas and neighbourhoods. As noted by McAuliffe (2012), the creative city has offered to street art new paths towards recognition. In the public discourse, street art has thus provided something like a mirror into which the contemporary city could mirror itself, finding beauty for once – after decades of graffiti ugliness! For an example of top-down strategic uses of street art, one can recall the commissioning of street art 'protected' interventions in the context of the London Olympic Games (Wainwright 2013). Not only major cities, but even a few remote villages such as Fanzara in Spain – which have come to be identified as street art hubs thanks to the efforts of a few relentless and passionate organizers – could hope to recover from their fate of semi-abandoned dying villages, turning into an instance of 'cultural triumph' (Kassam 2015). Success engendered a paradox of anonymity and stardom, in that a larger number of producers has fostered the fame of fewer bigger names. In economic terms, this has led to increasingly differentiated payoffs within the same market, according to a typical winner-takes-all scheme.

If we consider the two dynamics that characterize the divergent synthesis, a clear-cut opposition seems to have been put in place between, on the one hand, bad, defacing graffiti, and, on the other, good, decorative and marketable street art.[5] However, we should resist the temptation of simplifying thing in this way. Not only is the distinction between graffiti and street art not always easy to draw – as the lack of an established terminology testifies. The fact is that nowadays, as recalled above, an increasing number of cultural producers are positioning themselves against – or at least outside the boundaries of – street art. In this respect, one case is particularly illuminating. Back in 2007 and 2008, the Berlin-based street art curator Lutz Henke had invited the Italian artist Blu to paint a wall in the Kreuzberg neighbourhood. The pieces by Blu (one of which in collaboration with the French JR) have become quite notorious, to the point of being a naturalized part of the Berlin cityscape. Pictures of this artwork can be found on websites as diverse as the municipality of Berlin and a real estate agency currently redeveloping the zone. In reaction against this capture into the mainstream, in 2015 Henke put out a press release titled 'Blu Murals painted black'. In a public lecture, Henke (2015) explains that, in agreement with the artist, his collaborators have whitewashed the wall. 'We created something that contributed to gentrification and in the end we expelled ourselves from the neighborhood', Henke commented. At the same time, as the site of the artist reveals, Blu has completely dissociated himself from the street art mainstream, shifting to grass-root murals and working mainly if not exclusively with leftist squats, neighbourhood councils and social projects.

The Berlin piece by Blu has been recurrently described as 'iconic'. The problem, however, is that it was never clear of what it was an icon in the first place. This may have something to do with the inherent ambiguity of iconicity at large. Truly, icons are signs, but it is never clear of what they are signs. Despite their enhanced visibility, in fact, icons can never be reduced to 'established figurations'. Instead, they exist in a twilight region of the visible (Brighenti 2015). Icons are not systems, and cannot be. This is the reason why icons end up quite easily caught in the 'perverting' dynamics described in Stoic philosophy. Icons, in other words, are twisting operators that break unified designs and strategies: their most proper move is betrayal. They are as easily appropriable as they can get out of control again. The difficulties in circumscribing and stabilizing the meaning of icons deserves an in-depth inquiry that would probably drive us towards the core of social life – especially in connection with the question about why do we keep looking for them. However, for the moment, let us just content ourselves with observing how, in various cases, the iconicity of street art has intersected the discourse of urban creativity.

Urban creativity and the urban atmosphere

As discussed above, over the last couple of decades, the mantra of urban creativity has asserted itself as one large-scale narrative that a vast array of different actors ranging from local administrators to shop owners have strategically and tactically employed to talk about cities, imagine them and, ultimately, transform them. But, the rhetorical exploitation of the creativity narrative as an asset for urban development has increasingly experienced limitations, beginning from the fact that it is not entirely clear how such an asset can be produced, sustained, increased and, ultimately, turned into economic value. Among the attempted explanations of this phenomenon, Jack Katz (2010: 27) introduced the phrase 'urban alchemy' to describe 'the trick of selling versions of the public to the public'. What Katz refers to as 'urban alchemy' is simply the fact that people are attracted to cities because of their global human atmosphere, rather than just a specific set of tradable items. A series of economic opportunities derive from the very human density of cities. Katz takes the example of the bistro owner who,

> simply by orienting chairs toward the avenue or square, can charge extra for the espresso that comes with a landscape view of communal life that generations of others have made magnetic.
>
> (Katz 2010: 27)

This way, besides the pursuit of single goods, the city itself constitutes a preliminary *meta*-good people are willing to make sacrifices to afford. In our view, this happens because cities are coterminous with a public domain that constantly overcomes the plethora of objects and goods that are placed in it. In this context, *icons* lie precisely at the threshold between the plethora of objects and the immaterial enveloping milieu. From this perspective, it is impossible to conceptualize graffiti and street art without placing them within the larger ecology of the public domain and its specific dynamics.

The public domain can be imagined as an integral, enlarged public space beyond physical settings (Brighenti 2016b). Not only does the notion of public domain join together public space and the public sphere, it also moves beyond a topographical definition of public space, in order to apprehend the specific *publicness* that contradistinguishes public space and the public sphere. A theory of the public domain takes into account the fact that the existence of specific locales in the city is constantly prolonged towards other locales merged into circuits of imagination, discussion, affection and action. Spatially speaking, the public domain is infused (or scattered, disseminated) in the city in an interstitial way, through more or less visible paths and currents. Publicness corresponds to a specific degree of intensity in social life, and the intensity of the public domain is characterized by the on-going confrontation between a number of addresses that are released (or even 'shot') into an accessible, visible domain together with the reactions these addresses elicit or, in any way, meet (Iveson 2007). This is also why the public domain can never be fully occupied by anyone, least of all by the authorities. The public domain thus embodies the *limits of control* of public agencies. 'Reversible appropriations' could be a phrase that conveys the endless working of the public domain. In our case, a piece of graffiti or street art is cast or launched by its creators into the public domain through an inscription into the register of the visible and the accessible. By doing so, that piece of graffiti occupies a locale and from there begins to be spread out in a number of visual and discursive paths, including the reactions of passers-by, media coverage, discussions in forums and magazines, the wanted or unwanted 'attention' from the public administration, commercial actors and so on. A whole ecological circuit is thus drawn that incessantly passes through phases of closure (appropriation, privatization) and re-opening (further addresses, further changes made to the environment).

Part of the seduction of the urban atmosphere is a consequence of its eventful-ness, and part of the attraction of urban eventfulness lies in its never-perfectly-controllable status. This is the inherent life of the public domain, an ecology that no single actor can master thoroughly. Incidentally, this might be one of the reasons why the labels 'public' and 'urban' have increasingly come to flank, if not supplant, the 'street' in street art. In a sense, one of the problems with street art since its outset has always been that it has never been 'street' enough – at least, never as 'street' as the old graffiti tradition from which it stemmed (for some artists) or with which it hybridized (for others). 'The street' carries the connotation of a space that can never be fully tamed, where a degree of unruliness is true to type. This consideration has certainly constituted part of the coolness, thrill and excitement that welcomed street art in the early 2000s. In fact, however, unruliness, then perceived as conveying a liberating and empowering sense of freedom, itself facilitated the capture and re-inscription of graffiti art. The reason is to be sought in the peculiar, wide-ranging relationship between capitalism and governance that has been progressively asserting itself since the 1970s. As compellingly conceptualized by Michel Foucault (2004), the spread of 'ordoliberal' theory and the rise of neoliberal governance practically coincided with the project for a type of governance that includes freedom instead of excluding it. Rather than through norms and restrictions, the neoliberal individual can be governed through the environment – essentially, through market competition. From the moment street art has come to produce value, its unruly aspect has posed no problems to governance. To put it differently, the trick that critical theorists since at least the Situationists have called recuperation, or co-optation into the system, is deeply inscribed into one of the crucial contemporary models of power (albeit, arguably, not the only one in place).

Value-measure environments

So far, we have argued that graffiti and street art have been caught in an encompassing pattern of urban valorization. Consequently, the question now turns into the following: how is it that certain things acquire and, in turn, confer value? And, conversely, how is it that they lose value and, ultimately, detract it from its surroundings? More specifically, as seen above, with graffiti and street art we have been observing two mutually exclusive yet simultaneous processes of valorization, that is, simultaneously towards infamy and celebrity, towards expulsion and re-inscription. The existence of such simultaneous divergent circuits is to be related to the nature of value, and how it can be measured, if at all.

An ecological perspective invites us to observe the multifaceted composition of measuring tools deployed to capture value. To begin with, the notion of value must be liberated from both a narrowly economic and a narrowly moral understanding. Rather than a local phenomenon, value is best imagined as a total social fact – if not, probably, the *ultimate* social fact. To understand value, we need more than ecology: we need vitalism. Value – or, as it may also be called, worth – is a phenomenon that enables acts of creation and conversion across different social domains – fields or subsystems. Hence, its inherent instability, its polymorphic and metamorphic appearances. Not by chance, Katz (2010) chose an alchemic image to describe the process of urban valorization. The alchemic metaphor stresses the inherently metamorphic, converting aspect of value. Even better, we should speak of a 'conversive' feature, in the sense that not simply is value converted, but value is that which makes things be converted. What these things are, though, is not entirely clear yet. In connection with this, it should be remarked that, while value sparks from the middle of social life itself, it also mysteriously points towards an *outside* of social life, keeping the social domain open towards some kind of non-social space from which all sorts of innovations and unheard-of formations proceed.

Indeed, besides the notion of divergent synthesis, Deleuze also provides us with an important insight into art value (2004: 77): 'We know – he writes – there is only one value for art, and even for truth: the "first-hand," the authentic newness of something said, and the "unheard music" with which it is said.' A faithful vitalist, Deleuze ties value to novelty, immediacy, and its ensuing positive affections. In this view, the first-hand fresh experience that characterizes valuable art is akin to a *presence* (incidentally, here one can retrace a debt of Deleuze towards phenomenology, which he otherwise criticized). Elaborating a bit on the terminology, we could say that value is *expressive*. Now the puzzle becomes slightly more clear if we consider the extent to which such expressive innovations and unheard-of formations are difficult to integrate into social reality. What is interesting about the notion of divergent synthesis, or disjunctive conjunction, is that both convergence and divergence admit commensuration. They admit it in principle, yet practically they pose a series of considerable challenges to each single measurement. Therefore, the questions to be considered include the following: Can expression be measured? What is the relation between expression and measure? Do measures just capture expression or do they also produce it – and, if so, in what sense?

So intimate is the interplay between value and measure that it is possible to speak of veritable 'value-measure environments'. Actually, a measure provides not only a metric, but a whole environment where things can be apprehended and compared. In other words, the creation of new measures always entails the introduction of new ways of making, stabilizing and transforming how humans associate with their socii in a shared environment. Rather than simple tools, measures can be best conceived of as bundles of aspects, or selective gazes, packaged into every single measure unit and measurement act. The technological–material, the legal–political and the cultural dimensions of measures represent some such gazes bundled into each single measure environment. Every technical measurement system thus functions not only as an epistemic model but also, inherently, as a power tool. Not simply this: every measure system shapes and evokes a whole imagery. No power system, no institutional organization can exist without a whole ecology, cosmology and, eventually, a theodicy of measures. Towards the end of the nineteenth century, Gabriel Tarde (1890) observed that measures enable us to treat in logical – even quantitative, mathematical – terms things that, in fact, pertain to the field of teleology. In other words, measures turn what we want into what we believe.

Truly, measures enable us to objectify value. More precisely, perhaps, they enable us to *visibilize* it. Making value visible – such is the working of measures. In practice, we couldn't even imagine a manifestation of value that does not *ipso facto* conjure up a measurement system. A measure, understood as a procedure of visibilization, consists in the inscription and projection of value into the domain of the visible. Acts of visibilization are not innocent, though: they are acts that make things happen. Just as there is a magic of value, there is a corresponding magic of measures. But these two forms of magic should be carefully distinguished. The magic of measures is to be connected to two different yet superposed meanings contained in the word 'measure', namely: a) measure as the result of an act of measurement that records or gives back a certain value or worth;

b) measure as an explicit act meant to pursue or promote a given goal within a certain means–ends scheme (what might also be termed a 'policy'). The tension between recording an independent reality and creating the reality supposed to be ascertained or assessed, is the tension out of which the magic of measures springs. So, when it comes to understanding the 'vibrant urban environments' where graffiti and street art are produced, one clearly senses that urban vibrancy intimately resonates with excess, transgression and thrill – as said above, the public domain as the limits of control. In fact, however, it is only through measure that excess and transgression can be identified. Etymologically, both words contain a precise reference to the stepping or falling beyond measure. This is also why it is impossible to straightforwardly assign moral qualifications – such as good versus bad – to either measure or excess. If measures turn what we want into what we believe, then the quest for measure is intrinsically the quest for the *right* measure. It is an axiological quest. But the rightness of measure can only be commensurate to the value to be made visible, and the complication lies in the fact that, as noted above, there is no neutral act of visibilization.

Another crucial fact in the deployment of measures concerns the distinction between an object and an environment. Properly speaking, only an object can be measured, while the environment corresponds to the blind spot of measure – for the good reason that measure itself is such an environment. On the other hand, objects have no intrinsic value, rather, they draw their own value from the context and the situation in which they are inserted. This is particularly clear in the case of graffiti and street art, which have been described as precisely emplaced, topo-sensitive, situational, and embedded in unique spots (Chmielewska 2007, 2009; Ferrell and Weide 2010; Young 2014; Avramidis 2015). Thus, it is a matter of clarifying the nature of the urban interventions under scrutiny. Graffiti cannot be disembedded without altering its nature. But, applying a measure systematically entails severing the object from its environment. The transformation of value as a total social fact into value as economic asset – ultimately, as price – illustrates this dynamic. In order to 'cash' value, one has to circumscribe an artwork with definite boundaries, to turn an artwork into a tradable object. The paradox, however, is that severing the object from its environment also cuts the original link from which value itself stems. By doing so, value evades objectification and returns to the environment. What remains is, perhaps, a cherished decorative fetish, something that, in the short or long run, will lose liveliness and vigour. In the end, what remains is not even a fetish, but a *potiche*. In synthesis, here this is the unsettled relationship between value and measure: on the one hand, there is no value independently from the measures with which we attempt to grasp it; on the other, though, value can never be fully grasped by any act of measurement whatsoever.

Expressive measures and artful materials

The fact that 'urban creativity' has turned into an established, even major asset in contemporary capitalist urban valorization makes the relation between creativity and resistance not linear. Today, creativity per se is neither liberating nor capable of producing value. Indeed, the so-called process of capitalistic recuperation is always a recuperation of products, not value. However, from a political point of view, from the moment in which creativity has lost its novelty, those who want to resist the present state of affairs, and thus create a *new* novelty in the arts, find themselves in a complex situation – as we have seen in the Henke/Blu affair above. Like them, a whole cohort of people who were actively engaged in the scene in the early 2000s have felt increasingly expropriated of their own productions, with their own creative weapons of resistance turned against themselves. In this context, one can also read the bitter declarations by C215 (Guémy 2013). A certain dissatisfaction and maybe even hopelessness vis-à-vis street art has followed (the traditional graffiti community, on the other hand, has been much less affected). In this section, a proposal is made to reconsider a notion that represents, in a way, the uncanny alter ego of creativity – namely, the notion of *expression*. Perhaps, once this notion has been disentangled from creativity and decoration, an overall reassessment of current valorization patterns can be envisaged and, consequently, a space for new schemes may be imagined.

First, let us quickly review the imaginaries evoked by the words creation and creativity. Creation is, literally, a bloody enterprise. To begin with, the Latin verb *crĕor* is akin to the word *crŭŏr*, blood, and originally referred to childbirth – something that cannot happen without a certain expenditure of blood. It is a passive, not active verb. While we know that, in fact, the child is anything but passive during delivery, the ancient imagination encapsulated in the word creation tells that the child is being born because her mother is pushing her out. Also, one cannot help but notice the theological resonance of the imaginary of creation: we are all creatures because we have been created, and what we can create in turn is just a minor addition that never counterbalances our original debt towards our creator. Despite the original bloodiness of creation, in post-1968 Western culture the word creativity has been progressively transformed into a sanitized version of what is supposed to be an act of creation. Creativity seems to have become a sort of disembodied quality that has not much to do with creation itself and is instead to be connected with personal attitude or attribute. Psychologists have established all sorts of metrics to measure individual creativity; in parallel, urban studies scholars have employed it as the characterizing mark of local neighbourhoods, districts, as well entire cities – presumably on the basis that creative persons want to stay with other creative persons. Understood as an attitude of creation that prescinds from creation itself, creativity illustrates what Claude Lévi-Strauss (1950) once called a 'floating signifier', a vague catch-all phrase that can be deployed as a discursive resource to support valorization, albeit as simulacrum. At first sight, the discourse of creativity seems to stand in opposition to rationalist explanations of social action; in fact, both creativity and rational choice are grounded in an individualist model of society. As hinted above, the larger historical horizon in which such a trend makes sense is the rise of neoliberal governance where power works through free competition of individuals in the market. It is not by chance, then, that the discourse of creativity is inherently competitive and meritocratic.

Expression, by contrast, places us in a completely different register of imagination. What it offers is an essentially non-individualistic explanation of social life, one that fits with the ecological prism proposed at the outset of this chapter. In the previous sections, a conception of value as a form of expression has also been put forth. The ground for this view is that expression is contradistinguished by an accentuated *centrifugal* vector, a movement that goes from the core to the periphery. The core, however, is not an individual. Rather, expression proceeds from the heart of impersonal social life. Expression is not something that comes from within the individual and erupts outside of him/her; it is something that comes from within social life and erupts in a connective milieu of people. Thus, expression is a manifestation of the force of social life itself that connects individuals and envelops them within evolving environments. From this perspective, expressive persons, such as cultural producers of all sorts, represent singular points where the impersonal forces of expression coalesce and condense, and from which they are bounced and spread around. This view is not meant to downplay the importance of individual inventions; yet, it is important to distinguish expression from invention. While invention is something the individual confers to society, expression is something individuals come to embody by becoming receptors of social forces. In short, expression is another name for the mobility of preindividual and impersonal value. There is a further important connection to be established between expression and public life. As seen above, the public domain corresponds to a dynamic whereby a plural, even anonymous public is addressed. Such is also the dynamic of expression. In other words, if the centrifugal movement of expression draws outward trajectories, the outside towards which expression is directed is nothing else but the public domain itself.

No expression can be understood apart from a prolonged engagement with specific materials. Ethnographic studies of graffiti and street art have emphasized the skilled, sensuous and embodied work upon a range of specific materials that is being carried out by producers (Brighenti and Reghellin 2007; Young 2014). In every expressive act, a protracted faithfulness to an *art* is required. Here, the word art is to be understood in an extremely broadened sense, including all sorts of skilful domains where tools and tricks of the trade are deployed. There is nothing general about expression, given that expression cannot be but expression-in-something. In other words, expression is something that happens with or in materials themselves; it is an operation that proceeds through materials and their technologies. More precisely, expression consists in making materials expressive. After Duchamp, at the very least, all art is conceptual. But that is far from ruling out that artists – just as all humans, on another account – necessarily struggle with specific materials. The intimate physical, visible contact with materials always includes a kind of struggle and restlessness – together with commitment and, ultimately, enjoyment.

Having disentangled expression from creativity also offers an interesting entry point into the hypothesis of the *ornamental* nature of street art. In a recent contribution to the literature, Rafael Schacter (2014) offers a fresh and important insight into a thread of street art he has termed independent public art. In his work, based on a prolonged ethnography of the Madrid scene, street art is celebrated as urban ornament. The hypothesis is a fascinating one, which makes sense especially once ornament is neatly distinguished from decoration. Decoration (from the Latin *děcět*, bring appropriate) consists of *decent* embellishment, merely non-belligerent beautification. Ornament is a different story. The *ornamentum* is, originally, the equipment, the amour, the warrior's gear. It is also the jewellery and, by extension, the honour and distinction that come with it. Ornament is *parure, bijou, Schmuck*. To the modern eye, ornament may appear as tamed and domesticated in terms of elegance and distinction – just, slightly kitsch. Yet, as noted by Georg Simmel and Adolf Loos in two short, crucial essays, both from 1908, there is something inherently *excessive* in ornament. Loos was a modernist architect who passionately fought against ornamentation in architecture, regarding it as a sign of primitivism and lack of taste. This is exactly why he despised ornaments (Loos 2006 [1908]). From the point of view of modernist design, which should have been based on sober aesthetics, he stigmatized the ornament as 'criminal'. On the other hand, Simmel – the eclectic and highly refined cultural critic and theorist who remained an academic outsider throughout his whole life – offered a more rounded analysis of the ornament, describing it as the simultaneously egoistic and altruistic object *par excellence*. Egoistic, insofar as it is motivated by a careless desire to distinguish oneself and top others at any price, the ornament is also altruistic in the measure in which it proceeds by constantly offering aesthetic gifts to the beholder. The ornament thus represents a 'synthesis of having and being' that draws a strong give-and-take nexus between the individual and his/her milieu.

In clear contrast to decoration, the ornament lacks appropriateness; it is superfluous and frivolous, akin to the *bling* in hip-hop culture. Hence, the ornament constitutes a sort of graphism that is out-of-measure vis-à-vis the established and accepted aesthetic canon. The notion of *dépense* in Georges Bataille (1967), thought of as an unproductive expense of energy and goods, echoes a similar attention to a dynamic that the French author regarded as fundamentally anti-bourgeois. The ornament as an attitude, as 'ornamentality', is primitive, yet not restricted to far away tribes. In fact, it is the eruption of the primitive – such a childish mix of egoism and generosity beyond measure – in the heart of every modernity. There is, in other words, a rebellious stance in ornamentality that recalls the primitive rebellion of the social bandits described by Eric Hobsbawm (1959). The bandit is someone who has been banned and is searched for by the authorities. However, in rural societies the outlaws are often seen as beacons of popular resistance insofar as they represent peasant struggle against landlords, usurers and clergymen – let's just recall Robin Hood. Hence, the qualification of 'social' banditry. Excessive and dangerous to the establishment, social bandits steal and gift generously, measurelessly – they ornate their milieu.

The question, however, remains: can the ornament be subversive? Following the diverse insights from Loos, Simmel, Bataille and Hobsbawm, the ornament remains assigned to a status of ambiguity. While there is certainly an anarchic, unruly ingredient to it, the ornament lacks any overall political project. Indeed, Hobsbawm himself was the first to warn against the romanticization of social banditry, highlighting how in many cases social bandits had more of a conservative than revolutionary function, keeping rural society straddled in an impasse that inhibited any development. Like tattoos, ornamental practices entail an unleashed, joyous cruelty of the eye necessarily imbued with moral and political ambiguity. While ornaments lie outside of the aesthetic canon, they can still be captured by it and made functional. In the terms introduced by Deleuze and Guattari (1972), the primitive territorial coding ends up being overcoded by the barbarian despotic machine, that is, the central state. Whenever the state comes back in, the ambiguous graphism of ornamentality is replaced (or encaged) by proper writing. More than subversive, the ornament ends up being subverted.

Conclusions

Motivated by a rational strategy, the destruction of the wall by Blu in Kreuzberg has been a desperate attempt to resist the rise of creativity. The gesture is bold, yet per se incapable of elaborating alternative patterns of valorization. Probably, those who seek to resist current valorization patterns will find ornamentality similarly insufficient. Nonetheless, ornamentality retains an important indication. Indeed, the ornament conveys a deep sensuous engagement with materials. From this point of view, the ornament shares similarities with the work of expression that, as we have seen above, pivots around the transformation of materials into expressive materials. The ornament is expressive, although not all expression is ornamental.

More generally, this chapter has suggested that an in-depth analysis of expression might lead to novel insights into the overall issue of value-measure environments in contemporary society. In doing so, it should be kept in mind that art producers are not the only ones who handle expressive materials. Indeed, as the ecological point of view stresses, it is impossible to imagine the public domain without a plurality of heterogeneous materials of expression being worked upon, disseminated and coming into reciprocal contact. The contentious legal–political, economic and cultural dynamic surrounding graffiti and street art can be appreciated through the prism of the public domain – attending, that is, how the new measures of the urban are created, put in place, as well as challenged and undermined. Ultimately, the question to be tackled today concerns whether and how measures themselves can become expressive.

Notes

1   The author wishes to thank Konstantinos Avramidis and Myrto Tsilimpounidi for their careful reading of the first draft of the chapter, their generous comments and the wealth of suggestions to better it. Limitations are my own.

2   However, one should not overlook that street art traces back to at least the 1970s, stemming from independent and experimental art movements such as Fluxus and Situationism, whose avant-garde artists first engaged the materials of pop culture.

3   Such naive yet effective expression has been used by the New York-based street art tour guide Matt Levy (Holpuch 2014).

4 For an example drawn from British pop music, one can think back to the famous 'Cool Britannia' moment in the mid 1990s. (Available at: https://en.wikipedia.org/wiki/Cool_ Britannia. Accessed: 11 January 2016). More pointedly, recent conferences such as *(Dis)respectful Creativity Conference: Graffiti & Street Art on Contemporary Society & Urban Spaces* (6 June 2014, Athens) and *Lisbon Street Art & Urban Creativity International Conference* (3–4 July 2014, Lisbon) may be recalled (Available at: www.sgt.gr/en/programme/event/1692 and www.urbancreativity.org/ respectively. Accessed: 11 January 2016).

5 Two pieces by Lush make the point in a punchier way. Available at: http://lushsux. tumblr.com/post/111130182756/carry-on; http://lushsux.tumblr.com/post/11211963 2201/get-outta-jail-free-card. Accessed: 11 January 2016.

References

Avramidis, Konstantinos. 2015. 'Reading an Instance of Contemporary Urban Iconoclash: A Design Report from Athens'. *The Design Journal*. 18(4): 513–534.

Bataille, Georges. 1967. *La Part Maudite*. Paris: Minuit.

Brighenti, Andrea Mubi. 2015. 'Twilight of the Icons, or, How to Sociologize with Visibility'. *Sociologica*. 1: 1–17.

Brighenti, Andrea Mubi. 2016a. 'Graffiti, Street Art and the Divergent Synthesis of Place Valorisation in Contemporary Urbanism'. In Ross, Jeffrey Ian (ed.), *Routledge Handbook of Graffiti and Street Art*. London: Routledge, pp. 158–167.

Brighenti, Andrea Mubi. 2016b. 'The Public and the Common: Some Approximations of Their Contemporary Articulation'. *Critical Inquiry*. 42(2): 306–328.

Brighenti, Andrea Mubi and Reghellin, Michele. 2007. 'Writing. Etnografia di una Pratica Interstiziale'. *Polis*. XXI(3): 369–398.

Chmielewska, Ella. 2007. 'Framing [Con]text: Graffiti and Place'. *Space and Culture*. 10(2): 145–169.

Chmielewska, Ella. 2009. 'Writing on the Ruins, or Graffiti as a Design Gesture'. In Brighenti, Andrea Mubi (ed.), *The Wall and the City*. Trento: Professional Dreamers, pp. 31–45.

City of Toronto. 2013. 'StreetARToronto'. Available at: www1.toronto.ca/wps/portal/con tentonly?vgnextoid=bebb4074781e1410VgnVCM10000071d60f89RCRD. Accessed: 11 January 2016.

Cooper, Adam. 2014. 'Futures for Informal Urban Practice?' Speech delivered at *The Graffiti Sessions* Conference, Southbank Centre, London, December 3–5. Available at: www. youtube.com/watch?v=s1emhfuHGE0. Accessed: 11 January 2016.

Davies, Caroline. 2011. '"Tox" Graffiti Artist Convicted of Criminal Damage'. *The Guardian*, 7 June. Available at: www.theguardian.com/artanddesign/2011/jun/07/tox-graffiti-artist-criminal-damage. Accessed: 11 January 2016.

Deleuze, Gilles. 1969. *Logique du Sens*. Paris: Minuit.

Deleuze, Gilles. 2004. *Desert Islands*. Los Angeles, CA: Semiotext(e).

Deleuze, Gilles and Guattari, Félix. 1972. *L'Anti-Œdipe*. Paris: Minuit.

Ferrell, Jeff and Weide, Robert. 2010. 'Spot Theory'. *City*. 14(1–2): 48–62.

Foucault, Michel. 2004. *Naissance de la Biopolitique: Cours au Collège de France 1978–1979*. Paris: EHESS, Gallimard & Seuil.

Getty Images. 2006. 'Tony Blair Launches Respect Agenda'. Available at: www.getty images.co.uk/detail/news-photo/swindon-united-kingdom-british-prime-minister-tony-blair-news-photo/56557092. Accessed: 11 January 2016.

Guémy, Christian. 2013. 'Graffiti, Street Art, Muralisme . . . Et si on Arrêtait de tout Mélanger?'. *Rue 89/Le Nouvel Observateur*, 11 November. Available at: http://rue89. nouvelobs.com/rue89-culture/2013/11/06/graffiti-street-art-muralisme-si-arretait-tout-melanger-247235. Accessed: 11 January 2016.

Henke, Lutz. 2015. 'The Zombification of Berlin'. Public lecture. Available at: www. youtube.com/watch?v=BtSPCNCN-oU. Accessed: 11January 2016.

Hobsbawm, Eric. 1959. *Primitive Rebels*. Manchester: Manchester University Press.

Holpuch, Amanda. 2014. 'Is the Rise in Graffiti Complaints a Return to New York's Dark Days or a Golden Age of Street Art?'. *The Guardian*, 29 October. Available at: www. theguardian.com/artanddesign/2014/oct/29/new-york-graffiti-rise-police-complaints-street-art. Accessed: 11 January 2016.

Itinnerance Galerie. 2014. 'La Tour Paris 13: Une Exposition Collective Unique et Ephémère'. Available at: http://itinerrance.fr/hors-les-murs/la-tour-paris-13/. Accessed: 11 January 2016.

Iveson, Kurt. 2007. *Publics and the City*. Oxford: Blackwell.

Kassam, Ashifa. 2015. 'How Embracing Graffiti Stopped one Spanish Village Going to the Wall'. *The Guardian*, 11 April. Available at: www.theguardian.com/artanddesign/2015/apr/14/street-art-fanzara-spain-graffiti-artists. Accessed: 11 January 2016.

Katz, Jack. 2010. 'Time for New Urban Ethnographies'. *Ethnography*. 11(1): 25–44.

Lévi-Strauss, Claude. 1950. 'Introduction à l'œuvre de Marcel Mauss'. In Marcel Mauss, *Sociologie et anthropologie*. Paris: PUF.

Loos, Adolf. 2006 [1908]. 'Ornament and Crime'. In Miller, Bernie and Ward, Melony (eds), *Crime and Ornament: The Arts and Popular Culture in the Shadow of Adolf Loos*. New York, NY: YYZ Books, pp. 29–36.

McAuliffe, Cameron. 2012. 'Graffiti or Street Art? Negotiating the Moral Geographies of the Creative City'. *Journal of Urban Affairs*. 34(2): 189–206.

Robertson, Joshua. 2015. 'David Lynch Decries "Pathetic" Arts Funding Cuts – and Graffiti'. *The Guardian*, 13 March. Available at: www.theguardian.com/film/2015/mar/13/david-lynch-decries-pathetic-arts-funding-cuts-and-graffiti. Accessed: 11 January, 2016.

Schacter, Rafael. 2014. *Ornament and Order. Graffiti, Street Art and the Parergon*. Burlington, VT: Ashgate.

Simmel, Georg. 1908. 'Exkurs über den Schmuck'. In *Soziologie*. Frankfurt: Suhrkamp.

SocketSite. 2015. 'City Suing Prolific Tagger For $54K'. 21 August. Available at: www.socketsite.com/archives/2015/08/prolific-graffiti-vandal-is-in-the-citys-sights.html. Accessed: 11 January 2016.

Tarde, Gabriel.1890. *Les Lois de L'Imitation*. Paris: Alcan.

Van Loon, Jannes. 2014. ' "Just Writing your Name?" An Analysis of the Spatial Behaviour of Graffiti Writers in Amsterdam'. *Belgeo*. 3: 1–17.

Wainwright, Oliver. 2013. 'Olympic Legacy Murals met with Outrage by London Street Artists'. *The Guardian*, 6 August. Available at: www.theguardian.com/artanddesign/2013/aug/06/olympic-legacy-street-art-graffiti-fury. Accessed: 11 January 2016.

Wilson, James and Kelling, George. 1982. 'Broken Windows'. *Atlantic Monthly*. 249(3): 29–38.

York, Richard and Mancus, Philip. 2009. 'Critical Human Ecology: Historical Materialism and Natural Laws'. *Sociological Theory*. 27(2): 122–149.

Young, Alison. 2014. *Street Art, Public City: Law, Crime and the Urban Imagination*. London: Routledge.

8 Dead ends and urban insignias

Writing graffiti and street art (hi)stories along the UN buffer zone in Nicosia, 2010–2014

Panos Leventis

Introduction

The United Nations Buffer Zone is a strip of land of varied width that runs from west to east and divides the island of Cyprus in two. In the heart of Nicosia, the island's capital, the Buffer Zone (BZ), also called the Green Line, bisects the old city and its sixteenth-century fortifications (Figure 8.1). It is an urban landscape mentally and physically associated with a long history of armed conflict and violence.[1] During the last decade, the words, colours and messages of graffiti and street art have reappeared and proliferated in the midst of this landscape,[2] with often perception-altering results that affect both the place itself and its users.

This contribution identifies individuals and groups of artists who create on the walls of old Nicosia's no-man's land, 'writing' and 'telling' (hi)stories on the Buffer Zone's semi-destroyed urban fabric. It investigates whether specific sites are deliberately chosen, and inquires whether context influences content, theme or end-result of the work(s). From commenting (or refusing to comment) on military invasions, urban destruction and unresolved conflict, to engaging in past times of prosperity and rampant capitalism, and to pondering current realities of socio-economic crisis and uncertainty, street art along the Buffer Zone is discussed as a critique, a reflection, and an inseparable part of Nicosia's current and future urban processes.

The contribution is a phenomenological, composite urban walk comprised of narrations of experiences of the city's fabric, graffiti and street art. The walk progresses along the Buffer Zone of the Walled City, from Paphos Gate in the West to Famagusta Gate in the East. Each of the three short, two-part fictional narratives features a different protagonist who experiences events, spaces, the city, the graffiti and the street art. The protagonists are, in order, a reporter, activist and street artist in his twenties, a soon-to-be unemployed banker in his late thirties and, lastly, a multi-tasking architect – a refugee from the north of Cyprus – in her forties.

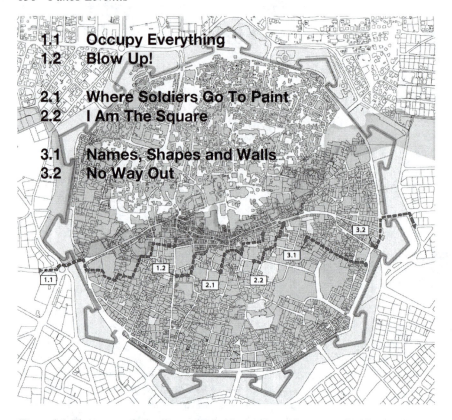

Figure 8.1 The centre of Nicosia surrounded by its sixteenth-century fortifications. The UN Buffer Zone or 'Green Line' bisects the city. The six paths corresponding to the narratives recounted in the chapter appear in dashed lines.

Illustration: Pavlina Platonos, 2015. Reproduced with permission of the illustrator.

1 Re-imaginings of a half-city: tags and stencils, 2010–2012

1.1 Occupy everything[3]

Date: Saturday, 15 October 2011

Path: Paphos Gate to Ledras barricade

> He entered the Walled City by Paphos Gate, turned left at the Castegliotissa, and hurried down Agiou Maronos street. He caught a glimpse of the two old men sitting outside the Maronite coffee shop – the same two old men that were always sitting outside the Maronite coffee shop – as they turned their heads toward him. They moved like some sort of ancient mechanical statues in an always-unfolding historical play.

He smiled. He took a tight turn. His bicycle flew through the narrow alley. Head first, he crash-landed on a dumpster in the middle of the street.

Maronites (Levantine Christians), Armenians and Latins (Cypriot Catholics) are, in addition to Turkish Cypriots, the other minorities officially recognized in the constitution of Cyprus. Prior to the division of Nicosia, and since mediaeval times, their religious and cultural core was the western edge of the Walled City, near the Porta San Domenico, the later Paphos Gate.[4] The Armenians have since been driven away from their area (north of the Buffer Zone), while the Catholic Cathedral of the Holy Cross and the adjoining embassy of the Vatican, both within the Buffer Zone, are still in use following special permission. The Maronite church, school and cultural centre are still in use, just south of the BZ, on Agiou Maronos Street.

He wasn't hurt. He sat on the pavement. Bathed in the warm, afternoon light, the dumpster was glowing. 'The treasure is found!' he thought.

Completely spray-painted in gold, and with the city's logo untouched at the centre, the dumpster had the words 'All that glitters is not gold' stencilled exactly where he hit his head. It wasn't one of his, but he would find whoever did this and shake their hand.

Figure 8.2 Unknown artist. ReCiproCity (tag) below Nicosia Municipal logo. Dumpster at Agiou Myrona Street.

Photograph: Panos Leventis, 2015.

Looking around, he thought: 'Spot-on!'
The freshly painted buildings and the shiny, renovated windows created a
welcoming backdrop.

The Nicosia Municipality logo features a white dove enclosed within a simplified version of the walled city plan, with eight (rather than the actual eleven) blue bastions and respective moats on a gold background. It is often stuck or stencilled onto urban furniture belonging to the Municipality (Figure 8.2).[5] Meanwhile, tags and stencil graffiti, often with political subjects, (re)-appeared in Nicosia during the months leading to the 2004 referendum on a UN-proposed solution to the Cyprus Problem and the country's accession to the European Union.[6]

Post-1974 urban renewal in the Walled City was initiated under the Nicosia Master Plan (NMP), a project dating to the late 1970s. Following a bi-communal initiative where the *two* mayors of Nicosia (south and north) reached an agreement to unify the city's sewage infrastructure, the NMP was created and approved in the 1980s as a larger project targeting residential, cultural and commercial areas within the Walled City for renovation and redevelopment.[7] The aim was to bring back inhabitants and visitors who had for years remained away from the Walled City, fearful of the BZ and the physical closeness to the conflict. During the 1990s, the first areas targeted were Chrysalyniotissa (south of the BZ) and Arab Ahmet (north of the BZ); pedestrianizations of, and adjoining, Ledra Street (north and south) followed, succeeded by rehabilitation of cultural cores around the Augustinian Church/Omeriye Mosque (south) and Saint Sophia Cathedral/ Selimiye Mosque (north) in the 2000s.[8]

The peace and tranquillity that surrounded him seemed picture perfect. But
he knew that it was nothing but a stage.
What the façades hid was what this place had been for decades, and what
this place still was: A place of pain and desolation. Behind the paint lay the
ruins of war, unused for as long as he could remember.
Well, except for cats and UN soldiers – that's who strolled the rubble and
the barricades. This was not construction. This was destruction.

The NMP has remained less successful in its treatment of areas adjacent to the BZ. Here, the plan's gentrifying projects were not reintroducing uses into targeted areas. By simply repainting building façades and having the BZ in the back remain a wasteland, the process was rather altering *perceptions* of the BZ. It became less of a project to revitalize an urban area, and more of an attempt to make it appear less threatening by erasure, by suppressing realities of conflict and division. Stencils that appeared in the western area of the walled city and read 'All That Glitters Is Not Gold', 'Cyprus Cola' (Figure 8.3a), and 'Under Destruct Experimental Project' (Figure 8.3b) echo this interpretation, calling on city dwellers immersed in this staged urban landscape to fall back to reality and to act so that this reality can be altered.

Figure 8.3 Unknown artists. **(**a) Cyprus Cola (stencil). Eleftherias Street, Nicosia; (b)
 Under Destruct [. . .] Experimental Project (stencil). Granikou Street, Nicosia.

Photographs: Panos Leventis, 2015.

His head still hurt, but he had to hurry to meet the others. They were probably already at the Ledras Crossing. He hadn't been able to meet them earlier at the demonstration – he had to be there now, at least. Their plan, sort-of a plan is what they had, was to take over the Crossing today, maybe again on the following Saturday, and perhaps in two weeks as well. Someone had proposed that they refuse to leave, set up tents and 'Occupy' the Buffer Zone. 'Occupy!' Yes. He had agreed, without hesitation.

This dead place had always been haunted by armies and occupiers. They would bring back some real life to it. He grabbed the bicycle, hopped on, and flew off.

Ledras, the Walled City's most commercial artery, is a 1-km-long long street that connects Eleftherias Square, outside the Walls in the south, with the Ledras barricade/crossing in the BZ and the Locmaci Caddesi barricade/crossing in the north. The barricade, along with the rest of the Green Line, was established in 1963 after intercommunal conflicts, and manned by UN soldiers. Following the 1974 invasion, occupation and division of the city, the barricade was sealed and became a roadblock into which one could peek and see UN soldiers and BZ desolation. In 1998, as part of the NMP, Ledras, along with Onasagorou Street to its east, was pedestrianized in a move designed to bring back leisure and entertainment uses to the Walled City. On 23 April 2008, following an agreement between Cyprus, authorities in the north, and the United Nations, the barricade became a crossing – the fifth one on the island, the third in metropolitan Nicosia, and the first in the Walled City.[9]

Echoing the stencil themes mentioned above, the protest movement Occupy Buffer Zone (OBZ) took place in Nicosia between fall 2011 and spring 2012. OBZ protestors, Greek and Turkish Cypriot 'children' of the global Occupy Movement, called for a solution to the division of Nicosia and Cyprus, and raised their voices in solidarity with the global Occupy Movement in its cause for a more just socio-economic system; the OBZ began on 15 October 2011 with a weekly takeover of the BZ between the Ledras and Locmaci barricades, and became a permanent inhabitation of the BZ in that area as of 19 November. Following a police raid on 6 April 2012, the movement lost its momentum, and had effectively ended by June 2012.[10]

1.2 Blow up!

Date: Wednesday, 11 July 2012

Path: Stoa Papadopoulou to Faneromenis barricade

The morning seemed unusually hot, and the coffee unusually bitter. He sipped it, unbearably slowly, out of the small cup. Around him, the young crowd that filled the tables of the Stoa Papadopoulou did the same. 'How can they tolerate so much hair in this weather?' His tongue and mouth felt dry. A drop of sweat fell on the wooden table. 'More water, please.'

Across from him, a pair of dice kept hitting the backgammon board. The
sound hit the porous stones of the walls and echoed in his head. It felt as if
he hadn't moved from that chair in weeks. What was he doing here, anyway?

Two blocks south of the Ledras Crossing, on the street's east side, an opening
leads into Stoa Papadopoulou, a narrow space between two wings of the same-
named building, which itself extends into a pedestrianized alley that connects
Ledras to Faneromeni Church and Street. This alley, part of the 1998 pedestrianizations, acquired new uses in the mid 2000s with the opening of coffee shops
and stores catering to alternative crowds that do not necessarily belong to the
consumer-oriented developments that the NMP perhaps had in mind for the area.
By the end of the 2000s, this mini block had acquired the character of an urban
resistance node. As gentrification and neoliberal processes transformed the area
with the addition of minimalist tavernas, wine bars and design stores, the Stoa
Papadopoulou–Faneromeni enclave added its own coffee shops, crafts and comic
book stores, and held its own cultural and activist events, with frequent calls for
protests and demonstrations.[11]

The proliferation of political stencils in the Walled City reached a climax during
2011–2012, in the aftermath of not only OBZ events, but also the worsening
national and international financial/debt 'crisis'. Adding insult to injury, the
destructive explosion at the Florakis Naval base (11 July 2011), an event that,
beyond human loss and suffering (13 dead and 62 injured), cost an estimated 2.8
billion US dollars, more than 10 per cent of the country's GDP. While the intense
gentrification process that the area is undergoing might appear to hinder the study
of stencil themes and application sites within Nicosia, the buildings along Stoa
Papadopoulou stubbornly resist their erasure, still bear witness to that time, and
fuse architecture, urban fabric, graffiti and street art into a narrative of a past that
is recent but unwelcome to the national collective.

Two sets of hands reached out from the wall next to him. He rubbed his face
to clear the sweat. The two starving, begging children faced a smiling,
beautiful woman, seated by a small table and having a coffee. She was about
to be joined by an also smiling young man who was approaching her table.
They were all stencilled right behind his chair, his small table and his coffee.
    Everyone around him looked like they were having a good time, just like
the woman in the stencil. What were they doing here, anyway?

A study of the stencils on the walls of this area yields an initial thematic
breakdown into three categories: first, the broader socio-political and/or lifestyle
commentary, maintaining the critical stance on current contexts and developments;
second, the overtly political, paying tribute to the most significant legacy of the
art of stencil; and third, the advertorial-commercial, which appears to try to
capture attention for self-proclaimed 'alternative' or 'avant-garde' social events
via stencils. In the first category one finds the 2014 'Penguin Mafia' stencil by
the artist SYD, perhaps a reference to the country's political system, the general

Figure 8.4 Blind [204 Crew]. Smiling adults and begging children (stencil). Nicosia, Stoa Papadopoulou.

Photograph: Panos Leventis, 2015.

social textual commentary 'Why Are You Wearing A Cage', and a powerful (though already buffed) visual by the artist Blind of 204 Crew that features a smiling woman sitting at a café and sipping her coffee, confronted by the ghostly images of two starving children that reach out their hands to beg for help (Figure 8.4).

> *Exactly one year to this day since the explosion, and no one was held accountable. Everyone remained in the dark. It was as if electricity never returned to Nicosia, as if no one bothered to switch the lights back on. Nine months since their first move into the Buffer Zone, and three months since they were brutally kicked out by their own police, and no one was held accountable.*
>
> *Everyone around him, all the so-called and self-styled revolutionaries of Nicosia, having a good fucking time, and not a single one held themselves accountable.*

In the second category one finds the stencil that features a Cyprus map featuring the Florakis Naval Base explosion, and below the word 'Katastrofias' (Figure 8.5a), a synthesis of 'catastrophe' and the last name of Cyprus' President (Christofias) during the fateful event of July 2011. Further east, stencils comment on the rise of the extreme right and the subsequent resistance to it, with versions of the 'Antifa[scist]' slogan and a depiction of a witch stirring up the Nazi swastika in her pot.

Figure 8.5 Unknown artists. Stoa Papadopoulou, Nicosia. (a) 'Katastrofias' (stencil);
(b) 'xorko.com' (stencil).

Photographs: Panos Leventis, 2015.

These stencils should be seen in the context of not only the OBZ movement, but also the rising wave of protests of 2012–13, either originating or ending at the heart of the Walled City, in the vicinity of the BZ at the Faneromeni area: demonstrations for solidarity with the victims of the 2011 explosion, against the feeling of non-accountability of the political system in relation to that event, for workers' rights, against the rise of the extreme right, against austerity and neoliberal policies overhauling the post-1970s socio-economic status quo, for demilitarizing Nicosia, against the city's division, etc. Remaining stencils around the Faneromeni area are a historical proof and fading archive of these events and voices.

> *How did this happen? Where were their dreams for this place? Where were their hopes for a better future? The void inside him was larger this morning. He had nothing left to give to these people, nothing left to give to this city. He got up and pushed his bicycle forward. He turned the corner and walked slowly towards the barricade. 'Berlin Wall Number 2,' he read on the wall.*
>
> *Into the void he disappeared.*

In the third category belong stencils that, among others, advertise music festivals such as 'xorko.com' (Figure 8.5b), for the summer festival held in 2012 and 2013), parties such as 'ZoGiaRomanzo' (organized by *klubd* on 12 August 2012), or dance events such as '3 Sept./Backroom/Ms. Lefki/Jonathan Reyes' (organized by Backroom Club on 3 September 2013). In their use of stencil, choice of sites and execution of this process as an advertising strategy, these businesses and teams evidence the adaptability of a market and a system that often knows how to subvert calls for resistance to it by masking itself in the resistance's own 'skin' in order to materialize its goals.

Meanwhile, exactly in front of the BZ barricade of Faneromenis Street lies a little taverna and kebab house called 'Berlin Wall Number 2'. Despite evident differences in the spatial politics and physical configurations, parallels between Nicosia and Berlin as divided cities existed for decades, especially in the 1970s and 1980s. Following the reunification of Berlin, Nicosia adopted the slogan 'Europe's Last Divided Capital', which it uses to this day.[12]

2 Crisis and the production of public space: street art, 2013

2.1 *Where soldiers go to paint*

Date: Wednesday, 2 January 2013

Path: Faneromeni parking structure to Eptanisou barricade

> *He gazed out of the large windows of 'The Weaving Mill' into the afternoon sky. Dark clouds gathered above, and strange crowds gathered below, filling*

the ramp across the street. Where were the cars? His holidays were over. The New Year was already here. Unlike the world outside, his glass of milk with rose syrup shone a bright pink. Next to it, the pink pages of the paper paled by comparison. The news was depressing. Rumours at the bank persisted. He had been working at that bank since the day he returned to Cyprus – already fifteen years. Could this really be the last year the bank even existed? He looked out of the window again. What were those kids doing across the street?

By the end of 2012, and in the context of the European and Greek debt and financial crisis, Cyprus faced multiple challenges to the survival of its post-1974 socio-economic system. Still, street life within the Walls of Nicosia and along the Buffer Zone continued: on 2 January 2013, a group of musicians and producers called *Sirius Productions Cy*, with the support of Nicosia Municipality, organized a 'Skates, Graffiti, Roots and Dub Sessions' event. It took place in the public parking structure under the athletics field of the Faneromeni Secondary School, one block from the BZ, just south of the middle of the Walled City. It was titled 'Love In The City'. The structure remained off-limits to cars for 24 hours.[13]

Love in the City gave a small taste of similar festivals organized for years in two coastal cities: Limassol's 'Street Life' festival, the island's largest, and the more modest 'LarnaCan' in Larnaca, with support from respective Municipalities, public agencies and private sponsors, introduced street art to urban fabrics and publics for the last decade. Street Life, organized annually since 2007, has become a part of urban life in Limassol, transforming neighbourhoods into areas of active participation and sharing. By 2014, it was the most attended outdoor public event in Cyprus. LarnaCan ran annually between 2010 and 2013 and had as sites Larnaca parking lots. By contrast, the authorities in Nicosia appeared at best hesitant. In a post-event announcement, the Municipality felt a need to give the reasoning for its active support of Love In The City: namely, the event aimed to 'improve the aesthetics' of the area, 'beautify' and give it a 'pleasant note'.[14]

He looked at his wife, immersed in her tablet universe. After all these years, she was still trying to get used to living in such a small city, in such a small country. Their baby daughter was playing with a doll on the large couch by the window. How would he care for her if he lost his job?

The street was by now full with crowds of youngsters. Anxiety overtook him. 'I need to get out. I'll be back soon.' His wife looked up, and shrugged her shoulders. His daughter didn't hear him. He opened the door in a hurry.

The crowd outside wasn't better: Noise, skating, loud music. Someone was drawing a plump baby face on the parking structure elevator. Still, the persistent sadness of the area filled the street.

Most of the area whose 'aesthetics' were to be 'improved' by the event was not directly within the urban fabric, but rather comprised of tag-riddled walls and

Figure 8.6 Paparazzi. 'I (Heart) You' (mural), 2013. Faneromenis parking structure, Lefkonos Street.

Photograph: Panos Leventis, 2015.

columns of the parking structure's first underground level. The event did nevertheless become somewhat of a public spectacle, particularly because of graffiti crews and street artists working on the structure's ramp and elevator, visible from Lefkonos Street. *Sirius Productions* invited the Limassol-based artist Achilleas Michaelides (a.k.a. Paparazzi) to create a piece as part of Love In The City, in order to 'up' the name brand of the event. Paparazzi, involved with street art in Thessaloniki (Greece) and Limassol, worked on the elevator shaft of the Faneromeni parking structure (Figure 8.6). Paparazzi had moved to Limassol in the 2000s, maintained an art studio, and became featured artist in a number of exhibitions. Via his recognizable and arguably unthreatening representational style, Paparazzi became widely known in Limassol. By 2013 he was working in Walled Nicosia, not only for Love In The City, but also on a piece in Stoa Papadopoulou, and on a large mural on Pythonos Street, four blocks south of the Faneromeni parking structure.[15]

> *He headed north towards the buffer zone. There was hardly anyone ever there. The walk, the cold air, the solitude, they would do him good. In no time, he found himself along a deserted street. 'Lidinis' read a crooked street sign.*

By now he couldn't see very well. The sun had already set. There was a café by the side of the barricade at the street's end. A café? Here? It was not open. The streetscape and the ruined buildings glimmered their last rays of daylight. The flags above the soldier post flapped in the cool breeze. He was not alone.

A kneeling silhouette was painting brightly coloured faces on the barricade. Was that a soldier? He stopped and surprised himself by asking, boldly: 'What are you doing?'

About 100 metres north of the Faneromeni parking structure lies the Christofidi barricade at the BZ; a further 200 metres east, following the BZ, at the corner with Lidinis Street, lies the Eptanisou Street barricade. The Eptanisou barricade and an adjoining roof wall structure bear two pieces by Cacao Rocks (Figure 8.7), executed in January and February 2013,[16] during a multi-month sojourn on the island as part of his military service in the Greek army. Cacao, who later that year proclaimed 'all graffiti and street art is a political action and an effort for communication', also said that through his work he is only 'try[ing] to change our environment and the city landscape' and that he 'first sees the *place* and then thinks of the *piece*'.[17]

Without turning, the silhouette answered: 'What do you think I am doing? Making my friends a little happier. Making this city a little happier. Making this city whole.' Those were the only words they exchanged. Time stood still while he watched the colours unfold until they covered the ruins of the barricade.

He simply said 'Thank You' and walked back into his life. He entered 'The Mill' with a wide smile on his face.

The *place* of Cacao's two colourful pieces, next to, and above, his favourite *Café Haratsi*, underwent intense gentrification during 2014–15, which included the repainting of all of Lidinis and Eptanisou streets' building façades. In spite of that, as of summer 2015, the two pieces, though fading in the harsh Nicosia sun, still 'claim' this corner of the city, reminders of Cacao's sojourn, the *Haratsi*, and the area's earlier era.

Cacao returned to Cyprus in November of 2014, this time not as a soldier: along with other international and Cypriot street artists, he was invited to take part in the first International Ayia Napa Street Art Festival by Paparazzi, who curated the event. Sponsored by the Municipality of the same-named, over-developed tourist resort, the festival targeted blank walls and aging buildings in key locations in order to provide a face-lift to the town's infrastructure and bring about some visual (if not urban) renewal. While in Ayia Napa, Cacao blogged a moving piece titled '322', reminiscing his Nicosia sojourn, adding context and reconfirming his connection to the *place*, people and locations of his Buffer Zone pieces.[18]

Figure 8.7 Cacao Rocks. Untitled works, 2013. (a) Lidinis Street 31–37 (rooftop), Nicosia; (b) Eptanisou street barricade, Nicosia.

Photographs: Panos Leventis, 2015.

2.2 I am the square

Date: Saturday, 1 June 2013

Path: Dimarcheias Square to Talou barricade

> *It was five months – on that cold evening back in January – since the last time he walked the same streets. Five months since his anxiety attack at the 'Mill' and the subsequent street art soldier encounter that reassured him. Five months that had torn his world apart. His worse fears had come true. As of last month, he had no job – the bank did not exist anymore.*
>
> *As of last week, his wife had no job either – her company filed for bankruptcy. His parents' pensions suffered deep cuts; their failing health was deteriorating quickly. They had discussed, time and again, the possibility of leaving the country. Where would they go? Who would care for his parents? And what about the kids' schools and friends? Earlier that evening, the discussion ended with a fight.*

In 2013 Cyprus found itself immersed in the centre of the global financial and debt crisis that originated in 2008–2009. Cypriot banks' exposure to Greek debt proved fateful for their survival, especially following the 2012 Greek debt 'haircut'. The state had to assume the debts of private banks, in order to avoid a complete meltdown of the financial system, and thus found itself with unsustainable amounts of (now) public debt. This led to the March 2013 assuming of a 10 billion euro loan and the signing of a 'memorandum' by Cyprus and its lenders, similar to ones already signed by Greece, Ireland, Portugal and Spain between 2010 and 2012. The terms of this memorandum meant heavy fiscal austerity for the state, and the end of the welfare state in the form that Cypriots had become used to in the post-1974 decades of economic development.

> *He called a friend and asked to meet for a drink. His friend was leaving soon for some party. He wouldn't go – what was a 'Party In The Street' anyway? The friend insisted. 'It starts at 7. It's at the Talou Street Barricade. You have no idea where that is, do you? I'll send you the map.' 'But a party at a buffer zone barricade?'*
>
> *It was already past 8. He was late. He reached in his pocket and unfolded the printed directions. Another street he had never walked before. Another turn he had never taken. Another barricade he had never faced. He had to lose himself, to forget himself.*
>
> *He didn't have to follow directions to find it: music and people became his guide. As the crowd thickened, his mood changed. He turned onto Talou Street and was immediately transported back to his college years. Memories mixed with hopes and desires: DJs, music, dancing, an outdoor bar, food stands, groups of friends and laughter. He didn't have to be persuaded anymore. He joined in.*

On Saturday, 1 June 2013, the Nicosia-based urban free-press project *Avant-Garde* organized a street party in celebration of their three years of existence. They chose to hold Party In The Street on Talou Street, an offshoot of Tritonos Street that once continued north into Ermou, Nicosia's commercial 'Main', now found within, and running parallel to, the BZ. The unmanned, deserted barricade blocking anyone on Talou Street from continuing north was to become a focus of social celebration, a site for a collective, public, urban process.[19]

> *A few drinks later, he still hadn't found his friend. In fact, he never searched for his friend. The rhythm and the beat carried him like a wave back in time. He wasn't tall. He couldn't see above the crowd. Only swaying bodies around him. He hadn't spotted where the DJs played out of, and neither had he looked at the wall on the east side of the street, next to the barricade, until he heard someone speak of it. He made his way through the crowd, and stood, frozen, in front of the wall. The piece was being finished as he watched. The moustached old man was reading a newspaper and commanding a sense of absolute tranquillity and reassurance.*

As part of Party In The Street, the organizers invited a street artist to work on-site and real-time, and 'contribute' a piece to the festivities. By extending this invitation to Twenty Three, a Larnaka-based artist who works with a hybrid of stencil, paste-up and painting techniques, the organizers, perhaps unknowingly so, added another urban narrative to the story of their party: on the side wall of the abandoned building east of the barricade, Twenty Three, who has described his work as 'a social critique on the post-war period of Cyprus',[20] created a piece depicting a seated old man reading a newspaper (Figure 8.8).

Avant Garde had run an interview with Twenty Three two weeks before Party In The Street: The journalist met Twenty Three in Limassol. As part of Street Life festival, Twenty Three had created a street art piece there, a 'precursor', or a 'twin' to the Talou piece, depicting an old, graceful Cypriot grandmother with an ample laughter. In the interview, Twenty Three discussed the difficulties of making street art in Cyprus, spoke of the island's conservatism and identity crisis, explained the process of stencil graffiti, and mentioned that his work revolves around the *tetraptych* 'thought, creativity, imagination, respect'.[21]

> *The music and the crowd faded. He moved even further back in time. He was a child in a peaceful village square. The war was a painful past. Adulthood and any new crises were unknown futures, nowhere to be seen. Only the village square existed, and this old man was sitting in its centre. Reading the newspaper, chatting with other elders. And he, an innocent child, ran, played and enjoyed himself along with the other children. This was the Nicosia he always searched for, the Cyprus he always wished he still lived in: simpler, happier, and nowhere to be found.*
>
> *Nowhere, except in front of that barricade wall.*

Figure 8.8 Twenty Three. Untitled, 2013. Talou Street Barricade, Nicosia.
Photograph: Panos Leventis, 2015.

While the festivities have long disappeared from Talou Street, *Avant-Garde* continues to celebrate its 'birthday' in Walled Nicosia: The fifth version of the event took place on Saturday, 9 May 2015, and was hosted in the spacious modernist building that during the day houses Nicosia's Farmers Market, adjacent to the city's new city hall, currently under construction.[22] Nearby, the piece by Twenty Three has weathered the façade renovations and 'sanitization' of the area, which has surprisingly spared the work from buffing, and calls on the occasional passer-by to pause, to 'remain' at the site, to claim the forgotten street and the barricade as an integral part of the city, as integral to Nicosia and to Cyprus as the old Cypriot male figure that the work depicted certainly is.[23]

3 Possible cities: Nicosia-themed graffiti and murals, 2014

3.1 Names, shapes and walls

Date: Wednesday, 22 October 2014

Path: Cyprus Technical Chamber to Famagusta Gate

> *She pushed the door of the Technical Chamber with her elbow and exited into the courtyard in a hurry. She was tired. Her hands were full of documents, her purse, her sunglasses, her phone. Her keys. Where were her keys? Oh, here they were.*

Fortunately, she decided to pay her licence dues today, or she would not have known about the lecture. She walked and read the invitation with excitement. Her mentor from Architecture School in the Netherlands was in Cyprus. He was to speak that same evening on the City, on centres and limits. Her schedule was full for the day, for the week, for the rest of forever, but she would attend, of course. Had he been to Nicosia before? What would he say to his famous ex-student for her new design of Nicosia's main square? Would he congratulate or critique her? Had he seen this city's 'centres and limits'?

Architectural culture, in Cyprus and in Nicosia, has flourished since the early 1980s, with numerous large scale national architectural competitions and resulting buildings, and has further been aided by the creation of the Technical Chamber (1990) and the inauguration of three Schools of Architecture in Nicosia between 2000 and 2010. The resulting multitude of lectures, exhibitions and symposia resulted in an increased awareness of architectural and urban culture by the public. A decision to award the remaking of Eleftherias Square, Nicosia's best approximation to a public plaza, located just south of the walls, to internationally known architect Zaha Hadid, and the subsequent saga of the project's ongoing construction, has been at the forefront of debates on urban space in the city.

She looked up. There was Nicosia, in all its history and faded glory, on the wall. It was already a decade since she attended the inauguration of that mural, already a decade since the inauguration of the Technical Chamber's renovated buildings. So much of the city had changed since then. So much of their lives had changed. She left the courtyard and turned right onto the street.

Commissioned and non-commissioned street art in Nicosia *about* Nicosia have almost always included either textual references to the city's name, or representational references to its eleven-bastioned renaissance walls. The formal strength of the fortifications plan is such that it has found its way onto emblems, seals and logos of a host of public and private organizations, all claiming familiarity, legitimization and authority via the city's plan.[24]

Muralists and street artists have followed a similar path. During the early 2000s, at a time when renovations edged closer to the BZ, the Technical Chamber (ETEK) renovated an old mansion (and unfortunately demolished two smaller structures) at the west end of Thisseos Street in the Walled City in order to house its headquarters. ETEK, along with the British Council, commissioned the artist Farhad Nargol O'Neill to design and execute a mural on the blind side wall of the Technical Chamber's Cultural Centre. Titled 'Constructing the Past' and unveiled on 6 April 2004, the mural features a series of graphics illustrating narratives and episodes from Nicosia's history, all within or edging out of a large plan of its Walls (Figure 8.9).[25]

Figure 8.9 Farhad Nargol O' Neill. 'Constructing the Past' (mural). 2004. Thisseos
    Street, Nicosia.

Photograph: Panos Leventis, 2015.

*She called a friend who had attended the same school. Surely she knew.
'Architecture and the City!' she shouted. 'What? I can't hear you.' 'Weak
signal.' 'Are you in the old city again?'*

*A car sped down the narrow street and hit her arm. The phone flew out of
her hand and landed in a flowerpot in the middle of a yard on her left. The
driver did not slow down.*

*She stood and looked at the car as it disappeared at the street's turn. 'The
bastards confused Thisseos with a highway.' On her right, the perimeter wall
of the high school, her old high school, sported some graffiti with 'Nicosia'
written across a large glob. A glob would have been useful. The city should
take its revenge on the unending sea of cars.*

Thisseos is a 350-metre-long and 3-metre-wide street that leads from the BZ to
Famagusta Gate. During the last twenty years, its humble residential fabric has
been altered significantly, with demolitions at both its west (Technical Chamber
renovations and parking lots), and east (demolitions by the Pancyprian Gymnasium
to increase its yard size). Simultaneously, pedestrianization and gentrification of
neighbouring areas have resulted in increased traffic on Thisseos, prohibiting
pedestrian activity or neighbourhood social life. Citizens formed groups calling

Figure 8.10 (a) Tano. Untitled (signature graffiti). Thisseos Street, Nicosia;
(b) Lympourouthkia. Thisseos Street (mural). Thisseos Street, Nicosia.

Photographs: Panos Leventis, 2015.

for renewed attention to urban issues facing the area. The group Awake Within The Walls started the blog 'Close Thisseos' in 2009, while the group Ariadne's Thread organized the three-day Thisseos Festival in April–May of 2010, with a goal 'to reclaim public space for the citizens and residents'.[26] In the last few years, a number of artists and crews have claimed the Pancyprian Gymnasium's perimeter walls that face Thisseos. One of the latest pieces is by Tano, bearing a rare 'Nicosia' tag with a glob (Figure 8.10a), and it can be read within the specific context of the school, the narrow width of Thisseos, or the competition of taggers to 'claim' this prime site.[27]

> *Her arm was okay. She was okay. She calmed down. The question now was how she would get her phone back, saved as it miraculously was by a flowerpot. The chicken wire and bamboo fence separating the yard from the street was high, and the metal door was locked. She asked, knocked, yelled. No one was home. The adjoining lot was empty, and the fence lower. She jumped in and grabbed the muddy phone. She looked up.*
>
> *Above the flowerpot, completely covering the house wall, stood another Nicosia, complete with its bastions, a fiddler, and an army of ants. Blacks and mauves swirled and twisted, and her tired eyes shut for a second. She sat on a dirty chair and stared at the wall. The city and its walls were lullabied to a peaceful, mid-day siesta by the sweet sound of violins. She fell asleep.*

The 'Thisseos Street' mural with Nicosia's Walls and the fiddler (Figure 8.10b), created in May of 2010 by a group who signed as 'Lympourouthkia' (little ants), is a product, a reflection, and a historic trace of the 2009–2010 time of mobilization for the future of the neighbourhood. Beyond the two Nicosia-themed murals and Tano's tag on Thisseos Street, a host of street art examples showcase the plan of Nicosia's fortifications: from the 'Cyprus Cola' stencil,[28] to the restrooms above the Feneromenis Parking Structure on Aischylou Street, and even as an abstract logo accompanying an anarchist call to arms, sprayed on a wall of Othellou Street at the Famagusta Gate area.

3.2 No way out

Date: Tuesday, 9 December 2014

Path: Famagusta Gate to corner of Makariou &
Stasandrou streets

> *She wanted to see the play for weeks, and this was her final chance: closing show, the coming Saturday. She left the theatre ticket box and walked toward her car. She had parked across from Famagusta Gate. She had to hurry back to the office.*
>
> *At least two projects waited, one for permit submission, and one for conceptual design. She would have been so excited had the times been*

different, but she had little energy to give. Still, she took them on. She could not refuse, not with such little new work. Construction supervision at the mountain house was constantly on her mind too, she had cancelled twice already. The clients were not amused. At least, she had tickets to the play.

The area around the renaissance Porta del Proveditore, the later Famagusta Gate, at the east end of the Walled City, was a rare exception to the post-invasion urban landscape of Nicosia: Though it was not far from the buffer zone, already by the early 1980s it hosted a number of cultural and entertainment venues, restaurants, theatres and cafés. Though the fortunes of some of those have varied through the years, the area has retained, if not strengthened, its mixed uses and lively character.

She got in her car, and turned the engine on. What was the Bishop doing in front of her? 'Our Godfather, our Brando, less sexy but even more scheming!' she thought. Even during the collapse of everything around them, the life and times of some were as good as they had ever been. She gave a sarcastic and angry smile at the wall, put the gear into reverse, and left the Bishop behind in a thick cloud of dust.

Figure 8.11 Nemesis. *The Godfather*, 2014 (stencil). Ammochostou street side-wall at Famagusta Gate.

Photograph: Panos Leventis, 2015.

The Limassol-based street artist Nemesis, who works primarily with stencils, created *The Godfather* in Nicosia during autumn 2014, on a sidewall bordering a parking lot across from Famagusta Gate (Figure 8.11). *The Godfather* features the black and white logo from Coppola's film poster of 1972, but in place of Marlon Brando, Nemesis placed the current Archbishop of Cyprus, Chrysostomos II. While the rich and powerful Church of Cyprus often commands a mix of awe and envy among ordinary Cypriots, the Archbishop's style and controversial views on socio-political issues made him a central figure in private and public discussions during the post-2008 context of crisis. Beyond Nemesis, other street artists have also depicted the Archbishop as a new Don Corleone, a powerful, rich figure who defies most forms of state and social control: a piece by Blind titled 'Church Co.' has him wearing a medallion with a large Euro sign, in Noa's 'Euro blessings' he sports a halo made of a euro coin, while Twenty Three has him relaxing in the jacuzzi that he reportedly ordered for Nicosia's Archbishopric.

Nemesis' themes and approach to street art as a visual–political medium echo contemporary work carried out in other cities where the financial crisis has become a catalyst for numerous and significant socio-political changes: in Barcelona, in Berlin, and particularly in Athens, where the work of a number of artists 'claims' urban space for a visual and political commentary on current events.[29]

She exited the Walls, and at the first traffic light she changed her mind. The Bishop had reminded her: No, she would not return to her office. Instead, she would attend the Street Art lecture at the Pop-Up Festival on Makariou Avenue. The University had a great schedule for that week and she wanted to see all the presentations. As for Makariou Avenue, well that was another story – nothing could revive that place for now.

The 2-km-long Makariou Avenue starts south of the Walls at D'Avila Bastion and leads to the southern suburbs. Between the 1970s and 2000s, Makariou was the city's primary commercial artery, with numerous businesses thriving along its course. A series of events changed this situation: the creation of large suburban malls, renovation of areas within the Walled City, and, finally, the post-2008 financial crisis, left Makariou largely empty. Its section closer to the Walled City has suffered the most. The Municipality announced initiatives that attempted to bring back some urban life to the street. The Nicosia Pop-Up festival, organized in 2013 and 2014, was arguably one of the most successful, using empty Makariou stores as venues for a month-long cultural itinerary.[30]

The semester was ending, the holidays approached. She had many things to take care of between now and then, before she could begin to think about kids out of school, presents, trees and parties. At the University, they asked for more of her time, energy and dedication, and offered fewer things in return. 'Part-Time', said her contract, 'Slave Labour' it should have read. But she loved the teaching and the students, and needed the extra income. The dove of peaceful days, of hard work, and of good pay for all, had flown far away.

To Poullin Epetasen ('The bird has flown away'), a stencil that appeared as early as 2009 in many locations in Nicosia (including a boarded-up door on Thisseos Street) is reportedly a creation of the artist Noa. Another commentary on the post-2008 situation on the island, it features the logo of the Republic of Cyprus, showing a white dove carrying an olive branch with the year 1960 (independence), but in this case the dove flies away from the rest of the logo.[31]

> *She parked the car with two tyres on the sidewalk. She missed the beginning of the talk. She would miss the end too – she had to go and pick up her daughter. She crossed the street diagonally, to save time, and saw her. The young lady with the Mona-Lisa smile and the traditional Cypriot dress was pasted right in front of the Street Art lecture venue, on a grey power cable box at the crossroads. It took a second before she recognized who Miss 'Me Yet' was. Yes, she probably did miss her.*

Miss Me Yet is one of the most popular designs of street artist Romeotees, who founded the same-named company in 2007. He manages the company, designs

Figure 8.12 Romeotees. *Miss Me Yet*, 2014 (paste up). Makariou Avenue, Nicosia.
Photograph: Panos Leventis, 2015.

shirts that 'represent Cypriots', and also 'draws on canvas and sprays on walls'. *Miss Me Yet* shows the young woman, dressed in traditional attire, who adorned Cyprus' one-pound banknote (Figure 8.12). The words 'Miss Me Yet', a play on 'Miss' and the young lady, refers to the post-crisis context and the romanticizing of pre-2008 times when Cyprus, with a strong currency, was not part of the mismanaged Eurozone project. The design also appeared, in late 2014, as a wheat-paste on the corner of Makariou Avenue and Stasandrou Street.[32]

Romeotees mentions that the project with the Cypriot dialect and visuals-inspired work is largely a result of the post-2013 context, a general wish for a return to a 'local[ized] culture', and a need for a redefinition of the identity of Cypriots, following the collapse of the lifestyle-driven culture of the past decades.[33] *Miss Me Yet* and its site, in the context of the de-commercialization of Makariou, impressed passers-by and visitors to the Nicosia Pop-Up Festival, hosted in the surrounding empty commercial properties in December 2014.[34]

Notes

1   Cyprus, an Ottoman province since 1571, was rented to the British in the late 1870s and then unilaterally annexed by them during World War I. As society and culture flourished under the new colonial power, along with development came calls by the Greek Cypriot majority, already since the 1920s, for political union with Greece, with whom the majority had obvious historic, cultural and linguistic bonds. Those calls for *Enosis* (union), a word often painted on village walls, were countered in the 1950s by calls from the Turkish Cypriot minority for a partition of the island into Greek and Turkish sectors, though the population was mixed throughout. *Taksim* (partition) became the antagonistic graffiti on Cypriot walls throughout the Greek Cypriot struggle against the British in the 1950s. With 1960 came not union with Greece, but independence, given to Cypriots along with a curiously unworkable constitution.

   Divisions and mistrust between the majority and the minority grew. By 1964, following fighting between extremists from both sides, a UN force arrived to keep an uneasy peace. Many Turkish Cypriots withdrew into self-imposed enclaves throughout the island, demanding a separate administration, while others continued to live and work alongside Greek Cypriots. The heart of Nicosia, surrounded by its star-shaped, eleven-bastioned Renaissance Walls, was by now divided into a Greek Cypriot south and a Turkish Cypriot north. That division became absolute after the Turkish invasion of 1974, and the resulting ethnic cleansing of the island into a north occupied by Turkish troops and populated by Turkish Cypriots and Turkish settlers, and a south inhabited by Greek Cypriots. 160,000 Greek Cypriots and 40,000 Turkish Cypriots became refugees in their own country. The slogan *Den Xehno* (I Do Not Forget) was a prevalent political graffiti in the south following 1974, sanctioned by state authorities, and held dear by families living and dying in refugee settlements. In the north, a massive slogan was carved in the early 1980s on a mountainside facing Nicosia, for all to see and be reminded of daily. A quote by Ataturk, it reads *Ne Mutlu Türk'üm Diyene* (How happy is he who calls himself a Turk), and was accompanied by a giant flag (425 × 250 metres) of the self-styled 'Republic' set up by Turkey in the north. More than any previous example, this slogan showcased the power and psychological influence that political graffiti and street art can exert.

   By the late 1980s, life in Cyprus returned to a seemingly peaceful normality. In the south, hard work and an economic 'miracle' aided by a quickly growing service sector was erasing, at least on the surface, the invasion's deep wounds. Refugee settlements were obscured behind rising skylines and commercial boulevards. Nicosia's buffer zone ruins were unmentioned backwaters to new narratives of coastal landscapes, resorts and crowded beaches. Resistance to Turkey's ethnic cleansing and occupation were few and far between to have lasting effects on the population, especially a youth increasingly addicted to consumerism. This was to change between 1987 and the 1990s, when the movement 'Women Return' organized unannounced marches, walks to ruined villages and churches within the buffer zone across the island, only to be fought back by Turkish and UN forces. Waves of student-led protests in 1990 and again in 1996 were often accompanied by political graffiti calling for peace and an end to the occupation.

2 During the twentieth century, political graffiti was a close companion to the history of Cyprus and its capital city. For a comprehensive review of, and commentary on, slogans and graffiti in Cyprus during the twentieth century and the first decade of the twenty-first, see Stylianou (2012).

3 After the same-titled book edited by Lunghi and Wheeler (2011).

4 See Leventis (2007).

5 See www.nicosia.org.cy. Accessed: 28 September 2015.

6 For a discussion on the history of stencil graffiti in Nicosia between 2004 and 2010 see Karathanasis (2008) and (2010). The author's interpretations of historical and socio-political events in Nicosia should be consulted carefully, and with a parallel reading of other relevant texts.

7 See Editors (1987).

8 See www.undp-pff.org/index.php?option=com_content&task=view&id=80&Itemid=140. Accessed: 28 September 2015.

9 For a post-2004 reading of Nicosia see Hadjichristos (2006); for a reappraisal of the NMP and catalytic urban design processes in Nicosia see Gaffikin, Mceldowney and Sterr (2010). For a reading on the post-2008 life of Ledras Street, its changing uses and Crossing, see Theophanous (2014).

10 On the OBZ against a wider context of social justice, via a Lefebvrian 'Right to the City' discussion, see Iliopoulou and Karathnasis (2012 and 2014); on the OBZ as a performance of emplaced resistance see Antonsich (2013).

11 For gentrification, neoliberal policies and street art in post-2008 Athens see Ioannides, Leventis and Petridou (2016).

12 See www.nicosia.org.cy/en-GB/home/. Accessed: 28 September 2015.

13 See https://vimeo.com/57527989. Accessed: 28 September 2015.

14 See www.nicosia.org.cy/el-GR/news/announcements/2013/47779/. Accessed: 28 September 2015.

15 For a discussion with Paparazzi on who can claim and act in public space, within the context of the Faneromeni area, see Kades (2015).

16 See http://cacaorocks.blogspot.gr/2013_01_01_archive.html. Accessed: 28 September 2015.

17 See Cacao Rock's interview in Tulke (2013).

18 See http://cacaorocks.blogspot.gr/2014/11/blog-post.html. Accessed: 28 September 2015.

19 See http://activecyprus.com/item/nicosia/party-in-the-street/5469. Accessed: 28 September 2015. *Avant-Garde* called for a public coming-together with DJ jams, street food and corporate sponsorship 'to have a good time, to drink, to forget ourselves'. See www.facebook.com/events/599535436730915/. Accessed: 28 September 2015.

20 See www.behance.net/gallery/21110483/The-language-of-trauma. Accessed: 28 September 2015.

21 See www.avant-garde.com.cy/twenty-three/. Accessed: 28 September 2015.

22 See www.facebook.com/events/816949771732378/. Accessed: 28 September 2015.

23 More than one year after Twenty Three finished his piece on Talou Street, the theme of the work was repeated, this time by Paparazzi, during the Ayia Napa Street Festival.

Paparazzi painted the side wall of the Napa Radio Station with a saluting, smiling old man, dressed in the traditional *vraka* attire and sipping his Cyprus coffee. For this, as well as some other notable street art works from 2013–2014 around the island, see http://mycyprusinsider.com/cyprus-uncovered/street-art-in-focus-10–1-must-see-works-around-cyprus/. Accessed: 28 September 2015.

24 The fact that the city is bisected by the Buffer Zone has also found its way in, for instance, the logo of Nicosia's (failed) bid to be named the 2017 European Cultural Capital, which shows only half of the Walled City, abstracted and traversed by a number of coloured lines. See www.facebook.com/nicosia2017. Accessed: 28 September 2015.

25 See www.farhadsculpture.com/PublicWorks/Construction_Past.htm. Accessed: 28 September 2015.

26 See http://closethiseos.blogspot.gr, http://anthropofagos.blogspot.gr/2010/04/3004-01-02052010.html, and https://falies3.wordpress.com/2010/04/22/φεστιβάλ-της-οδού-θησέως/. Accessed: 28 September 2015.

27 For more Tano signatures: http://streetartcy.com/artists-2/tano/. Accessed: 28 September 2015. On the act of writing, of placing and of siting signature graffiti see Avramidis (2014) and Avramidis and Drakopoulou (2015).

28 Already mentioned, found on Eleftherias Street in the west, and also on Tempon Street in the east.

29 For Athenian street art in the context of crisis see Avramidis (2012, 2014 and 2015), Leventis (2013 and 2015), Tsilimpounidi (2012 and 2015), Tulke (2013) and Zaimakis (2015).

30 See www.nicosia.org.cy/el-GR/news/events/2014/pop-up-festival/. Accessed: 28 September 2015.

31 As of August 2015, streetartcy.com has removed Noa from its list of artists active in Cyprus, and, lacking any other information at this time, the piece's creator remains unknown. For an in-depth study and contextualization of this stencil see Karathanasis (2015).

32 See www.romeotees.com/about/ and www.romeotees.com/urban-art/. Accessed: 28 September 2015.

33 Interview to A. Georgiou in *Lifo*, available at www.lifo.gr/team/u41183/53654. Accessed: 28 September 2015.

34 For an anti-Obama 2010 billboard in the US that featured the words 'Miss Me Yet' and a waving George W. Bush see www.npr.org/sections/thetwo-way/2010/02/bush_miss_me_yet_billboard_is.html.Accessed: 28 September 2015.

References

Antonsich, Marco. 2013. ' "Occupy Border [sic] Zone": Practices of Borderline Resistance in a Space of Exception'. *Area*. 45(2): 170–178.

Avramidis, Konstantinos. 2012. ' "Live your Greece in Myths": Reading the Crisis on Athens' Walls'. Professional Dreamers, *working paper no.8*. Available at: www.professionaldreamers.net/_prowp/wp-content/uploads/Avramides-Reading-the-Crisis-on-Athens-walls-fld.pdf. Accessed: 28 September 2015.

Avramidis, Konstantinos. 2014. 'Mapping the Geographical and Spatial Characteristics of Politicized Urban Art in the Athens of Crisis'. In Tsilimpounidi, Myrto and Walsh, Aylwyn (eds). *Remapping 'Crisis': A Guide to Athens*. London: Zero Books, pp. 183–203.

Avramidis, Konstantinos. 2015. 'Reading an Instance of Contemporary Urban Iconoclash: A Design Report from Athens'. *The Design Journal*. 18(4): 513–534.

Avramidis, Konstantinos and Drakopoulou, Konstantina. 2015. 'Moving From Urban to Virtual Spaces and Back: Learning In/From Signature Graffiti Subculture'. In Jandrić, Petar and Boras, Damir (eds), *Critical Learning in Digital Networks*. New York, NY: Springer, pp. 133–160.

Cacao Rocks. 2014. '322 [Blog Entry]', November 9. Available at: http://cacaorocks. blogspot.gr/2014/11/blog-post.html. Accessed: 28 September 2015.

Editors. 1987. *Restoring the Heart of Nicosia* [On the Nicosia Master Plan]. Nicosia: United Nations Development Program.

Gaffikina, Frank, Mceldowneya, Malachy and Sterretta, Ken. 2010. 'Creating Shared Public Space in the Contested City: The Role of Urban Design'. *Journal of Urban Design*. 15(4): 493–513.

Hadjichristos, Christos. 2006. 'Cyprus: Nicosia and its D-Visions'. *Architectural Design*, 76(3): 12–19.

Iliopoulou, Eirini and Karathanasis, Pafsanias. 2012. 'From a Buffer Zone to a Common Space: The Right to the City in a Landscape of Conflict'. Paper Presented in 'The Right to the City, the Right to the State: Social Justice in War and Peace' Conference, Nicosia, 22 September. Available at: www.academia.edu/4971785. Accessed: 28 September 2015.

Iliopoulou, Eirini and Karathanasis, Pafsanias. 2014. 'Towards a Radical Politics: Grassroots Urban Activism in the Walled City of Nicosia'. *The Cyprus Review*. 26(1): 169–192.

Ioannides, Dimitri, Leventis, Panos and Petridou, Evangelia. 2016. 'Urban Resistance Tourism in Stressed Cities: The Case of Athens'. In Russo, Antonio Paolo and Richards, Greg (eds), *Reinventing the Local: Travel Communities and Peer-Produced Place Experiences*. Bristol: Channel View, pp. 229–250.

Kades, Andria. 2015. 'The Great Divide Between Art and Vandalism'. *The Cyprus Mail*. 7 June. Available at: http://cyprus-mail.com/2015/06/07/the-great-divide-between-art-and-vandalism/. Accessed: 28 September 2015.

Karathanasis, Pafsanias. 2008. 'Street Art across the "Green Line": The Geographies of Graffiti in the Walled City of Nicosia, Cyprus'. Paper Presented in 'Border Crossings Conference', Korca, 25 May. Available at: www.academia.edu/4971720. Accessed: 28 September 2015.

Karathanasis, Pafsanias. 2010. 'Official Memory and Graffiti: Meanings of the Green Line in Cyprus as a Negotiated Field of Collective Memory' [Episimi Mnimi kai Graffiti: Oi Noimatodotiseis tis Prasinis Grammis tis Kyprou os Pedio Diapragmateusis tis Koinonikis Mnimis], *Outopia*. 89: 103–125. [in Greek]

Karathanasis, Pausanias. 2015. 'Cultural Biography of Stencils: Examining Methods for the Analysis of the Multiplicity of Meanings in Activist Stencils' [Politismiki Biographia ton Stencil: Eksetazontas Methodous gia tin Alalysi tis Pollaplotitas ton Noimaton sta Activistika Stencil]. In Pourkos, Marios (ed.), *Experience and Art-Based Qualitative Research Methods: Epistemological-Methodological Issues and New Perspectives* [*Vioma kai Vasismenes stin Techni Poiotikes Methodoi Ereynas: Epistimologika-Methodologika Zitimata kai Nees Prooptikes*]. Athens: Nisides, pp. 182–203. [in Greek]

Leventis, Panos. 2007. 'Projecting Utopia: The Refortification of Nicosia, 1567–1570'. In Pérez-Gómez, Alberto and Parcell, Stephen (eds), *CHORA5: Intervals in the Philosophy of Architecture*. Montréal: McGill-Queens University Press. pp. 227–258.

Leventis, Panos. 2013. 'Walls of Crisis: Street Art and Urban Fabric in Central Athens, 2000–2012'. *Architectural Histories*. 1(1): 1–10.

Leventis, Panos. 2015. 'Visualizing the Crisis on an Urban Canvas: Two Street Artists in the Historic Center of Athens, 2008–2014'. Invited talk at the American College of Greece, Athens, 19 November.

Lunghi, Alessio and Wheeler, Seth. 2012. *Occupy Everything. Reflections on Why It's Kicking Off Everywhere*. New York: Minor Compositions.

Stylianou, Philippos. 2012. *Walls Write History: Slogans, Paintings and Graffiti in Cyprus, 1892–2012* [*Oi Toihoi Grafoun Istoria: Synthimata, Zografies kai Graffiti stin Kypro, 1892–2012*]. Nicosia: Aigaion. [in Greek]

Theophanous, Christos. 2014. 'Ledras Street: "Under Construction"'. *Greka*, 19 February. Available at: http://grekamag.gr/3555/. Accessed: 28 September 2015.

Tsilimpounidi, Myrto. 2012. 'Athens 2012: Performances "in Crisis" or what Happens when a City goes Soft?'. *City*. 16(5): 546–556.

Tsilimpounidi, Myrto. 2015. '"If These Walls Could Talk": Street Art and Urban Belonging in the Athens of Crisis'. *Laboratorium*. 7(2): 71–91.

Tulke, Julia. 2013. *Aesthetics of Crisis: Political Street Art in Athens in the Context of the Crisis*. MA thesis. Berlin: Humboldt University. Available at: http://aestheticsofcrisis.org/thesis-publications/. Accessed: 28 September 2015.

Zaimakis, Yannis. 2015. '"Welcome to the Civilization of Fear": On Political Graffiti Heterotopias in Greece in Times of Crisis'. *Visual Communication*. 14(4): 373–396.

9 The December 2008 uprising's stencil images in Athens

Writing or inventing traces of the future?

Stavros Stavrides

Introduction

December 2008 marked an important turning point in the history of urban struggles in Athens. If by the term urban struggles we may describe not only struggles that have explicitly urban demands (e.g. affordable housing, transportation, anti-gentrification mobilizations, etc.) but also those that explicitly or implicitly target urban order, then December's youth uprising was mainly expressed in actions of the second type.

On 6 December of that year, an incident took place in Exarchia, one of the central neighbourhoods in Athens, that triggered an unprecedented series of dissident actions. A young schoolboy was murdered in cold blood by a policeman who 'felt insulted' by the boy's attitude. Exarchia is well known as an area of alternative culture, a place where young people from all over Athens tend to go, especially during the weekend days, to participate in musical or political events that usually depart from mainstream ones. In Exarchia many publishing houses, bookstores and neighbourhood cultural and political initiatives are located, including immigrant and refugee support centres, an occupied self-managed park (Navarinou), offices of non-parliamentary political groups, autonomous politico-cultural centres etc. This is a neighbourhood to which many demonstrations end sometimes in almost ritualized anti-police actions. Mainstream media often demonize the neighbourhood as an area of anomie, beyond state control, but actually in Exarchia police raids are quite frequent (either triggered and legitimized by actions that feed the spectacle of 'anomie' or with the alleged scope to control illegal actions – occupations or illegal immigrants). And routine police presence is expressed by patrol cars and motorcycles that hastily cross the neighbourhood and by groups of police riot squads in full gear that are stationed in strategic entrance points to the neighbourhood.

In such a setting, a verbal confrontation between a policeman and a young schoolboy could appear more explosive than in any other area. But it could have ended in one more show of police implicit or explicit brutality – not a murder. The fact that a violent incident happens in Exarchia makes it immediately a focus of attention both for the media and movement activists. This is why also in many cases the state has chosen to paradigmatically confront Exarchias's alleged 'anomic stronghold' in order to send a message to the rest of the city. What followed the murder of the boy was indeed amazing (Mentinis 2009; Sotiris 2009; Memos 2010; Stavrides 2010). Violent clashes with the police forces in huge demonstrations throughout the country, an immense number of school and university occupations, public building occupations that converted them to political centres and dissident culture laboratories (among them the occupied National Opera building and municipal buildings in many cities including Athens municipalities). All those actions and initiatives were organized with no dependence on established groups of the left and anarchist movements although people and activists from those movements actively participated. It was more like a series of violent and non-violent movement actions that had no controlling or planning political centre but were spreading throughout the country in a kind of metastatic almost contagious way. The December virus, or the December spirit, carried with it a shared distrust or even a hate against the state, a shared anger against accumulating injustices (epitomized in experiences of being marginalized and humiliated at work, at school or in the streets especially shared by youngsters, immigrants and jobless people). The city and its public space were both the site of such shared experiences and the site of rebellious and dissident collective acts (Petropoulou 2009).

'Reclaim the city', 'take back the city', 'take back our lives'. In those words – not necessarily literal slogans of the uprising – a collective expressive effort may be condensed. It was not only that young people felt that the schoolboy's murder by a policeman could epitomize the everydayness of state violence especially against those who were suffering the results of crisis (youth and immigrants included). Rebellious people felt that the city itself had been converted to the testing ground of unjust and aggressive policies. In the city they experienced austerity as devastating everydayness: pervasive armed police presence, street controls for illegal immigrants, humiliating treatment of vulnerable people by the police and the neo-Nazi groups, everyday experiences of a deteriorating transport system, high rents and no jobs for the youth, criminalization of public protests (some were considered suspects or criminals in advance), public schools with diminishing public funding and lack of democratic administration, advancing privatizations of outdoor public space etc.

We can perhaps see then why the December uprising was not simply an urban conflict phenomenon but that it used the city to express a shared spirit of anger as well as to develop a shared, albeit fragmentary and ambiguous, effort to devise forms of organization and life-in-common that opposed dominant values and dominant urban order. This is perhaps why collective and individual inventiveness was truly remarkably expressed in ephemeral acts of public space appropriation. The hooded ballerinas dancing their rebellious dance in front of the occupied National Opera building, the ironic December slogans that travelled through cell-phones and social media, the inventive posters and clown-like dressings meant to ridicule the policemen warrior outfit, the happenings in front of the state authorities' buildings, the flower-offering in place of stone throwing gestures, the burning of the huge Christmas tree erected by the municipality at the central square of Athens: all those events were using the city as the stage of the uprising and at the same time as the necessary means to spread the values and experiences of December (Stavrides 2010).

This is why the December stencil images that appeared on the walls of Athens' neighbourhoods and were reproduced through the social media, were not one more means to spread and disseminate the uprising's messages. These stencil images, as we will see, were actually stencil-acts, gestures that were both using and challenging the city. Calls to struggle and forms of struggle, those images were more like invented traces of an uprising in progress.

Presences that challenge the spectacle

Let us attempt first of all to approach the December stencil images as, indeed, images. What kind of images could those stencils be? Illustrations of events that need to be kept in collective memory? Emblematic condensations of ideas related to the uprising's motivating ideologies? Slogans turned into images? Signatures of anonymous artists in support of the uprising? 'Political trademarks', that is recognizable signs of activist groups or political views? It is true that stencils can be all those kinds. But December stencils seem to have acquired a somewhat distinct, albeit precarious status as images that emerge at the crossroads of seemingly conflicting signification trajectories.

It is difficult to separate today the problem of the image, namely the problem of the relation of an image to what it refers to, from the problem of the image's presence: Where and how do we meet images today? Images address us in contemporary metropolitan urban settings in ways that directly affect our understanding and perception of their context. We can possibly follow Jean-Luc Nancy's suggestions that we see images insofar as those images are 'distinct' (2005). According to his argument, an image is an image and not merely 'decoration or illustration, that is, the support of a signification' (ibid.: 12), only when it is distinct, only when it establishes itself in the 'obviousness of the distinct' (ibid.). There is a kind of force that throws an image to us, that makes us consider something as an image.

Limiting Nancy's understanding of images to this is probably misleading. But it can offer an entrance to the problem of the image's presence. It is easy to say that we see images all around us today, that we are constantly forced to see images. But do all these images matter in the same way? Do we distinguish images from other images? Is the stream of images simply a form of ambient setting that educates and controls our ocular perception or do we possess the means to control the stream, to divert, to select or even to not see? What Nancy seems to suggest is that images, insofar as they are indeed images, have the power to distinguish themselves from the visual stream that engulfs our senses. He even goes on to explore a certain violence that is inherent in images. Images do not represent something absent, they are themselves presences. Through them the 'thing presents itself'. It is 'posited as subject' (ibid.: 21).Thus, there is a kind of 'competition for presence' (ibid.) between the thing and the image of the thing.

This could offer a glimpse into a possible dynamics of image presence that may include and characterize the December stencils. Could it be that those images were really distinct, that they possessed the power to show because they went beyond a mere imitation of what they depicted and thus reached a point of expressing without illustrating? Such images thus became presences of and in the December uprising. Frozen and immobile as they were, they, nevertheless, seemed to capture the momentum of unfolding events. As distinct presences, stencils were December events too that together with all the other December actions demanded to be seen.

The most emblematic of such stencil-presences was, of course, the stencil image of the murdered boy himself (Figure 9.1a). Derived from a photographic image circulated in the media that depicted the young student smiling (probably taken in front of a coffee shop similar to the one in which he was shot) this stencil-image appeared in lots of places and in lots of versions during the December days. This was indeed an act of bringing to presence a murdered boy turned to a symbol. But it was not probably meant to represent or show how the boy actually looked. The stencil art's characteristic minimalism helped in transforming the boy's photo to a generic image of Greek youth: 'we are all Alexis', 'we are everywhere in the city demanding to be seen' could have been the meaning of this stencil–act.

One more example: a hooded ballerina stencil image attempted to transmit the dynamics of a coordinated expressive performance staged by hooded artists in ballerina style gestures in front of the occupied National Opera building (Figure 9.1b). By explicitly combining emblematic movement's 'combat outfit' with the fragile stylized acts of ballet, this event loosely represented the December uprising's effort to combine creativity with rage, art with direct action. A stencil image of a hooded ballerina, thus, somehow reproduced the presence of an event meant to be repeated throughout the city. Perhaps a bit cryptic, at least for those who did not witness the inaugurating event, which was nevertheless widely presented in alternative social media, this stencil seems to have contributed to a symbolic proliferation of hooded ballerinas in action rather than to the representation of the actual event.

Equally interesting was the case of a stencil that appeared mostly near the trendy coffee shops of Kolonaki, a neighbourhood of conservative upper-middle class that nevertheless borders Exarchia (Figure 9.1c). With a stylized image of a Molotov cocktail at its centre the stencil reads 'Relax you trendy guys and enjoy your drink. Your car is burning nearby'. Stencil presence acquires here the per-formative character of a real threat: 'You are not safe anywhere in the city, you, who are responsible for injustice and inequality.'

We know, at least after Guy Debord's *The Society of the Spectacle*, that in spectacle, relations between images shape relations between people: 'The spectacle is not a collection of images; rather, it is a social relationship between people that is mediated by images' (Debord 1994 [1967] thesis 4). If the spectacle, as an alien-ating and control mechanism, is considered to be omnipresent and omnipotent, then every act, no matter how much aggressively oriented against the established rules and values it aspires to be, is bound to succumb to the enclosure of the spec-tacle. Anti-politics becomes spectacular, it is being reduced to one more spectacle.

Figure 9.1
Stencils that challenge the spectacle.
(a) Alexandros Grigoropoulos stencil
on the National Mortgage Bank building.
Panepistimiou Avenue, Athens city centre;
(b) Hooded ballerina stencil on the Greek
National Opera building. Akadimias Street,
Athens city center; (c) Stencil at Kolonaki
district, Athens city centre. It reads: 'Relax
you trendy guys and enjoy your drink. Your
car is burning nearby.'

Photographs: Stavros Stavrides, 2009.

Could there be a way out? This is a kind of political riddle that we have inherited from the Situationist critique. And it can be emphatically expressed in the words of a graffito as recorded by Myrto Tsilimpounidi: 'What you say on the wall would not be said on the news, because if that was the case then something else would happen. I think the name is [*whispering*] revolution' (2015: 80).

True, many of the December actions can be considered as spectacular according to Debord's definition. They were treated by the media as a spectacle of horror and anarchy, ambiguously seductive and repulsive when shown on TV 'news'. Some of those actions had even been performed with the tacit aim of being reproduced through the media, sometimes in the hope that this will (and it possibly had) make them exemplary actions for potential imitators. However, not every image, not every image-action or action-image is necessarily bound to a 'spectacular' appropriation. And the December stencil images seem to have offered this kind of resistance to appropriation. First of all, they lack the tremendous power of resemblance that emphatically affirms that something has existed. Let us remember that Roland Barthes claimed that the affirmation 'this has happened' is at the heart of the photographic image: '[I]n Photography I can never deny that *the thing has been there*' (1981: 76). And this is true, one might add, even if photographic image's falsification was possible from the very beginning of its history.

Spectacle may indeed appropriate images of reality. Spectacle is organized in and by the media in the name of reality, in the name of truth. Spectacular December images pretend to simply document what was happening in those days. This is why they can trap us: seductive as they are for potential or active participants, in the December uprising and the uprisings to come, they indeed reduce the December events to a recurrent spectacle.

Are stencil images seductive in this way? They might be considered 'nice', 'beautiful', or objects of street 'art', but tamed spectacular images probably they are not. In their ephemeral presence in public space, those images were presences rather than re-presentations. Different objections may be raised against this interpretation. Not only in the name of spectacle's alleged omnipotence but also in view of the potential spectator's apathy or, perhaps in line with Georg Simmel's famous 'blasé attitude' (1997 [1903]). This last objection may simply trivialize the alleged power of presence connected to such images in the context of a supposedly prevailing mode of image perception, namely distraction: we don't really see when we see those images because there is a kind of mithridatism instilled by visual hyper-presence, by the incessant proliferation of images.

We know, however, that Walter Benjamin attempted to extract from this somewhat pessimistic understanding of visual culture – in which the subjects of looking are really de-subjectified – an optimistic remainder: distracted approach to images contains the grain of critical appropriation. The grain of distanciation. It thus possibly nourishes forms of reaction against what he describes as 'phantasmagoria' (Benjamin 1999: 10).

In his well-known distinction between distraction and concentration before a work of art, Benjamin argues that he or she who concentrates before such a work is absorbed by it whereas 'the distracted mass absorbs the work of art' (1992 [1936]: 232). In the latter case, which according to Benjamin is exemplified in film viewing, '[t]he public is an examiner, but an absent minded one' (ibid.: 234). The idea is that film is the non-auratic art *par excellence*, so it lacks what makes works of art unique, non-reproducible, 'authentic'. The 'decay of the aura' is, supposedly, one of the important results of the mechanical reproducibility of works of art (ibid.: 234).

Benjamin was not successful in predicting cinema's future, since, perhaps already at his own time but, surely, with the advent of mass culture, cinema became an art to be saturated with aura. No critical examination or distanciation can be inherently connected with cinema, especially with the culture industry cinema (Koepnick 2002). The idea, however, of distraction as a form of absent-minded critical approach to art, or to phantasmagoria and spectacle, seems to be promising in the context of today's visual culture.

True, the boundaries that differentiate the distracted from the concentrated approach to images are not absolutely clear. When we look at a billboard advertisement do we actually look? Perhaps we sometimes become fascinated by a new advertising campaign and seductive or 'strange' images capture our attention for time enough to consider our approach as concentrated. But, how often does this really happen? And how soon does our interest wither away along with our potential concentration?

A distracted perception seems to be the rule against which all advertising experts and designers need to fight all the time. Sneaking their messages through the distracted gaze is however an alternative strategy that may indeed be successful although always open to failure as when acts of misrecognition guide consumers to choices that are not the promoted ones. Consumers may have trouble in distinguishing between different brands by attributing to each one the corresponding image campaign. This is why, of course, repetition is critical: we need to be bombarded by image repetitions, by imagistic repetitions.

Image reproduction as an act

Stencil images are reproducible too. Stencils are actually designed and executed in ways that make them repeatable, recurrent. So, they can somehow attempt to infiltrate the distracted person's perception and affect his or her unconscious memory. However, stencils lack some of the guarantees and privileges of the publicity billboards. Stencils appear in unexpected and not in designated places, they are usually small and not dominating, they have no assigned frames, they lack the seductive and alluring power of bright-colour posters with the advertising image's over-realistic emphasis on texture and body expressions. Stencils are more like sketches, gestures based on emphatic abstraction or minimalistic depiction. And, what is more, stencils are being potentially reproduced not the way an image-based campaign can conquer the city: someone has to paint them each time, someone, who is considered to commit an offence to the law. Reproducing a stencil image, then, is an act that has to face ever-new contingencies, that has to be a distinct performance each time someone dares to repeat, or insists on repeating a gesture in order to address others. And, as Andrea Mubi Brighenti insists, these acts of addressing others are not simply adding words or images to public space but actually shape public space (2013).

This is why the presence of stencils, especially during an urban uprising that engenders and diffuses them, is taken to be an ever new act rather than a recurrent familiar image presentation. Distracted approach seems to be somewhat short-circuited in such a context. Not that people necessarily examined thoroughly those stencils. But their presence became an indicator of a presence of actors and an unfolding of events. This happens much in the same way we sense presences when we perceive danger in an urban context without exactly being aware of the danger's source and its form. The December stencil images, thus, were more like signs, danger signs perhaps, that could either activate embedded fears of lawlessness or dormant anger connected to perceived injustices.

Maybe the December stencils were nothing more than writings on the walls, images near or over other images, indifferent extensions to incoherent patchworks of messages in and through images that seem to only temporarily, if at all, attract a fleeting look. And indeed, if someone separates those stencil images from the context and the contingencies of December, one can't easily consider them as 'distinct' or eye-caching. As Yannis Zaimakis observes by studying political graffiti in crisis-ridden Greece, 'The art of timing in political graffiti is important. Writers make their creations during times of political tensions' (2015: 394). It is through this site-specific and time-specific awareness that graffiti may construct ephemeral 'counter hegemonic sites' (ibid.) and treat 'walls as contestable spaces' (Avramidis 2014: 201).

During the December days those images were present in a peculiarly emphatic way. They were announcing something in a city that was experiencing excessive (and expressive) blows on urban order. And they were also marking the city's body by leaving traces, showing areas in which events of a different kind were taking place. Those images, then, inculcated as they were on the city's body, marked presences that were demanding attention. Those stencils could not easily be overlooked. But, what is more important perhaps, those stencils were made in an effort or even with the insistent claim that they could not be easily overlooked. A characteristic example is the stencil depicting policemen in 'anti-riot' gear that was usually sprayed with red-paint drops to apparently produce the effect of the omnipresence of police brutality (Figure 9.2a). This was of course possible in Athens during the December days and many days after since, indeed, aggressive police presence in full gear was an everyday experience.

Such stencils were addressing the young people by verifying the power of dissident acts to metastasize, to migrate throughout the city of Athens, the state as threats to public order and the anaesthetized citizens as shocks that might mobilize them. They were ridiculing, mocking or praising actions and looks. Richard Sennett almost offered a definition of such acts when he described what he called the battle cry of graffiti in the context of early New York graffiti writing: 'We exist and we are everywhere . . . we write all over you' (Sennett 1993: 207).

Figure 9.2 Stencils' (re)production as an act. (a) Stencil depicting policemen in anti-riot gear. Tositsa Street, Exarchia district, Athens city centre; (b) Stencil depicting famous whiskey label logo while changing its motto. Ermou Street, Athens city centre.

Photographs: Stavros Stavrides, 2008.

And it is the same author who clearly distinguished between 'tags' as identity obsessed graffiti and stencil gestures as opposed to 'stencilized' political messages (ibid.: 205–211). December stencils were not tags. But they were not necessarily explicit political messages expressed in stencil phrases or political emblems. They were more like vectors of engaged communication that were not directed by the deciphering of signs or by the reading of familiar (or new) slogans. Those vectors had distinctive presence, since they were able to show, to mark, to address and to indicate at the same time potential acts of collective anger and protest. Highly indicative on this respect is the sarcastic appropriation of the well-known whiskey label logo in the form of a stencil image that may be interpreted as a direct call to violent action: 'Keep on bombing'! (Figure 9.2b)

A peculiar re-appropriation of the city-space unfolded in the acts of painting such stencil images. As I've argued elsewhere, we can even consider them as acts of 'commoning-through-representations that criticizes, ironically deconstructs or, almost sacrilegiously, attacks dominant images of the city' (Stavrides 2016: 203).

Invented traces

For Benjamin, aura and trace have a somewhat contrasting meaning. If 'the aura is appearance of a distance, however close the thing that calls it forth', then 'trace is appearance of a nearness, however far removed the thing that left it behind may be' (Benjamin 1999: 447). And he adds: 'In the trace, we gain possession of the thing; in the aura, it takes possession of us' (ibid.). Taking possession of the thing in such a context possibly means being able to control one's relation to something by using the traces left by it. Aura, as we have already seen in the case of the concentrated look, absorbs us.

What if December stencils were actually traces of a peculiar kind? What if they were meant to be not simply the remains of acts by those who acted to produce them, but also the indicative remains of acts towards which those schematic images actually gestured? What if those peculiar traces, those marks on the walls, were indeed calls to action by being remains and promises of acts at the same time? It is indeed paradoxical to claim that a trace can precede the act of which it is supposed to be a trace. But we are forever immersed in a visual culture in which the repeatability of images is a dominant mode of instructive gestures. We know that repeatable images are there to guide us as passengers, as consumers, as citizens, as subjects of work or leisure etc. It is only a slight change, a small unexpected gesture, that makes the December stencils deviant calls that address the absent minded 'observer'. Traces of potentially unexpected acts, traces of events that acquire their meaning as protest cries and as acts of delegitimization of existing authorities only insofar as they are repeatable. Through the repeated but unique acts that produce them, December stencils were marking potential paths for 'taking back the city'. However, they were not guiding indications for an invading army. They were more like promises of collective dissident presences. Declarations of war against injustice, humiliation, racism and inequality. They were the hieroglyphics of an uprising in progress. Dissident hieroglyphics. Acts of call in a code that had been developing during those days in and through expressive acts, in and through emblematic images that escaped the spectacularization of discontent.

While auratic appreciation of images enchants spectators by immersing them in a universe of representation that has the power to engulf them, images-as-traces possibly hint towards meaningful relations with reality that are based on the participation of the spectators to the production of perceived realities. Active spectators are those who perceive images as indicators of possibilities to act and not only as depictions of what has already happened. However, potential acts can be prescribed and thus prefigured by images meant to reproduce existing social forms of life. Does this mean that the boundaries that separate dominant didactic images (advertising ones included) from those that gesture towards deviating visual potentialities are blurred? Probably yes, if we believe that those boundaries are not crafted through differentiated practices of viewing, differentiating practices of looking. 'Emancipation begins when we challenge the opposition between viewing and acting', says Jacques Rancière (2009: 13). The emancipated spectator is probably the one who establishes those boundaries because s/he 'observes, selects, compares, interprets' (ibid.) and thus challenges not only the limits of imagination but also the limits of reality. Perceiving an image as a trace of a possible reality to which the spectator may contribute, the way the December stencils might be interpreted, is a powerful means to empower emancipated spectators in-the-making.

Perhaps the most characteristic hieroglyphic of the December uprising – in its exceptional character and execution – is an image that survived many months after those days on the door of an unused building at one of the central streets in downtown Athens (Figure 9.3). It was made with white paint and it depicts in a very crude way the contour of a human figure with a raised hand, or more likely, with a raised fist. One can easily guess that this figure, hastily painted on a door in a city area under more or less heavy surveillance, was meant to recall those white line figures painted on the ground to mark the position of a corpse at a crime scene. Isn't the marking of the position and form of an absent dead body a kind of macabre stencil image? The body itself becomes the stencil's matrix. Death, a violent death always, motivates a delineation of the remains of life. A stencil that acquires the characteristics of a death mask is produced in the form of a trace, in the form of a marker of a violent event.

It was the murder of the young schoolboy that surely inspired this bizarre painting on a door. But the contour of the dead body was in this case transformed to a standing figure. In a gesture of utmost minimalism that can nevertheless convey

Figure 9.3 Stencils as invented traces. The contour of a human figure painted on an entrance door. Panepistimiou Street, Athens city centre.

Photograph: Stavros Stavrides, 2008.

the cool horror of a dead body's documented presence at a crime scene, this quasi-stencil somehow condenses the distinctive power of December stencil images. A trace that recalls a trace: what can be more definite as trace than the trace of death, the mark of a body on a site of death, on the place of a murder? But also a call. A call that is activated by a presence: the raised fist is a call for struggle, a sign of determination, a declaration of promise. Well beyond a realistic depiction this schematic representation of a human body, an almost clumsy sketch of a standing figure, is an image that calls for action by being a simulated, an invented trace. A trace that becomes the imprint of future actions because it recalls the imprint of a past action – a murder – that justifies, generates, inspires, motivates, shapes or even expresses them. A trace that retains the shaping force of human hands both in the event that has produced it (we can almost see the hasty hand making this contour with one continuous single movement of the paintbrush) and in the fatal act that triggered the uprising. Stencil art – stencil act. The December stencils might have been the ephemeral products of a series of gestures that challenged the limits of a so-called street art. Or is it that in more or less similar conditions of urban uprisings, stencil art continuously reinvents itself? Seeking to avoid being tamed by the urban spectacle and the surrounding academic discourses, to which possibly, although unwillingly, this text also contributes?

References

Avramidis, Konstantinos. 2014. 'Mapping the Geographical and Spatial Characteristics of Politicized Urban Art in the Athens of Crisis'. In Tsilimpounidi, Myrto and Walsh, Aylwyn (eds), *Remapping 'Crisis': A Guide to Athens*. London: Zero Books, pp. 183–203.

Barthes, Roland. 1981. *Camera Lucida: Reflections on Photography*. New York, NY: Hill & Wang.

Benjamin, Walter. 1992 [1936]. 'The Work of Art in the Age of Mechanical Reproduction'. In Arendt, Hannah (ed.), *Illuminations*. Zohn, Harry (trans.). London: Fontana Press, pp. 217–252.

Benjamin, Walter. 1999. *The Arcades Project*. Eiland, Howard and McLaughlin, Kevin (trans.). Cambridge, MA: The Belknap Press.

Brighenti, Andrea Mubi. 2013. 'A Territoriology of Graffiti Writing'. In Musso, Claudio and Naldi, Fabiola (eds), *Frontier: The Line of Style*. Bologna: Damiani, pp. 51–55.

Debord, Guy. 1994 [1967]. *The Society of the Spectacle*. Nicholson-Smith, Donald (trans.). New York, NY: Zone Books.

Koepnick, Lutz. 2002. 'Aura Reconsidered: Benjamin and Contemporary Visual Culture'. In Richter, Gerhard (ed.), *Benjamin's Ghosts: Interventions in Contemporary Literary and Cultural Theory*. Stanford, CA: Stanford University Press, pp. 95–120.

Memos, Christos. 2010. 'Neoliberalism, Identification Process and the Dialectics of Crisis'. *International Journal of Urban and Regional Research*. 34(1): 210–16.

Mentinis, Mihalis. 2009. 'Peace, Legality, Democracy'. *Radical Philosophy*. 154: 67–68.

Nancy, Jean-Luc. 2005. *The Ground of the Image*. New York, NY: Fordham University Press.

Petropoulou, Chryssanthi. 2009. 'From the December Youth Uprising to the Rebirth of Urban Social Movements: A Space–Time Approach'. *International Journal of Urban and Regional Research*. 34(1): 217–224.

Rancière, Jacques. 2009. *The Emancipated Spectator*. Elliott, Gregory (trans.). London: Verso.

Sennett Richard. 1993. *The Conscience of the Eye*. London: Faber & Faber.

Simmel, Georg. 1997 [1903]. 'The Metropolis and Mental Life'. In Leach, Neil (ed.), *Rethinking Architecture: A Reader in Cultural Theory*. London: Routledge, pp. 67–76.

Sotiris, Panagiotis. 2009. 'Rebellion of Greek Youth'. *Radical Philosophy*. 154: 65–67.

Stavrides, Stavros. 2010. 'The December 2008 Youth Uprising in Athens: Spatial Justice in an Emergent "City Of Thresholds" '. *Spatial Justice*. 2. Available at: www.jssj.org/wp-content/uploads/2012/12/JSSJ2-10en1.pdf. Accessed: 20 December 2015.

Stavrides, Stavros. 2016. *Common Space: The City as Commons*. London: Zed Books.

Tsilimpounidi, Myrto. 2015. ' "If these Walls Could Talk": Street Art and Urban Belonging in the Athens of Crisis'. *Laboratorium*. 7(2): 71–91.

Zaimakis, Yiannis. 2015. ' "Welcome to the Civilization of Fear": On Political Graffiti Heterotopias in Greece in Times of Crisis'. *Visual Communication*. 14(4): 373–396.

10 Repetitive repertoires

How writing about Cairene graffiti has turned into a serial monotony

Mona Abaza[1]

Once upon a time, a revolution . . .

> I think what I'm trying to note here is that over the past two years I felt like I was a service provider for many individuals and corporations. It was a one-way exchange of value. When some people say, "Give us your photos in return for us giving you traffic," that's nice of them. But traffic won't pay my bills, nor is it equal in value.
>
> (Abaza and Morayef 2015: 299)

The opening quote of this chapter is an extract from the interview I conducted in summer 2013 with blogger Soraya Morayef (n.d.), who is considered one of the most thorough documenters of Egyptian graffiti. Similar extracts are used throughout the chapter as a sort of navigating compass, rather as snapshots that open the transitional passages. I hope to engage dialectically with the ethical paradoxes that many have encountered in post-January 2011 Egypt in the 'field of cultural production' (Bourdieu 2002 [1993]), but in particular in street art, under a withering revolutionary moment that is spiraling into a collective despair. The aim of this chapter is to trace the transmutations in the field itself, which have been affected not only by the major political shifts through the pervasive militarization of urban life since the military takeover in 2013, but also by the very commodification of the revolution and the appropriation of a myriad of symbols, languages and icons by a counter-revolution.

Graffiti witnessed an unprecedented boom at the beginning of the revolution, reaching a peak around 2012–2013, while continuing to flourish until 2014. Graffiti during the early years of the revolution dramatically told and retold the stories of the violent confrontations, killing and martyrdoms that took place in the streets. From day one, the painted walls of Cairo were vehemently wiped out by the authorities, to be instantly repainted by even more irreverent and mesmerizing graffiti that insult the police forces and the symbols of the state. It was the rapid pace of the whitening and repainting that created a significant public of followers, photographers and observers of the street. Graffiti then witnessed a definite decline with the military takeover in 2013. Nevertheless, not only graffiti but many symbols that were circulated in Tahrir (such as flags, badges, gadgets, Facebook cartoons, t-shirts) underwent a swift commodification and commercialization. From day one, graffiti was the field that attracted the most international attention, leading to an over-saturation in this form of cultural production. The current paradox lies in the fact that the branding and celebration of 'revolutionary art' on the global scale allowed the entrance of new young artists/players in the cultural field. These 'players' have gained international public visibility, but their graffiti did not escape obvious commodification and reification through curators, art galleries and media attention. Perhaps too the criminalization of graffiti after the military takeover was one of the reasons why graffiti was picked up by secluded spaces such as galleries, cultural centres, universities and museums.

The memory of Tahrir is fading away and turning into an agonizing nostalgia. Borrowing from Svetlana Boym's interpretation, nostalgia can be defined as 'a longing for home that no longer exists and never existed . . . a sentiment of displacement' (2001). Boym claims that 'outbreaks of nostalgia often follow revolutions; the French Revolution of 1789, the Russian Revolution, and the "Velvet" revolutions in Eastern Europe were accompanied by political and cultural manifestations of longing' (2001). The euphoric, carnivalesque and dramaturgical moments of January 2011 which caught the attention of numerous observers and lasted for almost four years seem to have withered away. This growing sense of loss coupled with nostalgia has recently influenced the domain of graffiti.

Four years after 2011, the entire region witnessed a different turn with the emergence of ISIS. The escalating 'war on terror' accompanied the decomposition of the state in a number of Arab countries such as Iraq, Syria and Yemen, and the suppression of the insurrection in Bahrain. Time and again, it is as if the entire region's predicament has been reduced to a 'swinging pendulum', this time, however, marked by the simplistic binary antagonism between extremist Islamists and military rule. This impression is enhanced by the culture of fear that characterizes the 'war on terror', as if it was the only alternative to counteract the chaos of the decomposing Arab states.

Was the Arab Spring a failure that merely led to further militarization of urban centres, costing countless lives? Punishment and the wrath of the wounded, re-emerging, aging regimes is perhaps the predicament of the entire region. Yet, even if pessimism reigns because Arab revolutions are considered to have failed politically as 'bread, freedom and social justice' are clearly far from being secured, hopefulness still shines in the field of culture and the arts, which have clearly blossomed since 2011. And graffiti, as an artistic field, has perhaps enjoyed disproportional attention compared to literature, music or documentary films, for reasons that are discussed below.

One can incessantly debate whether graffiti existed in Egypt prior to the January 2011 Revolution or not. In fact, it did exist but it was certainly the uniqueness of the insurrectional momentum that Egypt witnessed in January 2011 that gave birth to an unprecedented flowering not only of public art, but also of public performances, grief and biting satire against the long presence of suppressive authoritarian regimes. Above all, the Tunisian revolution, followed by Tahrir

Square, infested the entire globe with the virus of innovative forms of public protests in the squares. Thus, the symbol of the tent, V for 'vendetta', ironic text messages, songs, satire and graffiti travelled from one square to another, and from various Arab countries to Mediterranean and other European countries, to the Occupy movements in the US and Latin America, to Turkey and central Asia, and so on.

Since the military takeover in June 2014, one can argue that it is now 'once upon a time' that Egyptian cities witnessed this mesmerizing street art. They also experienced the criminalization of this very art, together with the banning of one English-language publication on the subject, even though numerous books on graffiti in the Arabic language remained unnoticed by the authorities (Mostafa 2015). It is as if what really matters in the official circles are the English publications and the Western gaze. It should also be recalled that, after the January revolution, the previous Ministry of Culture strongly encouraged the publication of numerous books on graffiti in the Arabic language that continue to escape censorship. However, the renewed tightening of censorship and the criminalization of street art go hand in hand with the disciplining and ordering of the street after four years of heightened street politics, demonstrations and violent confrontations with the police forces (cf. Abaza 2015). But that is not the whole story. It would be an easy task to merely blame the establishment for whitewashing the walls because of the unparalleled commercialization of what has been branded as 'revolutionary art'. The overwhelming international media attention, the countless foreign journalists, academics and writers briefly passing through Egypt and hoping to publish quick articles on the topic, the countless repetitive reports that recycled identical statements and information on street art, and last but not least the competition among some graffiti painters and the question of funding, all played an equal role in the phenomenon.

The iconic Mohammed Mahmud Street

> But what I'm trying to say is that I suspect there is a lazy habit of some researchers to just Google "street art in Egypt," pick the top four results, and then consider that adequate research. Or they visit one or two streets in Cairo with graffiti and decide that these visuals represent the whole scene. Some people may see a large mural in a convenient location, then fixate on that and make it the topic of their report, the focus of their exhibition, and the cover of their book. This leads to demand for that specific image and that artist.
>
> (Abaza and Morayef 2015: 298)

Graffiti, much like poems, satire, songs and words on the walls of the city, were spontaneous collective political actions that the effect of Tahrir Square has set free. What makes the Egyptian case unique is that one can read the graffiti as multilayered narratives, transforming walls into 'barometers' of the violent and tragic political events of the revolution (Abaza 2012b). Above all, some of these walls turned into 'memorial spaces' (Abaza 2012a) for the martyrs of the revolution in the street, nicknamed 'The Eyes of Freedom' (Figure 10.1a). During the shootings in Mohammed Mahmud Street in 2011, many protesters lost their eyes (Figure 10.1b); others were killed. It is no coincidence that these walls were continuously erased by the authorities, to be immediately repainted by 'young' street artists as a conscious rebellious act of offence against the 'aging' ruling elites, the internal security, and the military, as if it were a question of settling accounts (*règlement de comptes*). As violence escalated in the second half of 2011 and in 2012, and successive confrontations took place between demonstrators on the one hand, and the military regime, the police forces, and the subsequent government of the Muslim Brotherhood on the other, the walls developed a life of their own. The street artists also competed with each other to see who could most quickly fill the walls around Tahrir Square. Painting over and over again on the same walls produced endless layers (Figure 10.1c).

Beginning in the second half of 2011, Cairo witnessed an escalating militarization of urban life through the erection of further walls as buffer zones during the clashes. The city was turned into a genuine case study of the dystopian predictions of Stephen Graham on the 'new military urbanism' (2010). The numerous walls that were built around the Ministry of Interior following the Mohammed Mahmud clashes in 2011 testify to the vitality of research on walls and segregation (cf. Abaza 2012d). Here graffiti created an entire new interactive dialogue between artists and musicians, who produced satirical songs, and the countless passers-by who wanted to be photographed or filmed in front of the walls (Figure 10.1d). Painting *trompe l'oeil* landscapes on walls right across from the frightening building of the Ministry of Interior, and producing mock plaques with

Figure 10.1 Photographs of Mohammed Mahmud Street, depicting the changes of the murals and the passers-by posing in front of the wall. (a) The Arabic words translate as 'The Street of the Eyes of Freedom', as a metaphor for the victims who were blinded by snipers who specialized in targeting the eyes, 7 December 2012; (b) First portrait of the martyr Alaa Abdel Hadi killed during the incidents of the Council of Ministers in December 2011. Second portrait on the left, Ahmed Harara, who lost both eyes: the first on 28 January 2011 and the second during the first Mohammed Mahmud incidents in November 2011, 13 October 2012; (c) On the right is written 'Glory to the martyrs'. Ammar Abo Bakr painted in Arabic calligraphy over previous graffiti of the massacre of the Ultra Ahli football team in Port Said. The calligraphy reads: 'Forget what has passed and stand behind the elections'. It was meant to be an ironic statement against the electoral procedure that led to the election of the Muslim Brothers' president Morsi, 4 June 2012; (d) This image was taken on 23 November 2012 during the second set of violent incidents in Mohammed Mahmud Street. A graffiti artist is painting at the end of Mohammed Mahmud Street, while violent confrontations are taking place in the same street just across from the gate of the American University in Cairo; (e) Panorama of Mohamed Mahmud Street, 22 February 2013.

Photographs: Mona Abaza.

invented names such as 'The Street of No Walls' right near the newly erected walls, certainly produced an amazing visual effect (Figure 10.1e). Besieged residents, whose buildings were trapped in between walls, were often seen jumping ramps or trying to cross through pierced walls to reach their destination. These became common daily Cairene scenes, depicting the ordeal of navigating through a town centre that was barricaded with numerous checkpoints, barbed-wire barriers and tanks. Some even tried to mock these walls by bringing chairs, tables and bookshelves to squat, but they were quickly removed.

What made Cairene graffiti unique from 2011 until 2014 was that it evolved into a visible mode of street resistance, being on the spot in the midst of demonstrations and violent confrontations with the security. Spraying the walls became one way of taking part in these confrontations. It is also possible to identify specific repertoires in the representation of the portraits of the martyrs, which increased over time in both numbers and size (Figure 10.2a). Symbols of the revolution and countless signs related to funerary rites appeared and disappeared (e.g. the gas mask, revolutionaries depicted as angels with wings, the motorcycles that moved swiftly through the square to evacuate the wounded). The subjects of women and sexual harassment in Tahrir (Abaza 2013b) were all visualized by resorting not only to ancient Egyptian art, but equally to Islamic themes, such as the mythological figure of the *buraq* in Islamic tradition or the traditional paintings on mud-brick houses in the countryside depicting the hajj (Abaza 2012c). And last but not least, the same graffiti painter who produced Quranic verses in a wonderful classical calligraphic style – to challenge the Islamists and to send the message that the Quran and Arabic calligraphy belong to all, including secular Egyptians – later borrowed from Western popular culture, such as Andy Warhol's satire. This was graffiti artist Ammar Abo Bakr, who painted the entire Mohammed Mahmud wall in pink to reflect on the paradoxical relationship between the army and the people, at the exact moment when army tanks were occupying the entrance of Mohammed Mahmud Street in November 2013 (Figure 10.2b). Another example is the blue bra of an unknown female protester, which became an iconic symbol in December 2011.[2] Countless politicians were satirized through portraiture. Poems and words abounded to accompany the images. It is clear that graffiti became closely intertwined with the unfolding political events of the revolution.

Figure 10.2 Specific graffiti repertoires and the gradual wiping out of memory.
(a) All the faces and portraits on the wall represent successive martyrs of the revolution, including the iconic smashed face of martyr Khaled Said, killed after being tortured at a police station in Alexandria, the incident that triggered the January 2011 Revolution,12 January 2012; (b) Tanks occupying the Mohammed Mahmud Street after the ouster of President Morsi and the military takeover. The satirical pink wall, which refers to the military uniform, was painted by Ammar Abo Bakr while the soldiers were squatting the street, 22 November 2013; (c) The Mohammed Mahmud wall after creating a new gate, 21 September 2015.

Photographs: Mona Abaza.

The Rabea al-Adaweyya Square massacre in August 2013 which cost the life of almost one thousand followers of the ousted president Mohammed Morsi, the eruption of violence all over Egypt, the massive torching of churches, the public mutilation and killing of officers in police stations, the sporadic violent confrontations in the streets that followed, all marked a dramatic end to street politics. Curfews and draconian anti-demonstration laws were imposed. For the circle of street artists the death of the nineteen-year-old graffiti artist Hisham Rizq marked the end of an era in Cairene graffiti. After his corpse was found in the morgue, the authorized but highly dubious version of his death was that he drowned in the river Nile (*Ahram* 2014). With approximately forty thousand Egyptians being detained, many were sceptical with the official cause of Rizq's death. More recently, the numerous cases of 'forced disappearances' (Afifi 2016) raise questions of priority: street art became a secondary theme in the media, compared to the insurmountable economic problems and the endurance that most Egyptians have to exert in daily life, together with the blatant violation of human rights in police stations and jails.

Rizq's death marked a dramatic turn, signalling the danger of street politics under military rule. However, the walls of Mohammed Mahmud Street, which is one of the main streets leading to Tahrir Square, had hardly changed since November 2013, with the exception of Rizq's portrait. Since the second part of 2014, the Mohammed Mahmud wall art has not been countered with ironic, irreverent new paintings, as was the case in previous times. Because the paintings remained unchanged, the wall gradually turned into a depressing, rundown space, which little by little lost the attention of passers-by. In 2015, one hardly encountered any graffiti artists in the streets. In September 2015, the American University in Cairo decided to tear down the forty-year-old Science Building on the Tahrir Campus, removing with it a significant part of the iconic Mohammed Mahmud wall – which had witnessed the most important graffiti transmutations since the revolution – in order to construct one more entrance gate (Figure 10.2c). The official explanation was that the destruction was necessary in order to 'beautify' and restore the space of the university as it looked in earlier times (AUC Campus Community 2015). The modernist architecture of the science building did not match the authorized imagination of the clean, ordered postcards representing colonial and eventually orientalist Cairo. Certainly, too, renovation meant one more erasure and destruction of the iconic Mohammed Mahmud graffiti wall. It could also be that the repetitive portraiture of the city's martyrs, multiplying through time, has in fact lost the powerful effect that it produced at the beginning of the revolution (cf. Abaza 2013a). Possibly, one also needs to reflect on the very nature of the convivial, ecstatic moment that can only be ephemeral and fleeting, impossible to sustain in the long run. Clearly here, the magical spontaneous interactions that were experienced in the street have withered away, and with them the effect of the graffiti.

Since the military takeover in 2013, it has seemed that the decisive fight for a better future will be replaced by the recording of political memory, since erasures and denials have become the favoured tactics of the counter revolutionary forces. Activists disappear or are imprisoned. Some graffiti artists have already left the country, while others seem to have been co-opted to become famous media stars. Perhaps it is because living in Cairo translates today into how to survive through endurance (Paul 2015) and most often 'despair', as Asef Bayat (2015) puts it – despair in the face of an extremely hard daily life that makes the process of writing itself a heroic endeavour – but pursuing an unfinished and wounded revolution seems to be much less appealing for the academic research agendas of the global North than graffiti.[3]

Today, in 2016, the flag atop a huge, shapeless flagpole at the centre of Tahrir Square that has recently been installed by the current military government, together with the building of another gigantic garage, make it look as if the revolution could be reducible to solving the problem of traffic and car parking. The euphoric momentum of public space being metamorphosed into an unprecedented explosion of a myriad of artistic expressions – from singing, dancing, joking and poking, to performing, drawing and creating instant installations – has been consciously erased by the symbolism of this monstrous but insignificant parking space. The banality of the garage and the flagpole says it all regarding the political symbolism of attempting to erase a traumatic collective memory. It is as if the revolution never occurred. Tahrir Square has returned to being just a busy and 'normalized' square. The fact that demonstrations have been banned is no news, nor is the fact that participating in them can turn lethal or lead to long years of imprisonment. Military trials, draconian anti-demonstration laws, disappearances of activists and journalists, and death sentences have been enforced, and the violation of human rights in police stations seems to be much worse than prior to 2011. It's enough to make many believe that Mubarak's rule was actually a blessing.

Encounter

> You are an academic and people reach out to you and ask you for an interview . . . you sit down with them in a coffee house. They buy a cup of coffee and say, "Tell us all about graffiti," and you realize that you end up dictating them, their report or their book . . . you are doing their research for them. In one case, a whole cultural report was compiled by a team who spent their whole day inside a café, interviewing sources like me. They didn't meet the artists, they didn't take the time to observe the art in action or photograph the walls. There are even people who have published whole books on graffiti in Egypt, among other countries, without having visited any of the countries, and using other people's photos, including mine, without personal permission and for personal profit.
>
> (Abaza and Morayef 2015: 302)

From Soraya Morayef's bitter and thoughtful remarks on the fleeting overseas passers-by, I move to a unique experience thanks to the magical moments that the Square fashioned. I recall a moving encounter in late November 2012 with a graffiti artist in Tahrir Square during the first anniversary commemoration of the violent clashes in Mohammed Mahmud Street in November 2011. This second

Figure 10.3
An encounter with artist al-Zeft and his work. (a–c) Artist al-Zeft heads towards Kasr al-Aini wall to paint his 'smiley', 27 November 2012; (d) Nefertiti in gas masque by al-Zeft, Mohamed Mahmud Street, 26 September 2012.

Photographs: Mona Abaza.

Mohammed Mahmud incident turned once again to a repertoire of violence, although not as violent as in 2011, when over seventy people were killed. However, it was as if nothing changed with the successive regimes: Mubarak's ouster, the Supreme Council of the Armed Forces (SCAF) takeover, then President Morsi. This particular incident took place during the rule of the Muslim Brotherhood under former president Morsi, and the confrontations looked quite similar to those that happened under the military rule. Early one morning al-Zeft, whom I knew from previous encounters, was heading to Tahrir Square in the direction of the Kasr al-Aini wall with a ladder in one hand and paint in another, as if he were on an extremely urgent mission (Figure 10.3a). He was determined to defy the police situated behind the walls by drawing the smiley that turned out to be one of the most satirical graffiti drawn in the midst of extremely violent confrontations between the police forces of the Morsi regime and the demonstrators (Figure 10.3b). There was something dramatic and quite frightening about the square with its campers in this early morning. It was scary because at any moment violence could have erupted, since the police forces were posted on the other side of the wall; at the same time, it was satirical too, because the young men did not seem to be really afraid of anything. I recall smiling to myself when I saw al-Zeft and his ladder heading toward the concrete buffer wall erected by the army. The moment al-Zeft reached the Kasr al-Aini wall, other young men immediately appeared willing to help him in painting the smiley on the wall (Figure 10.3c).

Al-Zeft's Nefertiti[4] wearing the gas mask turned into a global iconic graffito that was displayed in numerous cities in demonstrations, marches and sit-ins (Figure 10.3d). For example, in January 2013, a large crowd of members of Amnesty International protested in front of the German Reichstag against Morsi's visit to Berlin, all of them wearing varying styles of the Nefertiti gas mask. Today, al-Zeft's work can be followed on his Facebook account, on which he posted his filmings and documentation of the Mohammed Mahmud confrontations as a front-line eyewitness in 2011 and 2012. Al-Zeft never reveals his face, but he is easily recognized, and much information about his personal life, travels, political opinions and the places he frequents is public. This continually raises new questions about anonymity. Meanwhile, several films and videos have been made about al-Zeft's work (e.g. Momtaz 2016). Equally interesting is the fact that one of al-Zeft's texts published in Karl and Hamdy's *Walls of Freedom* (2014) has been reproduced in French and other languages in blogs and Internet journalism, thus drawing further international attention to his work.

Commercialization

There's a tendency towards rivalry when working on exhibitions, such as who gets the best wall, and of course if there's money involved, then the situation gets very complicated because some artists believe they deserve to be paid more than others. There's nothing extraordinary about this; in fact it's quite similar to the rivalry in any artist community anywhere in the world. I just find it fascinating how these relationships and tensions formed so organically in such a short time. It is as if the nature of the artist is inclined to an environment of risk and temperament that induces rivalry and ego in some.

(Abaza and Morayef 2015: 299)

Graffiti won the lion's share of attention in the sphere of media to become the visual metaphor of the revolution, leading to an explosion of academic and non-academic articles, documentaries and films, and numerous exhibitions in Cairo and overseas. Competition developed among the producers of knowledge, and numerous books have already come out. One can observe two main tracks of publications in Arabic and English.[5] The impression is that the English works ignore, or rather are parallel to, the Arabic-language productions.

Often the English publications ignore the rich analyses that can easily be found in the writings published in academic journals and websites. Here the lack of knowledge of the Arabic language on the part of the majority of researchers, journalists and filmmakers, a lacuna that is often consciously understated in academic works, leads one to reflect on the true nature of expertise and scholarship. An exception to this is the work of Georgiana Nicoarea (2015), who conscientiously investigated the dialogical relationship between the power of words, poetry and literature on the walls and the way these interact with the visual element in graffiti. The two articles of Sherief Gaber (2013) and Amr Shalakani (2014) are ground-breaking because of their biting criticism of the Western gaze of the flocks of journalists, artists and students who focused only on the visual side while often failing to read the metaphors and insults, since it has become possible to become an 'expert' even with poor proficiency in Arabic.

However, this popularization in printed works is only one part of the story, as the trend of commercialization and co-opting of street art into reputable galleries and Western cultural centres developed quickly during the revolution. This went hand in hand with the massive witch hunt and the coercive disappearance of young activists and other citizens that took place in 2015. While some street artists have played the game of reproducing entire walls for chic galleries or becoming media stars, others have regretted their previous actions. Some artists never minded appearing on television and on satellite channels in talk shows and interviews. In this respect, Facebook accounts and posts can be true guides to the ways in which some of the artists have been praised by the official channels of culture.

Since 2015, however, Egyptian graffiti has become less appealing for the media world. Graffiti seems to have lost the attention it obtained in the early years of the revolution, although this might not be the case for some artists who were perhaps less visible in the streets after 2015, but gained international recognition through documentaries, such as *Art War* (Wilms 2013) and *The Square* (Noujaim 2013). Countless other documentaries and YouTube videos have been produced on graffiti since 2011. The international focus on graffiti was followed by a mass of overseas invitations and offers to the street artists for painting walls and murals in various European cities. A good example is the compelling work of Ammar Abo Bakr, who became a celebrity by being invited to numerous cities, such as

Berlin, Amsterdam, Brussels and most recently to Paris to draw a fresco at the Institut du Monde Arabe. It is no coincidence that Abo Bakr's fresco at the Institut du Monde Arabe depicted a portrait of a famous Sufi Sheikh from Upper Egypt (i.e. rural southern Egypt) covering his face with his hand. Abo Bakr explains in the YouTube video (IMA 2015) that he resorted to the Sufi symbol to propose an alternative, more tolerant religious form in an attempt to rescue the tarnished image of Islam, a result of the horrendous massacre at Charlie Hebdo. Interesting here is how Abo Bakr has recently shifted his attention toward broader political issues beyond the Egyptian revolution, since he has been invited to European capitals to produce large murals rather than just graffiti or stencils.

Mia Gröndahl is a Swedish photographer residing in Cairo. She published a book on graffiti, obtained European funding to sponsor installations for graffiti artists in downtown Cairo, and launched projects to empower young female artists by painting on walls in 2013. The project was titled 'Women on Walls' (WOW). This is a good case to reveal the tensions among artists, art gatekeepers and foreign funders. As I learned through informal conversations, the installations and activities around gender issues seem to have triggered antagonism among some of the graffiti artists. The feeling of being patronized seemed to be a major source of resentment for some street artists, who complained about the unequal distribution of funds. Since the project was meant to fund mainly female artists, some well-known male graffiti artists conveyed to me their impression that, for the foreign funders, it was more important to be a woman than to be a real street artist. Moreover, it was argued that young girls unknown in the street art scene were brought in by the photographer/project leader to be filmed, pretending that there is such a thing as a vibrant feminine street art. But the strongest feeling was the resentment of 'being taught' what political correctness is by a 'foreigner' residing in Cairo, who was trying to promote a politically correct cause such as 'gender equality', and who provoked criticism for using gender-insensitive verbal abuse in the graffiti and messages to be found all over the walls of the city. These messages then seemed to become points of friction between the artists and the photographer. Gröndahl then became the subject of an attack on Facebook. She was even publicly satirized in a graffito mocking her for having received funds in 'hard currency'. The satirical graffito was drawn by the street artist Aboud in Youssef al-Guindi Street (Figure 10.4a). Gröndahl was portrayed mimicking former president Morsi when he gave his first speech in Tahrir and opened his shirt to the audience to symbolize that he feared no one. In fact, her portrait was painted over the existing portrait of Morsi (Figure 10.4b). She was posturing with the same open shirt, but displaying dollars and euros on her chest. In the middle of the chest was a logo with the letters CKU, standing for the self-governing Danish Centre for Culture and Development. In a way, this graffito is quite revealing of the problematic relationship of foreign donors and sponsors with the post-revolution art scene.

On the other hand, artist Mira Shehadeh, who painted powerful murals on sexual harassment, also worked as a coordinator of the WOW project. Shehadeh's narrative is certainly more nuanced. According to her, there was quite a bit of ego

Figure 10.4
Graffiti responding to the commercialization of Cairene graffiti. (a) Former President Morsi opening his shirt as he did when he gave the oath of office. On his shirt are satirically painted two crossing swords, mocking the logo of the Muslim Brotherhood. The letters underneath reads: 'As he speaks, he lies', 9 February 2013; (b) Mia Gröndahl's portrait painted over Morsi's portrait. She is depicted, in a similar fashion to Morsi's portrait, with her shirt open. On the shirt 'hard currency' bills are shown, 12 September 2014; (c) Mia Gröndahl's portait erased, 15 May 2015; (d) 'No commercial graffiti is allowed' written to mock the graffito painted by one of the 'women on walls' launched by Mia Gröndahl, 17 April 2015.

Photographs: Mona Abaza.

struggle and striving for recognition involved in these battles. Anonymity as the major characteristic of street artists globally seemed to be completely lost (Shehadeh 2015). In fact, Facebook accounts have exposed more than ever the lives and works of the artists, and the jokes circulating among them. Facebook accounts can be a tracking tool to identify in detail the circles of photographers, curators and editors who are closely related to each of the artists. For example, it is quite easy to track the numerous activities, travels and exhibitions these artist are accepting. On the other hand, the only graffiti artist I have known who requested that his face be kept anonymous when I photographed him is al-Zeft. Nevertheless, we are told that the Sad Panda, Kaizer and El Teneen are three other artists who have remained anonymous until today. This pattern could raise questions about the reversibility of the publicness that Facebook provides and the fact that many artists, from day one of the revolution, were never concerned about the question of anonymity, as would be the case with American or European street artists.

The story was not yet over. The ironic portrait of Gröndahl on Youssef al-Guindi Street was finally whitewashed by Ahmed al-Alfi, the tycoon who currently rents the Greek Campus of the American University (Figure 10.4c). Some people suspected that the WOW project was behind the whitewashing, so that they could offer the space for women to unleash their freedom, but they actually painted their graffiti on a different part of the wall (Eickhof 2015). Ammar Abu Bakr expressed his anger toward the WOW graffiti paintings by writing on top of the erasures, 'This street is a necropolis . . . no commercial graffiti allowed', thus publicly exposing the agenda of commodifying graffiti in the WOW project (Figure 10.4d). This story raised several questions in the press (Eickhof 2015) regarding the role of Gröndahl as photographer/author and equally as curator-cum-producer of knowledge in the shaping of the symbolic and economic capital of the graffiti artists. Moreover, the virulent verbal war that was conducted on some Facebook posts and the satirization of the photographer by the graffiti artists, pointed to the growing animosity that replaced close collaborations among the groups.

Conclusions, time and again . . .

It is not just the countless repetitive articles published in the press on graffiti that is so disturbing but the poor quality of some of them that leads to fascinating reflection on the question of repertoires in the choice of topics. The street-art knowledge producers seem to be stuck in repetitive, almost identical, repertoires of images. In much the same way, it has become a must for a standard edited volume on the so-called 'Arab Spring' to include a chapter on graffiti and art. Dare one say that this overproduction and thus overconsumption in the field has exhausted the conversation to the extent of becoming a monotonous, *déja vu* topic, mainly celebrated and recycled in the various European cultural centres based in Egypt. While preparing this chapter, I could not stop flirting with the thought that this might, or should, be the very last article I write about Cairene graffiti. Maybe as a principle or perhaps as a feeling, too many opportunists and profiteers have emerged from the revolution. In the process, they transformed the very nature of Cairene graffiti and distorted the ways in which it is practised and perceived.

In the difficult current political situation, particularly after the massacre of Morsi supporters in Rabea al-Adawiyya Square in 2014, which was followed by violent confrontations, street art has become a secondary theme. It has been transferred from the public spaces of the streets to the private inner spaces of galleries, since street politics have been curtailed by the enforcement of martial law that criminalized protests after the military takeover. It is easy to speculate that, even if graffiti has lost momentum temporarily, the numerous representations of the iconic martyrs of the revolution and the captivating visual public effect of the murals will be hard to erase from the collective memory.

Notes

1 I wish to thank Konstantinos Avramidis and Myrto Tsilimpounidi for their extensive comments and support in the numerous rewritings of this chapter. I would also like to thank Johanna Baboukis for editing and thoroughly commenting on the logic of the arguments.

2 In Tahrir, a veiled female protester was stripped of her black cloak and kicked in the belly by a soldier's boot. Millions watched the humiliating sight of her being dragged along the ground, exposing her blue bra. Since then, the city's murals and barricades have been filled with hundreds of blue bras, and an avalanche of blue bras appeared in graffiti all over the city. The blue bra has turned into a symbol of national contestation against SCAF (the Supreme Council of the Armed Forces), ever since some Salafi shaykhs and pro-Mubarak talk-show speakers used it to smear its wearer as a prostitute who deserved to be beaten up and stripped naked in public. These counter-revolutionaries saw fit to ignore the simple violation of human rights, not to mention the fact that this was a public humiliation that specifically targeted women. This led in December 2011 to one of the most significant women's demonstrations against SCAF policies which have only led to the systematic escalation of sexual harassment, rape, gender humiliation and violent attacks on protesters.

3 As in the case of the Cambridge PhD candidate from Italy, Guilio Regeni, who was conducting research on the working class in Egypt and found dead with brutal signs of torture. Regeni appears to have suffered a horrendous slow death, raising questions about the role of the internal security (Kirchgaessner 2016).

4 Nefertiti was an Egyptian Queen (1370–1330 BC). She and her brother worshiped monotheism. Her bust, displayed in the Berlin Neues Museum, reveals an exceptional beauty, reaching an exemplary perfection.

5 The Arabic works deserving most attention are *Wall Talk* (2012) edited by Sherif Borai, Heba Helmi's *Inside Me Is a Martyr* (2013), and Maliha Maslamani's *Graffiti of the Egyptian Revolution* (2013). Mia Gröndahl's *Revolution Graffiti* (2013) and Don Stone Karl and Basma Hamdy's *Walls of Freedom* (2014) are the two major recent books in English. The French and German publications have not been considered here.

References

Abaza, Mona. 2012a. 'An Emerging Memorial Space? In Praise of Mohammed Mahmud Street'. *Jadaliyya*, 10 March. Available at: www.jadaliyya.com/pages/index/4625/an-emerging-memorial-space-in-praise-of-mohammed-m. Accessed: 27 February 2016.

Abaza, Mona. 2012b. 'The Revolution's Barometer'. *Jadaliyya*, 12 June. Available at: www. jadaliyya.com/pages/index/5978/the-revolutions-barometer-. Accessed: 27 February 2016.

Abaza, Mona. 2012c. 'The Buraqs of "Tahrir"'. *Jadaliyya*, May 27. Available at: www. jadaliyya.com/pages/index/5725/the-buraqs-of-tahrir. Accessed: 27 February 2016.

Abaza, Mona. 2012d. 'Walls, Segregating Downtown Cairo and the Mohammed Mahmud Street Graffiti'. *Theory, Culture & Society*. 30(1): 122–139.

Abaza, Mona. 2013a. 'Mourning, Narratives and Interactions with the Martyrs through Cairo's Graffiti'. *E-International Relations*, 7 October. Available at: www.e-ir.info/2013/ 10/07/mourning-narratives-and-interactions-with-the-martyrs-through-cairos-graffiti/. Accessed: 27 February 2016.

Abaza, Mona. 2013b. 'Intimidation and Resistance: Imagining Gender in Cairene Graffiti'. *Jadaliyya,* 30 June. Available at: www.jadaliyya.com/pages/index/12469/intimidation-and-resistance_imagining-gender-in-ca. Accessed: 27 February 2016.

Abaza, Mona. 2015. 'Is Cairene Graffiti Losing Momentum?'. *Jadaliyya*, 25 January. Available at: www.jadaliyya.com/pages/index/20635/is-cairene-graffiti-losing-momentum. Accessed: 27 February 2016.

Abaza, Mona and Morayef, Soraya. 2015. 'Interview on the Graffiti Scene in Cairo'. In Youkhana, Eva and Förster, Larissa (eds), *Grafficity: Visual Practices and Contestations in Urban Space*. Paderborn: Wilhelm Fink Verlag, pp. 295–306.

Afify, Heba. 2016. 'How Forced Disappearance Broke the Silence Barrier'. *Mada Masr*, 16 February. Available at: www.madamasr.com/sections/politics/how-forced-disappearance-broke-silence-barrier. Accessed: 27 February 2016.

Ahram. 2014. 'Activists Mourn Graffiti Artist Hisham Rizk'. *Ahram*, 3 July. Available at: http://english.ahram.org.eg/NewsContent/1/64/105374/Egypt/Politics-/Activists-mourn-graffiti-artist-Hisham-Rizk.aspx. Accessed: 27 February 2016.

AUC Campus Community. 2015. 'Science Building Removal to Give Iconic Tahrir Campus Facelift'. *The American University in Cairo News*, 13 September. Available at: http:// aucegypt.edu/news/stories/science-building-removal-give-iconic-tahrir-campus-facelift. Accessed: 1 February 2016.

Bayat, Asef. 2015. 'Revolution and Despair'. *Mada Masr*, 25 January. Available at: www. madamasr.com/opinion/revolution-and-despair. Accessed: 15 December 2015.

Boraie, Sherif. (ed.). 2012. *Wall Talk: Graffiti of the Egyptian Revolution*. Cairo: Zeitouna.

Bourdieu, Pierre. 2002 [1993]. 'The Field of Cultural Production or: The Economic World Reversed'. In Calhoun, Craig, Gerteis, Joseph Moody, James, Pfaff, Steven and Virk, Indermohan (eds), *Contemporary Sociological Theory* (2nd edn). Oxford: Blackwell, pp. 359–374.

Boym, Svetlana. 2001. 'Nostalgia and Its Discontents'. Available at: www.iasc-culture. org/eNews/2007_10/9.2CBoym.pdf. Accessed: 27 February 2016.

Eickhof, Ilka. 2015. 'Graffiti, Capital and Deciding What's Inappropriate'. *Mada Masr*, 7 April. Available at: www.madamasr.com/sections/culture/graffiti-capital-and-deciding-whats-inappropriate. Accessed: 5 February 2016.

Gaber, Sherief. 2013. 'Beyond Icons: Graffiti, Anonymous Authors and the Messages on Cairo's Walls'. *Cairo Observer*, 3 December. Available at: http://cairobserver.com/post/ 68890839257/beyond-icons-graffiti-anonymous-authors-and-the#.VvBPU0cVZSE. Accessed: 27 February 2016.

Graham, Stephen. 2010. *Cities under Siege: The New Military Urbanism*. London: Verso.

Gröndhal, Mia. 2013. *Revolution Graffiti: Street Art of the New Egypt*. Cairo: The American University in Cairo Press.

Helmi, Heba. 2013. *Gowaya Shaheed [Inside Me Is a Martyr]*. Cairo: Dar Al-Ain Publishing. [in Arabic].

IMA. 2015. 'Portrait – Amar Abo Bakr – Fresque à l'IMA'. *IMA You Tube Channel*, 23 January. Available at: www.youtube.com/watch?v=7lkdsLBvLbQ. Accessed: 27 February 2016.

Karl, Don Stone and Basma, Hamdy. 2014. *Walls of Freedom: Street Art of the Egyptian Revolution*. Berlin: From Here to Fame Publishing.

Kirchgaessner, Stephanie. 2016. 'Italian Student Giulio Regeni Found Dead in Cairo "With Signs of Torture"'. *The Guardian*, 4 February. Available at: www.theguardian.com/world/2016/feb/04/italian-student-found-dead-egypt-giulio-regeni-torture. Accessed: 27 February 2016.

Maslamani, Maliha. 2013. *Graffiti of the Egyptian Revolution*. Doha: Arab Center for Research and Policy.

Momtaz, Islam. 2016. *Wall*. Available at: https://vimeo.com/channels/305367. Accessed 26 March 2016.

Morayef, Soraya. n.d. *Suzee in the City: Art on the Streets of Cairo*. Available at: http://suzeeinthecity.wordpress.com/. Accessed: 27 February 2016.

Mostafa, Mohamed. 2015. 'Egypt Confiscates Revolution-time Graffiti Book for 'Instigating Revolt'. *Egypt Independent*, 18 February. Available at: www.egyptindependent.com/news/update-egypt-confiscates-revolution-time-graffiti-book-%E2%80%9Cinstigating-revolt%E2%80%9D. Accessed: 27 February 2016.

Nicoarea, Georgiana. 2015. 'The Contentious Rhetoric of the Cairene Walls: When Graffiti Meets Popular Literature'. In Grigore, George and Sitaru, Laura (eds), *Graffiti, Writing and Street Art in the Arab World*. Bucharest: Center for Arab Studies, pp. 99–112.

Noujaim, Jehane. 2013. *The Square*. New York: Netflix.

Paul, Ian Alan. 2015. 'The Revolutionary Practice of Endurance'. *Jadaliyya*, 25 January. Available at: www.jadaliyya.com/pages/index/20636/the-revolutionary-practice-of-endurance. Accessed: 15 December 2015.

Shalakani, Amr. 2014. 'The Day the Graffiti Died'. *London Review of International Law*. 2 (2): 357–378.

Shehadeh, Mira. 2015. Interview with author. 15 April.

Wilms, Marco. 2013. *Art War*. Berlin: Heldenfilm.

Part III
Representing graffiti, street art and the city

11 São Paulo's pixação and street art

Representations of or responses to Brazilian modernism?

Alexander Lamazares

Introduction

In the first half of the twentieth century, Brazil aimed to couple political independence with cultural emancipation. The quest to define a national identity that was autonomous would serve as the basis of a new national project built on the premise of modernity. The formation of national identity was parallel to a modernist aesthetic – one that informed the growth of creative cities and Brazilian artistic production. While architecture and the arts once served to build a modern national identity, the chapter looks at how contemporary street art may be read as continuation or response to the modernist project. Pixação, São Paulo's unique style of tagging is presented as a possible dystopian representation, one that illustrates the shortcomings of modernism.

The first part of this chapter examines the city's journey and the challenges posed to become a modernized city. A critical analysis of Brazilian modernism serves as a focal point for the creation of a megacity. I argue that the evolution of a modern, vertical city is synonymous with national identity. By critically unpacking the relationship with street art, the city, and modernism, the second part of this chapter explores, by way of responses to the issues raised in the first section, the unique elements of pixação that challenge modernism – specifically its highly corporeal nature, its perpendicular development, and its transgressive, aesthetic style. A critical look at national building is illustrated through São Paulo's contemporary street art – which is welcomed as both local and national representations of pride. Does contemporary street art affirm, represent or call for a revision of national identity?

Constructing a modernized city: São Paulo's aesthetic and urban development

São Paulo is a contradictory city where a sea of concrete modernist buildings, slums, derelict buildings, the homeless, street vendors, squatters and a vibrant, creative youth culture share an urban context undergoing a process of revitalization. São Paulo is at once a world city linked to global networks, and a local city, where public spaces manifest a mix of vibrant artistic production, social inequality and urban dereliction. Seeking to remake São Paulo into a modernized city, elite reformers and boosters of the 1940s and 1950s embarked on ambitious urban renewal projects.

Like other developing global megacities, São Paulo is a creation of the twentieth century. In 1900, the population was 240,000 (Sá 2014). By 1950, the population had reached two million, and it has now ballooned to over 20 million residents. Fuelled by easy credit and an emerging economy, ambitious developers and aspirations for a New York-style skyline, São Paulo experienced an unprecedented building boom following the turn of the century. The boom was also a consequence of the nation's modernist project that would continue through the middle of the century. The city's best known modernist buildings date back to this period, including the esteemed Museu de São Paulo, David Libeskind's Conjunto Nacional, Franz Heep's Edifício Itália and Oscar Neimeyer's many iconic buildings, such as the S-shaped Copan building. The construction of Latin America's largest urban park, the Parque Ibirapuera, linked with a distinctively serpentine walkway and unique modernist structures is an astonishing work in public architecture. The main feature of São Paulo's urban boom, however, was its sea of modernist skyscrapers. This first part of the chapter contextualizes how the creation and rise of a modernized city is intrinsically tied to Brazilian modernism – an aesthetic movement that brought national identity to the fore. The challenges posed by the city's boom are presented as potential indicators to revise national identity and revisit the modernist project.

Urban sprawl, or what happens when the buildings go vertical

As Brazil's largest urban area, among the top ten most populous in the world, the growth of a vast vertical city led to urban sprawl. Like most megacities, its untenable growth caused social–spatial segregation and exclusion. What anthropologist Teresa Caldeira (1999) calls a 'new aesthetic' of security has become integrated into all new developments, and old houses, schools, offices and shopping areas have been retrofitted to accommodate these needs. High fences, remote-controlled gates and doors, bullet-proof glass, uniformed guards and electrified wire have become commonplace in a city where those desperate to isolate themselves from the insecurity that seemed to be sweeping through Brazil's cities simply had to pay to do so. Enclosed, fortified condominiums offer the wealthy a chance to withdraw from the surrounding dystopia and create a new order. The rise of vertical city appears as fragmented territory exposing local and national deficiencies to the modernist project.

While urban sprawl may have benefited better-off Paulistanos[1] who lived and worked in and around downtown São Paulo, they had an adverse effect on the lives of the city's working-class residents. To transform São Paulo into the modern city envisioned, large portions were demolished, especially the dilapidated buildings located in the downtown area, inhabited by the working poor and newcomers from the traditionally poor areas of the Northeast, to new waves of immigration from Africa, Asia and Latin America. Unable to find affordable housing in and around downtown, many working-class or poor Paulistanos were left with two imperfect options: join the urban poor in one of the city's growing favelas (slums) or relocate to the periphery.

Rapid change is gripping São Paulo, the largest city in all of the Americas. A rising economy fuelled by commodities trade with China and decades of stable government had made many Brazilians more prosperous. However, as the country faces the worst recession in over a century and the impeachment of President Dilma Roussef looms, the successes of the modernist project may now be in question. One may question how urban sprawl may affirm or challenge the values of national identity and nation building. To understand how these values were embodied in the creation of a modernized city, one must first look back to São Paulo's important historical connection with modernism.

National identity, or how we always wanted to be modern

Brazilian modernism played a pivotal role in the creation of national identity. Two events marked its birth; each defined a national consciousness with a look inward while placing itself outside the realm of the European and North American context. First, the inauguration of the *Semana de Arte Moderna* (Modern Art Week) in 1922 in São Paulo, which brought new internationalist tendencies to São Paulo, and also brought upon a rupture in the arts between the earlier realism and the new abstraction influenced by European models (i.e. Mondrian and Max Bill). Second, the publication of *Manifesto Antropófago* (Cannibalist Manifesto) in 1928 by the poet Oswald de Andrade. *Semana de Arte Moderna* brought into focus a cultural explosion in Brazilian arts and made São Paulo the radical centre of this new wave of creativity. The *Semana de Arte Moderna* of 1922 also coincided with Brazil's independence centenary which renewed a strong sense of nationalism and cultural independence.

De Andrade argued that Brazil has a history of 'cannibalizing' other cultures, digesting them and producing something entirely new – and this was the country's greatest strength. While he mocked the Brazilian elite's adoration of and obsession with more developed countries, he encouraged cultural cannibalism as a way for Brazil to assert itself against European domination and its pervasive influence on Brazilian national identity. A key passage from the *Manifesto Antropófago* reads: 'Only anthropophagy (cannibalism) unites us. Socially. Economically. Philosophically. The world's only law. The masked expression of all individualisms, of all collectivisms. Of all religions. Of all peace treaties. Tupí or not Tupí, that is the question' (1928; 1991: 38). The phrase 'Tupí or not tupí that is the question'[2] is a double-entendre that carries important significance with Brazilian modernism. First, as a historical reference, the Tupí Amerindians were the largest indigenous group at the time of conquest. The Tupí were once believed to be cannibals who ate their enemies to gain strength (Forsyth 1983). Second, as an act of cultural cannibalism, de Andrade utilizes Shakespeare's passage, 'To be or not to be', digests it, and applies it to the formation of a new Brazilian national identity.

Few images are as metaphorically effective as the act of swallowing: the indigenous Tupí eating the white European man, devouring and digesting him. That which will nourish is selected and the negative, undesirable parts are discarded. The manifesto called for appropriating external culture and a reimagining of national history with a new date-system, a chronological mark to uphold the importance of cultural cannibalism.[3] The symbol of man eating man would serve as a point of departure and inspiration by the Brazilian avant-garde. The critical act of swallowing proposed a new historical narrative that preserved indigenous elements and provided for a revolutionary articulation of national identity. Brazilian modernism thus proposed a national identity that desired to be modern – but only on its own terms. This narrative would serve to contextualize the development of a creative, modern city.

Dreams made of concrete or when 'less is a bore' encountered opposition

The trajectory of Brazilian modernist architecture also played a pivotal role in the development of a newly defined national consciousness. Modernist architecture, known for its minimalist style, transformed São Paulo with its functional and economic structural designs. Would Brazil continue with Ludwig Mies van der Rohe's modernist vision of 'less is more'? In the 1940s and 1950s, Brazil acquired unprecedented prestige in the world of modern architecture. While it was regarded as the country that had inherited the progressive modernism of the pre-war period in Europe, the creation of the 'Brazilian Style' was among the first national variations of European modernism (Quezado Deckker 2001: 168). Whereas the colonial period in Brazil utilized European styles that were highly ornamental and prototypically baroque, Brazilian modern architecture distinguished itself with the combination of stark lines, sensuous curves and organic forms that reinterpreted European modernism. Oscar Niemeyer, a pioneer of modern architecture and a mastermind of Brasilia[4] – the capital city that was designed and built from scratch, aiming to symbolize the nation's desire to become modernized – distinguished his style to reflect a new vision that was tied to national identity. What inspired him was the free and sensual curve: 'the curve I find in the mountains of my country, in the sinuous course of its rivers, in the body of the beloved woman' (Niemeyer 2000).

Architect Robert Venturi, in contrast, countered modernism with the postmodern antidote, 'Less is a bore.' Believing that buildings require necessary variety, Venturi's opposition called for more decoration, symbolism, colour, pattern and clever references to historic structures (1966). While his attempt to undermine modernism called for alternatives with anti-modernist themes (Quezado Deckker 2001), the trajectory of Brazilian modernist architecture took a different and unique path, as it co-opted references from these two opposing visions. The use of local elements and traditions played a critical role in its development. Lucio Costa – one of Brazil's foremost modernist architects – engaged in a lifetime investigation of colonial architecture, the principles of which, he claimed, could be integrated with modern architecture (Moreira 2006). While Brazilian modernism distinguished itself with organic curvilinear forms, it also valued local needs and cultural memories, and it turned repeatedly to local building traditions. While São Paulo produced a great deal of extraordinary, imaginative and visionary buildings, one could argue that it too created many cheap imitations at best, and misguided value engineered atrocities at worst. Brazil was unable to fully stray away from anaemic imitations of European formulas. As São Paulo continued to grow, it acceded to Le Corbusier's modernist logic of creating mass-produced buildings whose architectural language was devoid of tradition. What resulted in São Paulo was, for the most part, a sea of 'boring', off-white boxes that symbolized a utopian world of concrete. Modernist architecture stressed utilitarian living and working quarters, but many of these structures lacked ways to engage with the city. In São Paulo, scores of modernist façades eventually became targets of pixadores[5] in their attempt to playfully engage with the 'boring' city. Pixação could thus be read as a reaction to modernist architecture and one that parallels Venturi's postmodern turn – as pixadores imposed their own symbolism, patterns and clever references of historic alphabets on the city's urban fabric. While modernism brought about monotonous structures and Venturi's work led to the over exuberant collision of misunderstood historic styles, pixação and street art illustrate the ways architecture can be more interactive with the urban environment, more connected to our culture, and more responsive to the needs of its citizens.

São Paulo's pixação and street art respond to modernism

This part of the chapter examines the ways pixação and street art may be visualized as responses to modernism. Pixação is presented as a transgressive art form that challenges the normative standards of beauty, genre and behaviour. Where modernism subscribes to form over function, pixação embraces anti-form, as transgressive art blurs established boundaries and definitions, challenging citizens to see and live the city in a different light.

São Paulo appears to be one of the rare cities that has invented its own formal writing tradition, far from the much beaten track of an iconic New York. The city represents an original, urban signature of tagging practice with an alternative urban aesthetic. The stylistic expression of pixação remains distinct from other graffiti practices that are widely globalized and homogenized. Meaning 'trace' or 'stain' and dating back in its contemporary form to the mid 1980s, pixação is a striking form of graffiti unique to the city that developed when Paulistanos began creating imaginary calligraphic signatures influenced by hybrid black letters. François Chastanet's seminal work, *Pixação: São Paulo Signature* (2007), was one of the first to present the rise of this unique singular vernacular calligraphy while separating it from the emblematic American graffiti. Claiming the architectural façades of the city as their canvas, the omnipresence of pixação is a 'calligraphic shock that caused an aesthetic transformation of the city', as well as exposing deep rooted tensions (2007: 34).

Pixação is part of São Paulo's visual and cultural lexicon, one that is rooted in the Runic alphabet.[6] In true Brazilian fashion, pixadores cannibalized the Runic alphabet, digested it, and made it something entirely new. Many pixadores were fascinated by calligraphic games under the indisputable influence of heavy metal record sleeves (Chastanet 2007). They were also drawn to the immediate pictorial qualities of Gothic writing. They instinctively relied on the expression of Gothic lettering, associated for many with rebellion, aggression and power.

While pixação remains illegal and pixadores continue to *rodar* (slang for going to jail), its growth points to the deficiencies of the modernist project. Whereas most city dwellers view pixação as an illegal defacement of their cityscape, a generation of innovative artists, such as Herbert Baglione, Nunca, Eduardo Kobra and Os Gêmeos are working with murals that transform the urban fabric. These artists have gained prominent success, both locally and globally, becoming celebrities in their might. With major commissioned projects in many cities, site specific murals have taken over entire buildings, and have also moved inside the empty white spaces of galleries and museums.

The periphery invades the centre

Pixação may be viewed as a dystopian response to the modernized city. Its proliferation at the centre could be read as a 'cancer to the healthy metropolis, whereby petty acts of destruction are both a symptom and cause of urban decay' (King 2016). Its geographical dispersion is a reminder of the ongoing inequalities and the existence of the urban poor who are often marginalized in neighbourhoods that surround the periphery of São Paulo.[7] Pixos attest to the effects of a modernized city where we see a gentrified city centre, with the redevelopment of abandoned buildings into stylish residences for the wealthy. Pixadores may see their work as a protest against a system that has excluded and failed them. Pixação's preferred choice of location is at the centre of the city; spaces that are out of reach for virtually all of Brazil's urban poor.

While citizens may see pixação in São Paulo as simply an eyesore, it is remarkably political, even if the individual messages painted in pseudo-Runic letters that resemble Scandinavia's ancient Runic writing are not explicit. Local authorities and residents have been engaged in a battle to stem the flow of pixação since the early 1980s, when the practice first emerged. Yet, despite high-tech security cameras, neighbourhood watch groups, police intimidation, draconian laws and a special sanitary unit within the city government dedicated to covering up pixação, it is prevalent and widespread. To address its rise, Brazil passed a law in 2011 that prohibited the sale of spray paint to minors. Since then, all spray cans require two warning labels that read: 'Pixação is a Crime' and 'the Sale to Minors is Prohibited' (Rousseff 2011). The law also decriminalized other forms of street art that is made for the purpose of 'increasing the value of public or private property through an artistic manifestation, as long as the work is permitted by the owner' (Rousseff 2011). With the passing of this law, we witness the latest phase of street art in São Paulo. This phase illustrates an urban dichotomy: one that is

Figure 11.1 Pixação in São Paulo. (a) On the façade of the Edifício Wilton Almeida de Paes, 2015; (b) On a modernist building façade, 2013.

Photographs: (a) Stephanie Bleier; (b) Vladimir Estrella. Reproduced with permission of the photographers.

characterized by the illicit acts of pixação from the periphery and the other distinguished by a resurgence in street art at the centre that is celebrated by its citizens.

The city's residents have expressed the proliferation of pixação as the equivalent of visual guerrilla warfare against their city. According to one estimate, there are more than 5,000 active pixadores in São Paulo alone (Oliveira and Wainer 2009). In recent years, as seen in Figure 11.1, pixadores have targeted icons (and cheap imitations) of São Paulo's modernism, from the Wilton Paes de Almeida building to Oscar Niemeyer's famous pavilion located in Ibirapuera Park. Pixadores have also tarnished sites that are part of the city's historic patrimony, including the Ramos de Azevedo fountain in downtown São Paulo. The more sacred a site may be to national patrimony, the more attractive it is as a target for pixadores. Some pixadores approach their craft in terms of politics of activism and resistance. As one anonymous pixador puts it: 'we practice class warfare' (Oliveira and Wainer 2009). Others are more idealistic, hoping that their pixos (tags), by tarnishing the appearance of the more privileged areas of the city, will encourage better-off Paulistanos to reflect on the way working-class residents live, especially those in the marginalized periphery.

While pixadores remain active, and their movement continues from the periphery to the centre and beyond to other Brazilian cities, could their aesthetics be understood as a dystopian response to modernism? Brazilian modernist artists, writers and architects created a new aesthetic with stylistic innovations that stressed national culture. They made a new narrative for a utopian city and nation. Pixadores, on the other hand, introduced a new aesthetic with a language whose alphabet was designed for urban invasion. Their goal was to reach, tag and vandalize the apex of modernist façades.

A corporeal critique of the city, or when parkour met street art

Due to the highly corporeal nature of pixação, a second important element differentiates it from other styles of global graffiti, especially as it affects and is affected by the city's urban environment. Some assert that pixação is also inspired by São Paulo's vast, tall buildings (Caldeira 2012), i.e. the emblems of Brazilian modernity. The corporeal, parkour-like nature of pixação is central to understanding its relationship with the built environment. The act of securing tags on inaccessible pinnacles is achieved with parkour-like skill. Parkour is a popular lifestyle sport that began on the streets of Paris, and has turned into a global movement that turns the cityscape into a readymade obstacle course. It involves moving rapidly through an urban area by navigating through a city's obstacles by running, jumping and climbing. With pixação, the act may be achieved with climbing tall buildings and making 'body ladders' to reach the highest possible tag.[8]

The most daring acts of pixação, as seen in Figure 11.2, can be witnessed with pixadores scaling the outside of a building. Like contemporary Spidermen or trained acrobats, pixadores scale buildings using an external surge arrester cable. This is

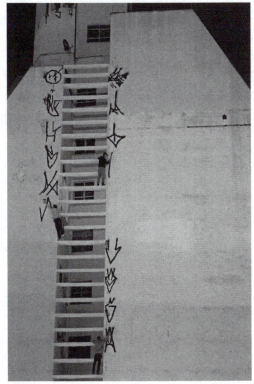

Figure 11.2 Pixadores scale modernist façades in São Paulo, 2011.
Photographs: Leandro Mantovani. Reproduced with permission of the photographer.

a particularly perilous way to climb a building, considering that the clamps used to hold the cable onto the façade are not built to withstand the weight of a person. Others do not use any climbing gear, and accidents are common and sometimes fatal. But for the adrenaline-seeking pixador, the pay-off is worth the risk. By scaling the building in such a way, they can access large sections of a façade that have never been touched by another pixador. It is also about visibility, particularly the kind that can only be achieved through daring acts of courage. Beyond fame, visibility and adrenaline, a motivation for pixadores is an ire directed against the city, and this is also reflected in their choice of language. Employing terms such as blow up, smash and destroy – these words are intended to degrade the urban environment. As one pixador puts it, 'pixação is an assault on the city' (Oliveira and Wainer 2009; cf. Siwi 2016).

The most extreme form of pixação takes place on the apex of a building, for which success is measured in terms of the height of a building, as well as its geographic and architectural importance. With geographical importance, the prize converges on the wealthier centre versus the periphery of the favelas. Whereas New York graffiti transformed the sides of subway trains into mass-media surfaces, São Paulo's modernist iconic architecture appears to be the indiscriminate prize target for many pixadores. With regards to architectural importance, the eye on the prize involves reaching the very top of a skyscraper or a cultural or historical landmark. Pixadores usually work at night in teams of two – climb a building's façade by grabbing on to its window ledges and pulling themselves up, floor by floor, leaving their pixos on each floor as they continue to scale to higher points. To extend their reach, pixadores may precariously dangle their bodies over a building or the ledge of a roof. Rooftop pixos require guts bravery, and the right equipment – black ink and a paint roller attached to a broomstick.

Both parkour and pixação could be read as a playful critique to modernist urban spaces – for they are typically performed in an urban environment with a transgressive character – both in constant negotiation with their right to exist. Both are daring balancing acts that involve leaping between walls, climbing buildings, and vaulting ledges to seamlessly move through the city's urban environment. As modernized cities become increasingly homogenous and restricted, parkour and pixação may be seen as practices that 'performatively display an alternative vision of urbanization, one which is more democratized, spontaneous, and free-for-all as it exercises its right to the city through re-appropriating capitalist spaces' (Raymen 2014).

Colourizing the concrete and inventing a different dream

The 2000s saw the rise of contemporary street art with a focus on murals that took over buildings, streets and walls – changing the personality and cityscape of neighbourhoods.[9] In recent years, street artists from São Paulo such as Herbert Baglione and Nunca have gained global notoriety with major exhibitions at Tate Modern in London and site specific street venues in many cities abroad. Baglione stands out for his explorations of elongated, contorted and ghostly looking forms.

His murals utilize monochromatic black and white, a possible reference to his roots in pixação (Figure 11.3a). Baglione replaced his image as a pixador/graffiti artist to conceptual artist. In 1997 he disseminated a written message on the streets of São Paulo announcing that his pseudonym as a pixador 'Cobal' was dead.[10] Since then, he has worked under his real name, and creates primarily melancholic, dreamlike, ghostly-looking creatures on streets, pavements and abandoned urban spaces. His murals may wrap around a ceiling and onto the pavement. His earlier phantasmagorical pieces draw attention to national identity, popular culture and its obsession with body image (i.e. anorexia and idealized body forms). Merging elements from sculpture, pixação and photography, his latest works are site-specific installations and murals that display ghost-like silhouettes with elongated limbs and emaciated, sinuous bodies. They populate the cracked walls, streets, stairs, the façades of buildings and abandoned spaces. Describing his creative approach with these spaces, Baglione explains that the ghost-like images and their shadows represent 'the path that the soul takes. It is as if the soul is leaving an invisible trail on these spaces' (Ginger 2014).

Francisco Rodrigues da Silva, popularly known as Nunca (meaning 'never' in Portuguese), speaks to national identity through indigenous elements and the effects of Brazilian cultural cannibalism. Nunca began painting the walls of his hometown São Paulo at the age of twelve and, since then, has moved from pixação to site-specific murals that blend consumer culture with indigenous motifs. By placing his images in urban settings such as motorway underpasses, he creates a timeless dialogue between history and modernity. Often improvised and playful, Nunca's street art reflects what he sees as the inner character of Brazilians, one that struggles for survival in the modern metropolis. The faces he depicts are based on ordinary citizens he sees on the streets of São Paulo. His works, even though created with spray paint and acrylic, often have the look of ancient woodcuts or etchings (Figure 11.3b). In recent years, his work has developed into a more pictorial form of communication whose vibrant colours and style evokes Brazilian indigenous rituals and traditions. Nunca responds to national identity through indigenous imagery and the use of dark red ochre, which similarly relates to *urucum*.[11]

The rise of street art transformed the city's urban fabric into a multi-coloured collage. Eduardo Kobra and Os Gêmeos are the street artists most renowned and fêted for large-scale murals. Kobra utilizes bright colours and bold lines while staying true to a kaleidoscope theme throughout his work. The technique of repeating squares and triangles allows him to bring to life historical cultural icons. In 2013, Kobra completed a 170-foot high mural that honoured the architect Oscar Niemeyer, who passed away just days before his 105th birthday (Figure 11.4a). Covering the entire side of a skyscraper in São Paulo's financial district, the artwork is inspired by Niemeyer's architecture, his love of concrete and Le Corbusier. Kobra's choice of architectural inspiration is noteworthy – Le Corbusier, as the father of European modernism, and Oscar Niemeyer, as Brazil's prodigal response to it. Niemeyer's began in the 1930s when he worked with Lucio Costa and Le Corbusier on the design of the Brazilian Ministry of Education and Health in Rio

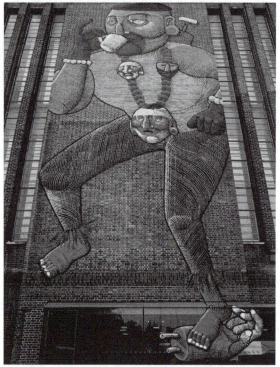

Figure 11.3 Paulistanos street artists around the world. (a) Herbert Baglione, *Street-Art Brazil*, Hauptwache Boden, 2013, (c) Schirn Kunsthalle Frankfurt, 2016; (b) Mural by Nunca on the façade of Tate Modern in London produced in the context of the *Street-Art* exhibition, 2008.

Photographs: (a) Norbert Miguletz; (b) Rafael Schacter. Reproduced with permission of the photographers.

Figure 11.4 Murals by Eduardo Kobra in São Paulo. (a) Mural of Oscar Niemeyer, 2014; (b) Mural of Ayrton Senna, 2015.

Photographs: (a) Antonio Marín; (b) Alan Teixeira. Reproduced with permission of the photographers.

– the first major modernist public building in Brazil. As Niemeyer began to establish his own style, more flowing and curvaceous than Le Corbusier's or Costa's, his signature style embodied the image of Brazilian modernism. Niemeyer appropriated the cannibalist tool – devouring modernist forms of architecture and digesting its foreign author. Both Niemeyer and Kobra may be read as poets of concrete and geometry. While Niemeyer constructed a new dream for Brazil, Kobra's trademark style – the kaleidoscope of colour – dreams in bright, bold colours and geometric forms, reimagining iconic images from the past and giving them an entirely new visual identity.[12] In 2015, Kobra made a tribute to the late racing driver Ayrton Senna (1960–1994) – a three-time Formula One champion – who is, for many Paulistanos, a symbol of local and national pride (Figure 11.4b). As a representation of national identity, the mural features the Brazilian flag floating like a halo over the iconic figure. Here, we see how the intersection of artistic production and national cultural icons contribute to the formation and reaffirmation of nation building and national identities.

Ordem e progresso? No thanks!

The street art of identical twins Gustavo and Octavio Pandolfo – who go by the name Os Gêmeos (meaning 'the twins' in Portuguese) – combines a visual language with a singular, unique aesthetic. Known for their yellow-skinned characters, Os Gêmeos have worked together since birth. Evoking folkloric, mythological, and national elements, their art is influenced by dreams and popular culture. Their murals are colourful and fantastical and also respond to love, politics, poverty and urban decay. The image of flags and its colours – yellow and green – are constant themes in their work.[13] The characters in their work may be the size of a person located on a street corner, or they can take over the entire façade of a structure. Playing with scale, their works have appeared on buildings, castles, planes and passenger trains. Improvisation plays an important role, and their work is shaped and informed by the urban environment and national identity.

Realizing that trains and subway systems are often objects of pride in the Brazilian context, Os Gêmeos persuaded the transportation authorities in 2007 to allow graffiti artists to paint entire trains without restrictions. The first train was painted in São Paulo, and due to the success of the project, 'Projeto Whole Train' expanded to many other cities across the country. Os Gêmeos celebrated national pride by covering the entire passenger train with the reimagined image of the national flag (Figure 11.5a). In another series of murals, 'Ordem e Progresso?' [Order and Progress?], the motto of Brazil's flag and the symbolic use of green and yellow again highlights national identity and nation building. The series, located on several street corners in São Paulo, however, makes strong social commentary on urban decay and is a rebuke that points to the failures of a nation. Brazil's promise of a modernized, democratic nation never fully materialized, in large part because the state never resolved the tension between the two goals enshrined in its national motto: order and progress.

In continuing with the theme of flags, Os Gêmeos collaborated with New York City graffiti artist Futura to create an 80-foot mural that took over the entire façade of a seven-story public school in the Chelsea neighbourhood of New York (Figure 11.5b). Blending in with the surrounding streets and playground, the large yellow fantastical character, popularly known as Gigante sports shorts is adorned with flags from around the globe. In a sign of global unity, the flags were reimagined and painted with the colours completely altered from their original form. Their idea was to create 'one world, one voice, no borders, no separation, just everything and everyone working together for a single cause that is a better world' (Os Gêmeos 2010). This mural could be read as a representation of postmodernism, where late capitalism is defined without borders, and where the pursuit of prosperity, democratic governance, and individual well-being are more important than national identity and state sovereignty (Van Ham 2013).

Could the work of Os Gêmeos also be read as a representation or response to modernism? For Os Gêmeos, cannibalism is a natural instinct that may be used to improvise and recycle everything that man creates. It allows them to change and reconstruct things to improve visual communication (Annear 2012). One may also consider a parallel reading between the work of Os Gêmeos and modernist artists, such as Anita Malfatti, who is credited with the development of Brazilian modernist painting. Like Os Gêmeos, Malfatti developed a style characterized by the discontinuity of shape and perspective, and by the jolting use of colour – primarily the bright yellow and green of the Brazilian flag (Nunes 2008: 26). While two of her most important pieces – 'The Yellow Man' (1916) and 'The Green-haired Woman' (1917) – caused sensation and were extraordinarily controversial, they also generated revolutionary changes in modernism. Given the conservative climate of a military-ruled republic, her earlier paintings were seen as daring, and denounced in the press as 'decadent', 'cross-eyed' and part of the boils in the 'excess of culture' (Leite 1994). Creating works that were non-realist and viewed as spatial anomalies, her work was rebuked as anti-nationalist. As a female artist, Malfatti not only strayed from academic convention but that of Brazilian society, rupturing the established etiquette by which women 'should' produce art. To a public that was guided by the colonial purview of the nineteenth century and in the process of forming a national identity, Malfatti was a trailblazer for painting portraits and landscapes in a new light. In many ways, Malfatti mirrored the journey of her native São Paulo – one that was in the process of carving out a unique identity and parting from the stifling rules of the past. Exploring new boundaries, Malfatti utilized new structural techniques – faces painted in blue and green shadows that flattened on the canvas, and bodies and faces that were unusually angular and painted in vivid, exaggerated colours (Congdon and Hallmark 2002). The characters in the fantastical and whimsical world of Os Gêmeos, in contrast, are inspired by the yellow-tinged skin experienced in their dreams. They feature rounded faces, angular, expressive eyes that are set widely apart, matchstick-thin limbs and bold coloured clothing.

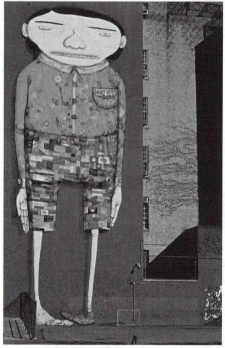

Figure 11.5 Murals by Os Gêmeos. (a) Projeto Whole Train, Estação Leopolidina, Rio de Janeiro, 2012; (b) Os Gêmeos and Futura, PS11: The William T. Harris School, New York, 2016.

Photographs: (a) Vladimir Estrella; (b) Alexander Lamazares. Reproduced with permission of the photographer.

Conclusion

As we trace the parallels of modernism with pixação and street art, it exposes many tensions and local divergences with nation building. Where the pioneers of Brazilian modernism created a language and aesthetic that defined national identity, the rise of pixação, in turn, responds to modernism's utopian vision. Pixação, rather, is a dystopian representation that reveals the failures of modernism, bringing to light urban decay, segregation and social polarization. Through the (mis-)use of the city's structures, pixação serves as a response to the city's evolving modernist landscape – one that is imagined and lived, and another that is planned and perceived.

By colonizing city spaces, pixação and contemporary street art rejects conventional modes of representation. We see this through the creation of a new art form, the playful engagement with the urban fabric, and the thrill of danger when tagging and climbing façades. We also see how street art interrupts the monotonous off-white buildings in São Paulo with fantastical and whimsical representations, offering new ways to engage with the city and the urban environment, and provoking a more dynamic and creative environment. The visual narrative of street art not only deconstructs national identity, but brings to light a reconceptualization of urban spaces and Brazilian modernity.

Notes

1 People from the city are known as Paulistanos. Sampa is a commonly used name by locals for the city of São Paulo. Paulistas refers to anyone from the greater state of São Paulo.
2 The Tupí inhabited almost all of Brazil's coast when the Portuguese colonized its land. In 1500 their population was estimated at one million people, nearly equal to the population of Portugal at the time.
3 While the *Manifesto Antropófago* was published in 1928, Oswald de Andrade playfully dated and signed off on the manifesto 'in Piratinga, Year 374 of the swallowing of Bishop Sardinha'. Piratinga refers the indigenous name for the area on which São Paulo was built. São Paulo was founded by Jesuit priests, who celebrated their first mass in 1554. By stating the year 374, de Andrade recognizes the birth of a city and a new nation.
4 Along with Niemeyer, architect Lucio Costa was the leading planner of the new Brazilian capital. Costa is considered the father of Latin American modernist design.
5 The Brazilian term pixadores roughly corresponds to the 'graffiti artists' or 'taggers' in contemporary English lexicon.
6 The Runic alphabet was used to write various Germanic languages before the adoption of the Latin alphabet and for specialized purposes thereafter. The earliest Runic inscriptions date from around 150 AD. The Runic characters were replaced by the Latin alphabet as the cultures that had used runes underwent Christianization by 700 AD in central Europe and 1100 AD in Northern Europe. However, the use of runes was in continued use throughout northern Europe and much of Scandinavia. Until the early twentieth century, runes were used in rural Sweden and on Runic calendars.
7 This is in contrast to Rio de Janeiro, where the existence of the urban poor is quite visible in the favelas that dot the city's mountainsides, often within view of some of the city's wealthiest neighbourhoods.

8 The spread of pixação's extent to other cities climbed to new heights when it appeared on the arm of Rio de Janeiro's landmark Christ the Redeemer statue, which is perched on the peak of the Corcovado Mountain (Giumbelli 2014).

9 São Paulo's street art culture has also experienced a considerable rise in video art installations and video mapping projects. Initiatives such as Vídeo Guerrilha, for instance, have been instrumental in transforming the façades of buildings into interactive canvases. Comprising video mapping artworks, Vídeo Guerrilha has utilized images to crawl up and down façades with spectacular interactive art pieces and digital forms of pixação (Lamazares 2014).

10 Of course, this is not new at all. For example, in the 1980s, Jean-Michel Basquiat (former graffiti artist and later famous painter) declared on the walls 'SAMO is dead' before moving from graffiti to high art.

11 *Urucum* is derived from *achiote*, a shrub or small tree indigenous to the Americas. Body-painting with *urucum* remains an important tradition with several Brazilian and other South American indigenous tribes.

12 Kobra has celebrated other national Brazilian icons in his work, such as the musician and songwriter, Chico Buarque and the writer Ariano Suassuno.

13 The yellow represents the wealth of the Brazilian soil, with an important reference to its gold reserves in Minas Gerais. Green symbolizes the country's lush flora and fauna, from the Amazon rainforest to the verdant jungle along the Atlantic Ocean and the Pantanal.

References

Annear, Steve. 2012. 'Giant Painting in Boston Spurs Racist Comments on Fox 25's Facebook Thread'. *BostInno*, 4 August. Available at: http://bostinno.streetwise.co/2012/08/04/giant-painting-in-boston-spurs-racist-comments-on-fox-25s-facebook-thread/. Accessed: 7 March 2016.

Caldeira, Teresa. 1999. 'Fortified Enclaves: The New Urban Segregation'. In Low, Setha M. (ed.), *Theorizing the City: A New Urban Anthropological Reader*. New Brunswick, NJ: Rutgers University Press, pp. 83–106.

Caldeira, Teresa. 2012. 'Imprinting and Moving Around: New Visibilities and Configurations of Public Space in São Paulo'. *Public Culture*. 24(2): 385–419.

Chastanet, François. 2007. *Pixação: São Paulo Signature*. Paris: XGpress,

Congdon, Kristin and Kara Kelley Hallmark. 2002. *Artists from Latin American Cultures: A Biographical Dictionary*. Westport, CT: Greenwood Publishing Group.

De Andrade, Oswald. 1991. 'Cannibalist Manifesto'. Bary, Leslie (trans.). *Latin American Literary Review*. 19(38): 38–47.

De Andrade, Oswald. 1928. 'Manifesto Antropófago'. *Nuevo Texto Crítico*. 12(1): 25–31.

Forsyth, Donald W. 1983. 'The Beginnings of Brazilian Anthropology: Jesuits and Tupinamba Cannibalism'. *Journal of Anthropological Research*. 1: 147–178.

Ginger. 2014. 'Herbert Baglione's 1000 Shadows Rise from Abandoned Psych Ward'. *HAHA – High On Arts Heavy on Antics*. Available at: http://hahamag.com/tag/herbert-baglione/ Accessed 26 March 2016.

Giumbelli, Emerson. 2014. *Símbolos Religiosos em Controvérsia*. São Paulo: Terceiro Nome.

King, Alex. 2016. 'Street art, utopia, and shattering boundaries.' *Huck Magazine*. Available at: www.huckmagazine.com/art-and-culture/art-2/worlds-top-street-artists-dismantle-graffitis-dystopian-reputation/. Accessed 15 March 2016.

Lamazares, Alexander. 2014. 'Exploring São Paulo's Visual Culture: Encounters with Art and Street Culture along Augusta Street'. *Visual Resources*. 30(4): 319–335.

Leite, José Roberto Teixeira. 1994. 'Brazilian Painting from 1900 to 1922'. *Bienal Brasil Século XX*. São Paulo: Fundação Bienal de São Paulo, pp. 24–37.

Moreira, Fernando Diniz. 2006. 'Lucio Costa: Tradition in the Architecture of Modern Brazil'. *National Identities*. 8(3): 259–275.

Niemeyer, Oscar. 2000. *The Curves of Time: The Memoirs of Oscar Niemeyer*. London: Phaidon.

Nunes, Zita. 2008. *Cultural Cannibalism: Race and Representation in the Literature of the Americas*. Minneapolis, MN: University of Minnesota Press.

Oliveira, Roberto T. and Wainer, João. 2009. *Pixo Documentary*. Available at: https://vimeo.com/29691112. Accessed: 20 February 2015.

Os Gêmeos. Artist Homepage. Available at: www.osgemeos.com.br/pt. Accessed 16 March 2016.

QuezadoDeckker, Zilah. 2001. *Brazil Built: the Architecture of the Modern Movement in Brazil*. London: Taylor & Francis.

Raymen, Thomas. 2014. 'Re-thinking Parkour as "Resistance": How Markets Dictate the Contextual Deviance of Parkour'. *Deviant Leisure*, 21 July. Available at: https://deviantleisure.wordpress.com/2014/07/21/re-thinking-parkour-as-resistance-how-markets-dictate-the-contextual-deviance-of-parkour/. Accessed 16 March 2016.

Rousseff, Dilma. 2011. 'Law Number 12.408. Decree to National Congress'. Available at: www.planalto.gov.br/ccivil_03/_ato2011-2014/2011/lei/l12408.htm. Accessed: 7 March 2016.

Sá, Lúcia. 2014. *Life in the Megalopolis: Mexico City and São Paulo*. London: Routledge.

Siwi, Marcio. 2016. 'Pixação: the Story behind São Paulo's "Angry" Alternative to Graffiti'. *The Guardian*, 6 January. Available at: www.theguardian.com/cities/2016/jan/06/pixacao-the-story-behind-sao-paulos-angry-alternative-to-graffiti. Accessed: 20 February 2016.

Van Ham, Peter. 2013. *European Integration and the Postmodern Condition: Governance, Democracy, Identity*. London: Routledge.

Venturi, Robert. 1966. *Complexity and Contradiction in Architecture*. New York, NY: The Museum of Modern Art Press.

12 Defensible aesthetics

Creative resistance to urban policies in Ottawa

Deborah Landry

Ottawa, we have a [graffiti] problem

Ottawa has a graffiti problem. This problem manifest recently in a conflict over who has a right to use one of the two legal graffiti walls permitted in the city. A local university based activist group, BlakCollectiv, painted the text 'Black Lives Matter' using white wash and masking tape, somewhat oblivious to the history and politics of the prominent and prestigious wall. By the next morning, graffiti writers discovered the text, and painted over it while the local press were on hand to capture writers painting over the message (Figure 12.1).

Soon the national press were taking sides: one Toronto Star opinion piece, intended as a passionate plea for readers to consider the problem of racism in Canada, captures the complexities of social exclusion in this case: 'In Ottawa, a mural memorializing Sandra Bland, a black woman who recently died in ominously suspicious circumstances while in the custody of a Texan police force, was defaced with graffiti' (Morgan 2015). The painted letters by one disen-franchised group were defined as 'a mural' worthy of archiving, while the arguably equally important work that went over it was defined as a 'defacement'. The drama over who was more disenfranchised unfolded on one of only two places in the city where the racialized aesthetic of graffiti could be applied without legal sanction. If written on any other wall in town, the activists would be breaking the law, same too for the writers. Weeks later, the wall continued to boil with painted messages over each other's work. Many claiming to support the BlakCollectiv cited the actions of the writers as white privilege, some writers accused the activists of colonist behaviour, others attempted to create a love themed piece in an attempt to find common ground, while others mocked the turf war, questioning the authenticity of activists not willing to get arrested and writers who would defend a state sanctioned wall. In the end, however, the tensions over scarce resources (public property) ended in the activists being called muralists, and the graffiti writers as vandals of a wall that they have historically taken care of for nearly two decades.

Graffiti is spatial practice; it challenges how the city is socially ordered and experienced by some citizens (Ferrell and Weide 2010; Dovey *et al.* 2012). This chapter discusses how graffiti, and responses to it, inscribes on the walls larger structural tensions at play in the city. These discursive inscriptions and

Figure 12.1 Two writers photographed by the local press as they discover a 'Black Lives Matter' whitewashed over a recent graffiti production at sanctioned graffiti wall, Piece Park/Tech Wall (Slater Street and Bronson Avenue).

Photograph: Haley Ritchie (*Metro News*), 2015. Reproduced with permission of the photographer.

representations of the City of Ottawa cast graffiti writers out of the community, literally and figuratively. Writers are presented in the mainstream press and in municipal records as contaminants to the ecology and aesthetics of a safe city, where 'boring' is equated with municipal security and graffiti is both the symptom and cause of an urban disease (cf. Cresswell 1992). The municipality's zero tolerance policy presents 'citizens' as victims and allies in the War on Graffiti, while graffiti writers are positioned as illogical parasitic enemies of the state. These institutional narratives foster violent and alienating responses to graffiti, while privileging the security for some citizens over the security of others (Cresswell 1992; Stewart and Kortright 2015).

Drawing the [urban] outline: how Ottawa transformed into a managerial city

Founded upon unceded Algonquin territory, Ottawa, Ontario is the capital city of Canada. It hosts an extensive system of federal bureaucratic agencies devoted to the task of managing a nation, two large universities and an average income that is second highest in the Nation (Government of Canada 2015). At one time it was a city devoted to the lumber industry, but in the 1900s the blue collar town – colonized by English, French and Irish immigrants – was transformed by a fire that destroyed most of the city. The city would rebuild. In the late 1940s, the Greber Plan was adopted to develop Ottawa into a sprawling park-like administrative town, decentralizing government buildings, removing Ottawa's railway system through town, and establishing national museums with an eye on tourism and Nationalism (City of Ottawa 2015a). Today, vast greenbelts, protected under the National Capital Commission, give the city a natural feel, while they simultaneously act as barriers between parts of the city, making many areas (such as water access to fishing spots) difficult to get through or to without a car. American-Canadian activist Jane Jacobs rallied against 1950s urban renewal policies that heralded in the dawn of administrative amalgamation and highways, in spite of how people traditionally formulated communities. Her activism and writings consistently posed the question: do we build cities for cars or people? Today, the answer to that question seems to be that Western cities, such as Ottawa, build and regulate their municipalities for the appearance of security.

Most of Ottawa's population is located in the suburbs of the city due in part to the cost and supply of housing in the core of the city. After a recent repeal of the Greber's urban plan to limit height restrictions on buildings, condos have begun to dominate our urban skylines. On weekends, government employees who fill the sandstone buildings and sidewalks give way to camera laden tourists posing with statues of former prime ministers, sampling high priced treats in the Byward Market, strolling along graffiti free market walls and malls. But the historic Byward Market has been looking run down these days because the area has been reorganized as a space for tourists, not the people who live here; businesses cannot sustain themselves on only three months of brisk business from tourists. Consequently, the only businesses that remain are largely those that appeal to the city's large university student population, bars and pubs, which increases real public health problems of over-consumption (Project for Public Spaces 2013).

Eradicating graffiti: no letters allowed, exceptions may be granted

Buddha, an award winning hip hop dancer and social worker, claims to have christened the hip hop graffiti scene in Ottawa in 1983, calling out then President Ronald Reagan on a visit to Ottawa (Melnyk 2011). At that time, there were a few train crews such as KWOTA writing in Canada who would bring traditional freight and wild style graffiti to the rail lines around town. The graffiti messages put forth by Buddha differed than the train crews' attention to style and script detail; Buddha's work centred on explicit commentary ('Reagan is a Psycho'). Both kinds of graffiti, however, were born out of a deep respect for Black and Latino hip hop traditions of the late 1970s. While there were no legal walls in Ottawa during the 1980s, there were many tolerated spaces for colourful pieces in back alleyways, along cement retainer walls and bike paths throughout the city and under low-traffic overpasses. Much has changed since then.

Around 1992, a group of young people active in the hip hop community approached the city council with a proposal to take care of an overpass in the centre of town that was becoming a burden to the city in terms of upkeep. The group convinced City Councilors to permit a pilot project: a legal graffiti space that came to be known as the House of PainT wall. The wall got its name from one of the first production pieces at the wall titled House of Pain, paying homage to the homonymous hip hop group. The space was indeed cared for by the writers and dancers of the hip hop community and the success acknowledged by the City of Ottawa lead to the sanctioning of a second legal graffiti wall. Christened 'Piece Park' by the writers – or 'The Tech Wall' because of its location in the former Ottawa Technical High school yard – it provides the only large scale art wall in the downtown core today. Both walls have easily become incorporated into mixed use spaces. A public walking path now winds along House of PainT while Piece Park stands amid a dog park and a public garden. New urban planning strategies have a bike path cutting through the park as the new light rail system construction moves forward. There are few spaces in this city where so many citizens with different interests find common ground. The walls in particular, however, were sanctioned for the graffiti community to use, because the graffiti aesthetic is not permitted in the city (unlike murals). Writers, who wanted to spend more time on pieces, or those who did not want the hassle of writing illegally, now had a place to go.

Community members have had to defend this space to city counsellors on numerous occasions. Additionally, many of the municipal funding programmes that commission 'graffiti murals' (employing a few writers a year) ask the applicants to justify their art in terms of crime prevention, something that is never expected of public art projects commissioned by local Business Improvement Associations (BIAs). While it has been typical for downtown city counsellors to support the legal wall, previous mayors and suburban city counsellors have suggested a move towards removing the sanction of the graffiti walls, assuming that the walls encourage illegal vandalism. Undeterred, House of PainT activists and writers – most notably Sabra Ripley and Mike Gall – have consistently showed up to defend the walls in meetings with the City and – in large part because of this determination and dedication to the local hip hop community – every year the hip hop community has garnered municipal funding to celebrate these spaces. House of PainT has since developed into an international non-profit urban arts festival that the City of Ottawa has benefited from greatly over the past twelve years.

In 1999 counsellors responded to some citizens who had voiced concerns about 'tagging' by attempting to manage graffiti through a pilot project facilitated by graduate students at a local university. Organizers were faced with a surprising challenge: they had to convince many citizens and business owners to cooperate with buffing or graffiti removal. The pilot project focused primarily on City of Ottawa property and utility buildings and structures in the downtown core. The students would offer to paint over graffiti if requested by citizens (if they owned the property) at the City's expense. This approach turned out to be a relatively cheap solution, costing thousands as opposed to the millions the city has recently claimed it spends on graffiti removal.

Prior to amalgamation, when graffiti was discussed in local newspapers, it was presented as an exotic art form that made foreign cities, such as New York, exciting and hip. In fact, even after two years of the pilot project's aims to educate citizens on how to report graffiti, many residents were unconvinced of the risk that graffiti was supposed to represent:

> We have laws against vandalism, which can be enforced when appropriate. We have paint to cover over offensive graffiti. In other cases, we can just live with it, not necessarily encouraging it, but not ordering a massive police operation against it, and praying that the continued existence of graffiti will not, as the editorial warns, cause people to barricade themselves in their homes. Neither massive police action nor an officially-sanctioned graffiti wall are going to stop it. It will stop when it stops, no thanks to us. Then something else will replace it, and we can hope it will not be worse. That may sound defeatist. But there are far bigger problems in our city than graffiti. Let's work on them.
>
> (Gordon 2001: D4)

It has taken almost two decades and millions of dollars in 'educating' citizens that graffiti causes crime, and is 'not nice', although many citizens remain indifferent to or resentful of the current legislation. Unsurprisingly, real estate organizations, condominium development companies and BIAs are among the biggest (and most organized) supporters of the 'zero tolerance' approach to graffiti that The City of Ottawa would formally adopt in 2008. While the rhetoric of 'crime prevention' fuelled the debate at this time, clearly the policies were supported most notably by those invested in concerns about property values, not public safety.

Not unlike other North American cities at the time, Ottawa adopted formal eradication strategies with a militaristic tone (cf. Iveson 2010); the use of such rhetoric by the municipal leaders can be traced back to the municipal election in 2003, which followed on the heels of a provincially forced amalgamation on Ontario's major cities. During the election, Ottawa suburban counsellors voiced concerns about what the amalgamation would mean for suburban and rural residents socially and financially. It is on this point then when city counsellor Alex Cullen announced via every media imaginable that the city was at 'war with graffiti'. Of course, this was not left unanswered; as Jennifer Barthel argues in her ethnographic study of the Ottawa graffiti scene of the late 1990s, 'writers from Ottawa responded with a campaign of their own. After many tedious hours of production, hundreds of stickers were affixed to numerous surfaces in the downtown core. The stickers asked "What war?"' (2001: 110). After five years of media attention on the 'problem' of graffiti, a formal graffiti bylaw was established in 2008. Given that there are already laws that address vandalism, this new bylaw focused on regulating what building owners could have painted on the outside of buildings; further, the new strategy would oversee the aesthetic of murals, whether commissioned privately or by the city.

Of course, trying to establish a clear definition of graffiti is not for the faint of heart (Wacławek 2011). As such, it is not surprising to find the bylaw would create opportunities for absurd situations. In one instance, an elementary school in an affluent neighbourhood had created a long chalk hopscotch drawing, which was power washed away the next day by the city because a resident complained of graffiti on the street. This resulted in an outcry from parents and so an amendment was made that excluded chalking from what counted as graffiti. Ottawa's regulators, instead of criminalizing graffiti, criminalized the mediums by which a piece on a wall (or street) is produced. Of course, this is not a new phenomenon as it happened in the US several years ago.

In another instance, I was invited by some former local writers to sit with them in an unexpected meeting they were called to with representatives from the City of Ottawa – Crime Prevention Ottawa mural programme. The meeting was called to inform those who were interested in the municipal funding offered by the programme that murals with 'letters' would no longer be tolerated. The young artists called to the meeting were largely former writers attempting to work legitimately as mural artists, while giving back to the city through mural programmes funded by the city to benefit committees deemed 'at risk' by municipal police. They sat before the committee in good faith, as young entrepreneurs with a foot in mural art businesses and another in urban art outreach programmes, trying to understand the new restrictions being presented to them. One former writer tried to appeal to the committee's sense of community, speaking of the relevance of graffiti to young urban youth; she spoke passionately about instances where the volunteer outreach work they did benefitted the very same population who the municipals' representatives from bylaw, local police and municipal council seemed most concerned about: poor racialized youth. On that point, the writer was dismissed by one municipal representative as being a 'poor business person' for overextending herself into uncompensated outreach work, while her business should be about providing 'the customer' what they want. The committee seemed to forget that they were providing funding for community groups to have murals in their neighbourhood that were focused on including 'at risk' youth.

We pressed on. I inquired how the committee proposed to tell the difference between a lowercase 'L' and a line; would hieroglyphics also be banned? I offered my professional concerns to the committee regarding problems that other municipalities faced when they create policies that are impossible to enforce. It was at this point that my credentials and relevance to the meeting were questioned, as our concerns fell upon deaf ears. The committee was not meeting with us to discuss the policy; they were meeting the young artists to warn them, 'as a courtesy'.

The committee justified the changes as a response to a few complaints made through the City's 3–1–1 line about one mural in particular. One caller apparently was upset with the writing by local writer Cens, feared graffiti was gang related messages. Instead of reassuring the caller that graffiti and gang activity was not related in the City of Ottawa, the style would instead be excluded from future murals. It soon became clear that the changes were fuelled more broadly by concerns over 'known' graffiti writers benefitting financially from participating in the mural programmes that were, ironically, set up to encourage graffiti writers to work legally and encourage younger generations to respect the community in which they were a part.

As the discussion heated up between the artists and the city representatives, a bylaw officer – impatient with our objections to their short-sighted assumption about graffiti – instructed the young writers to 'just stop calling it graffiti!' The representatives of the city concurred and, more diplomatically, attempted to explain that the mural programme funding would need be *defensible* to city council. Successful application would need to start using the language 'urban art' and proposed murals must exclude any typical graffiti styles. It soon became abundantly clear that the racialized aesthetic of traditional wild style and script graffiti was not welcome in this town. This echoes similar findings by Mark Halsey and Ben Pederick (2010): municipalities only sanction graffiti that promises not to be graffiti. It is important to note, here, that Canada does not provide the same 'freedom of speech' protections as our American neighbours who might benefit from challenging these kinds of discriminatory laws under the First Amendment (Mettler 2014).

Defensible aesthetics: sorry to see you go Bob and Jimmie

One of the greatest traditions of unsanctioned graffiti is to resist *existing social orders and create new ones* (Ferrell 1996; Iveson 2010). The graffiti community of Ottawa has continued to respond to absurdity with absurdity. A local writer (who does not sign his work and typically works with stencils) has taken to adding stitches to buffing, directing one to the reality that the grey is not neutral; it is an attempt at silencing (Figure 12.2). These productions are typically missed by bylaw enforcement.

Berserker/Bsrker has been working in Ottawa since before it had graffiti bylaws. He is particularly gifted at blurring lines between where a letter ends and a character or shape begins (Figure 12.3). A trickster, he has been known to return to where his work was buffed, only to repaint it just a little bit smaller so the buff is peeking out around the edges.

Any attempt to protect or defend graffiti is a tricky business because graffiti troubles mainstream ideological values about public and private space in ways that violate institutional norms (Ferrell 2009; Dovey *et al.* 2012; Stewart and Kortright 2015). As such, irony is a key feature of graffiti. Instead of eradication, the impact of increased regulation and fewer tolerated spaces in Ottawa has created a sense of martyrdom among the community, strengthening their resolve to 'bomb'. Further, more because fresh graffiti pieces are painted over shortly after they go up, writers spend less time on the colourful productions people tend to appreciate. Now, bombing is the primary form of graffiti one sees in Ottawa. Single colour quick style 'throwies' and tags make up a majority of the visible graffiti found it the core of the city, which was the kind of graffiti the bylaw intended to

Figure 12.2 Stitches around a buffed piece on Bank Street in Ottawa, 2014. Artist: JWC.
Photograph: Deborah Landry.

erase. The large spans of woodland and green space between the city and suburbia offer many spaces in which writers can work without fear of being detected by police or citizens. Graffiti has gone suburban, in large part, because suburban counsellors voted for zero tolerance policies based on fears about urban culture creep (Nayak 2009).

There is a problem of scale with mural or graffiti projects. Whereas nearby Canadian cities, such as Montreal or Toronto, foster the possibility of having a business creating large commission pieces that take up entire buildings, there are few local writers or artists who are able to work on that scale because they have been given no opportunities to develop such skills over the past twenty years. Those who have chosen to work on this scale have left town. Few businesses wish to go through the red tape of having to get a mural approved by City Council. Some resent the focus on property owners and so they refuse to take the chance on working with potential graffiti writers. While the city has made some exceptions to zero tolerance zones in town, there are still several cases such as this one: a local coffee shop discovers through a bylaw enforcement officer that the letter-free mural of Bob Dylan and Jimmie Hendrix he commissioned on the front of his building was not approved by the city. Initially the business was ordered to paint over the mural, but an exemption was applied for after the fact.

Even when the city invites urban art on overpasses the murals rarely reach higher than eight feet, even though there is a large wall to work with. Consequently, there is a strange 'eight foot' aesthetic to the street art in Ottawa (Figure 12.4).

Figure 12.3
With a linear style that incorporates a subtle aesthetic that typically is built to suit the shape and texture of the surface, Berserker's work typically fails to be recognized as graffiti by bylaw officers. (a) Centretown area, Ottawa Ontario, Ottawa, date unknown. Artist: Berserker; (b) O-Train line billboard, which ran until the sign was later torn down, date unknown. Artist: Berserker.

Photographs: Deborah Landry.

Figure 12.4 (a) Mural Title: 'The Heart of a City in Motion', 2015. Artist Group: AMPLove. Commissioned by the City of Ottawa; (b) While graffiti writers tend to leave the work of mural artists untouched, city branding masquerading as urban art is not granted such respect, particularly in lower income areas. This mural is positioned across the street from sanctioned overpass murals. The City of Ottawa branding murals commemorate Canada's upcoming 150th birthday, 2015. Artist: Nicole Belanger.

Photographs: Deborah Landry.

The City of Ottawa invites murals primarily as a method of excluding graffiti from the city. Mayor Jim Watson, who was newly elected in 2010 on a platform of a more liberal leadership, voiced support for more 'urban art'. I noticed he refrained from adopting military and pathological language from his speeches when addressing graffiti prevention programmes. I witnessed him gently correcting the war and pestilence metaphors used by long-standing 'anti-graffiti' councillors, who slipped in their political speaking on occasion at such ceremonies. The new liberal mayor's institutional support, however, remains steadfastly reserved for 'defensible art' that is inherently classist.

Following its first year success, four new murals have been installed on the City of Ottawa's underpasses in summer 2015. Murals were created by artists to beautify and enhance these underpasses as key gateways to the City with images that reflect and depict local culture, history or visions of artistic expression. Outdoor murals are effective in managing graffiti vandalism, supporting arts and culture and contributing to economic development.

(City of Ottawa, 2015b)

While the current Mayor seems to be disinterested in perpetuating the discourse of 'zero tolerance' in relation to graffiti, he has shown no interest in repealing the bylaws and policies that maintain this systemic inequality directed at 'kinds' of art and artists in the City of Ottawa. Indeed, there appears to be little motivation for such legal changes. It is rare that bylaws get repealed in Canada. When bylaws have been challenged at the Supreme Court of Ontario, the court has sided with the municipality each time, upholding mainstream ideologies about upper middle class aesthetics as a 'reasonable' expectation for municipal standards (Valverde 2012). So, while there *appears* to be an urban arts renaissance of sorts unfolding in the City of Ottawa, with increased calls for artists to create murals on urban overpasses, I suggest that these invitations are merely 'a kinder gentler' extension of our city's graffiti eradication policies. The new mural funding is not really about bringing colour to concrete structures that have long been popular painting places among graffiti writers. What is more, because the graffiti aesthetic is not permitted in deed or formal discourse, new mural programmes tend to benefit traditionally trained artists with arts funding backgrounds, with few exceptions. Certainly the CVs of the artists who were commissioned to paint the murals in Figure 12.4 indicate those with formal art training and a history of successful grant writing will be the population who benefit most from this urban art renaissance. The legacy of the zero tolerance policies has created limits for less privileged writers to benefit from these opportunities, simply because they are skilled in one kind of aesthetic that is not of liking to some state officials (McAuliffe 2012).

The zero tolerance approach to graffiti management limits economic mobility and encourages personal violence (Sampson and Raudenbush 2004; Greene 1999; Staples 2012; McAuliffe 2014; Young 2014). There are understandable resentments between those writers who believe graffiti must be illegal to be authentic, and those who do not, but such tensions rarely turn into more than words fired across social media. Some building owners, however, who understandably feel unfairly targeted by bylaw regulations, have physically assaulted writers. This was something that writers rarely encountered prior to the eradication legislation. At one point in my research, a writer and a restaurant owner told me similar stories verbatim, independent of each other: a group of business owners, tired of being threatened with fines over graffiti appearing on the rooftop areas of their building, set up a vigilante sting operation to catch the writers at work. Eventually they did: both writers (who were minors) were roughed up by the men, which escalated into police intervention, a problem that most police have little patience for (Ross and Wright 2014). Up until 2012 there were no actual fines issued to businesses (all building owners complied with bylaw warnings to paint over graffiti); nevertheless, frustration continues to manifest in divisive ways.

Ottawa, we still have a graffiti problem: but it's nice when it's legal

I had the pleasure of being a guest speaker for a summer university course being offered to privileged middle school youth. I brought them to a legal wall to talk about graffiti and upon our return to campus, I overheard one student say: 'yeah it's nice, when it's legal'. The commentary evinces how laws that govern public space can also shape what some of its citizens come to recognize as 'good' art: legislation and aesthetics become one. This exchange marked the challenging reality facing those of us passionate about graffiti in this city (legal or not): it is difficult to convince citizens on the benefits of fewer laws when an industry emerges directly tethered to these laws. Currently, the City of Ottawa maintains that it is spending one million dollars a year on what it vaguely calls 'graffiti management' but has yet to itemize what this cost is made up of. These costs, regardless, are directly related to the creation of bad policy. There are companies in town that rely on the city's 'graffiti management' programme to keep them in the business of buffing. Bylaw enforcement has in the past hired summer students to seek out graffiti for the city to manage. There are business improvement grants to be given to BIAs related to graffiti management. There is fencing to install, bylaw calls to tend to, and grey paint to be bought. The signs that inform writers that this is a municipally sanctioned legal wall (Figure 12.5) are consistently tagged heavily, replaced, and added to the cost of 'fighting graffiti'.

Figure 12.5 Tech wall tags cover up the City of Ottawa signage declaring the wall a 'Legal Graffiti Wall', 2011. Artists: Various.

Photograph: Deborah Landry.

The recent challenges to who is allowed to paint on these two legal graffiti walls had been brewing for some time before the BlackCollectiv showed up to paint on the Tech Wall. I was contacted other times prior to this by community members and former students concerned about whether they should be supporting ads placed on Kajiji trying to recruit volunteers to paint 'art' at Tech Wall, to 'take back' public space from those they feel had privilege. As interest in the wall by artists and activists who are not graffiti writers grows, and given the press coverage of the recent incident, more people will try to paint there, oblivious to the history and purpose of the wall. In the 'us vs them' debates that I suspect will follow in city council debates, I fear urban artists will continue to be presented as those with skill, and graffiti writer as the vandals of their own wall.

This case echoes sentiments raised by Cassie Findlay (2012) regarding the ephemeral and rebellious nature of script that is labelled graffiti and the reluctance to consider it worth keeping. Compared to other Canadian cities, such as Toronto and Montreal, Ottawa might be described in terms of an absence of graffiti, a concerning feature that speaks to the problem of silencing dissent (Bush 2013). It is not a coincidence that this is also an administrative town, where most citizens work in service to bureaucratic structures, where filling out the proper form is king. The context in which graffiti is produced and silenced is an important element to consider in figuring out what is happening at this wall, and on the streets of Ottawa. The markings on the wall have meaning in relation to the socio-political environment in which they are produced (Chmielewska 2007; Ferrell and Weide 2010; Avramidis 2015).

Writers challenge us to think about public space differently when there seems to be a mainstream assumption that a 'secure' city should look plain. Writers remind us that walls are strategies of power, territorial markers that begin the conversation about who may go here, not end it (Brighenti 2010). The City of Ottawa's 'zero tolerance' approach to graffiti and its mural-free zones was never in harmony with the living conditions of the lives of many people who call Ottawa home, particularly in the downtown core. Jane Jacobs (2005) warned of a kind of urban cultural annihilation: beware the power of ideology to make us blind to those things we 'really' need. The 'need' for a city that 'looks' secure has been an ideological ruse by the city officials or policymakers. Graffiti writers have responded to the falseness of this problem, and the absurdity of a graffiti management strategy that does little more than eradicate scarce public funds and opportunities for community engagement. City officials may claim to encourage urban art, but 'defensible murals' are truly the name of the game; in terms of policy and aesthetics of diversity, little has changed, even though the Mayor has. Murals celebrate crime prevention; graffiti represents criminal intention.

Patches of grey paint, wheat pasted posters, stickers and tagged up newspaper boxes hint at some kind of graffiti scene. Most traditional wild style graffiti has been pushed out of sight, although one may catch a glance of it tucked under a hidden overpass. Ottawa maintains a privileged urban aesthetic that equates scouring unauthorized voices and replacing them with the promise of security as a solid swath of beige or grey (Barthel 2002). The changing Western political climate over the last decade has only heightened the cultural value of security, whether real or imagined. The City of Ottawa embraced the zero tolerance approach to graffiti, as many Western cities did in the 1990s, blurring ideas about war and policing post 9/11; militaristic narratives circulate in an attempt to erase potential signs of disorder for fear that it will signal an urban vulnerability that may invite social disorder and chaos (Barthel 2002; Iveson 2010).

Ottawa has a graffiti problem. Erasing racialized art forms from the cityscape is systemic social exclusion. The legacy of zero tolerance graffiti management policies and legislation maintain systemic economic exclusion. The municipal government claims to choose art that represents its citizens, and yet the city chooses artists based on absurd rules of style, that omit an art form that many citizens like. Furthermore, this process relegates graffiti to the only two legal graffiti walls in the Nation's Capital City. Limiting this style to these spaces, out of sight or in a racially diverse residential downtown area, keeps this style 'in its place'. There are few spaces in which resistance can be registered on the walls of my city, which only exacerbates conflicts such as the one that unfolded between predominately working class graffiti writers and the university educated members of BlakCollectiv. This is a problem of representation and voice that the City of Ottawa cannot hope to keep buffing over.

References

Avramidis, Konstantinos. 2015. 'Reading an Instance of Contemporary Urban Iconoclash: A Design Report from Athens'. *The Design Journal.* 18(4): 513–534.

Barthel, Jennifer. 2002. *Perceptions of Graffiti in Ottawa: An Ethnographic Study of an Urban Landscape.* MA Thesis, Ottawa: Carleton University. Available at: https://curve. carleton.ca/8dc3e4d0-2ab4-4cbb-b20e-86b42444d3bf. Accessed: 14 May 2011.

Brighenti, Andrea Mubi. 2010. 'At the Wall: Graffiti Writers, Urban Territoriality, and the Public Domain'. *Space and Culture.* 13(3): 315–332.

Bush, Kenneth. 2013. 'The Politics of Post-conflict Space: The Mysterious Case of Missing Graffiti in "Post-troubles" Northern Ireland'. *Contemporary Politics.* 19(2): 167–189.

Chmielewska, Ella. 2007. 'Framing [Con]text: Graffiti and Place'. *Space and Culture.* 10(2): 145–169.

City of Ottawa. 2015a. *The Greber Report.* Available at: http://ottawa.ca/en/residents/arts-culture-and-community/museums-and-heritage/witness-change-visions-andrews-newton-7. Accessed: 30 June 2015.

City of Ottawa. 2015b. *Murals on Underpasses.* Available at http://ottawa.ca/en/residents/ water-and-environment/green-living/murals-underpasses. Accessed: 21 February 2015.

Cresswell, Tim. 1992. 'The Crucial "Where" of Graffiti: A Geographical Analysis of Reactions to Graffiti in New York'. *Environment and Planning D: Society and Space.* 10(3): 329–344.

Dovey, Kim, Wollan, Simon and Woodcock, Ian. 2012. 'Placing Graffiti: Creating and Contesting Character in Inner-city Melbourne'. *Journal of Urban Design.* 17(1): 21–41.

Ferrell, Jeff. 1996. *Crimes of Style: Urban Graffiti and the Politics of Criminality.* Boston, MA: Northeastern University Press.

Ferrell, Jeff. 2009. 'Hiding in the Light: Graffiti and the Visual'. *Criminal Justice Matters.* 78(1): 23–25.

Ferrell, Jeff and Weide, Robert. 2010. Spot Theory. *City*. 14(1–2): 48–62.

Findlay, Cassie. 2012. 'Witness and Trace: January 25 Graffiti and Public Art as Archive'. *Interface: A Journal for and about Social Movements*. 4(1): 178–182.

Gordon, C. 2001. 'Surviving the Graffiti Plague: Let us Spray'. *The Ottawa Citizen*, 21 August, p. D4.

Government of Canada. 2015. *Statistics Canada: Median Total Income, by Family Type, by Census Metropolitan Area (All Census Families)*. Available at: www.statcan.gc.ca/tables-tableaux/sum-som/l01/cst01/famil107a-eng.htm. Accessed: 30 June 2015.

Greene, Judith A. 1999. 'Zero Tolerance: A Case Study of Police Policies and Practices in New York City'. *Crime and Delinquency*. 45(2): 171–187.

Halsey, Mark and Pederick, Ben. 2010. 'The Game of Fame: Mural, Graffiti, Erasure'. *City*. 14(1–2): 82–98.

Iveson, Kurt. 2010. 'The Wars on Graffiti and the New Military Urbanism'. *City*. 14(1–2): 115–134.

Jacobs, Jane. 2005. *Dark Age Ahead*. Toronto: Random House.

McAuliffe, Cameron. 2012. 'Graffiti or Street Art? Negotiating the Moral Geographies of the Creative City'. *Journal of Urban Affairs*. 34(2): 189–206.

McAuliffe, Cameron. 2014. 'Legal Walls and Professional Paths: The Mobilities of Graffiti Writers in Sydney'. *Urban Studies*. 50(3): 518–537.

Melnyk, Adam. 2011. *Visual Orgasm: The Early Years of Canadian Graffiti*. Calgary: Frontenac House.

Mettler, Margaret. 2014. 'Graffiti Museum: A First Amendment Argument for Protecting Uncommissioned Art on Private Property'. *Michigan Law Review*. 111(2): 249–282.

Morgan, Anthony. 2015. 'The Suffocating Experience of being Black in Canada'. *The Star*, 31 July. Available at: www.thestar.com/opinion/commentary/2015/07/31/the-suffocating-experience-of-being-black-in-canada.html. Accessed: 30 August 2015.

Nayak, Anoop. 2010. 'Race, Affect, and Emotion: Young People, Racism, and Graffiti in the Postcolonial English Suburbs'. *Environment and Planning A*. 42(10): 2370–2392.

Project for Public Spaces. 2013. *Strengthening the Future of the Byward Market Report*. Available at: http://ottwatch.ca/meetings/file/66762/File_Doc_1_Strengthening_the_Future_of_the_ByWard_Martket_pdf_Item_BYWARD_MARKET_STRENGTHENING_THE_FUTURE_OF_THE_BYWARD_MARKET_Meeting_Planning_Committee_Date_2013_06_11_09_30_00. Accessed: 30 June 2015.

Ross, Jeffrey Ian and Wright, Benjamin. 2014. '"I've Got Better Things to Worry about": Police Perceptions of Graffiti and Street Art in a Large Mid-Atlantic City'. *Police Quarterly*. 17(2): 176–200.

Sampson, Robert and Raudenbush, Stephen. 2004. 'Seeing Disorder: Negotiating Stigmas and the Social Construction of "Broken Windows" '. *Social Psychology Quarterly*. 67(4): 319–342.

Staples, Brent. 2012. 'The Human Cost of "Zero Tolerance" '. *New York Times*, 29 April. Available at: www.nytimes.com/2012/04/29/opinion/sunday/the-cost-of-zero-tolerance.html. Accessed: 10 April 2013.

Stewart, Michelle and Kortright, Chris. 2015. 'Cracks and Contestation: Toward an Ecology of Graffiti and Abatement'. *Visual Anthropology*. 28(1): 67–87.

Valverde, Mariana. 2012. *Everyday Law on the Street: Governance in an Age of Diversity*. Chicago, IL: University of Chicago Press.

Wacławek, Anna. 2011. *Graffiti and Street Art*. London: Thames & Hudson.

Young, Alison. 2014. *Street Art, Public City: Law, Crime and the Urban Imagination*. London: Routledge Glass House.

13 #Instafame

Aesthetics, audiences, data

Lachlan MacDowall

Introduction

This chapter examines the ways in which graffiti and street art are increasingly produced as digital objects, shaped by the architecture of digital platforms and the aggregated responses of audiences, transmuted into data. This process is neatly captured by the title of a recent exhibition at the Steinberg Museum of Art in New York.[1] The 'From Concrete to Data' exhibition featured a mix of old school graffiti writers and documenters, street artists and contemporary artists working across all media, including many examples of screen-based media influenced by the aesthetics and practices of graffiti. Taken as a whole, this kind of work charts the transformation of graffiti from a form attached to the industrial landscape to one at home in the post-industrial city, one characterized not just by new materials and new economies – renovated buildings and gentrified neighbourhoods – but one in which graffiti and street art has become a set of mobile aesthetic features that, like the older industries, shift to new physical materials and then begin to dematerialize.

Graffiti and street art function as an index of this broader transformation from the industrial to the post-industrial age, simultaneously seeking out the remnants of the industrial age – bombing empty shop fronts or the hoardings of building sites – while also exploring the potential of digital platforms for 'getting up', graffiti parlance for the process of making one's name visible in the city. The notion of 'Instafame' explored in this chapter both emerges from and is set against this original fame-seeking and 'getting up' of early graffiti culture.

The shift of graffiti and street art from the context of the industrial age to the post-industrial city produces a complex dialectic between physical and digital spaces. The interior of an abandoned factory or a quiet laneway, already mediatized to some extent by more than a century of urban photography, becomes a different kind of space again when it is reproduced in digital social media. Under the right circumstances, the wall itself moves from being a spatial feature demarcating property boundaries and the division between interiors and exteriors to something else: a prop or scenic backdrop for the production of digital content. While graffiti and street art still seek the fame available from passers-by, the mediatization of the city allows for the amplification of more remote or inaccessible city spaces, where the (global) digital audience would likely exceed the local foot traffic, with small spaces sometimes yielding big data.

For street art, digital media forces a rethinking of the question posed by Nick Riggle (2010): what is the 'street' in street art? Riggle's analytic approach draws attention to the ways in which the context of the 'street' is intrinsic to the experience and meaning of street art; however, in order for this definition to be helpful, it must account for the 'street' as a multiple and shifting form (MacDowall 2014b). For example, the street has a long history as a highly racialized public space, while theorists such as a Saskia Sassen (2011) have taken issue with the dominance of European conceptions of the street – the boulevard, the promenade, etc. – instead pointing to the ways in which the street is now a global political form. Theorizations of street art that depend on concepts developed in European cities such as a the *flâneur* (Paris in the 1860s) or the Situationist's *dérive* (Paris in the late 1950s) seem less useful in accounting for its global reach, where the trajectories charted in the 'Hip-hop, From the Bronx to the Arab Streets' exhibition at the Global Arab Institute in Paris (Sassen's 'global street' in the 2000s) are more helpful.[2]Understanding contemporary graffiti and street art requires a sense of, at least, these two (interconnected) and changing aspects of the street: as a set or backdrop for the production of digital content and a site of globally connected political action.

Similarly, the analysis of contemporary street art is challenged by its rapid but uneven shift from a marginal, subcultural practice to a highly visible and main-stream, global formation. Currently, street art is in a phase of institutionalization, a process of being organized around a series of key artists, curators, galleries, festivals, magazines and websites, as well as new audiences, an element often neglected in the analysis of this process. Street art now represents a vast global field; it's scale and speed means that previous research tools and scholarly approaches – documentary photography, artist interviews and advocacy for the value of street art – may have limited value. In any case, they are now routinely undertaken by artists, curators and producers themselves, posing pressing questions about the role of academic research in this area.

The scale of the street art world means it is now difficult to fully conceive of it, to extrapolate from our personal, local experience to its global scale. As Fredric Jameson argues in *The Geopolitic Aesthetic* (2009), the scale of emerging 'world systems' often present challenges to existing tools, formats and aesthetic modes. Jameson asks, how is it possible

> to think a system so vast that it cannot be encompassed by the natural and historically developed categories of perception with which human beings normally orient themselves', to fuse our partial and local understanding with a sense of the global whole?
>
> (Jameson 2009: 2)

For Jameson, the key link between the domains of the local and the global is cognitive mapping, a concept he develops from the earlier work of urban planner

Kevin Lynch, whose 1960 book *The Image of the City* examined the ways in which people make sense of their urban environment, not through abstract diagrams but via local cues, a role now played by graffiti and street art as navigational markers and modes of informal place-making. Ultimately, the process of grasping a world system must be a self-reflective one, containing an analysis of the media and representational strategies through which it is constituted: 'any intent to map a network of just such productive nodes or provisional centres would have to include within the description an account of their mode of communicational relationship and command transmission' (Jameson 2009: 49).

Instagram and media histories

This chapter addresses the perceptual and methodological challenges posed by the global street art system by examining the role of the digital platform Instagram in producing graffiti and street art. It does this by considering Instagram's role as a central platform in the production of street art's 'communicational relationships', one that offers the promise of a glimpse at a global totality through a new aesthetic and interactive regime, a digital architecture that offers a kind of training in how to navigate a global archive of images. The chapter outlines some initial methods for representing and analysing the complex ecology of formats and feeds in which graffiti and street art exist and the potential of data-driven analysis for representing the global flows and fault lines of style and taste, using data from the Instagram accounts of the most-followed street artists and graffiti writers globally.

As many scholars have noted, in different ways graffiti and street art are part of a longer media history (Austin 1996; MacDowall 2008; Avramidis and Drakopoulou 2015). As a largely ephemeral and geographically dispersed form, visual media have played a key role in the documenting and disseminating of graffiti, from the original *New York Times* article reporting the exploits of early taggers in July 1971 to web videos documenting contemporary train painting, such as the series produces by the Grifters (2015).[3] Alongside the central role of photography and digital media, RJ Rushmore has broadened the notion to media of include house parties and 'meeting up at nightclubs', describing the vital social value of venues such as the Mudd Club in New York's downtown scene in the late 1970s and early 1980s (Rushmore 2013).

Each of these media forms and platforms provide new containers for graffiti and street art but also shape their practices and aesthetics. In his study of the nature and function of archives, Jacques Derrida (1998: 17) draws attention to these processes, by which the structures of media forms provide the point of origin and the horizon of the content: 'the technical structure of the archiving archive also determines the structure of the archivable content even in its very coming into existence and in its relationship to the future. The archivization produces as much as it records the event.' Sometimes this shaping takes the form of explicit interaction between users and is foregrounded in the art works or discourse. At other times, the impact of the media forms is more subtle, submerged within data flows or, leaving the works themselves seemingly unchanged, as the context, experience and meaning surrounding the artwork shift.

The architecture of Instagram

Initially launched in 2010 as a modest mobile photo-sharing application for Apple's iPhone that uploads images in a square format and adds filters that mimic vintage photographs, Instagram has grown to become one of the most-used social media platforms, alongside Facebook and Twitter. The reasons for this rise are complex, but include both 'technical' reasons (ease of use on mobile devices or the limitations of other platforms in processing images efficiently) and 'aesthetic' reasons (preferences for the clean, professional look of the filters and display, a preference for the speed of images over lengthy text or the availability of celebrity content). By the end of 2014, Instagram had more than 300 million users with over 30 billion images uploaded (Instagram 2015).

Media scholars have pointed to the importance of studying digital platforms within a context of a broader 'integrated ecology' of digital media (Tufekci 2014). Instagram is linked to a variety of other platforms; most directly to Facebook and current patterns usage suggest newer platforms such as Snapchat will rise in influence. And yet, with Instagram's privileging of flows of images tied to mobile devices that are carried through the city and the real-time battles for attention and impact that this generates, it is more closely synced with the aesthetics of graffiti and street art and the needs of its producers and consumers than any other digital platforms (MacDowall and de Souza 2016).

Like the street encounter with graffiti and street art, the design of the Instagram architecture allows for multiples ways to 'come across' an image, for example via the home page feed, by viewing an individual account, via a text search of hash-tags, via a page that displays images 'liked' by your followers or via the search page, where images identified as of interest via an Instagram algorithm are displayed or via a map that displays geo-tagged images. Depending on a user's preference for these methods (including their combination) the experience of the site will be different. As media theorists Nadav Hochman and Lev Manovich (2013) argue:

> it is the congruent operation of these elements within a single mobile application and the presentation – *i.e.*, how the application allowed users to create, share, and organize information – that might provide a plausible explanation for Instagram's widespread adoption, and how it meshes with current cultural trends.

While Facebook migrated from desktop computers to mobile devices, Instagram was more attuned to the mechanics of mobile devices through limited text comments and making use of the tactile features of scrolling and double tapping – a one-handed, street-based platform perfect for a highly mobile and distracted subject, Instagram's filters removed the need for image post-processing, collapsing the time from the image being taken to its publication.

For the majority of users, Instagram is a public, networked platform, social yet anonymous, allowing a mix of publicity and (relative) privacy that is also attractive to both graffiti writers and street artists, who must mediate these competing interests in different ways (MacDowall and de Souza 2016). Turning a mobile phone sideways, the scrolling Instagram feed resembles the fleeting view of graffiti from the windows of a moving train, the relation of moving train to a static wall matching that of a stationary subject viewing a scrolling screen. Just as viewing graffiti from a train both requires a certain retinal and cognitive agility and schools the viewer in this capacity, the Instagram interface both requires and develops certain visual scanning skills. In general, the aesthetic features of graffiti and street art are designed for visual impact, to be visible to this moving, distracted subject, and so are well suited to addressing the Instagram viewer.

Like most graffiti and street art, Instagram images are ephemeral or are glimpsed only fleetingly in a subjective endless present, from which the past rapidly recedes from M(inutes), to D(ays) to W(eeks) – no longer tied to a calendar date, but simply dated in relation to the present. As Hochman and Manovich (2013) argue, *Instagram* produces a multi-temporal image that suggests at least three different temporal references: the actual time when the picture was taken, the time evoked by a certain filter, and the time span indicated by the application when viewing the photo. At various points in this chapter I invoke the concept of the Instagram era to denote the shift in conditions; however, given the temporal complexity of the Instagram image, the concept of an 'era' is ambivalent, given how Instagram itself disrupts and reconstructs forms of history.

Analysing instafame

The term 'Instafame' is one of a sequence of popular invented hash-tags that use the 'Insta' prefix to point to the new practical and emotional conditions produced by the platform. In the context of graffiti and street art, #Instafame denotes an awareness and often a cynicism about the particular type of fame earned online, invoking a more genuine, robust reputation earned offline (or in the early analogue years of pre-millennial graffiti culture) (MacDowall 2014a). The term Instafame is used here to capture this tension, between an analysis that pertains only to conditions specific to the Insta-world, and the way in which it is impossible to completely demarcate the interior world of the platform from its broader effects.

Given this ambivalence, the chapter attempts to take a critical approach to analysing Instagram data, taking into account how it is constituted and querying its usefulness for cultural analysis (Manovich 2016). As danah boyd and Kate Crawford (2012) argue, big data should be considered as a conjunction of technical, cultural and scholarly formations that combines both seductive promises of large-scale, rational analysis and potential nightmares of abstraction, surveillance and control. Data analysis frequently uncritically mimics the language of quantification, comparison, interchangeability, scale and growth that are central to the logic of neoliberal capitalism. Instead, data analysis is used here not as a means to achieve a set of objective results or a total view but as a means of understanding the broader mechanics of how artists, art works and audiences are interacting, what Jameson (2009: 49) refers to as the 'mode of communicational relationship'.

This chapter examines only one aspect of the data – other forms of coding and analysis are possible. It also doesn't address some broader questions about what can and can't be displayed on Instagram and which artists – living and dead – are not represented on the platform. Instagram data exists as an expression of what Michael H. Goldhaber (1997) has termed the 'attention economy', a finite resource in an information age, which also shapes 'its own kind of wealth, its own class divisions – stars vs fans – and its own forms of property'. This division transposes onto the division between the fans of graffiti and street art 'paying attention' (following on Instagram) and those receiving it (being followed on Instagram). However, while Instagram appears to formalize the attention economy, it also undermines it, because 'following' does not have any necessary relationship to actual attention, and may be a replacement of actual attention, a proxy or deferral of attention. In one sense, following, as a marker of affiliation and as a component of a social network, might be the real content of Instagram, rather than the images posted or viewed.

Finally, it is important to understand both the official mechanics of the Instagram interface and the broader range of social and technical strategies that are employed to construct accounts and (primarily) boost follower numbers. Understanding both the structure and use of the platform are important in order to make distinctions between results as artefacts of the platform itself and those that more accurately reflect actual trends in tastes and behaviour, even though these two elements are structurally connected.

The handmade dataset

A number of artists and researchers have used large-scale forms of data to analyse graffiti, notably Evan Roth (2006) and the Graffiti Research Lab (2015), who developed a number of data-driven projects. Roth's pioneering design projects mapping graffiti letterforms in New York City led to a series of projects that combined technical ingenuity and a hacker ethos with the aesthetic energy of graffiti culture, though they also mirrored developments in law enforcement and surveillance, where the same techniques were used to build databases as evidence for the prosecution of graffiti writers (MacDowall 2008).

In 2012 Jake Dobkin developed the *GrafRank* project that appeared on the Gothamist website and used a variety of data sources including the photo-sharing site Flickr to create maps of trending artists in cities worldwide. Most recently, Hochman *et al.* (2014) mapped the spread of images of artwork produced by Banksy during his informal art residency in New York in 2013, as part of broader research into new modes of analysing social media and visual data. As Hochman and Manovich note in a related study:

> The use of quantitative analysis and visualization for the study of cultural visual data allows us to view cultural artifacts in new ways, to confirm and

describe more precisely the existing understanding of historical developments, and, potentially, to reveal previously unnoticed patterns.

(2014: 1)

Sitting behind these relatively modest goals is a more powerful promise of totality, what Hochman and Manovich (2013) refer to as an 'emerging operative cultural logic in which an individual photo is being related to a whole that potentially promises any image from any vantage point'. As with Jameson's analysis of cinema, which stresses that new aesthetic forms will be required to grasp this totality, Hochman and Manovich show how new mapping techniques can represent large numbers of images, using techniques that abstract colour data and tonal values and disperse them using radial projections or 'photo-trail' techniques. Just as *Instagram* offers the scrolling image feed as a mechanism for processing a large volume of images, these 'photo-trails', as a new aesthetic form, present a new way of reading and comprehending large banks or swarms of digital photographs, not as images but as collective variations in hues and tones.

As a starting point for analysis, a data table of the 100 most followed graffiti and street art Instagram accounts was constructed by hand using an iterative combination of methods:

- intuitive searching for accounts of artists with international profiles;
- examining the accounts of artists listed by well-known documenters of graffiti and street art, such as Instagrafite (@instagrafite) or Martha Cooper (@marthacoopergram);
- examining the accounts that high-profile artists are themselves following;
- searching for Instagram accounts from lists of artists derived from external sources (e.g. the participants of the major graffiti or street art exhibitions or publications or blog accounts of street art on Instagram);
- considering the users 'suggested' by Instagram. When a user 'follows' a new account they have the option of following three 'suggested' accounts. These 'Suggested Users' are curated by *Instagram* and matched to accounts via a private algorithm.[4]

This list was then refined over a number of months, with the total followers for each account on the list recorded in one session (12 June 2015) to minimize the changes in numbers of followers that happen every second.

The resulting Top 100 most followed accounts were then placed in ascending order, stretching from the 100th most followed account (Zes (@zesmsk) a graffiti writer with the Mad Society Kings crew in Los Angeles with 33,990 followers) up to the most followed account (Street Art Globe, an aggregated feed of new street art, which has 1.44 million followers) (Figure 13.1).

As the shape of the graph suggests, while the majority of the list have fewer than 100,000 followers, the top twenty accounts are considerably larger, ranging from 134,000 to the two accounts with more than 1 million followers (Street Art Globe and Instagrafite, another aggregated feed). Further analysis was then

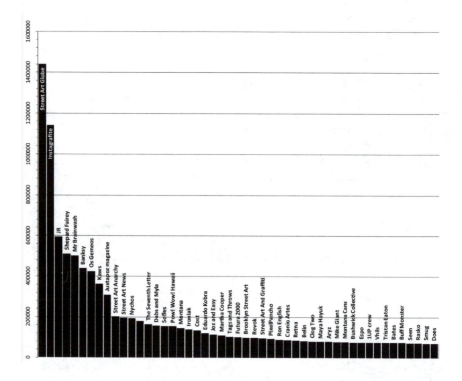

Figure 13.1 The top 100 most followed graffiti and street art accounts on Instagram
       (as at 12 June 2015) (simplified x axis).

Source: Lachlan MacDowall.

performed to orient the dataset towards two key questions facing contemporary
scholars of graffiti and street art, namely how to map the global contours of the
emerging institutionalization of street art and how to describe the complex
relationship between graffiti and street art, with their connected and competing
definitions, aesthetics and lived practices.

Coding graffiti and street art

In order to make sense of this list, the accounts were coded to distinguish between
the accounts of individual artists and those of 'other' accounts, which include
documenters (both individuals such as Martha Cooper and aggregated feeds),
publications (such as *Juxtapoz* magazine), spray paint manufacturers (Montana
and Ironlak), events (such as the Pow! Wow! Festival in Hawaii) and galleries
and curated spaces (for example the Bushwick Collective in Brooklyn or the
Seventh Letter in Los Angeles) (Figure 13.2).

The list was then further coded to explore the relationship between graffiti and
street art, formations that have both strong forms of affiliation and distinctive
characteristics, that has been a source of both collaboration and combative relations

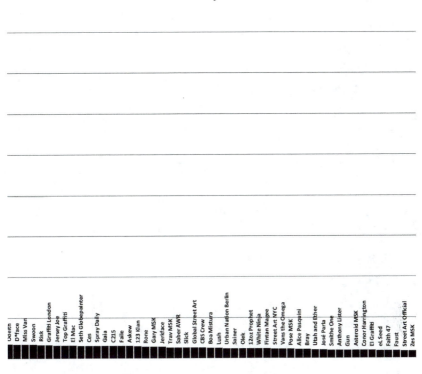

Figure 13.1 continued

in different contexts (MacDowall 2014a). Further distinctions were then made between street artists, graffiti writers and those that exhibited a combination of graffiti and street art, either in concurrent practice, in a hybrid form or over their career.

This coding exercise itself posed many interesting questions about the usefulness or not of these categories. As I have argued elsewhere, while it is important to note the distinctiveness of both graffiti and street art practices, they cannot be easily reduced to particular media and aesthetic features. Though they exist as global forms, both graffiti and street art have distinctive local variations and there are also many artists who work across the two forms (see MacDowall 2014a). In the process of coding, the many subtle distinctions across the shifting formations of graffiti, street art, muralism and urban art had to be collapsed into simple aesthetic explanations (the prevalence of graffiti-style letterforms) rather than more nuanced questions about the artist's history of practice (e.g., the extent of illegal, street-based activity).

However, the coding did reveal some clear trends. In terms of the numbers of accounts in each category the final list was weighted fairly evenly between the four categories: street artists (37 per cent), graffiti writers (25 per cent) and other

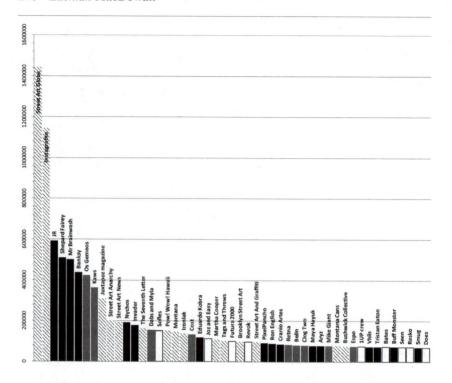

Figure 13.2 The top 100 most followed graffiti and street art accounts on Instagram (as artists (grey), graffiti writers (white) and others, which includes documenters, events and at June 2015), with the accounts classified into street artists (black), graffiti writers/street galleries (shaded).

Source: Lachlan MacDowall.

accounts (24 per cent), with the category of graffiti writer/street artists the smallest (14 per cent). However, it is clear from the distribution of accounts across the list that 'other' accounts and individual street artists dominate the upper half of the Top 100.

This is also evident when comparing the total followers in each category (noting that these are non-unique follows rather than actual followers, as there are many *Instagram* users following multiple accounts on the Top 100 list). Led by the million-plus followers of @streetartglobe and @instagrafite, these 'other' accounts comprised 38 per cent of all non-unique 'follows' (a figure derived from 4.8 million individual 'acts of following'). Strikingly, the accounts of graffiti writers were much less popular than street artists: of the 12.6 million 'acts of following' that generated the Top 100 list used in this study, only 1.6 million acts were for accounts that could be clearly defined as those of individual graffiti writers.

The top twenty accounts (Figure 13.3) also separates easily into a series of tiers, based on rough clusters of audience numbers, beginning with the two top aggregated accounts (Tier 1) and then a group of globally known street artists in

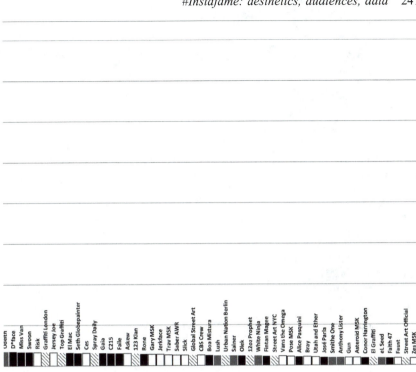

Figure 13.2 continued

Tier 2 (JR, Shepard Fairey, Mr Brainwash, Banksy, OsGemeos and Kaws, along with *Juxtapoz*, an established high-circulation arts and culture magazine that covers graffiti and street art).

The third Tier is dominated by a range of 'other' accounts: two aggregated news feeds (Street Art Anarchy and Street Art News), two spray paint manufacturers (Montana and Ironlak), an international festival (Pow! Wow!) and the shop and gallery of a well-known graffiti crew in Los Angeles (The Seventh Letter). The artists in the third Tier are well-known street artists who work internationally (Nychos, Invader, COST and a duo working under the name Dabs Myla) and Australian graffiti writer Sofles, the only graffiti writer in the top three Tiers and the most followed individual graffiti writer on the list.

Inevitably, the positions and relative numbers of followers on the list may conflict with one's broader perception of the popularity of an artist. For example, is Mr Brainwash more popular than Banksy, as the data suggests? Perhaps the small difference in followers can be attributed to the dramatic difference in the numbers of posts from each account: a few dozen for Banksy, more than 500 for

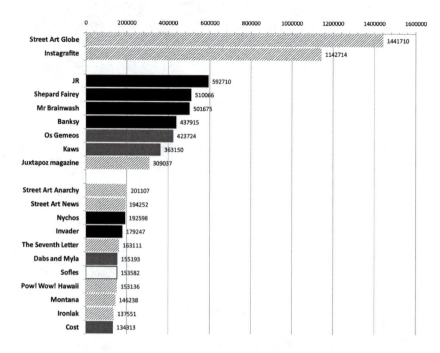

Figure 13.3 The top tiers of most followed graffiti and street accounts on Instagram (as at June 2015), with the accounts classified into street artists (black), graffiti writers/street artists (grey), graffiti writers (white) and others, which includes documenters, events and galleries (shaded).

Source: Lachlan MacDowall.

Mr Brainwash? Similarly, are OS Gemeos nearly three times more popular than Invader? This result (which has since narrowed to almost a 2:1 ratio) may be an effect of the duration of their Instagram accounts: OS Gemeos posted their first image in mid 2011, while Invader joined relatively late, in September 2013. The usefulness and limitations of the coding categories are also evident, demonstrating the complex position of an artist such as COST, who emerged in the context of New York graffiti culture but pioneered a number of forms in the 1990s (such as wheat paste posters and culture jamming pranks) that now seem more at home in street art culture.

The data can also be coded in a variety of ways, for instance to confirm and quantify the audiences of female street artists and graffiti writers (with train bomber Utah (@utah_ether) the only account falling into this last category). The coding does not include women who run or work in 'other' accounts (for example aggregated feeds or street art businesses) or who are part of large collectives (such as the Spanish Boa Mistura collective (@boamistura)). Though women artists feature strongly in aggregated feeds and the list of female artists and documenters includes many artists with high profiles who continue to exhibit internationally

(Swoon, Miss Van, Alice Pasquini, Olek, Myla, Faith 47, along with photographer Martha Cooper), statistically women make up only ten accounts from the Top 100 and a lowly 6 per cent of the total 'acts of following' (700,000 follows out of 12.6 million) (Figure 13.4).

In absolute terms, audiences comprising tens of thousands of self-identified followers represent a substantial base of viewers for an artist, particularly given

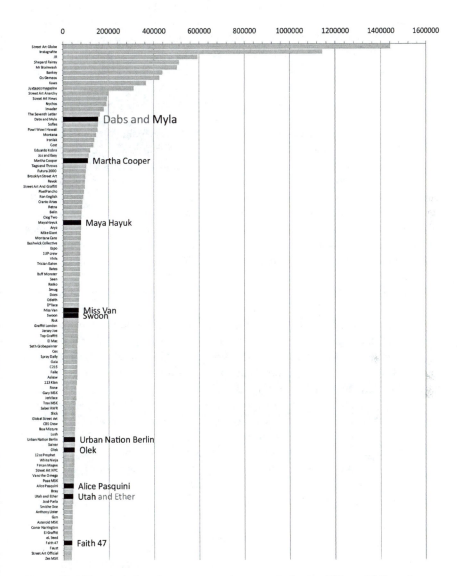

Figure 13.4 Female artists, documenters and curators in the top 100 most followed graffiti and street accounts on Instagram (as at June 2015).

Source: Lachlan MacDowall.

the low costs of communicating with them directly. However, perhaps the figures are more helpfully read in relative terms, allowing comparisons between the existing audiences for the cluster of seven accounts with from 40,000 to more than 60,000 followers, most of whom emerged in the pre-Instagram era, compared to Myla, the only female artist in the top three tiers, whose international rise (and move to Los Angeles from Melbourne) is roughly contemporaneous with the development of the Instagram platform itself. It is important to note the tension inherent in the Instagram platform, which has 'progressive' elements that allow new accounts to be established and grow in relative terms and 'regressive' elements that favour existing accounts and relatively larger accounts (which in turn, generally favours those accounts of early adopters or those who have had accounts for a longer period).

To be useful, the raw figures need to be given some further context, in terms of both the architecture of the platform and the practices and trajectories of the artists. For example, when I met Martha Cooper in 2013 she had embraced the new technology and had soaked up more than 100,000 followers, on the back of a busy schedule of international presentations and exhibitions. As a photographer she was intrigued by the possibilities of the iPhone and its convenience over her bulky Nikon camera. As with many professional photographers she initially maintained a distinction between iPhone images and those shot in the 35mm format with professional equipment (her @marthacoopergram account was labelled 'iPhone 5 only' and is now labelled 'iPhone 5 mostly'). Unlike Cooper's account, many of the top accounts are run by artists who operate with teams of hired assistants and full-time media managers.

In contrast to JR, whose photographic skills, high artistic output and collaborations with well-known artists and celebrities from other fields are perfectly aligned with Instagram form, the career of Swoon has shifted from easily recognizable iconography of paste-ups printed from wood blocks to more complex social practice and local activism, that perhaps are less suited to the speed and visual focus of the Instagram platform. Also, the number of followers in this dataset only include examples of the artist's work published on their own accounts – many artists receive exposure through images posted that do not identify the artist (given the anonymity of much of the work), or posted by other users with a hashtag, where they will often mingle with other images (#missvan has more than 13,000 entries, most referencing her artwork, while given her more generic name, the artwork of Swoon is hardly visible in the 385,000 entries under the hashtag of her name). More detailed research of the relationship between Instagram posting patterns and artistic production is continuing.

Rates of growth and surging accounts

The 'regressive' aspects of Instagram, that is, the relatively greater ability of accounts with large numbers of followers to reach an audience directly (through posting), indirectly (primarily through the 'likes' and comments of followers, which in turn makes the images visible to their own followers) and through algorithmic preferencing (the 'Suggested Users' feature among others) and thus expand their followers needs to be considered in any analysis, which will otherwise overly favour early adopters. One method is to discount the relative size of accounts and, within the Top 100 accounts, compare the relative rates of growth of accounts, paying attention to those accounts that are gathering followers at high rates.

Figure 13.5 lists the fastest growing accounts in the Top 100 from May/June 2015, which cluster into very high rates of growth, led by Australia muralist Fintan Magee (@fintan_magee).

Magee gained 2,621 followers over this period, ranking only twenty-fifth for number of new followers (compared to a rise of 42,238 new followers for Montana spray paint (@mtncolours)). However, when considered as a proportion of existing followers, his was the highest rate of growth. This is perhaps unsurprising given he completed an incredible landmark mural during this period in Werchter, Belgium. The work, titled 'Moving the Pointless Monument', was painted on a stack of seven shipping containers, showing a massive hunched figure carrying a square metal object on his back, with the surrounding sand foundations, tree line and sky continued into the painting, producing a convincing *trompe l'oeil* effect. The illusion is most powerful from a single point (where the tree line matches), viewed when the sky conditions match the painted sky blue tones. As such, the artwork is most effective in a single instant and place, best suited for Instagram display.

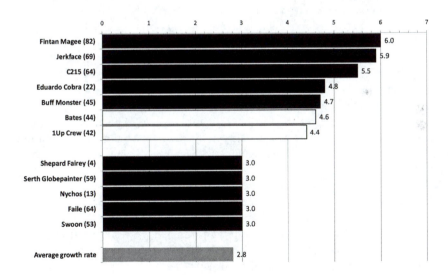

Figure 13.5 The highest rates of growth (in the month to 12 June 2015) among the 100 most followed graffiti and street art accounts on Instagram (as at June 2015, rank indicated in brackets) with the accounts classified into street artists (black) and graffiti writers (white).

Source: Lachlan MacDowall.

The average growth rate for all accounts in the Top 100 accounts during this period was 2.8 per cent, with most of the high rates of growth among accounts in the bottom half of the Top 100 (with Shepard Fairey and Nychos exceptions to this), perhaps reflecting the difficulty of continually reaching new audiences, once the account reaches a certain size. In a limited 'attention economy' it also raises questions about the saturating of followers and relative impact of Instagram posts. There were also a number of accounts that lost followers, potentially a more interesting site of analysis given the dominant rhetorical and mathematical drive of Instagram towards the amassing of followers.[5]

Conclusion

The popularity of Instagram for the publishing of graffiti and street art has shifted the terrain for fame-seeking street artists and graffiti writers. This chapter has set out to understand the key dynamics of these new conditions and the context of an emerging global system of graffiti and street art. In particular, the chapter examines how new methodologies of data mining and analysis can be used to sketch the contours of this global system, while remaining sceptical about the promise of data in general or Instagram in particular to enable us to grasp the system in its totality or allow us to exist in the endless new/now of Instagram feeds.

In many cases, graffiti and street art retain both the material messiness and ideological resonances of direct mark making. However, they are also becoming increasingly digital forms, affecting more audiences in the digital realm, and becoming designed and shaped more directly for digital platforms, with the space of the street often transformed into a set or backdrop for the production of digital content. Of all digital platforms, the speed and scale of Instagram (both its take-up and operation) has amplified this process, putting pressure on artists to trade in its 'attention economy' and leaving significant challenges for researchers.

This chapter does not argue that Instagram data provides a proxy for any kind of value, ranking or index of fame (other than Instafame) of graffiti writers and street artists. Aside from a range of philosophical objections, in practical terms it is not possible to fully distinguish between the many Instagram artefacts of the platform (from differences in demographics, language and time-zones to glitches, algorithms, bots, spams and scams) and surges of interest, especially given how, as I have argued, expressions of interest are shaped and organized by the platform itself (Parkinson 2014). And yet, while the number of followers does not provide a measure of value, the architecture of Instagram can illuminate to some extent the contours of interest in graffiti and street art within the network, and the patterns of Instagram do have significant material effects, shaping profiles, attention, exposure and reputation, as well as influencing the material practices of artists and the chosen and inherited aesthetics forms visible in the streets.

Further, I have argued that an analysis of Instagram also draws attention to the often neglected aspects of the audience within the street art system, though Instagram represents only one element of an array of possible audiences, that include both the ideal audience of street art's address, empirical viewers and the platform-specific forms of Instagram viewers and followers (see MacDowall, 2014b). Using this notion of audiences, the chapter also begins to outline the fault lines between the formations of graffiti and street art, potentially highlighting the overlaps and distinctiveness of their aesthetics and the asymmetry between the two, with the imagery of many forms of street art appealing to and addressing larger, perhaps more diverse audiences, though more analysis is needed in this area and several other important caveats remain. As Hochman and Manovich (2013) note, the technical architecture, context and user demographics of Instagram have evolved since 2010, so findings also may reflect a specific period in Instagram's history. Finally, there are ongoing questions for artists and researchers about the aspects of surveillance and data control with which Instagram is implicated, including the private ownership of data and opacity of algorithms and commercial arrangements. These are just some of the challenges of making and researching graffiti and street art in this Instafame era.

Notes

1   The 'From Concrete to Data' exhibition ran from 26 January 2015 – 21 March 2015 and was curated by Ryan Seslow. See www.concretetodata.com. Accessed: 17 December 2015.

2   The 'HIP-HOP, du Bronx aux Rues Arabes' exhibition was held at the Global Arab Institute, Paris from 28 April 2015 – 26 July 2015. Rapper Akhenation was the Artistic Director. See Cachin *et al.* (2015).

3   The article 'Taki 183 Spawns Pen Pals' was published in the New York Times on 21 July 1971 and is one of the earliest public profiles of New York graffiti writing. The article itself is often credited with contributing to the spread and popularity of graffiti in its early years. Available at: www.taki183.net/_pdf/taki_183_nytimes.pdf. Accessed: 17 December 2015.

4   The Instagram company describes the logic behind 'Suggested Users' as follows:

> To present people with a variety of talented Instagrammers to follow from around the globe, we continually review, add and remove people from our list of suggested accounts. The list always includes a mix of new and emerging voices as well as previously suggested community members.
>
> (Instagram Help Center webpage, 2015)

5   See for example reporting of rapper A$AP Rocky's Instagram posting. He reportedly 'lost 100,000 followers in 10 hours in May when he and [his creative team] AWGE posted a succession of 150 images, the majority of them plain grey, white or black' (Bakare 2015).

Bibliography

Austin, Joe. 1996. 'Rewriting New York City'. In Marcus, George (ed.), *Connected: Engagements with Media*. Chicago, IL: University of Chicago Press, pp. 271–312.

Avramidis, Konstaninos and Drakopoulou, Konstantina. 2015. 'Moving From Urban to Virtual Spaces and Back: Learning In/From Signature Graffiti Subculture'. In Jandrić, Petar and Boras, Damir (eds), *Critical Learning in Digital Networks*. New York, NY: Springer, pp. 133–160.

Bakare, Lanre. 2015. 'A$AP Rocky: 'Hanging out with Rod Stewart is Like Seeing Yourself 40 Years Older and White'. *The Guardian*, 2 July. Available at: www.the guardian.com/music/2015/jul/02/asap-rocky-hanging-out-with-rod-stewart-interview. Accessed: 16 December 2015.

boyd, danah and Crawford, Kate. 2012. 'Critical Questions for Big Data: Provocations for a Cultural, Technological, and Scholarly Phenomenon'. *Information, Communication & Society*. 15(5): 662–679.

Cachin, Olivier, Zekri, Bernard, Hammou, Karim, Collectif. 2015. *Hip-Hop: Du Bronx aux Rues Arabes*. Gent: Snoeck.

Derrida, Jacques. 1998. *Archive Fever: A Freudian Impression*. Eric Prenowitz (trans.). Chicago, IL: University of Chicago Press.

Goldhaber, Michael H. 1997. 'The Attention Economy and the Net'. *First Monday*. 2(4). Available at: http://firstmonday.org/ojs/index.php/fm/article/view/519/440. Accessed: 17 December 2015.

Graffiti Research Lab website. 2015. Available at: www.graffitiresearchlab.com/blog/. Accessed: 17 December 2015.

Grifter's Code videos series. 2015 Available at: http://thegrifters.org. Accessed: 17 December 2015.

Hochman, Nadav and Manovich, Lev. 2013. 'Zooming into an Instagram City: Reading the Local through Social Media'. *First Monday*. 18(7). Available at http://firstmonday. org/article/view/4711/3698. Accessed: 17 December 2015.

Hochman, Nadav and Manovich, Lev. 2014. 'A View from Above: Exploratory Visualizations of the Thomas Walther Collection'. In Abbaspour, Mitra, Daffner, Lee Ann and Hambourg, Maria Morris (eds), *Object: Photo. Modern Photographs: The Thomas Walther Collection 1909–1949*. New York, NY: Museum of Modern Art, pp. 1–6.

Hochman, Nadav, Manovich, Lev and Yazdani, Mehrdad. 2014. 'On Hyper-Locality: Performances of Place in Social Media'. Paper presented at the *8th International Conference on Weblogs and Social Media*, Ann Arbor, MI, June.

Instagram Help Centre webpage. 2015. Available at: http:// https://help.Instagram.com/2977 58797000260. Accessed: 18 August 2015.

Jameson, Fredric. 2009. *The Geopolitical Aesthetic: Cinema and Space in the World System*. Bloomington, IN: Indiana University Press.

MacDowall, Lachlan. 2008. 'The Graffiti Archive and the Digital City'. In Butt, Danny, Bywater, Jon and Paul, Nova (eds), *Place: Local Knowledge and New Media*. Newcastle Upon Tyne: Cambridge Scholars Press, pp. 134–147.

MacDowall, Lachlan. 2014a. 'GRAFFITIDOWNUNDERGROUND'. *Artlink.* 34(1): 16–19.

MacDowall, Lachlan. 2014b. 'Graffiti, Street Art and Stigmergy'. In Lossau, Julia and Stevens, Quentin (eds), *The Uses of Art in Public Space*. London: Routledge, pp. 33–48.

MacDowall, Lachlan and de Souza, Poppy. Forthcoming 2016. 'I'd Double Tap That!!: Street Art, Graffiti and Instagram Research'. *Journal of Media, Culture and Society*.

Manovich, Lev. Forthcoming 2016. 'The Science of Culture? Social Computing, Digital Humanities, and Cultural Analytics'. In Schaefer, Mirko Tobias and van Es, Karin (eds), *The Datafied Society: Social Research in the Age of Big Data*. Amsterdam: Amsterdam University Press.

Parkinson, Hannah Jane. 2014. 'Instagram Purge Costs Celebrities Millions of Followers'. *The Guardian*, 19 December. Available at: www.theguardian.com/technology/2014/dec/ 19/Instagram-purge-costs-celebrities-millions-of-followers. Accessed: 17 December 2015.

Riggle, Nicholas Alden. 2010. 'Street Art: The Transfiguration of the Commonplaces'. *Journal of Aesthetics and Art Criticism.* 68 (3): 243–257.

Roth, Evans. 2006. *Geek Graffiti: A Study in Computation, Gesture, and Graffiti Analysis.* (MFA). New York, NY: The New School University. Available at: www.ni9e.com/graffiti_analysis/graffiti_analysis_09.pdf. Accessed: 17 December 2015.

Rushmore, R.J. 2013. 'The Mudd Club and "Beyond Words"'. In *Viral Art: How the Internet has Shaped Street Art and Graffiti.* Available at: http://viralart.vandalog.com/read/. Accessed: 17 December 2015.

Sassen, Saskia. 2011. 'The Global Street: Making the Political'. *Globalizations.* 8(5): 573–579.

Tufekci, Zeynep. 2014. 'Big Questions for Social Media Big Data: Representativeness, Validity and Other Methodological Pitfalls'. In *ICWSM '14: Proceedings of the 8th International AAAI Conference on Weblogs and Social Media.*

14 Representations of graffiti and the city in the novel *El francotirador paciente*

Readings of the emergent urban body in Madrid

Stephen Luis Vilaseca

Introduction

The first decade and a half of the new millennium has both condemned and embraced graffiti and street art. Ordinances worldwide have been passed that have clearly restricted creative expression on public and private property. New York City's anti-graffiti campaign in the mid 1990s served as an urban renewal model for other global cities in the early 2000s.[1] In an effort to improve the quality of life of neighbourhoods across the United Kingdom, the Anti-Social Behaviour Act was passed in 2003. Among other outcomes, it facilitated graffiti abatement programmes by providing local councils the legal framework to remove graffiti from public property.[2] In 2005, the Bylaws for the Means to Foment and Guarantee Communal Living in Barcelona, Spain, established hefty fines of up to 3,000 euros for graphic expression on public space.[3] Madrid followed suit with similar laws in 2007 and 2009.[4] Los Angeles in the US, also in 2009, passed an ordinance requiring all new homes to be covered with a finish that resists spray paint. Although homes are private property, they are often visible from public spaces (sidewalks, streets) and hence graffiti and street art on private property affect how public space is experienced.

The very same cities that criminalized graffiti and street art in the early 2000s (e.g. Bristol and London in the UK, Barcelona and Madrid in Spain, and LA and New York City in the US) in order to make public space appealing to tourists and investors began to co-opt graffiti and street art and celebrate it in museums in order to achieve the very same end: the promotion of tourism and investment. In 2006, the Reina Sofia Museum in Madrid, in order to celebrate the twenty-fifth anniversary of the return of Picasso's *Guernica* to Spain, invited graffiti and street artists to reinterpret the famous painting. In 2008, Tate Modern in London opened 'Street Art', an exhibition displaying the street art of six artists from around the world. In 2011, the Museum of Contemporary Art (MOCA) in Los Angeles presented 'Art in the Streets', the first showing of graffiti and street art in the US. How have graffiti and street artists reacted to this contradictory legal and social context that has both criminalized and commodified graffiti and street art, and how has their reaction affected the city?

Arturo Pérez-Reverte's novel *El francotirador paciente* [*The Patient Sniper*] (2013) provides one possible point of entry into this complex issue surrounding graffiti and street art, and the lived space of cities.[5] It takes the reader on a wild ride from Madrid, Spain, to Lisbon, Portugal and Naples, Italy, in search of SNIPER, a fictitious, popular graffiti artist whose identity is unknown. Alejandra Varela is the art scout assigned to locate SNIPER and entice him to sign a lucrative book deal with a major publishing company. Since its release in November 2013, the novel has been translated into several languages and has become a bestseller in many countries, thus demonstrating how well it was received while highlighting its global, rather than merely local, impact.[6] Although the general readers embraced the novel, the response of Spanish graffitists and street artists has been mixed, ranging from complete rejection to cautious acceptance (Robles 2013). Their greatest fear is that the general public will think that all graffiti writers and street artists are like the odious, violent, radical main character.

Pérez-Reverte, the author of the novel, spent twenty-one years as a war correspondent in places such as Croatia and Bosnia and these experiences have informed the bellicose framework through which he understands graffiti and street art, and the territory of cities. Pérez-Reverte superimposes the relations of war onto the world of urban art. The illegal status of graffiti and street art forces practitioners to stealthily avoid the police in order to conquer new urban walls in much the same way that guerrilla fighters organize quick attacks in order to surprise and elude the dominant power. The figure of the sniper, as seen in previous novels by Pérez-Reverte such as *Territorio Comanche* [*Comanche Territory*] (1994) and *El pintor de batallas* [*The Painter of Battles*] (2006), reappears, not as a highly trained soldier, but as a rogue graffiti artist whose battlefield is the city.

The methodology that I use in this chapter is a humanities-driven approach to urban environments combining textual criticism with a social analysis of how we are to engage with the city. In order to contribute to the discussion on how we can think of and practice urbanism in a different way, I compare the actions of real street artists with the representation of the fictitious graffiti artist known as SNIPER. Instead of repeating an extensive explanation already elaborated in a previous article about the differences between graffiti and street art (Vilaseca 2012), I will offer here a more focused account.

Originally, graffiti was a means of protest against modernist urban strategies that ignored and abandoned certain neighbourhoods of New York City in the sixties. Graffiti's visual discourse was difficult to counter because it was a closed code only understood by the graffiti artists themselves. Its power and weakness derived from this incomprehensibility. Urban planners and politicians could not manipulate and distort a message that they did not understand. However, precisely because graffiti was not a logical protest, but rather a visceral one, the greater community of city dwellers often misinterpreted its presence as merely an aggression against the city. I would argue that graffiti today is oftentimes, but not always, an aggression against urban renewal plans that generate greater social inequality. That is to say, graffiti writers are no longer just poor, marginalized youth raging against the city. They are also rich, privileged sons and daughters of bankers, executives, real estate moguls and politicians (among other white collar jobs) who use graffiti to rebel against their comfortable lifestyles. In this sense, the line between graffiti and street art is becoming more blurred. Nevertheless, street artists, arguably, seem to be more open than graffiti writers to co-creating with the city, and communicating more directly with city dwellers.

The three terms 'graffiti', 'street art' and 'city' essential to the thematic section of the edited volume in which this chapter is placed are the same key terms found in my analysis. There is a fourth term that is also of great importance to this chapter – that is 'creativity'. I use it to mean, interchangeably, creative ideas, the result of those creative ideas (i.e. poetry, music, performance art, the plastic arts, graffiti, street art and cinema, among others) and the process of creating. My use of the term 'creativity' distances itself from Richard Florida's conceptualization of the 'creative class' because the creativity I am describing is that which rejects being reduced merely to exchange value. Instead of a 'creative class' whose creativity is manipulated to incite desire and consumption, the creativity I am detailing experiments with value systems that question capitalism.

SNIPER, the urban artist pursued by art scout Alejandra Varela, shares two positions held by many urban artists: a distrust of a value system in which economic profit is the only aim, and a phenomenological view of the city, that is, one that blurs the boundaries between built environment, body and art, and sees them as one. This entanglement of built environment, body and art, however, is tainted by Sniper's inability to imagine a better city. He violently breaks with a capitalist world without attempting to create another. I propose in this chapter to question Pérez-Reverte's view that urban artists have ripped the transformative power of creativity from their own practice and have given in to violence, and will argue exactly the reverse: that urban artists are modelling a new subjectivity with tremendous potential to short-circuit the fixed relations of capitalism.

SNIPER's atrophied imagination vs the emergent urban body

According to sociologist Stephen Duncombe, who travels the globe teaching socially engaged artists the political benefits of combining social activism with artistic practice (2010), the predominant political problem today is atrophied imagination. He argues that rational critique no longer has a critical function. Instead, radical utopian experiments will move people to take political action. For Duncombe, the absurd and the obviously impossible open up new spaces in people to contemplate real changes. For Pérez-Reverte, graffiti is not a utopian experiment, not absurd, not suggestive or provocative in a positive, creative sense. In fact, SNIPER struggles against his own atrophied imagination. He has lost faith in the power of art to transform society into a more socially just place. In my opinion, his cynicism has led him to a traditional reading of Marx. I argue that he believes, like a classical Marxist, that the symbolic is not a vehicle through which to create social or political change. Change occurs only when the material conditions for the change already exist (Marx 1970 [1859]: 21). However, unlike Marx, SNIPER is convinced that the material conditions for the downfall of capitalism will never appear. There is no alternative to capitalism and the only solution is its destruction. For SNIPER, the influence of the symbolic on urban space is destructive. In contrast with SNIPER, hispanists Malcolm Compitello and Susan Larson, who have written quite extensively on the relationship between cities, culture and capital, take into account the constructive possibilities of the symbolic on urban space. In fact, they stress:

> Studying cultural representations of place and urban space in particular is fruitful because one finds that they often play a reciprocal role in the creation of the urban environment itself. City planners and architects need some image, some inspiration to inspire them as they set about creating new urban environments in which people work and live.
>
> (2001: 237)

Nevertheless, the inspirational image is 'the image of capital' (Compitello 2002). Compitello, taking his lead from Marxist cultural geographer David Harvey, reminds us that even though urban consciousness may be 'both formative of and formed by cultural and social forms', we should never forget that 'capital shapes consciousness' (2002). In other words, Compitello and Larson acknowledge that imagination can have material consequences. What makes their approach to culture materialist, however, is, as they argue, that the symbolic primarily serves state or capitalist form. That is, the urban consciousness from which the symbolic emerges is organized according to the closed, internal logic of capital. For Compitello and Larson, the link between art and urban space is, thus, modern, urbanized consciousness. In other words, our subjectivity and our cities are produced in large part by capitalism. That is not to say, as Harvey points out in his article *The Art of Rent* (2002), that capitalism does not allow for instances of resistance. It does, but mostly on its own terms:

> And if capital is not to totally destroy the uniqueness that is the basis for the appropriation of monopoly rents (and there are many circumstances where it has done just that and been roundly condemned for so doing) then it must support a form of differentiation and allow of divergent and to some degree uncontrollable local cultural developments that can be antagonistic to its own smooth functioning. It can even support (though cautiously and often nervously) all manner of 'transgressive' cultural practices precisely because this is one way in which to be original, creative and authentic as well as unique.
>
> (2002: 108)

For those whose imagination has not atrophied and who can avoid being co-opted by capitalism, creativity still has the potential to create ruptures in the market system.

My concept of the emergent urban body arises from urban artists' attempt to understand and counter the alienation produced by modern urban life under capitalism. By writing their names, painting elaborate pieces, gluing paste-ups, spraying stencils, or placing stickers on public and sometimes private space, graffiti and street artists engage unexpectedly and unrestrictedly with the cityscape, demonstrating that, indeed, such an open interaction with the built environment is possible. Urban artists' imagination that is layered on top of edifices is as much a building material as are the bricks and mortar used in their construction. A component of urban artists' subjectivity, their imagination, mixes with the built environment to become a part of it. Therefore, personhood and city are inextricably linked. The blurring of the boundaries between the body, built environment and imagination reframes the body as not solely a physical body, but one that is at the same time a bundle of networked relations connecting art and constructed space. These series of relationships is the emergent urban body. It is a new subjectivity being modelled in the city by urban artists who are showing us that we can invent a subjectivity according to a self-determined logic and not according to that of capitalism.[7] By rethinking the relationship between citizen and built environment as continually constructive and not alienating, we can create a city more open to economic and social value systems other than capitalism, and, by extension, a sense of self programmed less by capitalism.

If all thought did not emerge from urbanized consciousness, and if some imagination poured forth from another source such as the body, then that thought and imagination would have the power to defy capitalism. Theories of embodied cognition and affect pose that very possibility.[8] Creativity that is not located in urbanized consciousness is not structured by the fixed relations of capitalism. Finding ways to harness the spontaneous connections between thoughts, words, bodily responses, and images would have tremendous potential in the fight against predatory capitalism. Creative activism is exploring how to do just that. Unlike SNIPER, urban artists who employ theories of embodied cognition and affect in tandem with, not in place of, a Marxist materialist approach to culture will strengthen the possibility of resistance in the future.

SNIPER: from artist to terrorist

> Él es un paracaidista en las calles, te dije antes. Un intruso. Dio con el grafiti como otros dan con una pistola cargada. Lo que le pone es disparar.

> He is a paratrooper in the streets, I told you before. An intruder. He discovered graffiti the way others accidentally come across a loaded pistol. What he does with it is shoot.[9]
>
> TOPO75, SNIPER's friend (Pérez-Reverte 2013: 84)

SNIPER agrees with urban artists that there is an unrestricted commingling between self, built environment, and imagination. Due to his conviction that the city is made in the image of capital, SNIPER attacks and, some would argue, terrorizes the built environment. As the opening quote of the paragraph suggests, his loaded gun is graffiti. In other words, he takes aim at the city because it is an extension of the capitalist body. He shares urban artists' phenomenological view of the city and their criticism of predatory capitalism. However, instead of building up a different body, he just wants to destroy it.

SNIPER, unlike the majority of urban artists, cannot imagine anymore. He goads Varela, the art scout assigned to entice him to sign a lucrative book deal, to visualize a utopic city knowing very well that it is not only futile, but impossible:

> Imagine … a city where there are no police officers nor art critics nor galleries nor museums … Streets where anyone could exhibit what they wanted, paint what and where they wanted. A city of colors, of impact, of phrases, of thoughts that would make you think, of real life messages. A type of urban party where everyone was invited and nobody was ever excluded … Can you imagine it?
>
> [Imagina … una ciudad donde no hubiera policías ni críticos de arte ni galerías ni museos … Unas calles donde cada cual pudiera exponer lo que quisiera, pintar lo que quisiera y donde quisiera. Una ciudad de colores, de impactos, de frases, de pensamientos que harían pensar, de mensajes reales de vida. Una especie de fiesta urbana donde todos estuvieran invitados y nadie quedase excluido jamás … ¿Puedes imaginarlo?]
>
> (2013: 240)

The response is 'no' because he is an artist who has lost faith in the transformative power of art, or maybe never had that faith. According to Police Inspector Pachón, 'he was always aggressive, even in his style … He preferred to be called a vandal before being called an artist' [siempre fue agresivo, hasta en el estilo … Prefería que lo llamasen vándalo antes que artista] (Pérez-Reverte 2013: 62). By identifying his street interventions as acts of vandalism instead of art, SNIPER shares the city officials' view that graffiti destroys the urban landscape. He recognizes that buildings are reified flows of capital and understands that graffiti does not enhance property value, but diminishes it.[10] SNIPER also acknowledges the power of art to impel people to consume. Creativity, for SNIPER, has become a prostitute that has sold herself to capitalism:

> we should support the electric signs, posters, advertisements, buses with their stupid announcements and messages … They appropriate all of the available surfaces, he told me. Even the construction sites for building repairs are covered with advertisements. And they deny us the space for our replies. As a result, the only art that I conceive, he repeated, is to fuck all of that.
>
> [nosotros debemos soportar los luminosos, los rótulos, la publicidad, los autobuses con sus anuncios y mensajes estúpidos … Se adueñan de toda superficie disponible, me dijo. Hasta las obras de restauración de edificios se cubren con lonas de publicidad. Y a nosotros nos niegan el espacio para nuestras respuestas. Por eso el único arte que concibo, repetía, es joder todo eso].
>
> (2013: 82–83)

Capitalism's harnessing of art to manipulate has blinded him to the constructive side of creativity. Because our subjectivity and our cities are produced more by capitalism than by ourselves, he harbours a hatred for capitalism that is indistinguishable from a hatred for people and places.

SNIPER's tag is his name with the cross-hares of a rifle painted over the letter *i*. He is a self-proclaimed urban street fighter participating in guerrilla warfare (2013: 237). Journalists have called him an art terrorist (2013: 42) and Pérez-Reverte, commenting on his own character, refers to him as an urban terrorist (Alfarmada 2013). How does SNIPER evolve from an artist to a terrorist? When does his relationship with the city and with others become more explosive? Police Inspector Luis Pachón looks to the evolution of his art for answers:

> That guy, Sniper, always was different from the others . . . Just look at the evolution of his artistic pieces. He had everything clear from the beginning. He had an ideology, understand? . . . Or he ended up knowing what it was.
>
> [Ese tío, Sniper, siempre fue diferente a los otros . . . Basta ver la evolución de sus piezas. Lo tuvo claro desde el principio. Tenía una ideología, ¿comprendes? . . . O acabó sabiendo cuál era].
>
> (2013: 65)

The fictitious SNIPER began painting in the street in the late 1980s with actual famed Spanish graffiti artist MUELLE whose real name was Juan Carlos Argüello Garzo (1966–1995). He was known for his tag *Muelle*, which in English means a coiled spring, and under which he would draw a spring followed by an arrow. According to SNIPER's childhood friend TOPO75 (also a fictional character), 'at that time . . . we signed under Muelle, imitating his spiral' [en esa época . . . firmábamos debajo de Muelle, imitando su espiral] (2013: 71). TOPO75 points out that SNIPER's tag was not always *Sniper*. He began by signing *Quo* because he liked the band Status Quo (2013: 73). During this initial stage, SNIPER's pieces were simple graffiti. However, it did not take long for him to develop his new moniker – *Sniper*. In fact, the first SNIPER tag also dates back to the late 1980s. In addition to graffiti (which is incomprehensible to anyone who is not a graffiti writer), he became interested in street art as a means to convey specific messages to a wider, more general public. He started to paint tourist buses with anti-capitalist phrases (2013: 43). However, he never abandoned graffiti. In fact, it was at this point when he distanced himself from Spanish urban artists and embraced wildstyle, the type of American graffiti that both exaggerates the letters to the point of illegibility and injects heightened risk and danger to the practice. T-KID 170, a well-known wildstyle graffitist from New York, explains:

> Wildstyle isn't really a style of letters, it's a way of life . . . And we reflected it in our graffiti and in our letters and that's how we expressed it. That was wildstyle. We would go to the top of the Brooklyn Bridge and we would do a piece right there. That's wildstyle. It doesn't matter that the letters are all

nasty . . . If my name is on the Brooklyn Bridge, you ain't fuckin' doing that, my man. That's wildstyle.

(Reiss 2008)

By the mid 1990s Sniper grew to be a skilled practitioner of wildstyle. TOPO75 recalls that it was at this stage when he progressively became more aggressive and alienated:

> in the last times together . . . he frequently used the word break, fuck, kill. We argued, and he closed himself up in his own thing. After was the Mexico trip.
>
> [en los últimos tiempos juntos . . . usaba mucho la palabra romper, joder, matar. Discutíamos, y él se cerraba en lo suyo. Después fue lo de México].

(2013: 79)

Traveling to Mexico and spending an extended period of time there was definitely transformative for both SNIPER's life and art. The Mexicans' open relationship with death and their tendency towards explosive behaviour in order to hide from themselves resonated with him. In *El laberinto de la soledad* [*The Labyrinth of Solitude*], Mexican writer Octavio Paz describes a general pattern of tumultuous Mexican behaviour with which SNIPER shares some characteristics:[11]

> The explosive, dramatic, sometimes even suicidal manner in which we strip ourselves, surrender ourselves, is evidence that something inhibits and suffocates us. Something impedes us from being. And since we cannot or dare not confront our own selves, we resort to the fiesta. It fires us into the void; it is a drunken rapture that burns itself out, a pistol shot in the air, a skyrocket.
>
> [La manera explosiva y dramática, a veces suicida, con que nos desnudamos y entregamos, inermes casi, revela que algo nos asfixia y cohibe. Algo nos impide ser. Y porque no nos atrevemos o no podemos enfrentarnos con nuestro ser, recurrimos a la Fiesta. Ella nos lanza al vacío, embriaguez que se quema a sí misma, disparo en el aire, fuego de artificio].

(1985: 53–54)

After SNIPER returned from Mexico in the early 2000s, Mexican-influenced skeletons and skulls populated his art. For SNIPER, death and the horror of life gave back to art a sense of seriousness that marketing and publicity had robbed from it. At that time, he broke with the art world by entering museums and secretly placing his own art.[12] For example, on a wall of the Thyssen Museum in Madrid, SNIPER spray-painted a stylized stencil of *The Moneychanger and his Wife* by Marinus van Reymerswaele in which he substituted the heads of the figures with skulls, and the coins with telescopic sights of a rifle. After a string of similar infiltrations, an influential critic praised SNIPER's actions as those of an art terrorist. Raymond Salvatore Harmon, in his book *Bomb: A Manifesto of Art Terrorism* (2011), defines an art terrorist as someone who fights for 'the secession of art from the financial/academic infrastructure of the supposed "art world"'. Museums, galleries and critics have definitely contributed to art's current status as a money-making game and as an investment opportunity for the rich. For SNIPER, the only art not trapped in the flows of capital is illegal street art. In direct defiance of capitalism's exaltation of exchange value over use value, SNIPER claims that 'art is not a product, but an activity' [el arte no es un producto, sino una actividad] (Pérez-Reverte 2013: 239). The same can be said of the city. Engaging in property speculation and the gentrification of centric working-class neighbourhoods converts urban space into merely a product that lower and middle-class people are unable to afford. SNIPER attacks urban renewal plans as he attacks museums. That is, not only is he an art terrorist, he is an urban terrorist as well, which is to say that he places in the city explosive doubts about consumption-based strategies of urban development as if they were bombs.

SNIPER is opposed to a form of urbanism whose aim is the development of a showcase city. In order to seduce tourists to visit and attract capital from possible investors, major metropolises undergo beautification processes and, essentially, become top-models (Degen 2004).On the temporary canvases that protect the façades of buildings during their facelifts are advertisements of attractive women in bikinis. The identification of city and seductress cannot be made more apparent. Against the alluring woman who is at once part of the built environment, SNIPER lashes out with an ad hominem attack: 'I use acid. Figurative, of course. Or not so much. Like throwing acid at the face of a stupid woman, satisfied with herself.' [Yo uso ácido. Figurado, claro. O no tanto. Como arrojar ácido a la cara de una mujer estúpida, satisfecha de sí misma] (2013: 268).

SNIPER sees no other alternative than to disfigure our subjectivity and our cities because both are produced by what he hates – capitalism. The coincidence between life and capitalism means that 'we do not deserve to survive . . . We deserve a bullet in the brain, one by one' [no merecemos sobrevivir . . . Merecemos una bala en la cabeza, uno por uno] (2013: 289). It is easy to understand why he chose his moniker. He sees himself as the sniper who will eliminate capitalism and us with it. However, despite self-identifying as a sniper, his methods include those of a 'bomber', the term graffiti writers use to describe themselves. That is, he 'bombs' or spray-paints public space. In the context of war, the bomber causes mass losses whereas the sniper has specific targets. Nevertheless, SNIPER's distinction has less to do with the number of 'casualties' than with the skill, dedication, and danger involved in producing those 'casualties'. Within a phenomenological framework of the city, 'casualties' occur when the destruction of built environment damages subjectivity. Anyone can physically place a bomb, but not everyone can kill a person with a rifle from a long distance. SNIPER criticizes those graffiti writers whose 'bombing' becomes too mundane, easy and safe:

> There are graffiti writers who return home and sit in front of the television or listen to music, satisfied with what they have done that day . . . I return home to think about how I am going to screw everyone over again.

[Hay grafiteros que vuelven a casa y se sientan a ver la tele o escuchar música, satisfechos de lo que han hecho ese día . . . Yo vuelvo a casa a pensar en cómo volver a joderlos a todos de nuevo].

(2013: 292)

The main character may consider himself a sniper among bombers, but, arguably, the true patient sniper of the title ends up being the art scout, Alejandra, who patiently tracks SNIPER during the course of the novel and eventually murders him.

Not only is there a correlation between city and top-model, but also city and domesticated bohemian. TOPO75, SNIPER's childhood graffiti partner, and Chueca, a once abandoned central neighbourhood in Madrid that is now a bustling zone of hipness, both 'let themselves be domesticated in order to have a hot meal' [se dejaron domesticar para comer caliente] (2013: 83). In the 1990s, members of the LGBT community moved into Chueca, a neglected part of Madrid known for drug trafficking and prostitution. Because of their significant capital, social and cultural investments, this once dilapidated, low-income area is now a thriving, trendy, up-scale gay quarter. Alejandra describes Chueca as 'half way between an atmosphere of barhopping and an against-the-system tradition' [a medio camino entre ambiente de copas y tradición antisistema] (2013: 69). Chueca's radical, gritty past, once a hindrance, has been stripped of its content and converted into a bohemian image that is manipulated to attract young, wealthy hipsters.

TOPO75, in his youth, used to tag buildings with his friend SNIPER. He has not done that in ten years. He now owns a store called Radikal located in Chueca that sells aerosol paint cans, books on graffiti, and clothing with anarchist symbols. Despite their radical posturing, both TOPO75 and Chueca are money-makers taking advantage of their nonconformist past. Because he betrayed his original ideals, TOPO75 recognizes that SNIPER will never forgive him (2013: 83).

Instead of succumbing to the logic of capitalism, SNIPER believes that we need to counter it with non-sense, with a different logic, with a different value system. He explains to Alejandra that 'I only introduce the absurd' [yo sólo planteo el absurdo] (2013: 289). Bringing forth the absurd – expounding a self-determined logic – is an objective that he shares with the emergent urban body. However, he differs from other real urban artists on how to reach that objective. Instead of experimenting with art to slowly and temporarily disconnect the standardized ties of order, SNIPER attempts to violently break with it. Activating the emergent urban body means becoming radically open to the world, not destroying it. The hatred towards capitalism should be a point of departure to create something better, not a destructive end in itself.

Telling stories about urban artists in Madrid: reality vs fiction in politics, literature and art

There is a storytelling – *El francotirador paciente* forms part of it – that surrounds popular notions of who and what graffiti and street artists are that contributes to the confusing context to which I allude in the introduction. Therefore, it is

necessary to examine not only the laws that are produced but the stories themselves, which are both formed by reality and also formative of reality, as they affect
public opinion. Because of the popularity of *El francotirador paciente* and Pérez-
Reverte's international fame and hence the novel's and the author's potential to
influence popular opinion as well as politicians, SNIPER – despite being fictional
– holds very real power. MUELLE used to always say that 'we give back to the
city the oxygen that the other aerosol cans (the ones that are not spray-paint cans
like hair sprays) steal from it' [le devolvemos a la ciudad el oxígeno que le roban
los esprays que no llevan pintura] (MUELLE quoted in Pérez-Reverte 2013: 73).
Being an oxygen-giver means using creativity to modify public space in order to
bring together the built environment with imagination. SNIPER is an oxygen-taker.
The purpose of this chapter has been to give back the oxygen that SNIPER (and
other urban artists like SNIPER) have stolen from street artists.

Returning to the question I posed in the introduction – How have graffiti and
street artists reacted to the contradictory legal and social context that has both
criminalized and commodified graffiti and street art, and how has their reaction
affected the city? – the answer is that they have reacted in three ways. The
categories are to facilitate our understanding of reality and are in no means fixed.
The first reaction is that of urban artists such as SNIPER who have become urban
terrorists with an explosive relationship with the city. The second is one of
capitulation in which graffiti writers and street artists such as TOPO75, tired of
the persecution, participate in the burgeoning market of commissioned graffiti.
The third is that of the emergent urban body that, through an unexpected and
unrestricted engagement with the built environment, co-creates with the city to
communicate openly with city dwellers. Each reaction has its own story to tell.
The narrative that will lead to a just city requires the radical imagination of both
future street artists and city dwellers everywhere.

Notes

1 There have been several anti-graffiti campaigns in NYC dating back to the early 1980s.
   I focus on Rudy Giuliani's campaign to clean up Times Square in the 1990s because
   its success and the subsequent media attention surrounding it introduced to the world
   the 'broken windows theory' (Wilson and Kelling 1982). Recent findings (Keizer
   et al. 2008) have reinforced the 1982 broken windows theory, and have led city
   governments worldwide to imitate Giuliani's model.
2 See Anti-social Behavior Act 2003, Part 6 – Articles 48–52.
3 See Ordenanzas de medidas para fomentar y garantizar la convivencia ciudadana en
   el espacio público, Article 20.2 (Ayuntamiento de Barcelona 2005).
4 See *Ley de medidas urgentes de modernización del gobierno local y de la administración
   de la Comunidad de Madrid*, Article 20, and *Ordenanza de limpieza de los espacios
   públicos y de gestión de residuos*, Article 17 (Ayuntamiento de Madrid 2007, 2009).
5 Another representation of graffiti that also informs my study is Maite Fernández
   Pérez's short film *Graffiti Area* (2014). The video was chosen as one of the four winners
   of the Bombay Sapphire Imagination Series Film Competition for 2013. The applicants
   had to use their imagination to interpret the same short film script written by Geoffrey
   Fletcher, Oscar winner for his screenplay for *Precious*. A graffiti artist paints a black
   beast on the wall of an underpass of a city. The monster is that part of himself that he

hates. His graffiti is at once a product of his subjectivity and a reaction against it. There is both a connection and a separation between artist and art, between artist and built environment. This is visualized through the point of view of the capitalist monster. Both beast and viewer look out at the graffiti artist as he stares back at us. The screen becomes the monster's eyes and the surface of the building. Such a framing emphasizes the graffiti artist's alienation and, at the same time, establishes an identification between spectator, beast and built environment. Cities are a reflection of who we are and our values. Both we and our cities have become monsters that establish relations of production and consumption that are oftentimes exploitative and violent. This current situation of heightened capitalist exploitation is what the graffiti artists need to get out of in the opening scene, and the built environment around them is what they look at that explains their predicament.

6 *The Patient Sniper* has been so far translated into Danish, French, Polish, Italian and Portuguese. According to Nielsen Book Scan, it was the ninth most purchased book in Spain for the year 2014. It was also wildly popular in Mexico, reaching number one on the Librería Gandhi's bestseller's list in January, 2014. Although not available in English, its aforementioned translations and popularity in Latin America have undeniably extended its impact beyond Spain's borders.

7 I first introduced the concept of the emergent urban body and its representation in an earlier article of mine (2012). There, I discuss *Symbiosis-Artists with Character*, a project by Barcelonan street artist DR. CASE, which mimics street artists' constantly evolving relationship with their exterior world. It does this by not only loosening the boundary between built environment and imagination, but, just as importantly, by softening the division between artist and art.

8 For an extended discussion on theories of embodied cognition and affect, see the introduction of my monograph (2013: ix–xxix). Also see Massumi (2002), Clough (2007) and Labanyi (2010).

9 All translations are those of the author unless otherwise noted.

10 This is not always the case. Graffiti and street art have also contributed to the skyrocketing of property values, leading to the gentrification of once marginalized neighbourhoods. For more see Vilaseca 2010.

11 Translation by Lysander Kemp, Yara Milos and Rachel Phillips Belash.

12 Banksy left his own art in Tate Britain in 2003. He also visited the British Museum and hung his own fake prehistoric art, a caveman with a shopping cart, in 2005.

References

Alfarmada, Alfonso. 2013. 'Arturo Pérez-Reverte: "El grafitero tiene derecho a llamarse escritor"'. *ABC*, 26 November. Available at: www.abc.es/cultura/libros/20131125/abci-arturo-perez-reverte-grafitero-201311242256.html. Accessed: 3 June 2015.

Ayuntamiento de Barcelona. 2005. *Ordenanza de medidas para fomentar y garantizar la convivencia ciudadana en el espacio público de Barcelona*. Available at: http://w110.bcn.cat/fitxers/ajuntament/ordenansacivismecast.189.pdf. Accessed: 10 June 2015.

Ayuntamiento de Madrid. 2007. *Ley de medidas urgentes de modernización del gobierno local y de la administración de la Comunidad de Madrid*. Available at: www.madrid.org/cs/Satellite?blobcol=urldata&blobheader=application%2Fpdf&blobheadblobhe1=Content-Disposition&blobheadervalue1=filename%3DLEY+32007+de+Medidas+Urgentes.pdf&blobkey=id&blobtable=MungoBlobs&blobwhere=1310999271310&ssbinary=true. Accessed: 29 July 2015.

Ayuntamiento de Madrid. 2009. *Ordenanza de limpieza de los espacios públicos y de gestión de residuos*. Available at: www.madrid.es/portales/munimadrid/es/Inicio/Ayuntamiento/

Normativa/ListadoNormativLi/ANM-2009-6-Ordenanza-de-Limpieza-de-los-Espacios-Publicos-y-Gestion-deResiduos?vgnextfmt=default&vgnextoid=4bde9faac2330210V gnVCM2000000c205a0aRCRD&vgnextchannel=00dfb351fd18d010VgnVCM1000009b 25680aRCRD. Accessed: 29 July 2015.

City of Los Angeles. 2009. 'Ordinance No. 180895 – Amending Section 91.6306 of the Los Angeles Municipal Code'. Available at: http://clkrep.lacity.org/onlinedocs/2008/08-3124_ord_180895.pdf. Accessed: 29 July 2015.

City of New York. 1995. 'Mayor's Anti-Graffiti Task Force Executive Order'. Available at: www.nyc.gov/html/records/rwg/nograffiti/html/executiveorder.html. Accessed: 29 July 2015.

Clough, Patricia Ticineto. 2007. *The Affective Turn: Theorizing the Social*. Durham, NC: Duke University Press.

Compitello, Malcolm Alan. 2002. 'Recasting Urban Identities: The Case of Madrid 1977–1997. Mapping Urban Spaces and Subjectivities'. *Arachne*. 2(1): unpaged.

Compitello, Malcolm Alan and Larson, Susan. 2001. 'Cities, Culture . . . Capital? Recent Cultural Studies Approaches to Spain's Cities'. *Journal of Spanish Cultural Studies*. 2(2): 232–238.

Degen, Monica. 2004. 'Passejant per la Passarel·la Global: Ciutats i Turisme Urbà'. *Transversal*. 23(July): 30–32.

Duncombe, Stephen. 2010. 'Utopia is No Place: The Art and Politics of Impossible Futures'. Invited talk Walker Art Center, Minneapolis MN, 29 July. Available at: www. youtube.com/watch?v=H8BhXKGOeeY. Accessed: 3 June 2015.

Fernández Pérez, Maite. 2014. *Graffiti Area*. Bombay Sapphire Film. Available at: https:// vimeo.com/channels/bombayimaginationseries/92659633. Accessed: 3 June 2015.

Harvey, David. 2002. 'The Art of Rent: Globalization, Monopoly and Cultural Production'. *Socialist Register*. 38: 93–110.

Harmon, Raymond Salvatore. 2011. *Bomb: A Manifesto of Art Terrorism*. Available at: http://raymondharmon.com/BOMB.html. Accessed: 3 June 2015.

Keizer, Kees, Lindenberg, Siegwart and Steg, Linda. 2008. 'The Spreading of Disorder'. *Science*. 322(5908): 1681–1685.

Labanyi, Jo. 2010. 'Doing Things: Emotion, Affect, and Materiality'. *Journal of Spanish Cultural Studies*. 11(3–4): 223–233.

Marx, Karl. 1970 [1859]. *A Contribution to the Critique of Political Economy*. New York, NY: International Publishers.

Massumi, Brian. 2002. *Parables for the Virtual: Movement, Affect, Sensation*. Durham, NC: Duke University Press.

Paz, Octavio. 1985. *The Labyrinth of Solitude*. Kemp, Lysander, Milos, Yara and Phillips Belash, Rachel (trans.). New York, NY: Grove Press.

Pérez-Reverte, Arturo. 2013. *El francotirador paciente*. Madrid: Santillana Ediciones Generales.

Reiss, Jon. 2008. *Bomb-It*. New York, NY: Antidote Films.

Robles, José María. 2013. 'Grafiteros y artistas urbanos, sobre Pérez-Reverte: "Se ha metido en terreno pantanoso"'. *El Mundo*, 8 October. Available at: www.elmundo.es/elmundo/ 2013/10/08/cultura/1381243134.html. Accessed: 3 June 2015.

United Kingdom, Ministry of Justice. 2003. *Anti-social Behaviour Act 2003*. Available at: www.legislation.gov.uk/ukpga/2003/38/contents. Accessed: 29 July 2015.

Vilaseca, Stephen Luis. 2010. 'The TriBall Case: 'Okupación Creativa ¡Ya!' vs. Okupa Hacktivismo'. *Arizona Journal of Hispanic Cultural Studies*. 14: 11–30.

Vilaseca, Stephen Luis. 2012. 'From Graffiti to Street Art: How Urban Artists are Democratizing Spanish City Centers and Streets'. *Transitions: Journal of Franco-Iberian Studies*. 8: 9–34.

Vilaseca, Stephen Luis. 2013. *Barcelonan Okupas: Squatter Power!*. Madison, NJ: Fairleigh Dickinson University Press.

Wilson, James and Kelling, George. 1982. 'Broken Windows'. *The Atlantic Monthly*. (March): 29–38.

15 Long live the tag

Representing the foundations of graffiti

Gregory J. Snyder

Introduction

This short chapter examines the inherent contradictions of graffiti often thought of in simple polarities, such as legal vs illegal, or art vs vandalism. My aim is to challenge these conceptual binaries by focusing on one of the most enduring and least understood aspects of graffiti writing, namely the tag. The impetus for this comes from a provocative legal piece produced with an 'illegal aesthetics', i.e. tags. The chapter starts by contextualizing my own first 'reading' of graffiti tags, then talks about how the 'writing' of graffiti is practised, and concludes with a detailed discussion of TWIST (Barry McGee) and AMAZE's (Josh Lazcano) collage of graffiti tags that vividly represents the contradictions of this subculture and its reception from the public. This chapter attempts to glorify in a small way, the most basic, and arguably the most hated, form of graffiti – the tag.

Graffiti tags represent the science of style – the aestheticized repetitive practice of writing the letters in a name in an effort to create a personal calligraphy. Tags are most often performed in public spaces under difficult circumstances and when done skilfully they are as beautiful as any mural. This is well known to the members of the subculture (and most who study it) but complete heresy to the rest of the world. Graffiti as we know it cannot exist without the tag. It is *the* essential component for learning, practising and mastering the form of graffiti as vandalistic art.

In the last two decades, as the mainstream has begrudgingly come to accept the artistic merit of graffiti murals or pieces, the notion that tags are done by unskilled vandals has become entrenched. Outsiders have been constructing writing as a criminal activity since its beginning, and as Joe Austin showed in *Taking the Train* (2001), the illegality of graffiti is a socially constructed phenomenon, more concerned with who is doing the writing rather than what is being inscribed.

Within graffiti subculture there is no strict division between the various forms of graffiti. Pieces, throw-ups and tags are all means for exploring style where writers attempt to get their name seen for the purpose of producing fame.[1] Writers practise their tags constantly and put lots of thought and energy into figuring out the best spots to put their names up. As Jeff Ferrell and Robert Weide describe, in their article 'Spot Theory', in addition to the aesthetic skills and taste for competition, writers are also skilled in the 'ability to select appropriate spots for writing graffiti' (2010: 49). Spots therefore can also be understood as a critical element of style. Where you write is as important as how you write.

Repetitive name painting on public surfaces plays a crucial role in a writer's development of a critical awareness. AME discusses how his experience 'bombing' has had an important impact on his development as an artist and as a person:

> You need to find a balance between not caring at all what people think and caring too much. Bombing makes you more thoughtful and you can't get there without it, because it provides the critique. It's like showing your portfolio, only it's not your whole portfolio, it's just a small portion of it. It's like a calling card, that says, 'This is me and a hint of what I'm about. If you remember this and you're curious enough, maybe you'll pursue it more and find out the rest of the story.'
>
> (1999)

Reading graffiti: the stories to be deciphered

There is a narrative to a wall that goes beyond individual tags claiming space. Numerous tags on a wall provide writers with the opportunity to tell stories about the exploits of their peers. Although tags are visually interesting on their own, it is not one tag alone that provides this impetus to the imagination. Rather, it is how the different tags play off one another that reveal the creative energy of a wall (MacDonald 2001; Snyder 2009; Avramidis 2014). There is an organic order to the way the space is divided, and a wall or door with heavy layers of graffiti reveals a history to its viewers in the same way that the sedimentary layers of ancient ruins inspire archaeologists to tell tales of past civilizations.

The first time I was able to understand this was in the fall of 1995. There was a door on First Avenue and 11th street in New York City that had about twelve tags on it. I will describe three that I came to know early in my studies, TWIST, DRANE and UFO (Figure 15.1). I have never personally met these writers, the entirety of my analysis is gleaned from conversations with writers, and my reading of the walls and magazines.

Even as early as 1995 San Francisco writer TWIST was a nationwide star, in fact the ubiquity of his tags in the summer and fall of 1995 were a direct result of his first solo show at the Drawing Center in Soho, NYC. He had done gallery shows in San Francisco and Brazil, bombed Washington, DC buses, tagged New York City mailboxes relentlessly, and in the words of AME (1999), 'He bombed the Great Wall of China'. TWIST's tag is thick and done with a home-made marker called a 'mop' filled with ink produced from fellow writer KR.[2] TWIST's tag is the largest on the door, which shows his confidence. TWIST's tag in the lower portion of the door is a testament to his skill and according to KEST (1999) shows how TWIST 'finds a way to make weird spaces work for him'.

Figure 15.1 TWIST, DRANE, UFO. East Village, New York City, 1996.
Photograph: Gregory J. Snyder.

DRANE also has a back-story, which I've picked up through reading his tags and talking to other writers. DRANE is up all over the East Village, but I hear he is from Ohio. DRANE's style is easy to read and thus I am able to recognize it all over downtown New York City. For many of his tags, DRANE also uses a mop to get a broad black ink stroke similar to TWIST.

The third writer under scrutiny I will call the UFO bomber because s/he doesn't have a name.[3] This writer has completely broken free from letters, and style. S/he tags up an ugly looking spaceship that I've seen everywhere in Williamsburg, Brooklyn and Manhattan. The frequency of this writer's work near more established writers suggests that this writer believes that the originality of his spaceship is on a par with the stylized writers. The drips look forced, sometimes s/he puts an eye in the middle and writes UFO or 907 crew next to it.

The UFO bomber is a fairly recent phenomenon so I assume that he was the last writer to tag the door. From this it follows that UFO is not intimidated by more established artists. There are numerous stories that we can now tell just by looking at this wall. TWIST's tag is big, taking up a large section of the door leaving only a small amount of space for other writers to get up. DRANE put his name in the awkward space that TWIST had left open. DRANE was careful not to 'go over' TWIST's tag showing his respect for him as well as announcing his own skills for accepting TWIST's indirect challenge, of putting his tag in a difficult spot without writing over TWIST. It takes skill to make your mark in this way therefore we can assume that DRANE is a pretty good writer. And finally how to assess what UFO is trying to say? Is this to be construed as a challenge to these writers' notions of style, or is it just a toy on a wall?[4]

The narrative possibilities that this door holds are almost endless, and further it matters little if my postulations are correct. Utilizing your imagination for storytelling is a creative act inspired by what many consider to be just ugly markings with no meaning behind them. The story I have just told only looked at three of the twelve tags on the beige door, but for ten minutes I was completely consumed and forgot that I was standing on a busy street in Manhattan.

Graffiti writing incites stories and the desire to write graffiti in part comes from the need to be part of the story. As famous Philadelphia and New York graffiti writer ESPO, aka Steve Powers, writes in the introduction to *The Art of Getting Over* (1999: 6): 'Stories are the most permanent medium for storing and sharing the graffiti experience . . . Good stories go across the world in minutes and last forever.'

Writing graffiti: the handstyle to be mastered

The process of writing graffiti begins with the creation and development of a tag, which is achieved through a commitment to constant repetition; writing the name over and over and over on paper and in public. Tagging is also the form where regional differences in style are most clearly noted, which means that where one starts writing has an enormous influence on style. Philadelphia signatures began in the late 1960s with CORNBREAD who is widely considered to be the first writer to go 'all city' as well as the inventor of putting the crown over his tag (Powers 1999: 10). Philadelphia writers, not New Yorkers, were the first handstyle masters and they have invented numerous styles. Every Philly writer has a 'gangster style' tag as well as a 'tall print', and a 'wicket'. Different styles of prints are used for different functions, tall prints work well on doors, rally prints, which is the name written over and over are used to cover lots of space. By far the most creative and enduring style to come out of Philadelphia was invented in the late 1970s by NB and his crew SAM (sly artistic masters) and is still used today (Acker 2013). This style is called 'wickets' (also 'wickeds') and it is a complex writing style that has a rhythmic requirement of at least eight beats per letter (Figure 15.2).[5] It also has never been copied by anyone outside of Philadelphia, which speaks to the master-apprentice relationships, which are still strong in Philly.

Los Angeles has its own style of cholo markings, or placas, that are rooted in Mexican culture and date back to the 1930s, and flourished during the height of the Zootsuiters in the 1950s (Kelley 1998; Chastanet 2009). These markings have a specific aesthetic form and are often used to promote the gang and its members (Phillips 1999). Although this style has evolved into an artform itself, as evidenced by the work of artist Chaz Bojoroquez, it is a separate culture from the name and famed-based graffiti. LA has both gang and NYC influences in their writing style. San Francisco also has a stylistic history that is fairly discernible; however, transplanted New York writers, such as KR who is the most notable, have had a huge impact on San Francisco writing style.

If style began in Philadelphia it was perfected in New York City. New York writers' handstyles have become iconic as graffiti calligraphy, and have influenced the style in every major city in the world (Schacter 2013). The early history of New York style begins when TOPCAT moved from Philadelphia to New York, added his street number, 126 and became TOPCAT 126. Christian Acker, in his thorough study of the calligraphy of graffiti tags (2013), suggests that TOPCAT transformed a Philadelphia 'gangster print' and created what came to be called 'Broadway Elegant'. This marked the beginning of New York writers creating 'logos' or 'lockups', which tended to connect the letters into a visual whole and were written without lifting the spray can or the marker from wall, done in one continuous stroke (Acker 2013: 97–98).

Other important NYC early style masters include PHASE II and STAN 153, but none has been as enduring as STAYHIGH 149. STAYHIGH's stick figure

Figure 15.2 Example of 'wicket' style of tagging. KASASKE, Williamsburg, Brooklyn, 2015.

Photograph: Gregory J. Snyder.

Figure 15.3 STAY HIGH 149, the inventor of the 'halo design', subway, New York City, 2010.

Photograph: Gregory J. Snyder.

was borrowed from the logo of an American TV show, The Saint, and the halo that STAYHIGH wrote over his tag, has since become of fixture of handstyle design the world over (Figure 15.3).[6]

Representing graffiti: the aesthetics of illegality

In order to understand how writers themselves blur the strict polarities between legal vs illegal graffiti it is interesting to analyse a piece by TWIST and AMAZE. The spot has been a fixture of New York legal walls for the last decade. The wall was sanctioned by Deitch Gallery and is known simply as the 'Deitch Wall', and various global superstars have been commissioned to paint. It is on the corner of Houston Street and the Bowery at the entrance to the art district of Soho. Originally, there was a Keith Haring replica done by ANGEL, and then it got murals from Brazilian twins OS GEMEOS, Shepard Fairey and Kenny Scharf, followed by TWIST and AMAZE'S piece. This is a legal spot in a fairly prominent area of downtown NYC and it is respected by viewers and writers who rarely ever (except in the case of Fairey) tag over it.[7]

Contemporary graffiti murals are almost exclusively legal and in many cities all over the world they have even become tourist attractions. Elaborate masterpieces most often require more time and more supplies than tags and throw ups, and therefore, most graffiti pieces done today are done on legal walls on which writers have been granted permission to paint. There are also spots all over the world that are specifically set aside for aerosol art. These legal spots have disarmed some of the controversy over graffiti vandalism. While some of the most ardent anti-graffiti folk worry that providing kids with a place to paint encourages more illegal graffiti, local Queens' websites listed 5POINTZ as one of the main attractions for tourists to visit in the neighbourhood. But as KEZAM warns (1999): 'Permission walls are pretty cool. Although you are more or less guaranteed to have the [police] make an appearance – so you better have permission slips from the owner of the property.'

Sadly, in 2013 the owner of the building that housed 5POINTZ buffed out all of the graffiti in the dark of the night and sold the building to developers seeking to create luxury condos. But for a while at least, 5POINTZ made Long Island City Queens a popular tourist attraction.

As mentioned, TWIST is one of the most successful graffiti writers to make the transition from graffiti to fine art. Barry McGee (TWIST), studied at San Francisco Art and Design and was featured at the Venice Biennial, and currently has works in the permanent collection of the San Francisco Museum of Art, the Whitney Museum in New York City, in addition to a recent (2012) retrospective of his art at the Berkeley Art Museum in Berkeley, California.

For graffiti artists in the early 1990s there were no longer opportunities to become professional artists right out of high school, so many put together portfolios of their graffiti work and got accepted at art schools (Snyder 2009). There they used the institutions' facilities to learn fine art, graphic design, photography, video editing and filmmaking. These skill sets would eventually help writers to produce professional looking graffiti magazines, videos and websites.

TWIST was one of the early pioneers to make this transition and his success created opportunities for others. Fellow former writers, Steve Powers (ESPO), Todd James (REAS), Greg Lemarche (SP.ONE) Craig Costello (KR) and so many others, have moved beyond piecing with spray cans to conceptual pieces that deal with signage, commercialism, fame and urban aesthetics. This artistic work is not graffiti but it is clear by their use of letters, graphics and sometimes aerosol paint, that each of these artists' vision was developed in conversation with the cities' built environment. But that doesn't mean that TWIST has left his roots behind.

When we examine the wall done by TWIST and AMAZE the fact that they chose to paint the tags of legendary and current writers shows their commitment to the subculture of graffiti, in addition to staking the claim that tags are also art.

TWIST and AMAZE's 'piece' is a challenge to those who want to dismiss graffiti tags as ugly vandalism.[8] Their piece is a painstaking conglomeration of tags from famous writers (Figure 15.4). All of the tags are done in red, which indicates that they were done by the same artists (TWIST and AMAZE) and they vary in style and size. The tags have an organic order as none of the tags go over any other

Figure 15.4 Deitch Wall, Soho, New York City. TWIST and AMAZE, 2010.

Photograph: Barry McGee, 2010. Reproduced with permission of Barry McGee and Ratio 3, San Francisco.

but there is almost no negative space on the entire wall; this is no easy feat. The tags are from writers all over the world in addition to some non-graffiti names. Interestingly there are not too many TWIST tags, instead it is an homage to the writers that Barry McGee, Josh Lazcano and CHINO (who showed up to lend a hand) respect. It is difficult to discern individuals' tags save for the numerous AMAZE, CHINO, TEMPT, SKREW and REVS tags and instead the piece has a wholeness to it that speaks to graffiti as a collective subculture rather than a mere conglomeration of individuals. This wall also works as a purely aesthetic testament to the graffiti tag, it is not necessary to know the back stories of the individual writers for the wall to be appealing.

During the process of painting the wall McGee and Lazcano got hassled by the police, who were desperately confused because these writers insisted they were painting a legal wall, even though they were inscribing it in a way that the police assumed was illegal.[9] It is here where we can understand that it is not always the act of graffiti that is illegal but its aesthetic that signifies its illegality. The public has come to understand that there is something called 'street art', which is good, and that there is something called graffiti tagging, which is bad. In this way of thinking graffiti murals are accepted as good and legal and artistic, while tags symbolize aggression, deviance and criminality. Police and (some) passers-by pride themselves on their ability to recognize graffiti tags, and connect them to vandalism, crime and deviance. Most could not conceive that anyone, let alone one of the most successful artists in the world, would choose to paint tags on a legal wall. Therefore it is the style of writing that marks it as deviant and represents it as illegal, rather than the act; or as Ferrell always reminds, style, especially in the case of criminalized subcultures, always matters (Ferrell 1996, 2007).

In painting this wall TWIST might be prodding the public and the art world to remember the foundations of graffiti (which also paved the way for street art), the lowly tag, in all of its beauty and elegance. This suggests that the illegality of graffiti goes beyond mere vandalism, and instead lies in the aesthetics of graffiti writing.

If TWIST and AMAZE were painting a fancy mural, even with aerosol paint, the police and others in the mainstream would not question them. By painting tags they are challenging the notion that it is not vandalism per se that the public despises but a particular aesthetic; an aesthetic that is associated with a particular subculture.

To those ignorant of the importance and elegance of the graffiti tag, tags represent deviance and criminality. TWIST and AMAZE seek to challenge this notion by making an illegal style of vandalism, legal art. In this way we are reminded that graffiti tags represent the foundations of a subculture that has become a worldwide phenomenon. The tag represents years and years of practice and hard work, and yet those writers who made a name for themselves with their hand styles did not do so by merely practising them on paper, they had to be applied to public space for all to see and to critique, and possibly diss. In this way the tag represents overcoming doubt and fear, risking health and safety and the possible wrath of the criminal justice system, all in the name of style. So while tags are executed in public space with the heat of scorn and criminality all around, this fire has consistently forced writers to progress and innovate while relying on their daring and creative courage. Long live the tag.

Notes

1   Recently a number of books have come out, written by former and current writers, focused on graffiti calligraphy, better known as 'handstyles', that showcase the history, science and art of tags. See Acker (2013) and Walde (2011).
2   This ink was developed by KR, and KRINK is now a fully developed artist supply company with markers and ink intended for use in pubic space. It should also be noted that mops, and other graffiti supplies are no longer homemade but are available in the marketplace.
3   During the course of my research I discovered that UFO is male.
4   UFO would remain a consistent writer for over a decade, and unlike most writers, his style never progressed.
5   This lesson in regional styles comes from conversations with Philadelphia writer DES (1998). See Powers (1999) and Acker (2013) for a complete history.
6   STAYHIGH 149 passed away in June 2012. R.I.P.
7   Fairey is a street artist and his piece was dissed largely because NYC writers viewed the work as studio art affixed to a wall rather than graffiti.
8   TWIST and AMAZE did a similar piece in Sydney a year after the one in New York. For more see Lowpro (2011).
9   For a detailed account of the process of painting the wall see Newman (2010).

References

Acker, Christian. 2013. *Flip the Script: A Guidebook for Aspiring Vandals and Typographers*. Berkeley, CA: Ginko Press.
AME. 1999. Interview with author. 8 March.
Austin, Joe. 2001. *Taking the Train: How Graffiti Art became an Urban Crisis in New York City*. New York, NY: Columbia University Press.
Avramidis, Konstantinos. 2014. 'Graffiti Subculture: The Meaning of Space on the Way to Fame'. In *(Dis)respectful Creativity Conference: The Impact of Graffiti & Street Art*

on *Contemporary Society & Urban Spaces*. Athens: Onassis Cultural Centre. Available at: www.sgt.gr/eng/SPG1032/?vid=1_8tk9k63f&pg=5&flt=151. Accessed: 25 September 2015.

Chastanet, François. 2009. *Cholo Writing: Latino Gang Graffiti in Los Angeles*. Stockholm: Dokument Press.

DES. 1998. Interview with author. 19 May.

Ferrell, Jeff. 1996. *Crimes of Style: Urban Graffiti and the Politics of Criminality*. Boston, MA: Northeastern University Press.

Ferrell, Jeff. 2007. 'For a Ruthless Cultural Criticism of Everything Existing'. *Crime, Media and Culture*. 3(1): 91–100.

Ferrell, Jeff and Weide, Robert. 2010. 'Spot Theory'. *City*. 14(1–2): 48–62.

Kelley, Robin. 1998. 'The Riddle of the Zoot: Malcolm Little and Black Cultural Politics During World War II'. In Austin, Joe and Willard, Michael Nevin (eds), *Generations of Youth: Youth Culture and History in Twentieth Century America*. New York, NY: NYU Press, pp. 161–181.

KEST. 1999. Interview with author. 6 June.

KEZAM. 1999. Interview with author. 5 May.

Lowpro. 2011. 'Streets: TWIST & AMAZE (Sydney)'. *Arrested Motion*, 16 September. Available at: http://arrestedmotion.com/2011/09/streets-twist-amaze-sydney/. Accessed: 25 September 2015.

Macdonald, Nancy. 2001. *The Graffiti Subculture: Youth, Masculinity and Identity in London and New York*. London: Palgrave Macmillan.

Newman, Jeff. 2010. 'Accidents Will Happen: Barry McGee Hits Houston Street'. *The Art Collectors*, 30 August. Available at: http://blog.theartcollectors.com/2010/08/30/accidents-will-happen-barry-mcgee-hits-houston-street/. Accessed: 25 September 2015.

Phillips, Susan. 1999. *Wallbangin': Graffiti and Gangs in L.A.* Chicago, IL: University of Chicago Press.

Powers, Stephen. 1999. *The Art of Getting Over: Graffiti at the Millennium*. New York, NY: St Martin's Press.

Schacter, Rafael. 2013. *The World Atlas of Street Art and Graffiti*. New Haven, CT: Yale University Press.

Snyder, Gregory. 2009. *Graffiti Lives: Beyond the Tag in New York's Urban Underground*. New York, NY: New York University Press.

Walde, Claudia. 2011. *Graffiti Alphabets: Street Fonts from Around the World*. London: Thames & Hudson.

Index

PGIL2021USA